Foreword by the Chairman

1   The present Royal Commission on the Press was set up in 1974 with the following terms of reference:

To inquire into the factors affecting the maintenance of the independence, diversity and editorial standards of newspapers and periodicals, and the public's freedom of choice of newspapers and periodicals, nationally, regionally and locally, with particular reference to:

a.   the economics of newspaper and periodical publishing and distribution;

b.   the interaction of the newspaper and periodical interests held by the companies concerned with their other interests and holdings, within and outside the communications industry;

c.   management and labour practices and relations in the newspaper and periodical industry;

d.   conditions and security of employment in the newspaper and periodical industry;

e.   the distribution and concentration of ownership of the newspaper and periodical industry, and the adequacy of existing law in relation thereto;

f.   the responsibilities, constitution and functioning of the Press Council;

and to make recommendations.

2   During its life, the Royal Commission took evidence from a large number of organisations and individuals, and commissioned work from those with special knowledge. This volume contains seven papers by Mr. Oliver Boyd-Barrett of the Open University, Dr Colin Seymour-Ure of the University of Kent and Professor Jeremy Tunstall of The City University, and is the third in the series of working papers which the Royal Commission is publishing with the object of promoting and informing public discussion.

3   Mr Boyd-Barrett surveys the collection of foreign news and the organisation and resources on which the British press can draw.

4   Dr Seymour-Ure wrote three studies for the Royal Commission. The first investigates the treatment by the British press of the specialist reporting of science and medicine. 'Parliament and Government' examines the relations between these institutions and the national and provincial press, and includes a study of the lobby system. In his third paper, Dr Seymour-Ure analyses the past and present connections between the party system and the national press.

5   Three papers by Professor Jeremy Tunstall are published in this volume. 'Letters to the Editor' reports on readers' letters to the press and shows who

writes and how and why the letters which are printed are chosen. His second paper traces changes in the status and function of editors in this country since early-Victorian times and considers some implications. Professor Tunstall's final paper investigates the reporting of news of industrial relations. This was also the subject of different treatment by Professor Denis McQuail, of the University of Southampton, whose report, *Analysis of Newspaper Content* (Cmnd. 6810–4) is published as a research paper of the Royal Commission. We have made the two reports available so that readers may compare their different approaches and conclusions.

6   These papers were prepared in order to assist members of the Royal Commission, but since the decision was taken to publish them, they have all been revised.

7   Finally, the papers express the views of their authors not of the Royal Commission.

O R McGregor

Royal Commission on the Press

June 1977

ROYAL COMMISSION
ON THE PRESS

Studies on the Press

by Oliver Boyd-Barrett
Dr Colin Seymour-Ure
and Professor Jeremy Tunstall

London: Her Majesty's Stationery Office

ISBN 0 11 730075 6

Contents

Part A

The collection of foreign news in the national press: organisation and resources

by Oliver Boyd-Barrett of the Open University

Contents

Author's note

The data on foreign correspondents was collected on two separate occasions in the first halves of 1974 and 1976 respectively. In 1974 a questionnaire was sent by the author to the foreign editors of the national news media organisations which requested information concerning the number of full-time staff correspondents, the number of additional staff correspondents temporarily assigned abroad, the number of retainer-paid stringers, the distribution of staff correspondents and retainer-paid stringers throughout the major world regions, and the news services to which each media organisation subscribed.

In 1976 much the same information was gathered by means of personal interview of foreign editors of the national newspapers or of persons delegated by them. These interviews were arranged and conducted by the author. In addition to the above items of information, the foreign editors were also asked to provide some information about London-based foreign news specialists, foreign desk staffing arrangements, foreign news-gathering, and relationships with news services. In all cases the respondents were most helpful, although not all were in a position to discuss financial aspects.

The data on the international news agencies were gathered by the author in the course of a four-year study financed by the Leverhulme Trust. The author wishes to acknowledge the assistance of Dr Michael Palmer in the gathering of material concerning AFP French operations, and of Mrs Hazel Grayson in the work of content analysis. The content categories used for the analysis, like those used in the study of foreign news content by Professor Denis McQuail,[1] were based on an earlier investigation of broadcast news carried out at the Centre for Mass Communication Research at the University of Leicester, but with certain modifications. Most notably, two new categories were introduced: internation and intranation violent political conflict; while some other categories were collapsed for the sake of this research. For full details of the research and the methodology employed, readers should consult the forthcoming publication by the author, *Les Agences de Presse Mondiales*, Alain Moreau, Paris, or the English-language report available at request to the author through the Open University.

O B-B
May 1977

---

1 Cmnd 6810–4.

Summary

The paper documents the decline in the number of staff correspondents working for British national dailies and resident overseas as foreign correspondents. This decline has been especially severe in the mid-seventies. The only daily papers to have increased their staff foreign correspondents in the period 1965–76 are the *Financial Times* and *The Guardian*. The overall decline has accentuated the concentration of all staff correspondents in North America and Western Europe, and in 1976 resulted in the absence of such representation in Communist Europe, South America and the Australasia/Oceania region. This decline may have been offset to some extent by greater use of London-based foreign specialists and general reporter 'fire-fighters', but there is no indication that there has been greater overall use of overseas 'stringers'.

The foreign news desks of the national papers enjoy a substantial measure of autonomy in their operations, especially amongst the 'quality' newspapers and in those cases where the sub-editing of foreign news is a function of the foreign desk. But there is considerable informal consultation between foreign editors and other colleagues. Among the 'popular' newspapers, however, *The Sun* has neither a foreign desk nor a foreign editor, and the *Daily Mirror* has no foreign desk but does have a foreign editor. A most important *external* constraint on foreign news reporting is identified in the paper as the existence of severe restrictions on press reporting that many overseas countries impose.

One possible future consequence of the overall decline of foreign news-gathering resources, the paper argues, may be more intensive use of the facilities of the international news agencies and, to a lesser extent, the smaller secondary news agencies associated with newspaper publishing groups. Among the major international news agencies, the leading American agencies and the French agency are characterised by high dependence on their respective domestic markets for overall revenue which restricts the extent to which they can respond to overseas market requirements.

The British agency, which is mainly owned by the British national and provincial newspaper press, combines a high degree of responsiveness to British market requirements with a much greater dependence on overseas markets for overall revenue than is true of the other agencies. Reuters is now mainly dependent on economic news services to non-media clients for the bulk of its revenues, and this together with the importance of overseas markets has cushioned the agency against the effect of a period of rapid inflation and the depreciation of sterling.

Content analysis of agency wires indicates that the regions of North America and Western Europe together account for around half or more than half the

13

content of all wires for the UK market, and that in terms of subject-matter politics and economics together account for around half the total. Substantial differences in the range of actual stories covered by the agencies were also observed, but all the agencies concentrated heavily on 'international' stories concerning two or more countries, and these accounted for half or more of all content.

1 Foreign news staff

1.1 Sources of foreign news

The two most important sources of foreign news for the national press are the correspondents they employ, and the international news agencies. These sources not only provide news directly gathered by themselves, they also relay news which they have culled from other news media around the world.

1.2 Three kinds of foreign correspondent

The three major types of foreign correspondent may usefully be identified as (i) the staff correspondent resident abroad; (ii) staff correspondents resident in the UK who regularly cover foreign news affairs and (iii) the 'stringer' or freelance correspondent resident abroad. The staff correspondent resident abroad has a full working contract with a single news organisation from which he derives the bulk of his earned income and which covers all his expenses. Of the staff correspondents resident in London or the UK who regularly cover foreign news some may be considered 'specialists' in given areas of the world and are likely to spend most of their working time in such coverage, while others may be general reporters who are flown out for coverage of major foreign crises and who are sometimes called 'fire-fighters'. Stringers generally fall into one of two categories. Some have a special relationship with one or more news organisations which is characterised by relatively frequent usage of their copy and some form of guaranteed income (retainer or guaranteed minimum lineage, possibly with some contribution to basic expenses), but the majority of stringers on the books of news organisations are paid only on a lineage basis and many of them are used only very occasionally.

1.3 Staff correspondents resident abroad

In the Spring of 1976, *The Times* employed more staff correspondents (18) in residential posts overseas than any other newspaper, followed by the other 'quality' newspapers, the *Financial Times* (16), *Daily Telegraph* (13), and *Guardian* (8)[1]. There was no clear distinction of category among the other dailies: the *Daily Mirror* (7) had as many as the *Daily Express* (7)[2], and more than the *Daily Mail* (4), while *The Sun* had no staff correspondents reporting to it exclusively from overseas, although it could call on the services of other papers in the *News International* group. The only Sunday papers with staff correspondents overseas, employed independently of daily sister papers, are *The Sunday Times* (5) and *The Observer* (5)[3]. The *Sunday Telegraph, Sunday*

---

1 Includes one whose salary is half paid by *The Observer*.
2 Includes one on 'full retainer' here considered equivalent to a staff correspondent.
3 Includes one on a 2-year contract; and one whose salary is half paid by *The Guardian*.

Express and *Sunday Mirror* largely depend on the correspondent resources of their sister daily papers; the *Sunday People* and *News of the World* may call on the resources of their respective publishing groups.

1.4 Decline in numbers

In many cases there has been a decline in the number of staff correspondents resident overseas working for national dailies, over the period 1974–76[1]. *The Times*, for instance, allows for a potential establishment of 22 overseas staff correspondents, but the actual number was 19 in 1974, 18 in 1976. In recent years the paper has dispensed with staff correspondents in Moscow and Peking and Latin America. The staff correspondent in India had recently been expelled at the time of interview and had not been replaced[2]. The strength of the New York bureau has been reduced by one. *The Daily Telegraph* has reduced the number of its staff correspondents resident abroad in a two-year period from 22 to 13. Centres which used to be covered by staff correspondents for *The Daily Telegraph* but which are now mainly covered by stringers or from other centres include Moscow, Vienna, Rome, New Delhi, Buenos Aires and Beirut. The *Daily Express* has in recent years closed its Rome bureau, its Beirut and Bonn offices, and recently reduced its New York bureau by 1. At the time of interview it contemplated closure of its Brussels bureau[3]. The *Daily Mirror* used to have a correspondent in the Middle East and one in Singapore for the Far East.

In the Spring of 1974, foreign editors of national dailies reported a total of 103 staff correspondents resident abroad; this figure had fallen to 73 in the Spring of 1976, a decline of 30%. While the earlier figures, gathered by questionnaire, may have been slightly inflated by the erroneous inclusion by respondents of some London-based specialists, the interview evidence in 1976 in nearly all cases indicated that a decline had taken place and that in some cases this decline had been substantial. Foreign news coverage is to some extent a fluid phenomenon and the commitment of resources to it occurs in response both to economic considerations and to the intensity of foreign news events at any given time, but the direction in the present climate of economic recession is clearly downward. The consequences of this downward drift have almost certainly been arrested to some extent by more intensive use of London specialists, general reporters or stringers. However, few go so far as to deny the advantages of having resident correspondents overseas, which include sustained cultivation of contacts and in-depth local knowledge for which it may be difficult to compensate entirely by other means.

The figures for 1974 show a slight decline from the figures for 1965 as provided in the 1966 report of the Economist Intelligence Unit. In 1965 the total number of foreign correspondents for the national dailies was 111. There were only 8 for the *Financial Times* at that time, and this paper has doubled its correspondents during the full period 1965–76. *The Guardian* also shows an increase from 6 to 8. However, *The Times* had 26 in 1965, *The Daily Telegraph* 30,

1 For a brief description of the methodology employed for this study see Author's note (p. 8). The study is valid up to the Summer of 1976. There will doubtless be some changes even by the time of publication.
2 Restrictions on foreign news reporting from India were lifted in September 1976 and the situation has further improved since the end of Emergency Rule. British news organisations will naturally review their reporting policies in the light of these events.
3 The Brussels bureau was closed in the latter half of 1976.

and the *Daily Express* and *Daily Mail* had 13 each. The *Daily Mirror* had 11 and the pre-Murdoch *Sun* had 4. The now defunct *Daily Sketch* had no staff foreign correspondents. The overall position of the Sundays has not changed greatly; *The Observer* reported 6 in that year, *The Sunday Times* 3. Also at that time, the *Sunday Telegraph* and the *Sunday Mirror* each reported one staff correspondent. The full extent of decline therefore in the period 1965–76 is 34%. For some papers, of course, the fall has been especially dramatic: 57% in the case of *The Daily Telegraph*, and 58% in the case of the *Daily Express* and *Daily Mail* combined. The evidence for the full period 1965–76 indicates the existence of a long-term trend of decline which has been accelerated by the economic recession of the 'seventies.[1]

1.5 Stringer correspondents

Assessment of the number of stringer correspondents working for Fleet Street dailies is complicated by the fact that a great many may be used only very rarely, and so the absolute number of stringers is not a good indication of actual commitment of resources. An attempt was made in interview evidence to elicit the number of stringers who have a special financial arrangement with the papers they work for, expressed in terms of the payment of a retainer, some form of guaranteed minimum income, or fixed contribution to expenses. The absolute number of stringers on the books of Fleet Street dailies may not show much variation between the 'quality' and 'popular' press, but the 'quality' papers are much more likely to enter into special financial arrangements with stringers. The *Financial Times* and *The Times* follow a policy of paying some form of retainer: 71 of the *Financial Times*' list of 83 stringers and all but one of *The Times*' 43 fall into this category. Thirty-four or rather more than one-third of *The Daily Telegraph*'s list of 90, and 10 of the *The Guardian*'s list of 32 stringers enjoy a special arrangement.

The 'popular' papers carry much less foreign news in total volume than the 'qualities', and are less interested in entering into financial commitments of this kind. Only 5 of the *Daily Mail*'s total list of 120 stringers are paid retainers of any kind; and only one of the 100 on the list of the *Daily Express*. The one retained man on the *Daily Express* is fully retained and is here considered a full-timer. The *Daily Mirror* pays extremely small retainers to four or five stringers only.

The available evidence is insufficient to permit the conclusion that the overall commitment of resources to the use of stringers has either increased or declined in recent years. The number of stringers paid retainers by *The Times* has fallen very slightly in the last few years (by between 2 and 5); similarly in the case of

---

1   A similar decline is evident in the case of US media foreign correspondents. Referring to recent data collected by Prof Ralph Kliesch of Ohio University, Jeffrey Blyth reported in *UK Press Gazette* (15 November 1976) that in 1975 there were only 429 American staff correspondents working abroad for US news organisations of whom some 100 were primarily desk men. This figure is lower than any year since the end of the war when there were something like 2500 correspondents and it also includes American news agency correspondents (agency and broadcast correspondents are excluded in the British figures provided above). Furthermore, Blyth reports that budget cuts have meant that foreign correspondents are obliged to do more office chores and relatively less thinking and writing. Improved communications may also have reduced the autonomy of the correspondent *vis-à-vis* the foreign news desk of his employing news organisation. New tax laws in the US from 15 April 1977 have abolished many income tax perks for Americans working overseas. This will mean a bigger bill for news organisations, some of whom will probably recall American staff and replace them with local employees, or even cut down completely (J Blyth, *UK Press Gazette*, 25 April 1977).

Numbers of staff correspondents 1975–76

	Financial Times	The Times	The Daily Telegraph	The Guardian	Daily Express	Daily Mail	Daily Mirror	The Sun[2]	The Sunday Times	The Observer
1965 ...	8	26	30	6	13	13	11	4	3	6
1974 ...	23	19	22	9	9	10	11		4	7
1976 ...	16	18	13	8	7[1]	4	7		5	5[3]

1 Includes one reporter on 'full retainer'.
2 The Sun may use 'News International' overseas reporting facilities.
3 Includes one reporter on two-year contract and one reporter shared with The Guardian.

18

the *Financial Times*. On the other hand both *The Guardian* and *The Daily Telegraph* have increased the number of stringers to whom they pay some form of retainer (by 4 in each case). Among the 'populars' the total list of stringers on the books of the *Daily Mail* has increased by 6 in the period 1974–76 but declined by 40 in the case of the *Daily Express*. In both cases some 10 or 11 stringers are considered to be 'regular' contributors. The *Daily Mirror*, as we have seen, pays only very small retainers and the number of these has declined slightly; while *The Sun* depends largely on the services of journalists employed by News International offices abroad.

1.6 Sundays: staff correspondents and stringers

In the case of the two Sundays with substantial independent foreign news resources, there is no very obvious drift. The *Sunday Times* reported four full-time staff correspondents abroad in 1974, and five in 1976 although it was likely that one of these would shortly leave the paper and not be replaced. There were four stringers on fairly substantial retainers, one of whom was such a regular contributor as to be thought of almost as full-time, and between nine and twelve other less regular contributors whose population shifted frequently. The *Observer* reported 7 staff correspondents in 1974 and three in 1976. However, in 1976 it also shared a correspondent with *The Guardian*, and had another full-time correspondent on a short-term contract; for the purpose of this report it is here considered that *The Observer* has the equivalent of 5 staff correspondents. There does appear to have been something of a decline in this case. Nine retainer-paid stringers were reported in 1974, 3–4 in 1976, with approximately twelve less-regular contributors.

1.7 UK-based foreign correspondents

In addition to staff correspondents and stringers abroad the Fleet Street dailies may also use reporters normally based in the UK for overseas coverage. There are as we have seen two kinds of such reporter. The first category is of foreign news specialists who spend all or almost all of their time working on foreign news stories, frequently travelling, and when so engaged fall under the general supervision of the Foreign Editor. The second category is of general reporters who are more or less frequently called on for 'fire-fighting' crisis coverage abroad. Some papers have a body of experienced general reporters who will be given preference for such assignments; on others the distribution of assignments among general reporting staff may be more democratic and used as a reward for good work, although experience and relevant expertise (language ability for example) will always be a consideration. Feature writers may also be sent out on foreign stories, at the initiative of the features desk and in close cooperation with the foreign desk. These two categories of home-based reporters who cover foreign news should be distinguished from the foreign desk staff who are largely desk-bound and who engage in much of the associated administrative work, editing and handling of agency tapes. While the two categories are not entirely distinct, the difference reflects day-to-day administrative reality. Foreign desk experience may also be a useful training for later foreign coverage.

The London-based foreign news specialists are mainly employed by the 'quality' papers, although some of the 'populars' have one or two general reporters who are especially experienced as 'fire-fighters'. There is a sense in which a paper's diplomatic correspondent is a foreign news specialist and in some cases (eg the *Financial Times*, *The Times*, *The Guardian*, *The Daily Telegraph* and the *Daily*

Mail) the diplomatic correspondent now reports to the Foreign Editor (on the *Financial Times* the diplomatic correspondent is deputy foreign editor). If we exclude diplomatic correspondents, however, there are six regional specialists on the *Financial Times* who travel regularly in their respective areas[1], and four regional specialists on *The Times*[2]. *The Guardian* has six journalists who form a regular corps of correspondents available for foreign news coverage but are based in the UK, and some eight to ten fall into this category on *The Daily Telegraph*, some of whom have been overseas resident correspondents in the past. *The Daily Telegraph*'s communist affairs correspondent also reports to the Foreign Desk. And on all papers, home correspondents such as the defence correspondent may liaise closely with the foreign desk when working on stories of international significance. The *Daily Express* has one London-based specialist, whose field is communist or Soviet affairs, and the *Daily Mail* has a chief foreign reporter who is called on for most of the 'brigade' work. The *Daily Mirror* has one or two correspondents who travel very regularly for coverage of major foreign news events. All papers, and especially those without any generally-recognised foreign news specialists, will call on general news reporters as necessary. The *Daily Mail* has three general reporters who are normally given priority in consideration of foreign assignments, *The Guardian* one to four in addition to the above-mentioned corps, and the *Daily Mirror* tries to distribute such assignments fairly widely amongst its general reporting staff.

1.8 Foreign desk staff

In contrast to these the Foreign Desk staff are relatively desk-bound: their functions include administrative responsibility, some writing, handling of agency tapes and other incoming material, logistics, payment of stringers, monitoring of performance, etc. At their head, and head of the entire foreign news operation, there is the Foreign Editor. The *Daily Mirror*, however, does not have a separate Foreign Desk, although it does have a Foreign Editor; *The Sun* has neither Foreign Desk nor Foreign Editor. In the case of these two papers the quantity and kind of foreign news consumed does not justify extensive departmentalisation. Aside from these the other papers may be distinguished between those which have integrated the foreign news desk with foreign news sub-editing, and those where the sub-editing function does not fall directly under the Foreign Editor's authority. The *Financial Times* and *The Guardian* follow a policy of integration. The entire foreign desk of the *Financial Times*, excluding the specialists already referred to, includes four journalists on the night desk (mainly sub-editors), seven on the day desk who both write and sub-edit, plus two writers who specialise in news for the international company news page (a quasi-autonomous operation), and two other specialists in economic news (eg Eurobonds, European business law), and of course the Foreign Editor. The *Financial Times* maintains the largest Foreign Desk. *The Guardian* has recently[3] brought its foreign desk down from Manchester to London, to set up an integrated foreign operation which it is hoped will increase flexibility and, possibly, transferability of functions among those working for it. It comprises three writer-administrators and 11 sub-editors. (All such figures are less than they seem, since the total numbers of staff actually work shift systems and must cover for holidays and absences.)

---

1 These are: the Middle East, W Europe, E Europe, Africa, Latin America and Asia.
2 These are: USSR and E Europe, Far East, Middle East, and 'former colonial territories'.
3 From September 1976.

Other papers do not have foreign desks which exercise direct authority over foreign news sub-editing, but on some of these there are sub-editors who specialise in foreign news, and there is generally the possibility of close liason wherever this is desired. *The Times'* foreign desk comprises the Foreign Editor and his deputy, and four other journalists who work a shift system between 10.00 a.m. and 2.00 a.m. There is a separate foreign news subs desk and a chief foreign sub-editor, who comes under the authority of the chief sub-editor but with whom the deputy foreign editor or foreign editor may work closely. *The Daily Telegraph's* foreign desk is five strong; there is a separate foreign subs desk with between two and four subs reporting to the chief sub-editor. On the *Daily Express* there is a Foreign Editor, his deputy, and five desk men. There is a sub-editor on the general subs desk who specialises in foreign news. On the *Daily Mail* there is a Foreign Editor and five other desk men. The sub-editing is separate, but the sub-editor responsible for the page that carries most foreign news will naturally liaise with the foreign desk where necessary. Both the *Daily Mirror* and *The Sun* have sub-editors who handle the agency tapes. In addition to around half a dozen regular travellers, both *The Sunday Times* and *The Observer* have foreign desks. *The Sunday Times* desk consists of the Foreign Editor and three others; *The Observer*, which until a few years ago had only a home desk, has just the Foreign Editor.

There is no comparable information to indicate whether there has been a decline or increase of London-based specialists or of foreign desk staff in recent years. In 1974, however, Foreign Editors were asked to state how many London-based reporters at the particular time of the survey were actually abroad on assignment, and this gives some idea of the extent of commitment of such manpower to overseas travel. At that time the national dailies had a total of twenty-two reporters normally based in the UK on foreign news assignments, of whom 14 were accounted for by the 'quality' press: *Financial Times* (4), *The Times* (2), *The Guardian* (4), and *The Daily Telegraph* (4). The remainder were accounted for by the *Daily Mail* (4), the *Daily Express* (1), and the *Daily Mirror* (3). *The Observer* and *The Sunday Times* each had four such reporters on foreign assignment.

1.9 Distribution of staff foreign correspondents

Of the total number of staff correspondents resident abroad working for the national dailies, over four-fifths are based in North America and Western Europe. In 1976, 60 or 82% were based in these two areas of the world. There were none at all in the USSR and Eastern Europe, South America or Australasia/Oceania. The other areas of the world were covered fairly evenly, with four correspondents each in Africa and the Far East and five in the Near East. *The Sunday Times* and *The Observer* distributed their smaller numbers more evenly than the national dailies, with 5 of their combined numbers in North America and Western Europe, and 5 in the Near East, Far East and Africa. The 'popular' papers had no residential correspondents outside Western Europe and North America, and the percentage of 'quality' paper journalists in these two areas was slightly lower than for all national dailies at 76%.

The situation was roughly similar in 1974, when 75% of all national daily journalists were based in North America and Western Europe. The decline in total numbers of residential correspondents abroad has been most dramatic in the USSR and Eastern Europe, South America and Australasia/Oceania. In 1974, there were 3 staff correspondents in the USSR and Eastern Europe,

21

and 2 each in South America and Australasia/Oceania. In 1976 there were none at all. The number of staff correspondents in North America and Western Europe declined from 77 to 60, from 8 to 5 in the Near East, from 7 to 4 in the Far East, while in Africa the total remained steady at 4 correspondents. Whereas the 'popular' papers had four correspondents outside North America and Western Europe in 1974, they had none in 1976. *The Sunday Times* and *The Observer* together have more correspondents outside North America and Western Europe in 1976 than in 1974 (5 in 1976, 4 in 1974).

Although there are many more capitals in Western Europe, the number of correspondents based there has fallen by twice as many as the number in North America (all USA): from 46 to 34 in Western Europe, from 31 to 26 in North America. (Falls of 26% and 16% respectively.) In an election year in the United States of course concentration in North America is to be expected.

These figures for staff correspondents overseas represent 'base' locations. This does not mean that such correspondents only cover the countries in which they are based. A correspondent in the Far East might also fly to Australia; a correspondent in, say, Tel Aviv or an Arab capital might also cover stories on the Indian sub-continent. But for the most part correspondents do specialise in the general region to which they are attached, and this distribution of manpower is a genuine reflection of news priorities of the Fleet Street press.

Within regions, certain capitals or countries rather than others tend to attract the national dailies as suitable for base offices. In North America almost all correspondents are based in Washington and New York; of the 25 residential correspondents in Western Europe employed by the *Financial Times*, *The Times* and *The Daily Telegraph*, for instance, 17 are based in Germany, France and Belgium; most African correspondents and stringers are based in Johannesburg and Salisbury.

1.10 Distribution of stringers

The concentration in North America and Western Europe as far as staff correspondents are concerned is offset by the distribution of stringers. Thus, for instance, of the full list of stringers on three 'quality' papers, *The Times*, *The Daily Telegraph* and *The Guardian*, 55 or only 35% were based in these centres. Out of a total of 155 for these three papers, 47 were based in Western Europe, 34 in the Far East, 26 in Africa, 18 in the Near East, 11 in Australasia and Oceania, eight in South America and four in Eastern Europe. Respondents to the 1974 questionnaire provided a breakdown of the distribution of stringers on 'retainer' or of equivalent status. Of the 167 retainer or equivalent stringers working for the four 'qualities' (*Financial Times*, *The Times*, *Guardian* and *Daily Telegraph*), 47 or 28% were based in Western Europe, 32 or 19% in the Far East, 26 or 16% in Africa, 16 or 10% in South America, 19 or 11% in the Middle East, 10 or 6% in Australasia/Oceania, nine or 5% in North America and seven or 3% in the USSR and Eastern Europe. Thus the balance in favour of Western Europe and North America in the case of residential correspondents is strongly redressed in the case of retainer or special status stringers, and especially as far as North America is concerned. However, these figures for stringers do not include those stringers who are employed by and report to staff correspondents resident abroad, as opposed to reporting directly to London. If these were included, the number of stringers in countries or regions where there are already staff correspondents would be increased. Even so, it is unlikely that many such stringers would be on a 'retainer' or equivalent basis, and it is certain that the use of stringers does, and indeed must, compensate to some extent for the geographical imbalance in the distribution of staff correspondents. One region which appears to do badly in such terms, both in the numbers of staff correspondents and stringers attached to it is the Soviet Union and Eastern Europe. This only partly reflects the political hindrances to reporting that are experienced in this part of the world; it also reflects financial difficulty in maintaining correspondents there, relatively poor pay-off in news terms from such investment of manpower, and is to some extent off-set by the presence in London or Vienna of a small number of specialists in communist affairs.

The use of stringers by the 'popular' papers is similar to that of the 'qualities', although there are far fewer regular or retainer stringers working for the 'populars'. Of some 15 regular (not necessarily retainer) stringers for the *Daily Express* for example, four are based in Western Europe, three each in Africa and Australasia/Oceania, two in the Near East and one each in the USSR, South America and the Far East.

There is some overlap between papers in the stringers they employ. But as a general rule daily papers prefer to avoid stringers who are already working for other dailies, and will tend to look instead to those working for overseas media or for Sunday or broadcast media in the UK. Almost all stringers used in any way regularly are professional journalists, but there have been instances of the employment of stringers who were widely thought to have had political beliefs likely to affect their reporting. There is no reason to believe, however, that such instances are typical, nor that the use of non-journalist stringers is anything other than occasional.

2 Foreign news collection

2.1 Foreign news budgets

The dailies differ in the extent to which they adopt fixed budgets for foreign news, and in the extent to which any fixed budgets are used as conspicuous instruments of control. They also differ in the items they include under foreign news budgets. These factors make meaningful comparisons difficult, and not all papers were willing to divulge this kind of information. It is clear, however, that for many papers, and especially for the popular papers, foreign news expenditure is considered a very heavy investment for relatively little return in usable news material, which is not to say that foreign news is considered unimportant but simply reflects the belief that there is a limited market for foreign news. This makes foreign news expenditure especially vulnerable in a time of recession. As we have seen this is reflected in the general cut-backs in staff correspondents overseas and also, when such cut-backs have been made as far as it is thought wise or possible, in general foreign news expenses (including travel of correspondents from London). Foreign news costs for the 'quality' papers run between £400,000 and over £800,000 a year; and for the 'popular' papers between £200,000 and £400,000. These figures will naturally break down in different ways between papers, but in the case of two 'quality' papers for which a percentage breakdown was provided, salaries were the highest cost (23–30%), followed by maintenance of overseas bureaux and foreign travel (20–27%), communications (16–19%), and other important items including news agency costs, payment to contributors, and allowance for inflation (£15,000 allowance on salaries in one case). News agency costs for two 'quality' papers varied between £10,000 and £84,000, representing about 7% and 22% of costs respectively. A paper spending less on its own staff correspondents, and less overall, might therefore commit a far larger proportion of its budget to agency costs.

2.2 Autonomy of foreign news operation

While the executive responsibility for the day-to-day running of the foreign news operation rests with the Foreign Editor in most papers, it is clear that here, as in other areas of news-gathering, there exists a great deal of informal consultation and cooperation between the Foreign Editor and his colleagues in other departments, including the Features, Sports and General News desks, as well as with the Editor. Ideas for foreign news coverage may arise in the course of editorial meetings from outside the foreign department; and the Foreign Editor will himself contribute to ideas put up for coverage by other departments.

The responsibility for the hiring and firing of staff correspondents naturally

25

rests with a newspaper's Editor, although a Foreign Editor would normally be consulted closely on such considerations in respect of the foreign news department. A Foreign Editor may generally exercise greater discretion as far as part-time or stringer correspondents are concerned, although he may consult with his Editor beforehand. As we have seen, the selection of foreign news is largely the responsibility of the Foreign Editor and his staff, subject to the general exchange of ideas in editorial meetings and in informal consultation. The editing of foreign news, on the other hand, for actual inclusion in the newspaper, in some cases comes primarily under the Foreign Editor's responsibility, where there is a subs desk reporting to the Foreign Editor and working on pages normally kept free for foreign news; elsewhere, and in the case of Page One and of other pages not necessarily kept free for foreign news, the subbing of foreign news is done by the general subs desk. In the latter case there may still be some subs who tend to be specialists in the handling of foreign news and who will liaise closely with the foreign desk. On the question of logistics, ie the decision-making process whereby certain correspondents are assigned to certain stories, there will normally be considerable consultation between the Foreign Editor and his colleagues, especially where there is time for advance planning as in the case of the US elections. While there is considerable scope for consultation and exchange of ideas, there may be times when a foreign eidtor will need to act unilaterally if a fast-moving story is to be adequately covered. In such circumstances discussion will take place after the event in post-mortem analysis.

While foreign news coverage is an expensive item and as such is vulnerable in a time of economic recession, nevertheless a number of senior editorial personnel have had experience in the foreign news field and are likely to be sympathetic to its problems. Most senior people on the *Financial Times* for instance have had such experience, including the Editor, Managing Editor, Deputy Editor, News Editor and two home news reporters. The Foreign Editor of *The Times* is also Deputy Editor and stands in for the Editor when he is away. The Editor of the *Daily Mail* is a former Foreign Editor. And on *The Sunday Times*, the Foreign Editor is also Deputy Editor.

2.3 External constraints on foreign news coverage

The decline in the number of staff foreign correspondents is exacerbated in its consequences for the quality and kind of foreign news reporting that occurs by the increasing difficulties which reporters face from modes of direct and indirect censorship imposed under foreign governments. Western media organisations, wrote *The Guardian*'s Asian correspondent, Martin Woollacott, in August 1975, are increasingly seen 'not as separate and diverse organisations but as elements in a system of cultural imperialism which gathers and interprets world news according to Western interests and values and then transmits it back to non-Western societies, overwhelming their own meagre news and propaganda resources'.[1] Justification for restrictions on foreign news reporters was less often expressed in terms of short-term political or military convenience during national emergencies, and more often in *ideological* terms. Such a trend can only have been furthered by the revelations in 1975–76 that the CIA had infiltrated western and foreign news organisations in the past, and that it would continue to use stringers.

---

1   Martin Woollacott: 'Where No News is Bad News'; *The Guardian*, 27 August 1975.

Anti-western sentiment in the sphere of international news gathering and dissemination was clearly active in two related developments in 1976. The first of these was the agreement among representatives of the 'non-aligned' nations at conferences in New Delhi and in Colombo to establish a Third World 'news pool', which would involve the exchange of information between their respective national news agencies. Such a measure, aimed at reducing Third World dependence on the western international news agencies, would rationalise existing exchange agreements, and would help to further the efforts, in particular, of the Yugoslav and Indian national news agencies in this direction. Because most Third World news agencies are directly controlled by Government ministries of information or their equivalent there was fear among many western media organisations that were such a news pool to be accompanied by greater restriction on the activities of the western international news agencies and other media, such a move would greatly impair the flow of information from Third World countries to the West. On the other hand it is true to say that the western international agencies have shown great durability throughout the course of their respective histories even in the face of attempted measures of the kind proposed by the non-aligned nations of 1976. It is also true that there is considerable weight behind some of the criticisms which many third world countries make about the undesirability of dependence on western international agencies. It is questionable however whether a news service operated by government-controlled news agencies would in fact help to improve the situation for these countries. Political disagreements between member countries would continually threaten the life of such an enterprise, while government sensitivities would considerably devalue its news-content. The scope for commercial revenue (in regions of the world where few media-systems are affluent) would be poor, and indeed, if the enterprise were to survive as a commercial operation, it might actually require a monopoly both in news-gathering and news-dissemination. This in turn would oblige the western agencies to become clients of the new agency for want of other news-sources, which is exactly the situation they now fear.

Such fears were further excited by a draft resolution presented to the UNESCO conference in Nairobi in November 1976 and supported by the Soviet bloc. This proposed that 'nations are responsible for activities in the international sphere of all mass media under their jurisdiction'. This was widely considered to encourage dictation to international media. The Conference however turned down the proposal and referred the draft to the drafting and negotiating committee for review. Voting in favour of this postponement was 78 to 15, with the West, most African and Asian countries and South America voting for, and the Soviets, some Africans and Iraq against. The issue will not arise again until the next UNESCO general conference in 1978.

Regardless of the success or otherwise of such proposals that directly seek the international legitimation of government control over international media, it is very common for governments to impose various restrictions on foreign news reporters – as for instance did India under Emergency Rule up until September 1976.[1] However, even the formal lifting of such restrictions, if accompanied by continued suppression of domestic media, greatly interferes with the work of

---

1   Some countries also have protective laws which add hugely to the cost of foreign news bureaux. Peru for example requires that there are three Peruvians for every American correspondent (J Blyth, *UK Press Gazette*, 25 April 1977).

foreign correspondents and with the quality of news reporting since domestic media are of considerable importance as news sources. There is no doubt as to the widespread occurrence of severe restrictions on domestic media activities, and these are regularly documented by several bodies, including the International Press Institute, the news agencies and Freedom House, a non-government US organisation. In its annual report for 1976, for example, Freedom House claimed that the percentage of the world's population living in countries with a free press stood at only 19·6%. Seventy-one out of 212 territories and dependencies in this report were categorised as 'not free', and a further 80 as 'partly free'.[1]

The concept of 'press freedom' however is not unambiguous, nor ideologically neutral. It is true that in defining press freedom for other parts of the world some western observers are blind to deficiencies in their own. However if it is accepted that the task of news-gathering by a professional corps of men and women who have no direct nor substantial political or other axes to grind or masters to obey (beyond their respective publics) and whose work is practised without fear of intervention from government, industrial or other external pressures – if these things are accepted as valuable and worthy of preservation, then there can be no doubt as to the current size and seriousness of the problem of the decline of such 'press freedom' in the world today. Only considerable diplomatic and professional vigilance is likely to arrest this trend. One possible mode of improvement might indeed be through the UN if, in the light of events in Nairobi 1976, a sufficient number of nations were to support a positive proposal supporting press freedom. Such a proposal might incorporate international agreements to refrain from infiltration of media organisations by intelligence agents, to recognise and protect the personal and professional freedoms of accredited correspondents and so on. Offending nations might be sanctioned by the reciprocal withdrawal of rights to foreign correspondents, or of training and other media-related aid schemes.

The increasing difficulties of international news reporting may be a contributory factor in the decline of staff foreign correspondents for the British national newspaper press. If the news from a certain country is so restricted that that country is no longer considered 'newsworthy' then a newspaper is unlikely to invest scarce manpower in reporting it. (The alternative option of greatly *increasing* such investment to overcome the obstacles is, sadly, rarely considered possible.) Furthermore where a news-centre is extremely dangerous to the life and property of correspondents assigned to it, then a newspaper will face difficulties, firstly, in finding suitable candidates for the assignment, and secondly, in finding candidates who are prepared to put up with such conditions for long periods of time.

2.4 Agency subscriptions

All the national daily papers subscribe to the overseas news services of Reuters, of which they are part owners through their membership of the NPA, and many also take the economic news services of the British agency. Likewise the Sunday papers, which in some cases have access to the same agency teleprinters as their sister dailies. All dailies take the service of the American news agency, Associated Press (AP), save the *Financial Times* and *The Guardian*, although these two,

---

1 Reported in *UK Press Gazette*, 3 January 1977.

in common with other 'quality' newspapers also subscribe to the economic service run by AP in conjunction with Dow Jones (the leading Wall Street news agency and publisher of the *Wall Street Journal*), AP–DJ. Those that do take AP also subscribe to the agency's photographic services. *The Observer* takes AP, but *The Sunday Times* does not. All dailies take the service of the second American agency, United Press International (UPI), save *The Times*, which only takes a limited service of UPI photos. *The Observer* does not take UPI, but *The Sunday Times* takes a limited weekend service. Most subscribers of UPI also take its photo service. *The Times* has an exclusive Fleet Street arrangement with a fourth international agency, Agence France Presse (AFP),[1] and *The Sunday Times* also makes use of this service.

In addition to their subscriptions to the major world news agencies, which provide by far the most comprehensive news services on general world affairs, some papers have arrangements with smaller and more localised agencies. *The Times* has an exchange arrangement with the expanding New York Times News Service, and also takes the English-language services of Tass and Novosti. *The Guardian* has access to the service of the *Washington Post* and *Los Angeles Times*, with which it joins in distributing a news service to Europe.[2] Staff correspondents of the national papers resident abroad in some cases receive national services or specialised services for foreign correspondents of some of the national news agencies. Some papers have access to AFP through the national service of AFP received in the Paris offices; in Germany some bureaux take the domestic service of Deutche Presseagentur (DPA) and so on. With the exception of *The Times*' decision to drop UPI news service, and *The Observer*'s similar decision to stop taking a limited weekend service of UPI, the basic position with regard to agency subscriptions has not changed markedly in the recent recession period.

2.5 Cost of agencies

One notable feature of agency subscriptions is the relatively high cost of the agency with which the national newspapers have the closest relationship, Reuters. Absolute costs vary from paper to paper, but relative to the charges imposed by the American agencies, Reuters' service is considerably more expensive. In the case of one of the popular papers the subscription paid to Reuters was almost four times greater than that paid to the more expensive of the two American agencies (£30,000 as against £8,175). This differential is slightly less if the cost of the American services is made to include the separate subscriptions to domestic American agency services in the United States (eg the special Washington service of UPI, which goes to many newspaper bureaux).[3] Otherwise, the British nationals are getting in return for this greatly additional outlay a world news service which is more responsive to the British market than the American agencies, since it is of course mainly owned by British interests, draws a far higher proportion of its revenues from the British market than do the American agencies, and is *controlled* mainly by British nationals

---

1 The only other national media organisation subscribing to the AFP's world service is the BBC.
2 Thus some papers, including *The Times* and *The Guardian*, have their own foreign news services. *The Observer*'s foreign service for instance is marketed to 400 overseas clients by the New York Times News Service.
3 In addition to subscriptions to Reuters, AP and UPI for full world services in London, one of the 'popular' papers also pays an additional £1,300 to UPI and £2,500 to AP for domestic US services. But it also pays to Reuters an additional £1,850 in Paris for its European service.

(although a large proportion of its total staff are overseas nationals). And in certain respects the make-up of its news service may reflect British interests rather more than the services provided by the American agencies.

2.6 Agency communication facilities

The agencies provide services other than direct news services. They also provide communication facilities. In a few cases, the national dailies sub-lease wires from the main news agencies which have surplus facilities for this purpose. This is a practice developed in recent years only, and is availed of mainly by the 'quality' newspapers which carry a sufficient weight of foreign news to justify the expense of a complete line. The *Financial Times* sub-leases a permanent open line from Reuters for transatlantic communications; likewise *The Times*; *The Daily Telegraph* sub-leases a line from AP for the same channel. The 'qualities' are also more likely to use agency facilities for 'piggy-backing' their copy from important news centres on a semi-regular basis; that is, they send news copy through the agencies' communication facilities rather than their own. In which centres such arrangements are made, and with which agencies, depends in part on the quality of personal relationships between the journalists on the spot. There are two problems with such arrangements which make the quality of personal relationships important. The first concerns exclusivity. The journalist of a paper which uses an agency's communications is naturally sensitive to the possibility that the contents of his copy, if unfamiliar to the agency, may be 'lifted' and disseminated or in some way used by the agency itself. The second is the problem of what happens in emergencies or news crises, when the agency may wish to keep open all its lines for its own use. In this case the needs of local journalists will be given relatively low priority, so that at the very time the service is most needed, the receptivity of the agency may be at its lowest.

There are two main reasons for using agency communication facilities: cost and convenience. Cost is at least as important a consideration as convenience for the 'quality' papers, given their more substantial copy needs; whereas the 'populars', unlikely to enter into regular arrangements of this kind, and needing their help only for major crisis stories, are more concerned for the convenience of being able to use an agency's assistance for getting copy out of a country at a time when other communication facilities may be out of order or inaccessible. But of course it is precisely at such a time, as we have seen, that an agency may want to retain as many of its facilities as possible for its own use, and when there is likely to be a queue of anxious users. Agencies extend such assistance not only to the British market of course. Reuters for instance handles much of the communications of the New York Times News Service (distributed in the same way as the services of the major international news agencies), and also handled the communications of the short-lived Asian News Agency. The agencies often handle the communications of foreign news bureaux of non-British newspapers

2.7 Reuters' service to UK provincial newspapers

The Reuters' service is of great importance not only to the national papers, but also to the provincial press. Under a long-standing agreement dating back to the last century, Reuters does not distribute its general news services for newspapers outside London directly, but indirectly through the Press Association, which, with the NPA, is the second largest owner of the agency. The Press Association makes a selection from Reuters' foreign news, and to a lesser

30

degree from the service of Associated Press, and compiles its own foreign news wire which then goes to its provincial members. Some of the larger newspaper groups may subscribe to the services of the international agencies in their London offices and distribute a selection of such news to their members.

2.8 Importance of agencies to the UK press

The importance of the agencies to the foreign news service of the British national press, however, is not especially clear from the evidence of the printed page where there tends to be relatively little acknowledgement of the agencies. The agencies themselves profess to find the British press the least inclined in the world to acknowledge any such dependence. One reason for this of course is that the British press has one of the strongest bodies of overseas newsmen to represent it, even despite recent cutbacks, and stands among the few nations which do possess such a facility, namely the United States, Japan, West Germany, France and the Soviet Union (not necessarily in that order). However, it is difficult to accept that the importance of the agencies is truly reflected by the extent of acknowledgement they receive. In the first place, the agencies have representatives (staff correspondents or regular stringers) in all the most important and most of the lesser capitals of the world, where the British press is able to cover relatively few capitals in this way. They therefore are or tend to be the most important initial or early warning system of an impending news development. A newspaper may pick up an on-going story and either ask its nearest staff foreign correspondent to fly in and write up the same story, or rewrite the story from London with some extra reporting effort by telephone calls to well-placed contacts. Secondly, the agencies provide certain key services to staff correspondents and stringers in the field. One of these we have discussed, the communication facility, which is generally paid for. But an experienced staff correspondent normally will have developed a good relationship with at least one of the agency bureaux in order to have access to the agency service in that bureau, and thus acquaint himself with latest news developments in his part of the world, and in the world generally (since the general state of play of world news is some indication of how important his own centre is likely to be, and he will adjust his own expenditure of time and energy according to the likelihood of its being productive). Thirdly, in their capacity as clients of an agency, newspapers may request the agencies to develop certain stories in which they are particularly interested, or may use the local agency representative in a news-centre as a news source. Finally, apart from their importance to the British market specifically, the agencies are of overwhelming importance as news sources for the media of most countries of the world, and in many cases rank even more highly as news sources for the diplomatic corps and foreign ministries of even the most prosperous countries, than internal diplomatic and intelligence channels.

The leading agencies of the world, those that aim both to gather and to distribute news in most or all countries of the world, are generally regarded as being AFP, AP, Reuters, Tass and UPI. There are in addition some strong national agencies which sell their services in particular areas of the world or in a limited number of countries outside their own (including, most notably, DPA and Kyodo), or whose services tend to concentrate only on certain areas of news. Finally there are a great many national agencies which often act as important news sources for the international agencies, and as important clients for the world agency services. In some less affluent countries the primary purpose of the national agency may be to collect and edit incoming world agency services.

31

Staff correspondents of newspapers may often consult the services of national agencies. In many cases, especially in Africa and ex-colonial territories, the national agencies have been established with the aid of the agencies of the ex-colonial powers (mainly Reuters and AFP), and may retain a special relationship with them.

The leading agencies of the world do not confine themselves to newspaper markets, nor do they deal only with print services. Both Reuters and AP for example are associated with extremely powerful financial news services, which are sold to the business and financial markets, as well as to media, through Reuters' Economic Services and Associated Press-Dow Jones respectively.[1] AP and UPI both provide photographic news services and as such are the leading news-photo services of the world. Reuters and UPI are leading in the world news-film market for television: Reuters through its part-ownership of Visnews, UPI through its part-ownership of UPITN.

The British newspaper industry is fortunate in having Reuters based in Britain, and in having ownership control over Reuters.[2] As the economic recession progresses, and as the condition of Fleet Street generally deteriorates, the deterioration of foreign news resources in the Press leads or may lead to greater dependence on the services of the news agencies. And while the agencies are not unaffected by recession either, Reuters own position is a strong one, for it depends for the bulk of its own revenue not on media subscriptions to its services, but on subscriptions from the business and finance community to its economic services. In some respects it is sheltered even from the effects of general business decline. The Reuters' Monitor Report for example provides a currency exchange news service which is of general interest and importance almost regardless of recession. Its substantial foreign currency earnings (84% of total turnover was earned overseas in 1975) have appreciated considerably in sterling terms. These help to offset the effects of domestic inflation in the UK where the agency incurs a high proportion of its total costs.

One possible danger in present circumstances may be that as a result of traditional pride in their own news services from overseas, the British national newspapers may be reluctant to exploit the advantages offered by the news agencies. For one thing they are concerned about the lack of exclusivity of agency services; but on the other hand it is possible for newspapers to commission special reports from the agencies at a price usually far less than the cost of covering for themselves. This is not to suggest that the agencies offer the only or the best means of preserving standards in the field of foreign news coverage. It may also be that papers need to consider more seriously the possibility of sharing correspondents in certain busy centres; or to reassess the advantages of strong New York/Washington bureaux in favour of more equitable distribution over continents; or to consider greater sharing of bureaux resources. Future application of new technology may also be helpful: the use of facsimile transmission for instance instead of telex for transatlantic communication is one such possibility.

The most important agency sources of news for Fleet Street as we have seen are Reuters, AP and UPI. Only *The Times* takes Tass in London. The usefulness of Tass to the western press is mainly as an indicator of political attitude and

---

1 These have now been joined by a joint venture between UPI and Commodity News Service (Kansas) on world markets, established in January 1977.
2 Broadcast media also benefit considerably.

opinion in Moscow rather than as a straight news service. Since the leading western agencies will quote from Tass, direct subscription to the service is dispensable. In the case of the fourth leading western agency, AFP, again it is only *The Times* which takes the service directly in London. It does so on an exclusive basis so that the French agency's English-language coverage of the world is not available to other newspapers (but is taken by the BBC). Some Paris bureaux of the nationals subscribe to or have access to its domestic news service for French news. There are differences of coverage between the agencies which justify subscriptions to more than one of the leading agencies, although AFP is in many ways more distinctive from the other three world agencies than these are from one another, yet is not widely used by the British press. While the saving from dropping any one agency service is not great, as a proportion of total foreign news costs, and while it is undeniably useful to have at least a second corroborating source on any developing story, there may be some advantage in the greater development of what are known in the United States as 'subsidiary' agencies, such as the New York Times News Service. One problem about the main US subsidiary agencies however is that they do concentrate very heavily on US news in their overseas news distribution. And because such services are generally compiled from news gathered by particularly strong news organisations, they are likely to reflect the same basic preoccupations of the Anglo-American press sphere. On the other hand they do offer a much heavier diet of interpretative commentary pieces which are not generally available from agency sources on the English market in any quantity, except to the relatively small readership of the *International Herald Tribune*, now printed in England as well as France. Greater use of such services might also justify reductions in the New York or Washington bureaux, freeing correspondents for work from other, possibly cheaper capitals.

3 The News Agencies

3.1 Ownership

One of the most important features of the four leading world agencies in their role as international news wholesalers is their fundamentally *national* character, although Reuters is in some respects less 'national' than the other three. AP is a newspaper co-operative owned by its member newspapers. Until recently when full AP membership was extended to Canadian papers in 1971, all full members of AP with the right of bond purchase were located in the United States. UPI is a private but media-associated commercial enterprise, a subsidiary of E W Scripps Co, which owns a controlling interest in the agency in addition to its interest in Scripps-Howard Newspapers (fourth largest US daily newspaper chain in control of circulation). The French agency AFP, is not actually 'owned' by anybody. It was given provisional status as a public body in 1944 and in 1957 was formally reconstituted in law, granted the rights of a private individual but outside all conventional judicial categories. The organisation is administered by the Conseil d'Administration on which sit 8 newspaper directors, 2 ORTF representatives, 3 representatives of public service clients of the agency and 2 representatives of the agency's personnel. In addition a Conseil Supérieur has the power to monitor the agency's fulfilment of its legal responsibilities and this body's membership includes 1 member of the Conseil d'Etat, 1 magistrate from the Cour de Cassation (Supreme Court of Appeal), 2 newspaper directors, 1 journalist, 1 representative of ORTF and 2 others. Finally a Commission Financière is charged with the surveillance of AFP's financial affairs, and comprises 2 members of the Cour des Comptes and 1 expert elected by the Minister of Finance.

Like AP, Reuters is also owned mainly by its national press, that of the UK. But although it is often considered to be a cooperative in the same spirit as AP, the similarity stops short. The UK press has never been financially powerful enough to support Reuters in the way the US press supports AP, not to mention UPI. Few of the structural characteristics of a cooperative which AP exhibits are to be found in the operation of Reuters. Reuters is a limited liability company incorporated under the Companies Act (UK); its capital is owned by the press of Britain, Australia and New Zealand. The Press Association, representing the provincial daily press of the UK, owns approximately 41·5%; the Newspaper Publishers Association representing London-based national newspapers, owns an equivalent share; while the remainder is divided between the Australian Associated Press, representing Australian daily newspapers, which has approximately 14% and the New Zealand Press Association, representing the dailies of New Zealand, which has approximately 3%. Ownership is therefore concentrated in the UK, and Australian and New Zealand representatives do

35

not normally attend the regular board meetings in London, although there are occasional board meetings in the Pacific area which they do attend for discussion of area-related issues. In practice, control of the organisation rests largely with the Managing Director appointed by the board and his staff.

3.2 Source of revenues

It is not ties of ownership alone which give the agencies their national character. Home markets for all the agencies account for a substantial proportion of total revenues. In the case of the American agencies the proportion of total revenue accounted for by the domestic United States market is certainly not less than 60% and is probably around 80%. AFP also looks to the home market for the bulk of its revenue. In the early seventies, overseas revenue accounted for approximately 17% of its overall revenue. And of its domestic revenue, some three-quarters is derived not from media clients but from organisations of the French state in their capacity as clients for AFP services. This heavy dependence on such revenue is the basis for claims that are sometimes made to the effect that the AFP is 'subsidised' by the State. But the question of revenues should be separated from the question of editorial control, in which matter AFP certainly enjoys as much autonomy in news reporting as, for example the BBC.

Reuters, unlike the other three agencies, has no domestic arm as such. The Press Association, which is part-owner of the agency, distributes international news from Reuters and AP to the provincial UK press. Reuters distributes its news services direct to the national newspapers in London and to the Press Association's London Head Office. It distributes financial and economic news services to clients throughout the country, whether media or non-media. Because of the arrangement with the PA, however, the importance of the domestic market may not be so evident in the case of Reuters as it is in the case of other leading agencies. Yet the proportion of UK revenue to the total is still considerable for just one country. In the early seventies, overseas trading revenue represented approximately 80% of Reuters' overall revenue, and the remaining 20% was mostly accounted for by the UK[1]. Outside its home market Reuters' most important market area, like that of AFP, is Continental Europe which in 1972 accounted for 38% of total trading revenue, followed by North America (17%), Asia (11%), Africa (7%), the Middle East (3%) and South America (3%). While Western Europe is of great importance to all four leading western agencies, there are differences with respect to the relative importance of other markets. AFP's trading position in North America is weak by comparison with Reuters' which has made a determined assault on the North American market in recent years. On the other hand, Reuters' activity in South America is relatively limited in comparison with that of the North American agencies.

The domestic markets are unusually wealthy markets for the agencies partly because they are countries which happen to be saturated with media. Each domestic market accounts for a large percentage of the total number of clients served by its agency. Less than a third of all UPI clients are overseas clients. On the US market the agency served, in 1976, 1,146 newspapers and 3,680 broadcast stations, out of a worldwide client total of 6,911. Leading overseas markets for UPI as for AP are Western Europe and South America. Although

---

1 The proportion of overseas revenue has however risen fairly steadily over the past two decades, and stood as high as 84% in 1975.

directly comparable figures are not available, the proportion of direct overseas clients for AP's services is higher than in the case of UPI, and approaches half the world total of approximately 9,000. AFP's smaller world total in 1972 amounted to over 700 (including other agencies), of which the home market, excluding the State clients, accounted for 23%.[1] It cannot be said that the proportion of UK clients to the total of Reuters' clients is as great as in the case of the other agencies, but just as Reuters' revenue base tends to be Continental Europe, which in conjunction with the UK accounts for over half of the total trading revenue, this same area almost certainly accounts for a similar majority of its clients. For instance, Reuters in 1969 distributed directly or indirectly to 3,154 newspapers around the world: 52% of these, or 1,640, were located in Europe.

3.3 Distribution of resources

Concentration of ownership, revenue and clients within national boundaries appears to influence the distribution of agency resources in favour of the home markets in the case of the American agencies and, to a lesser degree, the French agency. The number of AP's domestic bureaux (110) in the early seventies represented 65% of the total; and UPI's domestic bureaux represent almost 60% of the total. Moreover, many middle-ranking US bureaux are as large as or larger than some of the larger overseas bureaux. The Philadelphia bureaux of the two agencies were considered more important, in terms of manpower resources, than Austria or Holland (with almost three times and seven times greater population respectively than Philadelphia), and about as important as Italy with some 26 times the population. With the exception of major capitals such as Tokyo or Buenos Aires, the non-European and non-US bureaux of the leading agencies are not generally as well staffed as the European. The proportion of domestic to overseas bureaux is less striking than in the case of the American agencies, but France is a much smaller country and requires fewer resources for adequate coverage. In 1973, in addition to the Paris Head Office, there were 12 principal AFP bureaux in France. Overseas there were 82 principal bureaux. Comparison with Reuters does not arise since Reuters does not cover the UK for the UK market. Excluding those staff in Paris handling foreign news, 17% of AFP's editorial manpower was concentrated in France in 1972, and 19% of its technical support staff.

Distribution of resources in favour of the home market is accompanied as the figures would indicate by a superiority of service, very evident in the case of the American agencies and to a lesser degree in the case of AFP. The American agencies in the first place offer a much greater variety of services for their domestic clients or members than are generally available overseas: for instance, in the case of AP, two national trunk wires and a variety of state or regional wires, a special broadcast wire for radio and television stations, and special sports and financial wires. Most newspaper clients can receive their services in teletypesetter form which means that they can transmit agency material into print without the need for further typesetting on their part. From 1975 an increasing number of the larger clients receive datastream services which allow

---

1 These figures compare interestingly with those for *Tass* which in 1976 had under 400 overseas subscribers, including other agencies, but which served 3744 print media in the Soviet Union and 38 broadcast media. The figures were given by the agency's director-manager in New York in a talk to the VII Public Relations World Congress, 1976, and quoted by Robert V Brown in *Editor and Publisher*, 11 September 1976, p 52.

the client to dial the stories he requires in advance and to receive those stories in a matter of seconds. Overseas clients do not enjoy the same proliferation of different services. There is generally only one wire to choose from; in many cases, although AP more than UPI has resisted the trend, this wire is distributed through a national news agency which may translate the service and in any case generally shortens it greatly. While this is convenient in some important respects it does also narrow the range of choice. In the UK, however, the national papers have access to the complete one-wire services of both American agencies. There is no provision yet for delivery of these services via teletypesetter or by datastream, not least because of the state of technology outside the United States.

3.4 Refinements of service on home markets

United States clients or members of the American agencies enjoy certain refinements in the news-coverage they receive, refinements which affect overseas clients only indirectly, if at all. AP, for instance, unlike UPI, maintains a 'Special Assignments' team in Washington whose members work on longer-term projects that require the kind of 'digging' and 'investigative reporting' that is not common on ordinary news beats for the wire services. This team tends to concentrate on Washington or federal stories which are of primarily domestic significance, not geared specifically for the overseas market and often not transmitted overseas in any form. Much the same could be said of AP's 'enterprise' output from New York, which has its own editor to put up ideas for unusual coverage, and here again the domestic news stories appear to get most attention. The enterprise reporting is based on a bank of specialists maintained in New York, and includes writers on racial developments, consumer interests, science, aerospace, education, religion, urban affairs, auto racing and golf. There are few such specialists working for the major news agencies outside the United States. Provision for special client requests (for coverage beyond that regularly provided) is unusually generous in the case of Washington, and yet does not occur as a separate organisational feature in any other bureau. Thus UPI's Washington bureau houses a regional desk to handle special client requests from the domestic market, and an International desk which serves the interests of overseas clients in a similar way. Both AP and UPI maintain organisations representing their members or clients (primarily US members and clients).

The Associated Press Managing Editors (APME), representing AP member newspapers, meet each year and elect committees which sit to discuss and organise research into aspects of AP functioning and general newspaper functions. More than 500 editors sat on APME committees in 1971. The Association also offers various awards for outstanding coverage each year. There can be little doubt that the AP relationship with its members through APME helps create a unity of identity amongst members, a reliable and powerful means of feedback, an impetus to excellence in professional practice and a forum for new ideas that is not matched by the European agencies. This, of course, should not obscure the fact that all agencies have very important informal relationships with their clients; and in the case of the European agencies the smaller numbers of domestic clients, as well as the great importance of a heterogenous overseas market to Reuters, militate against the usefulness of an APME-type association. UPI's nearest equivalent to APME is the recently established Newspaper Advisory Board, which grew out of the annual Edicon conferences for UPI's clients, which has also set up committees similar to those of APME.

AFP shares something in common with the American agencies in the importance it gives to the domestic French market. France is its most important source of revenue, as we have seen, accounting for almost 80% of the total, largely because of funds injected through State clients; and France attracts the heaviest expenditure, around two-thirds of the total. A sizeable proportion of all clients are situated within the country, approximately 23% if State clients in Paris are excluded, and 15% of all major bureaux. Just as some of the middle-ranking North American bureaux of the US agencies are better endowed with resources than some of the middle-ranking European bureaux of the same agencies, some of AFP's French provincial bureaux are more heavily manned than certain bureaux which cover whole European countries. Each of the major French regions has a regional director and between two and six full-time editorial staff and auxiliary staff. By contrast, the Madrid bureau, which is additionally important as a source of news of interest to AFP's South American clients, has a staff of four editorial journalists in addition to a director and auxiliary staff; the bureau in Vienna, which covers much of Eastern Europe, consists of one director and three editors; Athens has an editorial staff of three. Just as the scope of client choice for clients of the US agencies is greater within the US market than outside it, French clients of AFP generally have access to both national and regional material and other specialist services, whereas overseas (but not in the UK) AFP is in most countries distributed via national news agencies, and the service very much truncated. (Where there is no legal requirement for foreign agency services to pass through national agencies, clients often have the option of subscribing to the original full-length service.)

3.5 Bureaux: area of coverage and size

Whereas most European countries attract their own bureau coverage, with three or four bureaux of the major news agencies located in their capitals, this is not quite so common in the less developed world. Bureau chiefs in Nairobi, Kenya, for example, are responsible for coverage of up to six or more countries in the East African region. Of course they do have stringers as assistants in these countries, who, because of the character of communications in Africa, file direct to head offices in London or Paris, but these stringers are in other respects junior to the Nairobi office which can direct coverage and if necessary take over. Until the recent Lebanese crisis, Beirut bureaux generally acted as bases for coverage of up to five other Arab countries. The largest bureaux also tend to be those situated in the major capitals of the developed world or which are well-situated to serve as regional centres. The most highly staffed (editorial) bureaux of one American agency in the early seventies were London (40), Paris (26), Rio de Janeiro (21), Tokyo (16), Beirut (15), Saigon (14) and Buenos Aires (13). Less well-staffed bureaux included Cairo (9), Bangkok (7) Bogota (3) and Dacca (2). A large percentage of such staff numbers however are engaged in routine monitoring, translation and similar work.

The agencies tend to employ more local journalists (citizens of the countries covered) than they employ from their own countries – up to three and a half times as many locals as non-locals. However, despite the high number of local journalists employed it is clear that the agencies prefer *control* to rest in the hands of nationals of their own countries or nationals of the Anglo-Saxon world. Available evidence suggests that two-thirds of all bureaux are headed by nationals of the agencies' own base countries and a further percentage by white commonwealth or West European journalists, while a quarter only are headed by locally recruited journalists or other nationals. A higher percentage of all stringers are locally recruited journalists than staff correspondents, and non-journalist 'support' staff are also mostly locals.

3.6 News regionalisation

One important consequence of Reuter's greater dependence on overseas revenues than is the case with the other agencies has been its decision to greatly expand the extent to which it *regionalises* its news services overseas; that is to say, since the 1960's Reuters has focused more heavily on *regional* news as opposed to general global news requirements. This involves the gathering of African, Middle Eastern and Asian news which is primarily of use only to countries within those regions. In recent years it started an Arabic news service for Arabic news clients in the Middle East. It claims that relatively high proportions of some of its African wires for example carry news primarily of interest to Africa, and the extent to which these services are regionalised is certainly greater than is the case with the other agencies.[1] The American agencies, depending mainly for their revenues on the home market, and conscious of the limited demand for foreign news on the US market, do not regionalise their news services to the same extent.[2] AP basically distributes the same service throughout the world, and although it used to make provision in London for the insertion of regional European news and African news, the extent to which this facility is utilised has fallen off in recent years. UPI's services, making use of computer centres in Brussels and Hong Kong are more regionalised than those of AP, and its service to London for instance shows greater concentration on news of Western European affairs than AP's.[3] AFP regionalises its news services more extensively than the American agencies, especially on its African wires, and to a lesser extent for its service to Asia.

3.7 Reuters' market diversification

The continued viability and strength of Reuters as a leading international news agency has been greatly helped by major developments over the past decade and a half. Some of these have occurred on the traditional news side: in some of the most important world media markets – in particular France, Germany and the United States – Reuters no longer depends on the domestic agency services of other agencies to help it in its coverage of these countries, and this has given it greater freedom of manoeuvre in capturing markets in these affluent regions. But much the most important developments have occurred outside the traditional news media. In particular the economic services, which have a history going back to the original Baron de Reuter, have been greatly expanded since the early sixties helped by the great increase in communications capacity that came about with the introduction and exploitation of telephonic cable and multiplex lines, and the arrangement with Ultronic Systems in 1964 which gave Reuters the world rights outside of the United States to Ultronic's market quotation, interrogation and display system. Reuters economic services have now become the major source of revenue for Reuters, contributing to well over half of trading revenue. This marked the entry of Reuters into the field of computerised services in which it has led the way for all the agencies. The

---

1 Available content analysis indicates the actual figure may be up to 30%.
2 In some respects regionalisation of news on US agency wires has diminished in recent years.
3 Although AP has followed Reuters and UPI in computerising its world news services, it is unlikely that the facility of greater news regionalisation which computerisation offers will be availed of.

growth of computer services such as Stockmaster and Videomaster was accompanied by an equally rapid development of teleprinter services in the economic field. In the United States, Reuters entered into strong competition for the first time against the well-established Dow Jones, and particularly successful competition in the commodity market against the Kansas-based Commodity News Service.[1] Depression in the early 'seventies hit the economic services and reduced their rate of growth as activity on stock markets declined drastically. But at least one new service was designed to offset even this obstacle to profit. The innovation was the Monitor Service, which provided immediate and direct access to the money market rates of leading world banks. Other ventures by Reuters include its entry into CATV news provision in the United States; its continued partnership with the BBC in the newsfilm business, Visnews; the establishment of 'audio' or voicecast news reports for radio; and the establishment of a research and development subsidiary, IDR Inc., in the US, to facilitate its exploitation of computer services. The only major agency activity in which Reuters has no part is in wirephoto or photo transmission systems, which have traditionally been the preserve of the American agencies on the international markets. Nor does it generally provide teleprinter news services specifically designed for broadcast clients in the manner of the American agencies for US broadcast clients.

3.8 Agency content

A 1974 comparative study of AP's general European wire with Reuters' South European wire over a five-day period and of UPI's UK wire with AFP's English-language wire for the UK for a three-day period, suggested a number of general features of content distribution on the services of the major international news agencies available on the UK market. (Note: Reuters' South European wire showed a 75% similarity of stories with the agency's UK wire in a one-day pilot study, the difference partly accounted for by the exclusion of UK stories on the UK wire.) For the most part, these broad characteristics, unless otherwise stated, broadly conform to patterns observed on international news services of the major western agencies in other parts of the world.

A word count of the Reuters and AP wires on one Friday in March 1974, showed approximate totals of 49,500 and 54,000 respectively; and for the UPI and AFP wires for one Friday in May 1974, approximate totals of 38,000 and 32,400 respectively. The wires of AFP and UPI were somewhat shorter, by between a third and a quarter, than the wires of Reuters and AP. Although UPI carried more dispatches than AFP (15%), 936 as against 814 for the *three*-day period in April 1974, AFP carried many more stories (which may be made up of a number of dispatches). In the three-day period, AFP carried 418 stories, UPI carried 256; thus AFP carried 63% more stories than UPI, although these stories were on average shorter than those of UPI in length. In the five-day study of the Reuters and AP wires in August 1974, AP's European wire carried some 14% more stories than Reuters' South European wire (totals of 602 and 528 respectively for the full period), but Reuters carried about 18% more dispatches than AP. AFP's daily average of stories was higher than for any of the other wires.

The dominant area of coverage on all four wires, except for the AP wire, was Western Europe, which accounted for between 28–37% of all dispatches and between 26–37% of all stories. AP gave greater priority to news from North America (39% of all dispatches, 43% of all stories).

1 In 1977 CNS joined with UPI to provide a new agency economic service outside the US to compete both with AP-Dow Jones and RES.

(Note: because the basis of determination was the individual dispatch, and because in some cases dispatches referred to more than one country, the figures for dispatches in this particular context of geographical breakdown are more reliable than the figures for stories. But in general terms the breakdown by story reflects the breakdown by dispatch.)

The second most important area of coverage was North America except for AP which gave second priority to Western Europe. North America accounted for between 11 and 24% of all dispatches and between 11 and 27% of all stories on the wires of Reuters, UPI and AFP, and AP devoted 31% of dispatches, 26% of stories to Western Europe.

These two regions, Western Europe and North America, accounted for well over half of all dispatches and stories on the wires of Reuters, UPI and AP, and rather less in the case of AFP, accounting for between 48% and 61% of all dispatches on the wires of Reuters, AP and UPI, and between 57% and 67% of all stories, and 39% of dispatches, 38% of stories on the AFP wire.

Reuters and AP gave approximately equal attention to the Middle East and the Far East (7–11% of stories, 8–12% of dispatches). UPI gave considerably more attention to the Middle East, and more attention to Africa than the Far East. Of these three areas, AFP gave relatively considerable attention to both the Far East and Africa, each area accounting for about a fifth of the agency's total output. In most cases, Eastern Europe and South America received little attention in proportionate terms, Eastern Europe faring better (4–10% of all dispatches and stories) than South America (2–7%). Extremely little attention was given to Australasia and Oceania (0–1% of all dispatches and stories of all agencies).

In terms of the number of stories carried by, say, Reuters, these figures indicate that the daily average for the five-day period amounted to no more than 52 and 28 stories from Western Europe and North America respectively, 15 from the Middle East, 14 from Asia, 12 from Africa, 9 each from Eastern Europe and South America, and 2 from Australasia and Oceania. Naturally, many of these stories would have continued over the five-day period, but in this study each day was treated separately, so that the weekly total would greatly exaggerate the number of *distinct* stories in one week.

The content of the wires was in all cases dominated by politics and economics. Politics accounted for 40% of UPI's wire, 37% of Reuters', 36% of AFP's and 29% of AP's. Economics accounted for 20% of AFP's wire, 15% of UPI's and AP's, 12% of Reuters'. These two categories together accounted for over half of the entire content of AFP and UPI, and a little under half of the entire content of Reuters and AP.

The next most important single category was sport, accounting for 6% of the AFP wire and 9% in the case of each of the other agencies. An aggregate category of 'sensational' news made up of stories concerning intra-national and inter-national violent political conflict, business and political crime, crime and legal, tragedy, disaster and accident, accounted for approximately a quarter of all news on the wires of Reuters, AP and UPI, and rather less in the case of AFP. A second aggregate category, 'social and welfare' made up of news of science and technology, social and welfare, education, religion and culture accounted for around 8% of all stories on the wires of UPI, AP and Reuters, a little higher in the case of AFP. Human Interest stories accounted for around 10 % of the coverage of UPI and AP, but half of that in the case of Reuters and AFP. Coverage of labour relations and of industry together accounted for between 2 and 4 % of the total in all cases.

Measures of wire similarity were constructed in comparison of UPI with AFP and Reuters with AP. There was little similarity between AFP and UPI. On one of the three days they were examined, for instance, only 27 stories were carried on both wires, and these constituted only 21·7 % of all AFP stories and 42·1 % of all UPI stories. From other sources it seems highly likely that UPI would be closer in this respect to AP and Reuters. Between 35 % and 44 % of Reuters' wire content in the five-day period examined, in terms of numbers of stories, also appeared on the AP wire, accounting for 31–40 % of AP's wire. It is surprising to find that over half of the Reuters' wire consisted of material different to that to be found on the AP wire and vice versa, in terms of story numbers. However, a great deal of this must be accounted for by the substantially greater coverage of North America on the AP wire. In the case of AFP's difference from UPI the most likely source of difference is the greater priority given by AFP to the Far East and to Africa, and to the tendency, also to be found in the data, for AFP to draw its news from a wider variety of datelines in any given area, thus helping to account also for its higher number of stories.

The agencies' coverage was examined for an indication of the extent to which its stories dealt mainly with events concerning individual countries (national), or with events involving two or more countries (the 'international' stories par excellence). The most striking finding to emerge is the very heavy emphasis of all agencies on stories of international significance in this sense of pertaining to two or more countries. Postulated reasons for this include the possibility that such stories are considered to have more immediate global market appeal by organisations which have clients in many countries; also that in many countries stories of 'internal' or 'national' significance are more difficult to report because of censorship and other restrictions, and that international news is relatively safer. Certain categories of news, such as sport, do not have much impact beyond national boundaries. 60 % of all UPI dispatches were international, 59 % of all AFP dispatches. On Reuters, 69 % were international; and on AP, 66 %. It is probable that if this analysis were done on a story basis, the percentage in favour of international stories would fall, but would still exceed the number of national stories and a 'mixed' category. This is because international stories are more likely to be compiled from several dispatches than national stories. This was tested for the UPI wire, and it was found that 48 % of UPI stories were international, 40 % national and the remainder fell into a 'mixed' category where it was impossible to allocate stories to one or other of the main categories.

Part B Section 1

Science and medicine and the press

by Dr Colin Seymour-Ure of the University of Kent

Contents

Author's note

This study, conducted between October and December 1975, is impressionistic and selective. It focuses on Science Correspondents, many of whom also cover aspects of medicine. The evidence illustrates but does not 'prove' propositions. I have sought to present it informally and without solemnity.

C K S-U
December 1975

Summary

1 This report examines factors governing the content about science and medical research in the national press.

2 **Science as a subject**

Science is a private world. The science writer is thus a translator to the lay audience. News values and the values of the scientific world often clash. The social significance of science writing has increased with the growth of science and its influence on public policy. Science writing is very diverse. At present much of it is 'indignant'.

3 **Science as news**

Some science subjects are difficult to translate or hang on topical pegs. None remains subject to taboos. All are subject to fashion. Medicine, including research with animals, is always in fashion. Some fashions are triggered off (Flixborough). Others grow gradually (Pollution), reflect research priorities (Space) or personalities. Subjects move away from Science Correspondents when they are developed (computers, oil).

Criticisms include: mistakes, premature publicity, misconstruction, superficiality, selectivity (eg 'good news is no news'), sensationalism, betrayal of professional confidentiality, excess of anti-science stories.

Alleged consequences: blurring of popular conception of scientific insights, confusion of advice received by government, arbitrary decision-making (eg on safety standards), loss of scientists' morale, increased 'doomwatch' potentiality (on 'Wolf!' principle).

Criticisms defended: science is publicly funded and must be socially responsible; exaggerated enthusiasm invites exaggerated reaction; scientific PR is insidious; scientists may exploit the press in pursuit of funds.

4 **Science writers as a group**

It is said to be a cosy and 'reactive' job, but with varied organisational arrangements that reflect the diversity of subject matter (medicine, defence, aviation, etc).

Most correspondents have a scientific background but consider it unimportant.

Familiar practices of competition and co-operation with colleagues are followed, leaving plenty of scope for differing treatment of the same subjects (eg nuclear energy) and for pursuing hobby-horses.

The science writers' and medical journalists' Associations overlap. Membership is not essential.

5 Science writers and news organisations

Competition for space is tougher in the populars than in the qualities, whose correspondents think their position quite strong. Clare Dover (*The Daily Telegraph*) has her own column.

None of them knows much about his readers; nor finds libel etc inhibiting; nor encounters the advertising department except for Special Supplements.

6 Some notes on sources

Sources divide into: 'events', diary items, documentary, personal contacts (most valued). Some scientists are defensive; some are extrovert – often in search of funds.

Conferences are useful pegs. The *British Association for the Advancement of Science* (BAAS) is a hardy annual.

Lobbying: the Chemical and Pharmaceutical Industries. Journalists mistrust the industries' 'public misinformation sessions'. Some companies have been known apparently to put pressure on employers. Some refused in February 1975 to pay for advertisements in *The Guardian* when accompanying copy was unfavourable. *Free medical journals*, financed by drugs advertising, are a useful source of stories. Not all are completely independent. *British Society for Social Responsibility in Science* (BSSRS) is a good example of an 'indignant' lobby in this field. Press publicity is one of its methods. Its own Quarterly is an occasional source of stories. The *Chemical Industries Association* (CIA) protects the industry's interests. Its external relations director thinks the press fairer than TV, regards BSSRS as 'politically motivated' and runs a considerable information exercise. The case of Vinyl Chloride Monomer, a carcinogenic gas associated with production of PVC, is examined.

Journals. Specialists and semi-specialist journals – *Nature, New Scientist, British Medical Journal* (BMJ), *Lancet* and important American ones – are important spontaneous sources. *The Times*' relations with *Nature* are institutionalised in its daily Science Report (Appendix II). Some correspondents file twenty or more journals and throw away many more.

1 Science as a subject

Science has several distinctive features as a subject for the press.

1.1 A private world

Science is the extreme case of a subject at once incomprehensible to the layman yet of intense potential relevance. White-coated scientists hide away in laboratories (itself a specialist word: contrast 'office' or 'workshop'), and emerge to tell us about synthetic meat and fluoridated toothpaste.

During the few weeks of this study science stories that made news included:

'*Plan to Make Britain World's Nuclear Dustbin*'; (the storage of near-indestructible nuclear waste; *Daily Mirror* headline, 21 October 1975);

'*The Time-bomb that Ticks in a Tin of Aerosol*'; (chemicals destroy the earth's ozone layer that protects us from ultra-violet radiation; *Sunday Times*, 26 October 1975).

Errors in the preliminary diagnosis of breast cancer.

Experiments at Cambridge in which the eyes of live kittens are rotated in their sockets (designed to mimic a visual disorder in infants called cyclotropia).

The accidental killing of Professor Hamilton-Fairley, a leukaemia specialist, by a car bomb.

Science is private almost by definition. Readers catch up with particular subjects (eg the principles of nuclear fission) but the scientist, because he is working at the frontiers, works with concepts, language and perhaps a methodology that are beyond the layman's grasp.

1.2 Science writer as translator

A distinctive feature of science writers, therefore, is that they 'translate' the specialist's work to the general audience. For this purpose scientists seem to accept that journalistic skills are more important than scientific training. (Science writers on general newspapers say their own science backgrounds have little relevance to their particular interests within the field.)

The job of translation makes much science writing *difficult, prone to error* and open to *misinterpretation by readers*.

1.3 Tension between science and news values

The elements making some science stories excellent news do not all please the scientists. Subjects may get little attention because they are very difficult to translate, or they lack a topical peg or don't involve an 'event'. They may get a lot of attention by being personalised or linked to a passing fashion.

1.4 The social significance of science writing

'Scientific knowledge is at least doubling every decade. If you left your formal education 30 years ago . . . the conception of the universe in all its aspects as it was then understood was no more than one-eighth as rich as it is today'. (Stafford Beer, *The Listener*, 25 February 1971.)

1.4.1 *Science and Government*. One cause/effect of this growth is the involvement of science with government. ' . . . there is barely any issue of government, whether it be public health, or the devising of new weapons, or the planning of cities, or the improvement of agriculture, which is not beset by scientific and technical considerations' (Lord Zuckermann, Romanes Lecture, Oxford University, 27 February 1975).

1.4.2 *Science writer as opinion-former*. Another result, since most of our scientific education is through mass media, is that the science writer 'plays a far more important part in moulding public opinion about scientific matters than does the researcher who publishes his findings in professional journals' (Zuckermann, *ibid*).

1.4.3 *Status of science writing*. The growth of scientific research raised the status of scientists and stimulated science writing. The atom bomb and moonshots were key events. (See Appendix I on the growth of science journalism.)

1.4.4 *Diversity of science writing*. The range of scientific activity gives science writers a wide brief compared with some newspaper specialists. Subject to the normal constraints of not missing a good story carried by competitors, there is considerable diversity of approach.

1.5 'Positive' and 'Negative' approaches to science

'The two faces of science' is a common theme in the discussion of science writing. Nuclear energy brought power stations but also the bomb. Heart transplants brought recipients (temporary) benefit but sometimes involved 'switching off' donors and drawing nice distinctions about the moment of death.

At present we are in an *indignation phase* (contrasting with what American literature calls a 'Gee-Whizz' approach). As well as translating science, science writers often discuss the social implications. The current emphasis is on damaging side-effects like environmental pollution and health hazards in the chemical industry.

2 Science as news

2.1 General News Values

General news values stress topicality, personalities, élites, the dramatic and the unexpected. The more a science subject fits these, the greater its chance of being published. 'Conventionally, publicity surrounding a scientific paper awaits the day of its publication, but much of what is reported in "science" comes from other sources and for this most journalists and editors require some sort of "peg".' (David Davies, editor of *Nature*.) Science correspondents on dailies tend to divide their stories into *events* (eg the chemical plant explosion at Flixborough), *routine diary items* (eg annual conferences of the BAAS, BMA) and stories culled from *documents* (journals, reports) and their *contacts*. Quoting three examples of journal-based stories, Phil Tucker (*The Guardian*) used the word 'advance' each time: 'advances in laser holography'; 'sudden advances in catalysts'; 'advances in medicine'. Clare Dover (*The Daily Telegraph*) thinks branches of engineering are in at least as sorry a state as the medical profession: but stories about medics fit news values much better. Miranda Robertson (*Nature*), who chooses items for the daily *Times/Nature* science report, quoted particle physics and molecular biology as two subjects underrepresented because of the difficulty of writing them up intelligibly. (A story about Quarks, she had the impression, had nearly sent the sub-editors up the wall. Pearce Wright (*The Times*) confirmed her impression before I even asked.) Her selection procedure involves 'a constant tussle' between two criteria – 'general interest to readers of *The Times*' and 'Is it scientifically important?' 'The quality of scientific work is just about the last criterion'. This distresses her.

2.2 Taboos

No correspondent could think of subjects that would be ruled out even if they fitted news values, though one (now retired) editor was quoted as 'very lukewarm' on cancer stories. In particular there seem no longer any taboos on sexual matters. The old *Sunday Pictorial* was credited by one correspondent with having demolished the taboo on VD.

2.3 Subject fashions

General news values govern the day-to-day appearance of science stories. On a longer time-scale, subject fashions are important.

2.3.1 *Medicine is always in fashion.* Heavies take it as axiomatic that the popular papers are even more interested in medicine than they. Certainly Ronnie Bedford, *Daily Mirror* Science editor, was engrossed in October 1975 in the Junior Hospital Doctors' dispute with the Minister; while at *The Times* that

story was not a responsibility of the Science editor – nor of the Medical Correspondent – but of a reporter specialising in the NHS and Social Services. David Davies (*Nature* editor) recalled not bothering to give *The Times* a coffee-causes-cancer story. But *The Sun* picked it up from the magazine, and *The Times* wanted to know then why Davies had not sent it along. He was able to persuade them it was not worth fussing about. *Nature* consider medicine (and psychology) heavily over-represented in the *Times/Nature* column – a choice of *Nature*'s but made by criteria of what *The Times* and its readers are thought to want. Pinned on a board in *Nature*'s office was a note of the three articles in *Nature* itself during the previous six months about which most enquiries had been received. Two were directly medical:

Do Coffee Beans Cause Cancer? (10 April 1975)

Do Hair Colourants Cause Cancer? (5 June 1975)

The third had medical implications (radiation hazards):

Do Aerosol Sprays Endanger the Ozone Layer? (25 September 1975)

2.3.2   *Medical research involving animals* is always popular. The story about the kittens' eye-balls being rotated became an item on the news pages after first appearing in the *Times/Nature* report. It was the first such story *Nature*'s editor could remember starting a row in his eighteen months with the magazine. A similar story more recently was about Beagles being forced to 'smoke' cigarettes.

2.3.3   *Some fashions are triggered off by events.* The Flixborough plant explosion, Clare Dover thought, made it easier than before to write about problems of chemical safety. Heart transplant surgery is also an obvious example.

2.3.4   *Fashions that have developed more gradually* include 'pollution', 'the environment', nuclear energy and subjects that simply reflect fashions in research – eg the present interest in immunology. David Fishlock (*Financial Times*) estimates half his time is spent on nuclear energy. The subject did not generate many stories in the late 1960s. Now, to quote Lord Zuckermann's Romanes Lecture again, it is a field of constant dispute: 'The main points at issue are the safety of nuclear power stations, the toxicity and handling of plutonium, and the disposal of the radio-active products of fission.' Fishlock likes it partly because it is a good international subject. 'Pollution' and 'the environment' grew popular to some extent by American example. (Some American writers attribute them to concern caused by the Viet-Nam war.) The most active lobbies, like the British Society for Social Responsibility in Science (BSSRS) and Friends of the Earth, have been subject to American influence.

2.3.5   *Space* was an obvious fashion. Ronnie Bedford (*Daily Mirror*) recalled having 'Front page after Front page' on it in the 1960s. Now it is difficult to get anything in. Clare Dover's predecessor on *The Daily Telegraph* was fascinated by it. She herself was not; as his deputy, she used to make sure the Russian space effort got a good showing. Some of her own interests at the time – eg computers and nuclear energy – were developed in reaction against space.

2.3.6   *Some fashions are a matter of personality.* An interest by a member of the *Financial Times* in contraception meant that this was covered more thoroughly while she was on the paper than afterwards. Ronnie Bedford 'uses every opportunity' to write stories about smoking and lung cancer for the *Daily Mirror. The Times* has a reputation among science writers for articles about astronomy. Clare Dover 'virtually drummed into being' – in her own opinion – the public discussion of whether to invest in English or American nuclear reactors. Phil Tucker (*The Guardian*), a *New Scientist* writer was annoyed to realise, must be scanning an American astronomy journal which the *New Scientist* man thought he himself was about the only journalist in England to see.

2.3.7 *Movement of subjects away from science writers.* Several correspondents mentioned that subjects can reach a point where they cease to be a science speciality and pass to some other specialist. Clare Dover quoted *computers* as an example: they passed to business writers six or seven years ago. *Oil* had been a geological subject and was now going the same way. (The Hovertrain was going through the same progression when it was axed.) David Fishlock (*Financial Times*) listed *cellulose-based smoking materials*, *semi-synthetic proteins* and *new technology of administering drugs.* Pearce Wright (*The Times*) quoted *Law of the Sea* questions. If the shift is from 'science' to 'technology' the connection for the science correspondent may not altogether disappear.

These different kinds of subject fashion confirm the great *potential variety* of what can be included in science writing.

2.4 Criticisms of science news

Nature's 'constant tussle' between the criteria of general interest and scientific importance when choosing items for *The Times* epitomises the tension between science and news values. There is a long list of criticisms of the press, many of which overlap.

2.4.1 *Mistakes.* 'The professional scientist's constant complaint against science writers is that they get it wrong; that they imbue with all the authority of science some observation, opinion or conclusion which at best is open to argument and at worst is factually incorrect or misleading. It is a grievance I hear in many laboratories I visit, as well as in Whitehall and corporate head-quarters.' (David Fishlock, *Nature*, Vol 250, pp 747–49, 30 August 1974.) One example: Professor Roy Calne, a leading kidney and liver transplant surgeon at Cambridge, is on record as saying that 'untruthful reports about his work had deterred relatives from giving their permission for removal of organs from dead next-of-kin, with the result that patients had died without being given the chance of receiving a transplanted organ'. (BMJ 3 May 1969, p 263, quoting *The Times*, 28 April 1969.)

2.4.2 *Premature publication.* 'Major Breakthrough' and 'Miracle Cure' are two phrases cropping up again and again in criticism of science writing. Ronnie Bedford (*Daily Mirror*) thinks 'Breakthrough' was a late 'fifties and early 'sixties word. (He compares it with the ubiquitous 'Housewife' in the 1940s – 'Tell the Housewives how you make an H-Bomb, Ronnie'.) He claims to have killed lots of 'breakthroughs', 'miracles' and 'cures' that subs have wanted to use. David Davies (editor, *Nature*) writes of scientists flying kites. 'A lot of these kites will come to grief within a year or two, but that is the way science works. What can a correspondent write? Very often too much. It is far too tempting to extrapolate from 10 mice to a million humans and add the *fortissimo* amen that the scientist has carefully eschewed at the end of his *mezzo piano* composition.' (*Nature* supplement, n.d.) General Practitioners confirm that these stories are reflected in their surgery attendances.

2.4.3 *Misconstruction and superficiality.* Lord Zuckermann devoted part of a *Times Literary Supplement* Lecture (published in the TLS 12 November 1971) to illustrations of this criticism. He quoted pesticides in food, the controversy about mercury levels in fish and coverage of the Torrey Canyon disaster (about which he was scientific adviser). The latter involved a classic human error. Tucker (*The Guardian*) calculated that the quantity of detergent used to disperse the oil would 'remain as a mass' and be catastrophic to marine life in most of the English Channel. Lord Zuckermann and his committee were highly concerned and halted operations. They checked and rechecked their figures. 'But try as we could, we could not confirm Mr Tucker's conclusions. Direct communication with him revealed that he had made a mistake in his sums. In calculating the concentration of detergent in a cubic mile of sea, he had apparently multiplied length by breadth, but not by depth – and, not surprisingly, obtained estimates of concentration of detergent far higher than our own.'

David Davies considers that claims of 'British achievements' which are *not* are a common form of superficiality.

A variation on this criticism is:

2.4.4 *Selectivity of news.* Fishlock (*FT*), who views the nuclear energy industry sympathetically, quotes an example about the toxicity of plutonium. At a time when much publicity suggested 'scientists were playing fast and loose with the nation's well being' by underestimating plutonium's toxicity, the Medical Research Council published a report refuting such criticisms. For the most part, the science writer critics simply ignored it.

Another variation is:

2.4.5 *'Good news is no news'.* 'If we set aside dramatic matters like heart transplantations or the separation of Siamese twins, it is rarely that we hear about the new practices which . . . have resulted only in good. But the echoes of the uproar which followed the dreadful thalidomide tragedy will never die down.' (Lord Zuckermann, Romanes Lecture.)

2.4.6 *Sensationalism.* 'It is inherent in the nature of news that it should be new. In medicine and science this often means that what has been common knowledge for ten years is suddenly announced in the daily press as a world-shaking discovery.' (Henry Miller, Vice-Chancellor of Newcastle University and formerly Professor of Neurology; *Listener*, 23 April 1970.) To the lobbyist these lags may look like 'huge delays in disclosure' and be an aspect of secretiveness. To BSSRS, for example, the discovery that ICL was selling computers in South Africa that were used in operating the Pass Laws was none the less significant because five years had elapsed before the fact became known to it. (BSSRS passed the story to *The Guardian*, where it made the front page.)

Correspondents of the heavy papers tend to take for granted that 'it's easier to get stories about sex into the tabloids'. Is there a tabloid ring about the example Ronnie Bedford (*Daily Mirror*) plucked from the air to illustrate the usefulness of *The Lancet* as a news source? Female anaesthetists, the story said, have a significantly higher rate of spontaneous abortion than other women.

2.4.7 *Breaking professional confidentiality.* This is mainly a medical concern, often centering on the question of disclosure by newspapers of patients' names. It became an issue about Heart Transplants, both in South Africa and the UK (*The Daily Telegraph* disclosed a donor's name against the wishes of surgeons). It had earlier been an issue when blood transfusion was developed: newspapers had printed photos of donor and recipient shaking hands. (Subsequently strict anonymity became the rule.)

2.4.8 *Too many anti-science stories.* The current phase of 'indignation' writing is naturally unpopular with scientists. Fishlock (*FT*) is worried by it too, especially as 'this kind of story is so much easier to write, and so much easier to get past many of the news editors of our national newspapers'. One science writer on a heavy Sunday told him he knew he could get more articles into his paper 'if he were willing to twist them a bit to turn them into a "scare" story or a "scandal" story'. Much 'indignation' writing is about the social and environmental implications of science. Scientists feel themselves vulnerable because the argument may not be about facts. 'If you say I've got a wart on my nose, I can deny it. But if you just say I'm one of the ugliest men in town, all I can do is argue that I'm really quite pretty.' (Edward Condon, US Physicist. Quoted by Fishlock in *Nature* 250, 30 August 1974.)

2.5 Consequences alleged by critics

Allied with the criticisms listed above, emphasis on the negative aspects of science produces several dangers, the critics argue:

2.5.1 Newspapers (and TV) paradoxically '*stand between the public and the real insights of science*' (Stafford Beer, *Listener*, 25 February 1971).

2.5.2 Official scientific advice to government has become more complex since it is 'now almost always tendered against a background of well-publicised but not infrequently superficial, fact and opinion'. Worse still, 'the voice of the responsible official adviser becomes drowned by the warnings of the doomwatcher'. (Lord Zuckermann, Romanes Lecture.)

2.5.3 There may be a loss of confidence among the scientific community. Fishlock (*FT*) illustrates this danger with the nuclear energy industry. No paper has a 'Nuclear Industry Correspondent', so the commercial side tends to be neglected and science correspondents have a free rein. The topic provides easy copy for horror stories. As the industry is 'young and vulnerable', in his view, it is not well placed to defend itself – in marked contrast with the coal industry, which he believes is much more unhealthy yet strongly equipped for defence.

2.5.4 Sensationalists 'run the risk of overdrawing on the fund of public belief. Credulity can be stretched too far. The day could well dawn when a true 'doomwatch' story will fall on deaf ears . . .' (Lord Zuckermann, TLS, 12 November 1971).

2.5.5 The confusion of scientific and (in essence) moral arguments increases arbitrariness in decisions about, say, safety standards in the use of toxic materials. Again, 'politicians who have to shoulder the responsibility for decisions about nuclear power programmes may have their faith in their official advisers shaken because of public innuendoes of complacency, even irresponsibility . . . ' (Lord Zuckermann, Romanes Lecture.)

2.6 Adjustments used in defence

The main arguments justifying the emphasis on 'indignation' stories are these:

2.6.1 Scientific research is not carried on in a social vacuum; environmentalists, those concerned with health and safety at work etc, perform an important social function. They complement, for instance, the work of the Select Committee on Science and Technology (which received several unsolicited bouquets from interviewees).

2.6.2 The more scientific research is funded by public money and bears on government policy, the greater the need for scrutiny of its results. Scientists have been insulated too long by public money and private workplaces.

2.6.3 The existence of public relations and information officers seeking to spread the good news is presumptive evidence of the existence of bad news.

2.6.4 Too uncritical a view of science (the 'Gee-Whizz' reaction) would simply risk a swing to an equally exaggerated critical view.

2.6.5 The recent drying-up of research funds is making scientists more aggressive in their efforts to get their share. Science writers must be on their guard against extravagant claims. (American scientists traditionally seek to use the mass media as instruments to raise funds – especially from Congress.)

Bernard Dixon, editor of the *New Scientist* (considered by Fishlock to have been 'deeply infected' by indignation at one time) has argued along most of those lines. While sceptical of the more extreme arguments of what may be termed the Zuckermann line, he agrees that 'recent years have certainly seen some very silly and nihilistic onslaughts on the scientific community' and that 'interpretative' science writing can just mean that 'every story, every news item, is presented with a large dose of the writer's own views and prejudices'.

3 Science writers as a group

The editor of one science magazine, with the perspective of an ex-professional scientist, views the science correspondents as 'a terribly heterogeneous branch, including some real hacks'. Theirs is a cosy life with easy hours (except the occasional night 'phone call if they have missed a story). They get 'locked in to the job'. It does not lead anywhere: longevity could become a serious problem.

He doubts if they carry much weight in their papers. There is no 'giant', head and shoulders above the rest – one man's view, avowedly from the scientists' camp; but it pinpoints several aspects of science writers as a group.

3.1 Variety of organisational arrangements
The wide range of topics that might be included in 'science', plus the movement of particular developments in and out of the field, is reflected in the variety of papers' arrangements for science writing. The commonest connection – which is no guide to whether a paper has separate correspondents or not – is between *science and medicine*. Other common connections are with *technology, defence* (decreasingly) and *aviation*.

Examples (approximate):
The Times
  Science Editor
  Medical Correspondent
  Medical Reporter (Part-time)
  Technology Correspondent
  Aviation Correspondent
  Daily 'Science Report' provided by *Nature*

The Daily Telegraph
  Science Correspondent
  Medical Correspondent
  Aviation Correspondent

The Guardian
  Science Correspondent (shares office with Defence Correspondent)
  Medical Correspondent
  Aviation Correspondent

Financial Times
  Science Editor
  Aviation Correspondent
  Energy Correspondent
  Technology Page (4 people)

Daily Express
  Science Editor
  Medical and Science Reporter
  Aviation Correspondent

Daily Mirror
  Science Editor
  Science Correspondent
  Aviation Correspondent

Press Association
  Science and Medical Correspondent
  Energy Correspondent

3.2 Background

Most Science Correspondents have 'science' somewhere in their background. 'Background' is the right word: their journalistic skills are what really matter. The point is best made by the example of Ronnie Bedford (*Daily Mirror*). The *Daily Mirror* audience and format require greater expertise in 'translation' than *The Times*. Bedford, appropriately, is a traditional 'hard school' journalist, inspired to the job as a boy by the chance purchase of Hamilton Fyfe's biography of Northcliffe. In 1945 he was a Reuters' man with the American army in England. Hiroshima made him decide to specialise post-war in science, and he built up contacts with atomic scientists like Cockcroft and Penney. He has been writing on Science and Medicine for the *Daily Mirror* (with a spell on *The Sun*) for nearly thirty years.

Other Examples:

The Daily Telegraph Clare Dover has a degree in Physics, Chemistry and Metallurgy. She joined the paper fourteen years ago after three years with the magazine *Understanding Science*. She answered an advertisement in *The Daily Telegraph* for an Assistant Science Correspondent. She was main Science Correspondent for three years. She finds being a woman helps – except that she was barred by an oil company from going on a North Sea rig, until the paper made a fuss.

The Times Pearce Wright trained as an 'engineer'. He started on *Electronics Weekly* and was hired by Sir William Haley twelve years ago as a Science and Technology reporter. (The science editor then was not a full-time staff man.)

Financial Times David Fishlock is a chemist. He worked for McGraw-Hill and then the *New Scientist* (mainly as Technology Editor). He joined the *FT* ten years ago.

3.3 A 'reactive' job?

Compared with some specialisms much news comes *to* the science writer, rather than having to be hunted down. Clare Dover broke down 120 of her recent stories and columns by their origins (though she doubts if the period was typical). Only one-third were 'self-initiated'. Obviously this does not mean the writer has no need to look for his news and to 'make' it like other journalists. The variety of science writing in different papers, whose existence science writers themselves and observers on specialist journals continually assert, testifies to that. But the science writer has available a large number of routines and accessible sources if he wishes to use them. Much science writing therefore does consist in relaying to the reader, in translation, the findings and doings of researchers, industries, government committees. The weekday Technology page of the *Financial Times*, for example, contains a lot of copy printed largely verbatim from publicity handouts. The usefulness of the page lies less in its authorship than in drawing together information with a common theme from a variety of sources that would take an interested reader too long to cull for himself. Clare Dover's predecessor, to quote a different kind of example, was allegedly told when he took the job some eleven years ago that he was not to rock the boat and should just concentrate on diary items, but in practice this was not enforced and made no difference to his handling of the job.

The idea that science writing is 'reactive' is linked to the argument about indignation. To Lord Zuckermann the science writer should be a reporter pure and simple ('one does not expect them to behave like art critics . . .') – TLS 12 November 1971). To Bernard Dixon (*New Society*) and overwhelmingly to the Science Correspondents themselves, this role is much too passive. Clare Dover plainly distinguishes her own, highly active, definition of her job from the definition apparently given to her predecessor. The subjects correspondents name spontaneously as of particular concern – public health, nuclear safety, 'social awareness issues' – reflect their view.

This represents, on the other hand, an active, watchful *stance*. Watchful *activity* is much less. Partly, science writers simply do not have the resources to mount great investigations. Partly, one suspects, they would not want to. Approaching subjects with a healthy scepticism and doing some quiet nosing around is one thing; but, in the opinion of Andy Solandt, Director of BSSRS, the science writers do not have activist expectations of their jobs. On the whole the interviews conducted during the researching of this paper confirm his impression.

3.4 Diversity of interests

The diversity of approach claimed of correspondents undoubtedly exists. But it is not easy to pin down and evaluate. An important limitation is the need all have in common to report 'events'. 'We do have a tendency to follow each other around', said David Fishlock (*FT*). When the *Daily Mirror* ran its front page story on 'Britain as a Nuclear Waste Dump' (see 1.1) he had felt obliged to pick the topic up again even though he had been writing frequently about reprocessing and the contract in dispute. Clare Dover claimed not to make a point of over-reacting to what the opposition are doing – but added that of course the News Desk let her know soon enough if she has missed something. Fishlock covers himself against *The Times* particularly. But he feels under no pressure at all in the office to develop either fields (like Astronomy) developed by a competitor or fields in which he acknowledges himself weak (like medicine and 'the rarefied end of biology').

The Times and *The Guardian* clearly cover one another. Wright and Tucker enjoy a 'competitor-colleague' relationship of the type Jeremy Tunstall found widespread in his study of other specialist correspondents (*Journalists At Work*, Constable, 1971). Among the tabloids, Bedford (*Daily Mirror*) is undoubtedly under greater pressure to cover himself than are the heavies. Reading the rest of the press is 'the first thing I do'. He insists that the main paper to cover himself against is not *The Sun* but the *Daily Mail*.

This is routine newspaper practice, and it may well be that science writers need to watch each other less than, say, Lobby Correspondents. But it means that their diversity consists firstly in *differing treatment of the same subjects* and, secondly, in the *areas in which they specialise* in their 'uncommitted' time. *The Times, The Guardian, The Daily Telegraph* and the *Financial Times* 'all handle things quite differently', for instance, in Fishlock's view. Nuclear safety is an example quoted by all the 'heavy' correspondents independently. Wright (*The Times*) and Tucker (*The Guardian*) take a different line, they all agree, from Fishlock (*FT*). Tucker feels *The Daily Telegraph* (and *Daily Express*) tend to take an establishment view of the issue.

Areas of Specialisation are easier to get a definite idea about. Between one-third and one-half of a correspondent's time is perhaps free of unavoidable routines. We have seen that one-third of Clare Dover's stories are self-generated, and that Fishlock spends about half his time on his main interest – nuclear power. Tucker named his 'personal network of communicants' as more important than all the rest of his sources.

Some correspondents' special interests have already been indicated. Other examples are:

Tucker (*The Guardian*):   Environmental and 'social awareness' questions.

Wright (*The Times*):   Known for an interest in Astronomy.

Bedford (*Daily Mirror*):   Public Health issues.

Dover (*The Daily Telegraph*):   Nuclear power.

Fishlock (*FT*):   Nuclear power.

Silcock (*Sunday Times*):   Reputed to have a special interest in diseases transmitted from dogs.

Pincher (*Daily Express*):   Defence questions.

The importance of fashions must not be forgotten. Those interests (the dog diseases perhaps excepted) might be called 'underlying'. Aerosol sprays and the ozone layer, for instance, had an especially adrenal quality for most correspondents at the time.

3.5 Group identity

Diversity of interests is doubtless one reason why the Science Writers' group, the *Association of British Science Writers* (ASBW), is less important, whether as 'postbox', organiser of newsworthy events or gatekeeper to essential sources, than groups like the Lobby or Industrial Correspondents. The Association was founded soon after the war. Dr Martin Sherwood, the Chairman, says 'anyone can join'. The corollary is that not everyone does. Many of the 195 members are from trade and technical publications. Pearce Wright (*The Times*) and David Davies (editor, *Nature*) find no disadvantage in not belonging. The Association organises an activity on average once a month. Most of these are lunches addressed by prominent guest speakers (eg the Secretary for Energy). Attendance is not high, partly because of disagreement among members about whether the occasions should be for off-the-record 'back-grounding' or for on-the-record news. The venue – until recently the Dorchester – has not been very convenient. The Association has organised successful receptions for its members to meet groups like the Select Committee on Science and Technology and the Science Attachés' Club.

The Medical Journalists' Association (MJA), though more recent (founded in 1967), is more exclusive; a fact symbolised perhaps by its having a badge – a snake entwining a quill. The Membership overlaps with the Science Writers' Association. Those journalists who want a story out of a meeting (eg Clare Dover) find its lunches more useful than the ABSW's.

Membership figures:

ABSW: Full: 150. Associate: 32. Academic: 13 (195).

MJA: Full: 118. Affiliate: 59 (177).

Twenty-two people are a full member of both. Six of these are on national dailies or Sundays.

4 Science writers and news organisations

The kinds of correspondent kept by individual newspapers have already been briefly indicated. This section concentrates on working arrangements inside the organisations.

A correspondent's activities are conditioned by distinctive features of his paper as well as by the factors already mentioned. For example the *Daily Mirror* carries Marje Proops' weekly advice column; and Bedford may be consulted by her sometimes about medical questions. *The Times'* role as a journal of record means Pearce Wright has to cover various official publications carefully and have regard to the long term importance of a subject as well as to more ephemeral news values. Fishlock (*FT*) obviously writes for an audience interested specially in industry, applied technology and the financial side of science.

4.1 Competition for space

'The sub-editors who put the programme to bed and decide what goes in have got to strike a balance. And if there's a lot of serious material on a particular night, and there's also a serious science story, the odds are that it will get hurled out – not simply because it's science but because it doesn't fit the picture.' (Chapman Pincher, *Daily Express*.) That is one part of competition – getting space at all. The other part is, how much? Bedford points out that the longest *Daily Mirror* article is never more than 1,000 words. Pincher says: 'When I first went to the *Daily Express*, the average feature was 1,500 words. Now the average feature is 700 words, and if you make it longer they cut it.' Fishlock, on a heavy paper, reckons to publish over seventy feature articles a year of up to 2,000 words. Wright comments that space in *The Times* is always much easier when Parliament is in recess.

Competition for space in both senses is much harder in the Populars, as Bedford readily agrees. (He thinks the copy in some of the heavies could do with a bit more subbing anyway.) In the heavies the position varies. Dover (*The Daily Telegraph*) takes rather a different view from Pincher: she thinks science, not being 'mundane', competes on *more* than equal terms for space. Tucker (*The Guardian*) 'is prepared to fight' for some subjects and can get a whole page occasionally. Wright (*The Times*) feels the existence of *The Times/ Nature* Science Report strengthens his own position rather than weakening it, by giving the subject a certain status. He has a number of masters – Features Desk, News Desk, as well as writing leaders – and can manoeuvre for space. Another distinctive point is that he can suggest a story might be a good one for opening up a correspondence. When Fishlock joined the *Financial Times* the job was put to him as mainly feature writing – like many other *FT* specialists.

He thinks this distinguishes him from other Fleet Street science writers. Unlike some *FT* specialists, however, he does not have a guaranteed column. He prefers anyway to have to earn his space and not be tied to a specific weekly column.

4.2 Autonomy in the news organisation

The constraints provided by the general character of a paper and the demands of the news executives vary. The clearest form of autonomy is the possession of a regular column. This is the basis of *The Times/Nature* arrangement (described in Appendix II). Clare Dover and Ken Owen, technology correspondents of *The Times*, are the only national daily science writers with such a column. It appears fortnightly on Mondays (alternating with Education). Until five years ago it appeared only monthly. Fortnightly suits her well: she would need help if it were more frequent. What she writes is her own affair. Only once could she recall writing on a suggestion of the editor.

Relations with sub-editors are like those of any journalist. The Populars, again, are the more vulnerable. Bedford (*Daily Mirror*) reckons that 'Every two or three years a sub-editor makes a real mess, or mistake, with something'. Bedford defines the relationship normally as himself providing 'something more than a pint for the sub to put in a pint pot'. He agrees that subs have more control over his copy than over, say, Tuckers. Tucker and Fishlock are satisfied with the discretion left to them. 'The great majority' of Fishlock's features are initiated by himself and 'only a small proportion' by the editor. He has a good relationship with the Technology page. Wright is satisfied that his judgment is accepted on whether there is a 'science angle' to a story.

4.3 Relations with readers

One piece of American research suggested news executives underestimated their readers' threshold of interest in and comprehension of science writing. British Science Correspondents certainly know very little about their readers. Their own mailbags are characteristically eccentric. She gets most response to the 'idiot pieces', said Clare Dover. An example was an archaeologist's discovery of a bird whose wings seemed to have been formed by the back legs not the front legs. Practically every RAF officer in the country, she said, wrote in to suggest that this must be the bird which flew backwards in ever-decreasing circles ...

The correspondents' awareness of, let alone familiarity with, even JICNARS (Joint Industry Committee for National Readership Surveys) data seem sketchy or non-existent. Apart from the special case of *The Times* correspondence columns, they rely on their own journalistic instincts and those of their editors ('... at the end of the day', etc). Bedford said he could assume far more knowledge in readers than when he started in the '40s. He attributed this partly to TV.

4.4 Advertising departments

The growth of 'special supplements' in the heavies (excluding *The Daily Telegraph*) has had some peripheral impact on science correspondents, mainly perhaps as perks. (A case from *The Guardian* involving pressure from advertisers is considered below.)

4.5 Legal hazards

Correspondents bump inadvertently into libel but none saw it as a 'problem'.

5 Some notes on sources

Clare Dover's breakdown of the origins of her stories was:

Self-initiated	37
Conference	26
Suggested by news desk	19
Scientific journals	10
Annual reports, etc	10
Press Conference	7
Agency copy	7
Postbag	3
Incoming 'phone call	1
	120

These can also be classified, as was suggested in the introduction, into 'events', diary items, documentation and personal contacts. Correspondents see most scope for individuality in the latter.

5.1 Scientists

Many of the personal contacts are with scientists working in government, industry and the universities. Illustrating the 'areas I keep an eye on', Bedford reeled off Harwell, Aldermaston, Dounreay and the universities of Manchester (for dermatology) and Leeds. Fishlock said most of his features originate in talking to people – mainly industrial or government scientists.

Correspondents are understandably less willing to particularise about their scientific contacts than about other questions. It was impossible also for me to tap a 'representative' group of scientists. I can only relay general impressions.

There are obvious differences in scientists' attitudes to the press. An extreme defensive reaction came from Professor Douglas Bevis of Leeds. He told a BMA Conference in Hull in 1974 that there were, to his knowledge, three individuals then living who had been born as a result of a technique in which a woman's egg had been fertilised outside her body and then re-implanted in the uterus to grow normally to its full term. He was so astonished and offended by the publicity following this remark that he said he had decided to abandon his own work in that field. (*Listener*, 15 August, 1974.) At the other extreme correspondents quote scientists who 'forever call the press' – about their latest findings, to do down their rivals, and so on. Some of these are simply extrovert:

69

one, for example, was described as 'emerging' into an all-purpose media scientist. Others are struggling against conventional wisdom: an elderly professor who believes relativity is rubbish, and another man who does not accept the connection between smoking and lung cancer. Clare Dover generalised about subject differences: Doctors are 'itching to get on the 'phone'; Archaeologists 'are held to get talking'.

Bernard Dixon (*New Scientist*) has discussed such differences at some length. 'Today there are innumerable press conferences, press releases, briefing sessions, visits, demonstrations, public relations officers, and press officers, to provide the press with a copious flow of information from the laboratory bench'. The main aim is to attract funds. This creates two problems. 'Some medical researchers, for example, are keen to use publicity where it will help them in attracting cash to their research projects . . . but become unhappy about discussing the political and social implications of their work.' Secondly, the 'wrong' scientists are often the most effective publicists. Science correspondents therefore increasingly have to play a role comparable to the referees who serve academic journals. In Dixon's view most of them have enough 'knowledge and acumen' to cope with the situation, but some have not. The role of trusted scientific contacts clearly extends beyond that of useful sources to include advice. The Department of Education and Science Annual Directory of *Scientific Research in British Universities and Colleges*, listed by name, institution and subject, is also invaluable for this purpose.

5.2 Conferences

Scientific conferences are useful pegs on which to hang stories that might otherwise lack the right topicality. Correspondents naturally find parts of them also rather a bore. Pearce Wright is glad, for example, that the Medical Reporter John Roper does the bulk of the BMA Annual Conference reporting. Clare Dover distinguishes the usefulness of conference papers and topicality from the actual conferring; and she may prefer to see participants independently.

5.2.1 The British Association annual conference is still for news editors the one week of the year when science is entrenched. It is by far the best example of a topical peg and a routine diary item, coming round yearly like Harvest (and at Harvest time).

5.3 Lobbying: the chemical and pharmaceutical industries

This topic was chosen because:

(*a*) it is plainly an area of tension between science writers and their sources (quite apart from the past history of thalidomide, which is not dealt with in this paper);

(*b*) it involves journalistic horror stories and even elements of a mythology;

(*c*) these industries are rich, well organised, and resourceful;

(*d*) there are counterbalancing lobbies;

(*e*) it is at the medical end of science.

5.3.1 *Science writers' perspectives*

(*a*) '*Public misinformation*'. Science writers hold – and quickly air – their prejudices about these industries, based on the normal journalistic suspicion of PR activities, including parties and facility trips. (British practice is increasingly to accept free travel but on the clear understanding that no strings are attached. American papers, in contrast, are more likely not to accept it.) A common accusation is that big drug houses (eg Pfizers, Beechams, Cyanamid, Roche etc) organise 'public misinformation sessions' under the guise of straightforward conferences, sometimes in 'neutral' premises. Independent authoritative figures, similarly, have sometimes been hired to write papers which are published without the origin and finance being made clear.

Bernard Dixon (*New Scientist*) has documented one example fully in his book *What Is Science For?* (Collins, 1973). This concerned the activities of Cyanamid following publication of the Swann Report (1969) recommending restrictions on the agricultural use of antibiotics. Cyanamid sponsored a symposium. 'Neither invitations to the symposium nor the programmes carried the sponsor's name. But they did include the name of the Royal Society of Medicine – the venue booked for the occasion by Cyanamid – in such a way that invitees might well have concluded that the RSM had sponsored the meeting. The RSM, a prestigious learned Society which holds regular meetings of its own, became aware of this critical omission only when an unwanted invitation was returned to them' (p.139). Three of the platform speakers were strongly opposed to the Swann recommendations; the fourth was neutral. The RSM later tightened the rules for hiring its premises. After criticisms in *New Scientist*, Cyanamid wrote to the Chairman of IPC (owners of the magazine) drawing attention to the 'very grave charges indeed' and the 'damaging allegations' *New Scientist* had made and 'clearly expecting the Chairman to take internal action'. The Chairman backed Dixon up and the matter ended.

(b) *Advertising.* One recent horror story is about a special supplement in *The Guardian* in February 1975 on synthetic protein sources like soya bean textured into 'meat'. As a counterweight to the rest of the articles, Phil Tucker (*The Guardian* Science Correspondent) proposed including an article by Colin Tudge, Science editor of the magazine *World Medicine* and well known as an 'arch-enemy' of synthetic foods. There was some discussion whether to include it, but it went ahead. (Tudge sees such developments as a mis-application of research effort.) The advertisers in the supplement then got together and complained to *The Guardian* that there had been no mention of the article in the original prospectus. On that ground some, possibly all, refused to pay for their advertisements. *The Guardian* has apparently not insisted on payment.

(c) *Free medical journals.* Known euphemistically as 'controlled circulation' journals, these are financed by advertisements almost entirely for drugs. Those of its products that are not on public sale have to be promoted by the pharmaceutical industry by specialist advertising and by travelling reps. During the last ten years the use of free, glossy magazines has proliferated. Few, if any, are owned by drug companies. But at least one has a drug company director on its Board. He is named on its masthead but his connection with that company is not.

One General Practitioner showed me the following unsolicited journals in his mail:

	Published Owner
Modern Medicine	Modern Medicine Publications
Modern Geriatrics	Modern Medicine Publications
General Practitioner	Haymarket

71

Doctor	Sutton-Siebert Publications
Medical News	Medical News-Tribune
British Journal of Sexual Medicine	Medical News-Tribune
*World Medicine	New Medical Journals
*Pulse	Morgan-Grampian
Medical Interface	Interface Periodicals
*Update	Update Publications
MIMS Magazine (Sc. Monthly Index of Medical Specialities)	Haymarket

There is quite a high turnover: perhaps two or three a year. *Medical Interface*, for instance, was launched as *Interface* by a Haymarket man and then taken over and relaunched by an American firm. Those marked with an asterisk were considered by the GP and one or two science writers to be the more useful and independent of the industry. Some are aimed at only part of the market – eg the under-40s.

One copy of *Medical Interface* had an article by Lord George-Brown on pay beds. But mainly they provide reminders of mortality and of the wide range of diseases from which it is soon clear the lay reader must be suffering. Some science correspondents – Bedford (*Daily Mirror*) and Dover (*The Daily Telegraph*), for instance – readily acknowledge them as a useful source of stories. *World Medicine* is among the list of journals Fishlock files (see Appendix III).

The journals are of interest for two other reasons. Firstly (and predictably) they make twice the impact of the *Prescribers Journal*, the DHSS vehicle for keeping GPs up to date about drugs. GPs, it was argued to me, therefore get much of their continuing drugs education from these magazines (and from the non-commercial journals like the *BMJ* and *Lancet*, presumably). Advertisements, further, may be more influential than the articles. It is a surreal experience to see the everyday techniques of advertisements for beer and cigarettes applied to drugs ('Down with Linctified Expectorant – Up with Mucus'), including the suggestive use of children and sexuality. Some advertisements, it was claimed, seem to define clinical conditions which their product can then 'cure', particularly in the grey area of depressive illness, 'stress' and so on.

The second cause of interest is the effect of free journals on the professional journals. Dixon (*New Scientist*) thinks the free journals grew up, partly beeause the others were becoming too specialised for all the GP's needs. The *BMJ*'s evidence to the Royal Commission on the Press stresses the difficulty a journal linked to membership of a professional group has in responding quickly enough to cost increases to avoid temporary losses. The DHSS are apparently seeking ways both of cutting down the amount spent on drugs advertising and of channelling more of it into the 'non-commercial' journals. Economic recession has begun to hit the free journals anyway. *World Medicine*, for instance, has asked doctors to write in if they wish to continue receiving it.

5.3.2 *Lobbyists' perspectives*

(a) *British Society for Social Responsibility in Science*. 'The main field of action for the society is in health hazards in industry.' Methods include 'publicity in the dailies, science journals, radio, television and trade union publications'. BSSRS stands well to the 'left' among groups interested in science. It is therefore sometimes used by science writers for an 'alternative' view to that of spokesmen of the chemical industry, or in areas like occupational health where scientific research is relatively thin. The society publishes a Quarterly, *Science For People*, which has a somewhat 'alternative' air. Much of it is argument and analysis, not facts. Even so, Andy Solandt (General Secretary) estimates that once every three or four numbers a story gets picked up from it by the nationals (frequently *The Guardian*). BSSRS claim credit for starting the discussion in this country about the health hazard from Vinyl Chloride Monomer, a gas involved in the manufacture of PVC.

BSSRS also publishes pamphlets (eg *The Environment: A Radical Agenda*) and has active local branches. Founded in 1969, its 800 members are mainly 'under forty, university educated and critical'. Its more specific interests trail off into the democratisation of laboratories and sexism in science. They exist in a context of thought that sees much science as oppressive and irresponsible, because divorced from its proper social setting by the mystification process of the mass media. In the terms of the earlier discussion, BSSRS is 'indignation' institutionalised.

(*b*) *Chemical Industries Association.* Bill McMillan, External Relations Director of the CIA, thinks that 95% of the reporting of the chemical industry is objective and fair (though he does not always like it). The Science correspondents of the nationals are 'first-class'; he has a particular regard for Bedford (*Daily Mirror*). Any sensationalism comes from headlines and subs – he has often heard science writers grumble about it. Troubles come otherwise from 'the occasional opportunist' and from people who are 'politically motivated'. (This phrase cropped up three or four times and was pejorative. BSSRS, obviously, is 'politically motivated'; so are a few of the *New Scientist* staff.) Problems also arise when a paper's science man is not available – say on a Sunday evening – and some junior picks up a story from the United States.

Mr McMillan's confidence in the press is interesting for two reasons. Firstly, it is in strong contrast to his opinion of TV (especially documentary makers). He often recommends his members simply not to take part in TV programmes, whereas he positively encourages them to talk to the press. Secondly, his industry, which includes paints, medicines, plastics, dyestuffs, etc, is capital-intensive and generally harmonious. It is 'politically identifiable as a successful private enterprise and is therefore ripe for kicking'. The CIA, with 300 members, defends the interests of about 95% of the industry from ICI downwards.

Mr McMillan draws a clear distinction between the role of the Association and that of PR firms. The CIA does not seek to 'use editorial copy for advertising'. Equally, he feels journalists prefer to quote the CIA because it is a spokesman of the whole industry rather than of a particular company. His general policy therefore is 'not to push too hard'. Correspondents are not flooded with stuff. The two-monthly bulletin for members gets sent to some of them for backgrounding, but the Quarterly Economic Bulletin is more useful for stories as it contains original material.

(*c*)   An example of the CIA's approach is the controversy over Vinyl Chloride Monomer. Against a background of occasional research since 1949, an American company, B.F. Goodrich, announced in January 1974 that three former employees had died from the rare liver cancer angiosarcoma. The association of the chemical and the disease is unusually clear, but whereas there have been about

73

50 cases round the world, there have been only two in the UK. In Britain four companies manufacture Vinyl Chloride (in Wales, Aycliffe, Chesterfield and Blackpool). The press over here took up the story on some scale – McMillan does not attribute it so definitely to BSSRS as BSSRS does. He now has a 15-inch-high pile of cuttings, including some from his contacts and counterparts in the United States and throughout the world. Argument has focused on the safety levels of the gas in the air in the polymerisation plant. Within weeks of the Goodrich announcement, the industry set up a committee under the CIA's umbrella to consider plant modification and the considerable problems of measurement of small traces of the gas. A committee with Government, Trades Union and CIA representatives was also set up under the Health and Safety Executive. In dealing with the press McMillan is partly concerned with local papers in the areas of the plants. The companies seek to keep their own staff informed; but local papers may pick up stories independently, often from America. These need monitoring; and McMillan put out statements on behalf of all four companies, including 'reassurance'. At the national level McMillan early 'got the experts together' for a press conference at the Royal Society of Medicine. Thereafter he 'topped up' with press releases, phone calls, etc. The Association was also involved, at the same venue (McMillan, though an engineer by training, is a Fellow of the Society), in a conference on Vinyl Chloride Health problems, with some twenty DHSS, industrial and hospital speakers, on 12 September 1975.

The discovery that Vinyl Chloride was a human carcinogen was the first major health hazard in the plastics industry and was correspondingly important for McMillan. In a *post mortem* at a plastics industry conference an ICI spokesman, after detailed examination of press coverage, concluded that press treatment had been generally fair. Difficulties came from news 'injected into the debate from abroad' – because of context and verification difficulties. ' "Action groups", because they have a view which appears to challenge, can get a prominence in the media: in situations where their action is not required, this can sow the seeds of misunderstanding between journalists and those who carry the real responsibility for action. To be telephoned, without warning, with the request for a rapid reply to an action group statement can be a frustrating experience for those who, at the time, are actually working on the problem: for the journalist who asks the question and has a press-time to meet, the slowness of the reply must be equally irritating, and may even suggest an inability to respond.'

5.4 Journals

The free medical journals and BSSRS *Science for People* have already been quoted as providing stories for the general-interest press. They are examples of a general practice. Since publication in a learned journal is one of the chief ways of announcing results of scientific research, it is only natural that the journals are acknowledged by the science writers to be an important source. The *New Scientist*, Fishlock has written, has been invaluable 'as the first stage of breaking down a complex piece of research or "emerging opportunity" into a simple but lucid newspaper story'. In the extreme case, the arrangement between *The Times* and *Nature*, the relationship has been institutionalised: *Nature* undertakes to provide material for a daily column and *The Times* sets aside a permanent spot, with only an informal negative veto over the choice of subjects and the minimum of subbing, evidently. (See Appendix II.)

Fishlock files *twenty-five* journals, not counting the trade and technical press, and discards many more. (They are listed, with Clare Dover's, at Appendix III.) Since so much science is American, many of the important journals are American. Clare Dover finds *Science* (USA) a better source than *New Scientist*, for example. Also, the letters show her what people are going to start arguing about. She also likes *Scientific American*.

The medical journals are a regular source. Twenty of the nearly 300 *Times/ Nature* stories in the calendar year ending 31 October 1975 were credited to the *BMJ* and twelve to *Lancet*. Bedford (*Daily Mirror*) reckons he gets one story a month from the *BMJ* (and others, as we have seen, from *Lancet*). The press receive the *BMJ* ahead of subscribers. Some doctors dislike this.

Nature, and *New Scientist* rather more, are to some extent directed towards less specialised audiences or at least to mediating one type of specialist to another. John Maddox, editor of *Nature* in the 1960s, refers to its 'unique blend of journalism and learned journal'. His successor, David Davies, feels that when it comes to the crunch the scientific community 'probably regard us as being on their side'. Maddox claims that his attempts to make science more intelligible 'turned out to be more widely appreciated by scientists than by the wider public'. *Nature* began in 1869 as a weekly vehicle of news and comment and, in Maddox's view, almost 'stumbled' into being a learned journal.

New Scientist (founded 1956; first editor, Percy Cudlipp) was meant, Cudlipp wrote, to be a link between science and industry, translating science to the inexpert businessman. In fact its appeal proved to be rather broader, to the inexpert of many kinds. (It sells a lot to schools, obviously.) A reflection of the journalistic side of both these publications is that, unlike strictly specialised journals, they positively encourage publicity. Press releases go round with each number. There is quite a long 'free list' at *New Scientist* (including members of the Commons Committee on Science and Technology). The Press Association science correspondent, Nick Timmins, is ex-*Nature*. In Davies' opinion he picks up more than average, and this is reflected in the provincials' science coverage. Martin Sherwood (Science Policy Editor) quoted several examples of *New Scientist* stories picked up by the press and broadcasters, often without attribution (which, again, matters more than with academic publications) and sometimes complete with an original slip or two.

Another aspect of the scientist/journalist character of *New Scientist* and *Nature* is that they rely heavily on outside contributors. (This creates its own 'skew': contributors are easier to get in some fields than others.) Both editors mentioned spontaneously their concern at the possible consequences of closed shop regulations.

Appendix I
A note on the growth of science journalism

Benjamin Harris's *Publick Occurrences*, published in 1690, was the first American newspaper. Hillier Krieghbaum points out in his book *Science and the Mass Media* (London, 1968) that it contained two paragraphs on 'science', exhibiting characteristics still found in today's press: a concern with public health and medicine, a local angle ('the NIH factor' – 'Not Invented Here'), a stress on progress and a vague connection with the military. ('Public Health and Medicine', ranked top by 166 American daily newspaper editors in a 1951 survey, was second to 'Satellites and Outer Space' as the subject having 'special interest' in 1958 and 1965. 'Atomic Energy' dropped from second to fourth.)

In 1939, soon after the National Association of Science Writers was founded, there were only thirty-four recognised newspaper science correspondents in the USA. In 1961 there were 477. The atomic bomb was a key event. Thereafter, the launching of Sputnik in 1957 received greater public awareness than any event. Then in 1969, when Apollo 11 landed on the moon, 53.5 million households in the USA watched an average of $15\frac{1}{2}$ hours TV coverage. The launching was covered by 4,000 reporters from 55 countries.

Until the 1930s science journalism in Britain, as in the USA, was done either by scientists writing largely in their own fields, or by reporters expounding the wonders (and commercial possibilities) of modern inventions. A few of the former continued after the second world war. The Science Correspondent of the *Financial Times* from 1947–52, for instance, was Sir Francis Simon, Professor of Thermodynamics at Oxford. (Fishlock says his writing on nuclear energy was very farsighted and stands up well today.)

Between the wars a new kind of professional science journalist developed. One of the first, along with Ritchie Calder, was J G Crowther, who reviewed the growth of his subject in a British Association paper some years ago. He submitted a number of articles to *The Guardian* on aspects of science and society, then went to see C P Scott. He said he wished to become a scientific journalist. Scott said: 'The trouble is, Mr Crowther, that there isn't such a profession'. 'To this I answered: "No, but I propose to invent it".' Crowther won his point and became *The Guardian*'s scientific correspondent until the time of CND. Between the wars he ranged widely, visiting Moscow in 1929, following the development of atomic physics, observing the interaction of metallurgy and architecture in the work of the Bauhaus school.

Crowther notes these changes in science writing since the 1930s:

– the ratio of interpretation to information has decreased;

77

- the development of information control in the interests of security (eg in atomic energy) and the ambiguous significance of PR: you never know what is being hidden;
- less access: in the 1930s 'it was possible to meet Rutherford and Bohr, and have quite frank discussions with them';
- subjects are often intrinsically more difficult to explain;
- scientists travel much more and themselves rely on the peripatetic scientific journalist for gossip and information much less.

Crowther was a founder-member of the Association of British Science Writers in 1947.

78

Appendix II
The Times/Nature Science Report

Every day *The Times* publishes a Science Report, usually produced by *The Times/Nature* News Service. It is a unique feature of British science journalism. The subjects range over all the sciences and into technology. The Report normally appears on the Court Page.

Origins

Science Report was apparently an idea of John Maddox when he was editor of *Nature*. It was suggested by him informally to John Grant, then Home Editor of *The Times*, shortly after the Thomson takeover in 1967. It was a time of major Thomson spending, and William Rees-Mogg, the new editor, decided to take it on. The idea was distilled into the proposal for a column modelled on *The Times* Law Report. This explains why the column is put in a box with lines round it and an unvarying heading. Once drawn to one's attention, the analogy with the Law Report is discernible (fairly timeless, written according to strict professional, non-journalistic standards, as a matter of record, etc).

Responsibility for contents

One of the most distinctive features of the Science Report is that *The Times* has in effect delegated responsibility for its contents. *The Times* is not technically obliged to print what *Nature* offers: occasional pieces get held up or put on one side, and a piece by a staff man might perhaps be used instead. But everything that is printed goes in relatively untouched; and because of that, the Chief Sub has to control the order in which reports appear so that he can fit the right length to the available space. (*Nature* therefore supply them in varying lengths.) If a piece has not been used, it will have been the decision of the Chief Sub, who will have considered it too complicated for readers. Periodically of course there is liaison about the column variously between Pearce Wright (*The Times* Science Editor), Miranda Robertson (*Nature*'s organiser of the section) and *The Times* Chief Sub. Very occasionally *The Times* suggests a subject – for instance comments on the Nobel Prize list – or query a story picked up by other papers and not sent in by *Nature*. Similarly Miranda Robertson might contact *The Times* medical correspondent if he seems to have missed something she thinks is important in the *BMJ* or *Lancet*.

Organisation in Nature

Miranda Robertson has been able to throw her weight about (her phrase) for some eighteen months; she combines this job with other *Nature* editorial duties. Four or five staff members write a minimum of three pieces each per month. About half are solicited by her and half suggested to her. She herself writes two or so a week. She looks each week at the forthcoming contents of *Nature* and decides which pieces *must* be written up for *The Times*, which pieces *could* be, and who should be asked to write them. Many other journals are also used as a source – especially *Science* and the Proceedings of the National Academy of Sciences.

Criteria of selection of Science Report

Miranda Robertson sees 'a constant tussle' between the criteria of general interest to *The Times* readers and 'Is it scientifically important?'. With up to six pieces a week, a few of those at the margin would be in one week but not another; stories that are easy to write up obviously get a certain preference. A consideration for *The Times* is the traditional 'journal of record' idea: an item might be chosen because in five years' time it could turn out to get the Nobel Prize. (The 1975 chemistry Nobel work had not been written about: chemistry is difficult to put across.)

Miranda Robertson feels, like Pearce Wright, that the Report has in the past been too technical and that the balance between the two general criteria is not quite right yet. Scientifically important work is sometimes excluded because of the difficulty of exposition. (Quarks, as I have indicated in the main text, have apparently caused dismay to sub-editors.)

The balance of stories between different sciences partly reflects difficulties of exposition but it also reflects the specialist interests of various members of staff. With immense subdivisions in science, however well *Nature*'s staff keep up with what is going on, they undoubtedly do miss important material on occasions.

General impressions, mistakes etc

Overall, Miranda Robertson thinks the Report gives a reasonably good idea of what is topical, and is a bridge between the cultures. Scientists remark spontaneously that they like it, though *Nature* has no systematic feedback. Occasionally a piece starts a hare in *The Times* correspondence columns. Other letters are passed on for answer from *The Times*. A story about kittens' eyes being rotated in the interests of research became a news story in October 1975 in its own right. Mistakes inevitably creep in, but they are usually insignificant rather than major matters of misreporting or misinterpretation.

Appendix III

Journals filed by David Fishlock (*Financial Times*) **and Clare Dover** (*The Daily Telegraph*)

David Fishlock appeared to keep journals more systematically than Clare Dover. The lists should not be thought of as presented for strict comparison. Only the eight journals marked with an asterisk seemed to be filed by both of them.

Fishlock

New Scientist*
World Medicine*
Lancet*
British Medical Journal*
The Practitioner*
World Health (WHO)
Naval Research (US Navy)
Weather
Science and Government Report (USA)
Nucleonics Week (USA)
Weekly Energy Report (USA)
CERN Courier
Atom (AEA)
Science* (USA)
Scientific American* (USA)
Physics Today
IAEA Bulletin
Science Journal (now folded)
Research Policy (Sussex University)
Nature*
Economist
Pharmaceutical Journal
Toxicology
Physics Bulletin
Nuclear Engineering International

Plus

The Times
The Guardian
'. . . and the Trade, Business and Technical press and the flow from the Foreign Desk . . . .'

Dover

New Scientist*
Science* (USA)
The Practitioner*
Trade and Industry (DTI)
Scientific American* (USA)
Sky and Telescope (USA)
British Medical Journal*
Lancet*
Medical Week
World Medicine*
Nature*

Odd copies of

Modern Medicine
Chemistry and Industry
New Society
Electronics Weekly
Bulletin of Atomic Scientists (USA)

The In–Tray contained

CERN Courier
Health Visitor
American Medical News (USA)
Blesmag (Limbless Ex-Servicemen)
Marine Pollution Bulletin
Flash (Trinity House)
Profile (ITT House Magazine)
ABPI News
Health and Social Service Journal
Aviation Week (USA)
General Practitioner
Intercom (Home Office Tele-communications)
Electronics and Power (IEE)

Part B   Section 2

Parliament and Government

by Dr Colin Seymour-Ure of the University of Kent

Contents

Author's note

This paper discusses four factors governing newspaper content under the general heading of 'Parliament and Government'.

As with my other papers, this one contains no policy proposals (nor are any intentionally implied). Nor does it offer sweeping judgments about editorial standards. It is necessarily impressionistic.

The paper is based on interviews with national and provincial editors, specialist journalists, parliamentary officials and civil servants, MPs etc; and on documentary information. The interviews were carried out in 1976 by myself and Professor Jeremy Tunstall of The City University, some of whose work is included in this volume.

Parliament is discussed because of its links with notions of press diversity and independence through its connection with the party system; because of its considerable dependence on the press; and because it illustrates so well the perennial tensions between British politicians and the press.

The Lobby Correspondents were chosen because they are still at the centre of the machinery of political journalism; they have been the subject of a (frequently polemical) 'debate'; and there have been important additions to the literature about them since the main lines of the argument were set.

Economic journalism is included because it has been a relatively 'new' subject; it overlaps political journalism; and it is a field where Government depends considerably upon successful communication of its policies to the public.

Local Government and the local press is a subject not widely studied and about which there is little secondary literature.

C K S-U
August 1976.

1 Parliament

1.1 Press and Parliament: Tensions

The relations of Parliament and the Press are full of tension, mutual suspicion and potential conflict. This is a commonplace. Newspapers share a golden age myth about the quality and influence of Parliament, particularly in their comment on elections. Parliamentary memoirs suggest a golden age myth about the press. Michael Macdonagh, a *Times* press gallery veteran writing in 1902, recalled the amount of grumbles in the Victorian age about coverage not being what it used to be; and O'Connell was complaining even in 1833. Asquith grumbled in his memoirs published in 1926. Attlee grumbled in the 1940s. Within weeks of becoming Leader of the Commons in 1976 Michael Foot grumbled: 'Broadcasting of the proceedings of the House would be a proper development', *The Times* report ran (adjournment debate, 13 April 1976), 'particularly in view of the scandalous misreporting, under-reporting and improper reporting of the House which [goes] on by practically all the newspapers of the country . . . Reporting is a travesty of what it used to be, even when I came to the House . . . The *Express, The Sun* and most of the others are an absolute disgrace to journalism.' This provoked a letter to *The Times* (to which Mr Foot gave a bouquet) from Sir Max Aitken: Mr Foot 'ought, in the stillness of the night, to reflect whether the blame attaches to the newspapers or to Parliament. Many people now hold the view that Parliament is so intrusive into our lives that any discouragement of this is in the national interest and in the interest of democracy.' (15 April 1976.) Perhaps there was exaggeration in both opinions: if so, it further reflects the mutual suspicion. Another illustration in the 1975–76 session was a breach of privilege complaint against the *Economist*. Such complaints – a handful every year – are a constant symptom of the tension. They often reach a peak at times when the Commons are unsure of their standing with the electorate and are particularly sensitive to the tone of their coverage – for example during the Suez Crisis and when the balance of parties is very fine. The *Economist* published on 11 October 1975 a story based on the draft report of the Select Committee inquiring into a Wealth Tax. Since the report had not yet been presented to the House, this was technically a contempt, though no evidence was produced by the Committee of Privileges to justify its view that the offence was not merely technical. The Committee recommended that the *Economist* be fined, and that the Editor and responsible reporter be excluded not only from the Lobby for six months but from the entire precincts of the Palace of Westminster (except for the express purpose of seeing their local MPs). In 1974 a similar 'premature publication' offence led to the exclusion of the *Daily Mail*'s lobby Correspondent being mooted. In neither case was the suggestion adopted, but each illustrated the Commons' touchiness. Technical offences against Commons' rules were certainly committed: the point about the Commons' reaction is a sledgehammer-and-nut one.

The following sections seek to explore the basis of the tension between Parliament and the Press, with the aim of providing a context in which the coverage of Parliament – and the Government in Parliament – can be judged.

(a) Parliament depends on the Press

(i) *Historical origin.* The parliamentary idea of consultation precedes Parliament as an institution. When the institution took shape the only practical way of talking together was by meeting together. The shape of Parliament has always been governed by communications technology. At first the critical factor was the relationship of horsepower to mileage; and the parliamentary timetable was determined by the cycle of the seasons, since members could not meet at seedtime and harvest. A vestige of these constraints remains in the shortness of Friday sittings, which enables MPs to get back to their constituencies for the weekend. The growth of newspapers and of parliamentary responsibility to the electorate have encouraged the institution's procedures continually to adapt to the needs of the Press. Newspapers deadline times in the late 19th century meant that if speeches were to be reported they must be shorter and made much earlier in the day than before. The *Westminster Gazette* editor J A Spender, comparing the mid-19th century Commons with the 1920s, remarked that the great moments then 'were nearly always after dinner and generally after midnight, but in these days the newspapers which impose their timetable upon Parliament are more and more aggrieved if anything important is said after the dinner-hour'. The decision in 1902 to change Question Time to the early afternoon took account of newspaper convenience: 'We must arrange our proceedings, I presume,' said A J Balfour, Leader of the House, 'so that they may be reported in the newspapers that have currency all over the country.'

It may be argued at the extreme that communications media are 'bigger' than institutions. If Parliament, for example, fails to adapt to new media like TV, Parliament not the new media will in the long run be the loser.

(ii) *Need for publicity.* The point that Parliament needs the Press to report its proceedings requires no labouring. In the 1890s even *Hansard* was contracted out to reporters on *The Times* (William Law, *Our Hansard*, Pitman, 1950 pp 16–17). Since a public right to reports of debates was conceded at the end of the 18th century Parliament has always subsidised the press through the provision of press gallery accommodation. On the rare occasions when the Chamber has been rebuilt, account has been taken of newspapers' wishes. The new Chamber opened in 1950 contained 161 seats, an increase of 68, and provincial evening newspapers were admitted for the first time. The focus of tension about Gallery facilities has often been catering. The Gallery's dining room is a useful facility and, in the words of Speaker Morrison, an ally, in 1958, 'essential to [its] tradition and dignity'. But it has generally made a loss and in 1958 the Commons Kitchen Committee precipitated a crisis by deciding unilaterally to abolish it. After strong lobbying the decision was rescinded. Accommodation generally is cramped, although there have been improvements since a Gallery Working Party detailed the inadequacies in a report in 1964. The report ranged from high matters of status and principle, embellished with quotations from Macaulay and Dr Johnson, to the general feeling that the Bar 'should be brighter, with crisps and peanuts and such things lying around'. But the Gallery has always been a poor relation. Parliament has provided facilities which are essential to the journalists' work and cost little or nothing – for instance

Lobbymen have privileged access to private parts of the buildings. Copies of parliamentary documents are available in advance of general publication; which frequently puts journalists at an advantage over MPs – a sore point that causes regular complaints. Physical facilities, however, are at risk whenever money is involved; and irritating episodes like the installation of a lift in the Serjeant-at-Arms' house in 1934, which absorbed half one of the Gallery's writing rooms, litter the institution's history. In the last resort, though, Parliament's need for publicity obliges it to cooperate. The Press Gallery seating in the 1950 Chamber is twice the size originally proposed.

(iii) *Implications of Broadcast Debates*. Both the main points in these previous two sections on the shape of the parliamentary institution and its need for publicity are at the core of the argument about televising Parliament. Can Parliament afford not to televise its proceedings? Will it be bypassed and supplanted by programmes that do televise politics? Or will the new radio broadcasts be sufficient adaptation for the time being? In either case, an increased role for broadcasting in parliamentary coverage may affect press attitudes unpredictably. The public may want to read more as a result of what they hear (and perhaps eventually see). Alternatively newspapers may move even further in the direction deplored by Mr Foot, on the grounds that broadcast coverage makes press coverage redundant. (This latter view is sometimes taken about at least one country, Australia, in which debates have been broadcast by radio since 1946.)

(iv) *The Press and the 'Parliamentary Agenda'*. Parliament needs the Press for a source of information just as much as for publicity. The results can be seen in any Question Time or Adjournment Debate, and in many of the inquiries by Select Committees. If one thinks of a 'parliamentary agenda' consisting of a number of topics to which at any given moment MPs attach priority, then the Press can be said to have a major influence over it. Partly this may be a matter of sign-posting – articles highlighting a particular subject; and partly, of course, the actual views of specialist writers may influence the attitudes Members adopt. It is an area in which a very broad view of the necessary *diversity* in the Press can be justified. This point is explored further in the sections on Select Committees and on the Opposition; but it is worth noting here one refinement – the role of the Press in the definition of political crises. When is something a political crisis? One answer is: when the Press (and broadcasting) say it is. At what stage does the rate or level of inflation become a 'crisis'? At what stage in its intended reduction will it cease to be one? How far does the £ have to fall, and how quickly, before there is a foreign exchange crisis? How big can a balance of payments deficit be before it is a crisis? Is there an Energy Crisis? How far is it simply a financial crisis? Since the application of the word is arbitrary, the Press can be more influential than when reporting hard 'facts'; and since a 'crisis' denotes something unexpected and urgent, an immediate and visible response is demanded – preferably action not words. Political crises in which Parliament becomes involved are thus excited, intense occasions, whose seriousness in the eyes of Ministers may be affected considerably by the amount of publicity.

The Liberal Party's leadership crisis in Spring 1976 was not strictly a parliamentary crisis nor probably of lasting significance, but it illustrates the argument clearly. Mr Thorpe's decision to resign was a response to circumstances that had recently changed in only one particular – the cry taken up in the mass media. His authority was at risk essentially because the media said it was and the Party reacted to the crisis in a predictable way – by choosing as temporary replacement the familiar, reliable figure of Mr Grimmond. In an equally clear cut example, Mr Heath sacked Mr Powell from his Shadow Cabinet in 1968 after a speech on immigration that was typically presented as POWELL RACE BLOCKBUSTER: A CRISIS FOR HEATH (the *Sunday Express* headline). The substance of Mr Powell's speech was less objectionable to the Conservative leadership than the *tone* – it was the tone to which Mr Heath referred in his letter of dismissal. Newspapers' construction of the speech as a challenge obliged Mr Heath to treat it as a crisis and to be seen to respond with more than words.

Those examples refer to personalities. Others could be drawn from legislation. One of the best in recent years might be the rushed legislation about Kenya Asian immigrants in 1968 which followed an intensive campaign by Conservative backbenchers and newspapers.

The importance of the Press as a source of information is emphasised, lastly, by that interpretation of parliamentary influence which rests on the axiom 'Knowledge is power'. This is often attractive to those who look for influence in MPs but feel the emptiness of the formal powers to overturn Governments and control the purse. The 'knowledge is power' argument involves the slow accumulation of expertise by Members; the embarrassing disclosure by a Select Committee; the awkward Question requiring a Departmental adjustment in Whitehall; and the alleged effect of all such activities on the 'climate' of policy as well as, occasionally, on someone's career. Insofar as MPs do exert influence in these ways, they are continually nourished by the Press; and the value to them of a 'diverse' press must be great.

(b) The Press depends on Parliament

While some tension derives from the ambivalence of parliamentarians who both recognise and dislike their dependence on the Press, some derives also from the dependence of the Press on Parliament.

Parliament exercises formal control over the Press just like any other industry. As well as laws with fairly specific application – libel, Official Secrets, Monopolies and Mergers, the Press is likely to see its interests affected by wider measures, the most obvious example in the 1975–76 Session being the Trade Union legislation affecting the closed shop principle. Parliament has exercised its legislative sovereignty over broadcasting more than the Press, as far as intrusion into content goes (*Yesterday in Parliament* is broadcast obligatorily, for example).

A more direct form of control is over the terms on which the Press gets information about Parliament (including the Government in Parliament). Attitudes towards the exercise of its formal contempt powers, as described in the *Economist* example in the introduction, can be frustrating to newspapers having a well meaning desire to inform their readers. So can problems with gallery facilities. Parliament's control gains an edge from newspaper competitiveness.

The most striking general example of the control is the institution of the Lobby. This is discussed in a separate section. Its effectiveness, in the unsensational form of the efficient reporting and exposition of great quantities of routine news about government activities, depends wholly on cooperation by Parliament (which is not to say there would be no political journalism without it). The Lobby relationship is nicely illustrated by one of its rules (which are the kind that Members evidently do not normally need to read): 'Do not run after a

Minister', this rule begins, indicating the regard Lobby men must have to their status as 'licensed intruders' in the Westminster precincts. 'It is nearly always possible', the rule continues, recognising the politicians' acceptance of the usefulness of the system, 'to place oneself in a position to avoid this'.

The Press, in law and in practice, desire the cooperation of Parliament; and Parliament thus has some control over them.

(c) Conflicting Goals of Press and Parliament

Neither Press nor Parliament defines its goals by reference exclusively to the other. This too explains the tension between them.

In brief, Parliament wants publicity for what it considers important and at the time of its choice: hence the arguments about premature publication and press concentration on the froth of parliamentary business. (Eg 'Reports of Committee hearings receive infinitely less press coverage than proceedings on the floor of the House' – Dick Taverne, formerly Chairman, Public Expenditure Committee General Sub-Committee, *The Listener* 23 November 1972.) Newspapers, on the other hand, have to take account of their target audience; the presumed and expressed interests of that audience; their partisanship and attitude to the Government; conventional news values; and the economic factors affecting the paper. (Of the latter, I wondered if the flow of advertising through the year fitted well with the peaks of parliamentary activity. From asking a few newspapers about their average paging, it appears that there is at least no serious imbalance. When papers need space for Parliamentary/Government news – eg October–December – papers are normally at their biggest.)

The result is that many Parliamentarians share Mr Foot's view that press coverage is trivial and inadequate, overstressing personalities and short-run issues; and no doubt many journalists share Sir Max Aitken's view. The divergence is most acute over subjects like the legislation for British membership of the EEC, which did not fit news values at all tidily.

To some extent Parliament's own attitudes are consistent with newspapers' tendencies. For example, the focus of parliamentary procedure still remains the floor of the Commons Chamber. The constant presentation of Questions for debate in terms of AYE and NO, reinforced by the party-conflict, Government *v* Opposition model of doing business – even down to the plurality, winner-takes-all method of choosing MPs from the electorate and the Executive from MPs – all these fit in well with newspaper preferences for clashes, confrontation and excitement. They are symbolised by the faithful reporting of the exact votes in Commons division lists whose political importance is normally trivial.

Perhaps the Prime Minister's Question Time epitomises the parliamentary conflict best. Marcia Williams notes that Harold Wilson 'was certainly more tense than usual on the nights before Questions, and anxious to get away to the study, so that he might look through the Questions in peace'; the reason being the effect of drubbing the Opposition on party morale. Questions have 'repercussions on television and in the newspapers. There is nothing like a good Press on the following morning for heartening a Party Leader. Afterwards it is possible to sense the reaction in the country as the effect of newspaper stories and the reports of MPs to their constituencies have their effect throughout the rest of Britain' (*Inside Number Ten*, New English Library edn 1972, pp 67–68). The British Parliament, in strong contrast, say, to the French, West German or

93

United States', does not use procedures seeking compromise and agreement. Quite the opposite: the floor of the House conventionally exaggerates the differences between parties. 'Westminster is strong on drama and weak on influence. It thrives on the big debate, the motion of censure, the clash on Second Reading . . . The main Parliamentary occasions are, in fact, a kind of theatre, and a number of political commentators are essentially political drama critics.' That is a common view, even when not expressed, as here, in the context of an argument (by Dick Taverne, already quoted) for wider use of Committees.

Significantly, one attempt at procedural reform to which great importance was initially attached failed in the early 1970s, precisely because it did not fit into the 'adversary' format and link to some particular political issue. This was the institution of a two-day debate on the annual Public Expenditure White Paper setting out the Government's expenditure projections for the next five years. The debates have generally fallen flat. Commenting in *The Times* on the 1971 debate, David Wood confirmed the obvious explanation. 'Mr Macmillan himself [Chief Secretary to the Treasury] put it well to the deserted benches on Thursday night: "The White Paper does not convey any news. By definition, as a rule, it has nothing new in it. It is the result, not the cause, of Government decisions, and the policies it described are themselves continuing in time and therefore are not essentially new policies." Precisely. It is last year's political battles, already lost and won, eked out with the predictions from the Treasury's very own Gypsy Lee' (13 December 1971).

1.2 Select Committees and Press Publicity

(a) Growth of Committees and of their interest in publicity

Most of the points raised in discussing the tensions between Parliament and the Press are illustrated by an examination of the publicity given to Commons Select Committees.

The work done by these Committees has grown enormously in the last ten years. The list at Appendix I, dated 1 April 1976, names no less than forty-two (including sub-committees). (A later list, dated 16 June, had forty-five.) A few are domestic and/or rarely burdensome (eg Committee on Members' Interests; Privileges Committee). Most are concerned with matters that are not in the least arcane. Appendix II shows which of them met (in public) in the week beginning 8 March 1976. (It also includes seven Standing Committees dealing with legislation.) On Wednesday, the heaviest day, ten committees met. The Select Committees sitting that day heard evidence about Chrysler, the Inshore Fishing industry, Alternative Sources of Energy (wind power), National Parks, Industry and Scientific Research, and Preventive Medicine.

The Select Committee system developed since the mid-1960s is a patchwork; but it has the common characteristic of a much greater interest than before in openness and communication with the public. Typically, the Press are invited to report the proceedings as they go along instead of waiting for the final report; and the range of witnesses is far wider than before. (The older tradition is maintained by the prestigious Public Accounts Committee, which still hears evidence in private, though the evidence is eventually published.) The present system contains long established Committees like the Statutory Instruments Committee and the Nationalised Industries Committee. The interest in publicity, however, is identified more with the so-called 'Crossman Committees' set up from 1966, when Mr Crossman was Leader of the House. Some reformers had great hopes of them as instruments of executive scrutiny and accountability. Overseas Development, Race Relations and Science and Technology are remaining examples. Others were superseded by the big Public Expenditure Committee (49 members) with its six sub-committees specialising in subjects broadly coinciding with Whitehall Departments (Environment, Trade and Industry, etc). This Committee was given wider terms of reference that might make it more newsworthy anyway: it was allowed to scrutinise policy, not just (in theory) the appropriateness of expenditure for existing policy – and it was supposed to gear its inquiries to the new five-year Public Expenditure Survey system in the Departments. In practice the Sub-Committees have followed their noses in whatever directions they fancy.

Membership of the EEC has prompted a new Select Committee (with three sub-committees) to monitor the large volume of European Secondary Legislation. *Ad hoc* committees of inquiry are also set up (reverting to a much older practice): on 1 April and 16 June lists these included Abortion, Cyprus, Violence in the Family and Direct Elections to the European Assembly. In the previous session this method had been used to canvass proposals for a Wealth Tax – an inquiry which came nearer than most to the reformers' fancy for a 'pre-legislation committee'.

(b) Getting Publicity for Committee

(i) The problem of 'Skew'. The Committees start at a disadvantage because of the 'Skew' in Commons proceedings towards the floor of the Chamber. The Press quite literally do not always know what the Committees are doing, even when they may be hearing evidence on a traditionally good news subject. The work of the Committee on Violence in the Family, for example, led to a big feature in the *News of the World*, making use of the report of oral evidence conveyed by the Committee Clerk to the journalists concerned. Other tabloids, for which this might be thought a likely subject, may simply not have taken in that the inquiry was going on. The Committee's public sessions were attended by three or four people from the heavy papers and the PA and by virtually no one else.

The Commons Committee Office, which has general responsibility for pro-gramming sessions, circulates to the Press Gallery and Lobby each week a summary notice of forthcoming sessions (an example is at Appendix III). But witnesses are not always known even that near in advance; nor may it be easy to judge which of them will be interesting. 'It has been hard work', one observer of the process over several years has concluded, 'for any interested pressmen or member of the public to keep himself informed of what might be going on in Select Committees on subjects of interest to him.' In contrast the 'Business Statement' in the Commons each Thursday by the Leader of the House about the programme for next week is usually a lively parliamentary occasion that catches journalists' attention anyway.

Part of the problem is that the Press Gallery and Lobby – again reflecting their orientation to the floor of the House – do not contain the specialist journalists whom the Committees need to attract. The story at Appendix IV, for example, a routine report of evidence to the Abortion Committee, is by *The Times* Social Services Correspondent not a member of the Gallery. One instance was quoted to me of a paper – *The Daily Telegraph* – apparently assigning a staff man specifically to cover Select Committees (in liaison with the paper's specialists);

but it seems unlikely that many other papers do the same. Successful contact with appropriate specialists can bring its own difficulties of coordination too. One Committee appointed a specialist adviser (an increasingly common habit, itself capable of raising the level of publicity) but did not wish to announce it until he had left another job. The Lobby agreed to hold the story over (and were not particularly interested). But a non-parliamentary journalist, having discovered the adviser's name elsewhere, intended to publish it and rang the Commons for confirmation. The cooperation of the paper's editor and lobbyman then had to be sought in keeping publication back. (Ever since, in an attempt to mollify him, the journalist has been sent all the Committee's handouts.) Such episodes are inevitable and generally trivial. But they underline the fact that in winning press publicity the Committees need to get beyond the long established arrangements for parliamentary publicity.

(ii) Mechanics of Publicity: Handouts and Contacts. Parliamentary officials consider it a minor triumph that, having lobbied Fleet Street news editors, *The Times* and *The Daily Telegraph* regularly publish the weekly programme of public Committee sessions. Committees also announce themselves in a press release when they start a new inquiry, usually including an open invitation to submit evidence. An example from the Environment Sub-Committee of the Public Expenditure Committee, which decided in April 1976 to investigate planning procedures, is at Appendix V. Attached to it is a resulting news item in *The Times*, filled out slightly by its Planning Reporter.

At the other end of the process, advance copies of Committee reports are now allowed under standing order 85 to be given to the Press up to 48 hours before publication – although not until they have been technically laid on the Table and presented to the House. For many years lobby correspondents have had advance copies, but now the practice has extended much more widely. Undoubtedly reports do find their way also to journalists even earlier, when still in draft stage. This is strictly a contempt and can cause considerable resentment – as in the *Economist*'s publication of details of the Wealth Tax Committee report in 1975.

What happens between the start and finish of an inquiry varies with the personalities of Committee members and officials, the subject and, more particularly, the kind of Committee. Committees that are permanent, if they have a well defined ambit (Science and Technology; PEC General (Economic)) have built up press relations for which the imagery of 'Machinery' seems too smooth and highly organised. The effect is of bits of string more than a seamless drivebelt. *Ad hoc* committees, or those which dart around more (Trade and Industry, Employment and Social Services) have arrangements breezily described to me as 'pretty chaotic'. The latter tend to be reactive, while the former may take initiatives for publicity.

One simple innovation, though it took some time to establish, has been the introduction of lists of specialist journalists to whom appropriate stuff is circularised. This had worked well for the Public Expenditure General Sub-Committee, which has carried on a kind of dialogue with the Treasury and various outside observers, with the authoritative assistance of its specialist adviser, Mr Wynn Godley. The 'audience' of journalists for this sub-committee is small but influential. In April 1976 the list contained 52 entries, which are broken down by news organisations in the List opposite. Most of the entries are anonymous (eg 'News Editor'). Only 17 are named individuals. Apart from

Public Expenditure Committee

General Sub-Committee Press List 1976

News organisations listed

Organisation	No. of Copies	
Financial Times	5	W Keegan, A Harris, S Brittan, News ed, City ed.
The Times	4	T Congden, P Jay, Business News ed, Gen News ed.
BBC	4	D Harrod, B Griffiths (TV) ed TV News, ed Radio News.
The Guardian	3	F Cairncross, J Stead, News ed.
The Observer	3	C Raw, News ed, Business ed.
The Daily Telegraph	3	M Becket, C German, News ed.
Sunday Telegraph	3	P Hutber, L McGrandle, City ed.
The Sunday Times	2	News ed, Business News ed.
Evening News	2	M Rothwell, News ed.
Economist	2	M Schreiber, ed.
Evening Standard	1	News ed.
Spectator	1	Ed.
New Statesman	1	Ed.
ITN	1	News ed.
Granada TV	1	Norma Percy
Glasgow Herald	1	Ed.
The Scotsman	1	Ed.
Press Association	1	News ed.
Press Gallery Secretary	6	
Lobby Correspondents' Secretary	6	
Treasury	1	
	52	

The Scotsman and *The Glasgow Herald* no provincial newspaper is included, though the copies sent to the Press Gallery and Lobby are no doubt generally available. None of the popular nationals is included either. The General Sub-Committee list was compiled on the initiative of a Commons Official, in an informal way, and 'is all run by an intelligent secretary in the Clerk's Department'. It started out as a list for the activities of the Expenditure Committee as a whole; but its economic slant made it especially suitable for the General Sub-Committee, and other sub-committees have their own lists. The Environment Committee, for instance, circulates information to at least twice as many journalists as the General Sub-Committee. It includes representatives of Local Government associations and interest groups. The Science and Technology Committee, similarly, has quite longstanding links with Science Journalists. The Association of British Science Writers exchanges hospitality with the Committee.

The *ad hoc* Committee on Violence in the Family makes a good contrast. (February–August 1975, mainly; and February onwards, 1976.) This sent out no press notices about its proceedings at all, although it dealt with a number of spontaneous inquiries (including only one telephone call from any of the specialist publications that one might have expected to be interested). The Committee gave a press conference on the publication of its main report, but no journalist seems to have built up a 'special relationship' with it along the way, and the Clerk could not identify the press representatives at its sessions.

(iii) Importance of the subject of inquiry. Subjects coinciding with conventional news values obviously attract most publicity. Abortion is such a natural one that the Abortion Committee (set up in February 1976) had a press conference about its main report more from a feeling that it could not get away without one than from any general enthusiasm among its members for the idea. More than thirty journalists came along and produced some strong questioning.

That and Violence in the Family exemplify 'human interest' subjects. Others are politically controversial. One of the earliest Expenditure Committee reports to make headlines was about private practice in the NHS (1972). It produced a report polarised on party lines. An unlikely subject, the Charity Commission, drew coverage because it had implications for the status and costs of private schools. The Committee on Cyprus attracted attention because it criticised Mr Callaghan for decisions about Cyprus policy during the Turkish invasion of 1974 when he was Foreign Secretary. The PEC General Sub-Committee attracted attention before the 1976 Budget by saying it would take 'an economic miracle' to fulfil the Government's objectives set out in the recent White Paper on Expenditure cuts (ie Public Expenditure to 1979–80). The report was rushed out so that MPs would have the weekend to read it before the Budget. An added factor ensuring publicity was that the Chairman of the Sub-Committee, Mr Michael English, is a Labour Member, and the final report had been agreed by the 49 members of the full Expenditure Committee, on which the Government has a majority (as on the sub-committee). The Chancellor took up the phrase in his Budget speech, and so did Sir Geoffrey Howe, Shadow Chancellor, in his broadcast reply. Perhaps the best example of general press publicity has been the Trade and Industry sub-committee's inquiry into wages paid by British firms in South Africa (1973). This directly followed articles in *The Guardian*, which gave it great topicality. In eighteen sittings 28 companies gave oral evidence. One hundred others gave written evidence. The hearings were followed keenly. 'Powerful industrialists have been subjected to close and aggressive

98

questioning', a *Times* report commented at the end. 'British commercial morality has never been so mercilessly examined . . . There [is] ample evidence that British companies were previously in ignorance of the situation in their South African interests.'

Perhaps because of the general importance of economic management the specialised work of the General Sub-Committee (eg on the Treasury's forecasting, control and monitoring of public expenditure) has had attention outside specialist economic publications – for example from Peter Jay, in *The Times* and David Watt and Samuel Brittan in the *Financial Times*. Specialist publications also keep track of the Committees, though I have no detailed studies of them. The *Economist* naturally follows economic inquiries carefully. Indeed its problems with the Privileges Committee were a result of its thoroughness: the editor reckoned he published a story about it at least every fortnight. When I visited a Science and Technology sub-committee session in April 1976, Lord Bowden was discussing Science policy (valedictory remarks before retiring as Principal of UMIST) before a small audience including two journalists, one of whom was assistant editor of *New Scientist*.

(iv) Influence of Chairman. Some Chairmen take great trouble with publicity – sending out signed press releases themselves and so on. Others are less interested. Committee officials often do not know whether Chairmen – and other members – are keeping in touch with the Press or not. In other cases (eg the General Sub-Committee sometimes) Chairmen tell the Clerks to make sure particular journalists are kept informed. Again, some Chairmen happen to be favourites of the Press. Mr William Hamilton may not have needed to work very hard to attract attention as Chairman of the Violence in the Family Committee. His successor, Mrs Joyce Butler, is a less publicised figure.

It is not easy to provide more detail, partly because publicity shades into public relations and the topic invites discretion (certainly among officials). There is no doubt, however, that the personality of Chairmen is one of the most important determinants of publicity for Select Committees.

(v) Publicity ripples. MPs willing to devote time to Select Committees probably favour the 'knowledge is power' interpretation of backbench influence. Possibly they exaggerate the catalytic effects of Committee inquiries and reports. For all the fuss about British firms' wages in South Africa, the immediate visible effects were not tremendous: 'some firms left the impression that although they had the power to intervene, they had no intention of doing so. Not one company said it would withdraw from South Africa.' (*The Times*, 12 July 1973.) But certainly publicity does ripple outwards. Sir Henry d'Avigdor-Goldsmid, when Chairman of the Expenditure Committee, observed that his general sub-committee's report in December 1972 'set the keynote for the debate on the White Paper and for subsequent discussion in the press'. The Science and Technology Committee is also widely regarded as having this sort of impact – for example in its hearings on Lord Rothschild's proposals for the financing of research. The Treasury organise press conferences of their own to publicise their replies – specialised affairs to which only a handful of journalists are invited and all turn up. Many of the interest groups whose evidence may form the bulk of a Committee's inquiry have good press connections. A few have virtually no existence outside the columns of the press (especially in the social policy area). Written evidence may therefore be publicised independently. So

99

too, of course, are groups' reactions to reports. The Abortion Committee found that some pro-Abortionists refused to submit evidence (technically an offence), because they considered the Committee biased. Instead they publicised their views independently, including comments on other witnesses' evidence.

This argument, again, is not easy to document thoroughly. But in general it is plausible.

(vi) Publicity and Committee's priorities. The subjects that committees choose to examine – or that they are set up to examine – are part of the 'parliamentary agenda' and thus reflect to some extent the 'exchange' between Press and Parliament. A case like the Trade and Industry sub-committee's inquiry into South African wages is particularly clear. Adam Raphael's articles in *The Guardian* led to parliamentary Questions and agreement by the Front Benches that something should be done, with the sub-committee in effect being told to volunteer. Back in 1967 an inquiry into the Torrey Canyon tanker disaster was similarly bounced onto the Science and Technology Committee, whose members were evidently not all pleased. The Committee on a Wealth Tax followed the Chancellor's announcement of approval of such a tax in the Budget. While hardly a response to popular demand, the idea had been floated in articles and pamphlets. Violence in the Family was a subject taken up by Jack Ashley, an MP specialising in social policy areas (subsequently PPS to the appropriate Minister). It was a characteristic pressure-group field, with Women's Rights overtones (most of the violence being done by men) and some well publicised case histories (eg Mrs Pizzey). Publicity (including parliamentary Questions) put the topic on the agenda: undoubtedly Departmental willingness to let MPs explore it was important in getting the Committee set up – not least because the DHSS had no clear idea what to do.

Ad hoc Committees like that one require impetus to set them up. The regular Committees simply need impetus to choose one subject not another. In the Expenditure Committee, the six sub-committees choose their own subjects. The personality of the Chairman here too is crucial. Some Chairmen have their pet causes. Some adopt suggestions of other members. There have been some splendidly haphazard choices – members getting ideas looking out of train windows, etc. Sometimes Committee Clerks make the key suggestion – and have shopping lists for that purpose. Clerks, in fact, can be influential; feeding a suggestion to a sympathetic member or even (at a later stage) a key witness. Because long delays can occur between publication of a report and a Departmental reply (up to two years at the DES; very short at the Treasury; and an average of four or five months), Sir Henry d'Avigdor-Goldsmid considered that Committees have tended to favour subjects where the taking and publication of evidence can of itself have immediate repercussions. (Eg the Environment Sub-Committee inquiry on Improvement Grants; the South African Wages inquiry.)

'Topicality', then, is in various ways a criterion of what the specialist Select Committees decide to explore. It is clearly linked to publicity. As for the Commons as a whole, its Committees need the press both for publicising their activities and for helping determine what those activities should be.

1.3 The Opposition

Almost by definition the practice of Opposition excludes a precise formal 'theory' of its role. But the main characteristics are uncontentious: the Opposition seeks office, expects office, is loyal to the principles of the constitution, and is single-party. These characteristics govern its attitudes to the Press. To some extent they produce contradictory behaviour – most obviously in the tension between confrontation of the Government and 'loyalty' to particular policies (eg broadly, Defence). Opposition attitudes to the Press, therefore, like those of the Government, are ambivalent.

Two key points about its relationship with the Press, however, distinguish the Opposition from the Government most sharply.

(i) *The Opposition could barely survive without the Press* (and broadcasting). The Government at least has something to *do*: its authority and action would come home to the people like a tax return through the letter box even if there were no mass media. Opposition, by comparison, is all talk.

(ii) Journalists may plausibly claim that *all the functions of Opposition short of taking Office (at which point it is no longer the Opposition anyway) can be performed better by the Press*. Not only is this true in the general sense that Press and Opposition both see themselves as watchdogs of the Government; but even at the level of detailed scrutiny of legislation the Press may be more informed and alert. For example, John Whale, writing in 1971, suggested that the most effective criticism of the Conservative Industrial Relations Bill came from the Press: 'A number of newspapers followed the Bill in detail through its Committee stage, drawing on expert opinion: a number of the changes made in the Bill had been suggested in newspaper comment.' (*Journalism and Government*, Macmillan, 1972, p 39). The opposition to Stansted as London's third airport is another case, he considers, where newspapers were more effective than the parliamentary Opposition in compelling a departmental reappraisal.

In one way this congruence between the attitudes of Press and Opposition is a boon to the Opposition. It is well exemplified in *The Times*. Long thought of as in broad support of the Government of the day, *The Times* deliberately 'went into opposition' under Sir William Haley's editorship; and it now feels a conscious responsibility to give adequate coverage to 'out parties'. All the editors interviewed by Professor Tunstall and myself had a concept of 'the duty story' – and Opposition are one beneficiary of it. But of course the Press need not be positively pro-Opposition just because it is anti-Government. Their identity of interests is modified by press partisanship and differences on particular issues, quite apart from the non-political interests of newspapers. Papers can also swamp the Opposition, providing publicity in some way inappropriate. While the Opposition needs publicity, most of the points made below show that it is not an unmixed blessing. 'An out-party sometimes forgets that the power it exercises as an opposition', reflects John Whale, 'is to some extent in the hands of journalists' (*op cit* p 38).

(a) *To get publicity, the Opposition needs to be seen to be doing something.*

(i) On the floor of the Commons, talk *is* action. The tendency of the Press to concentrate on debates therefore suits the Opposition. (In a book about politics and television, John Whale makes a similar point about air travel. Politicians, when reaching or leaving airports, appear to be doing something: therefore airports are a good place for interviewing them, especially on film.) In the only full length study of the Opposition, published in 1973, R M Punnett (of Strathclyde University) writes: since 'the news media are interested in "action" rather than "opinion", and as the Government controls events in a

101

way that the Opposition does not, there is a great temptation for the Opposition to try to attract news coverage to itself by all means possible, including dramatic and vigorous outbursts against the Government's "villainy".' (*Front-Bench Opposition*, Heinemann, 1973, p 196.) More than any other facet of parliamentary work, probably, the set-pieces in the Chamber, with Question Time to the fore, meet conventional news values of personalisation, clashes, crises, the unpredictable and unexpected.

Opposition coverage on the floor of the House can bring problems. Rip-roaring attacks may keep backbenchers and party loyalists happy, but leaders may not feel they are always the right way to win votes. In Punnett's words, the Opposition Leader 'can all too easily appear carping and even unpatriotic' (*op cit* p 100). One senior Conservative Opposition spokesman recently remarked to a Fleet Street editor that he felt he had to 'go beyond the mark' and be more sensational than his predecessors between the Wars, in order to get reported. Secondly, remorseless criticism may run counter to the Opposition's 'alternative government' goal. Thirdly, coverage of the Chamber may over-stress the Leader at the expense of his Shadow Cabinet colleagues. In an ingenious measurement, Punnett counted references in *The Times*' index to members of the Cabinet and the Shadow Cabinet in 1961 and 1968 (half-way years in the lives of two Parliaments). Predictably the Leader of the Opposition received only half the coverage of the Prime Minister – but his share of total Shadow Cabinet's references was much higher than the Prime Minister's share of the Cabinet's. From this and other evidence Punnett asserts: 'The Leader of the Opposition is almost alone among Opposition figures in receiving regular coverage by the news media. . . . General responsibility for the conduct of opposition is seen by press and public to rest very much on [his] shoulders.' (*Ibid* p 100.) The Leader thus has 'responsibility without power' and gets undue blame or praise. Whether this is good or bad depends on whether the Leader is behind or ahead of his party in the polls. Mr Wilson was normally more popular with the electorate than was the Labour Party. Support for Mr Heath consistently trailed behind support for the Conservative Party as a whole.

(ii) If it is to avoid the accusation of being a one-man band, says Punnett, the Shadow Cabinet, distinct from the Opposition in general, has to be *seen* to be active. 'Thus the press is kept informed of special Shadow Cabinet meetings, and of important Shadow Cabinet "decisions".' (*Ibid* p 108.) Before elections photographs may be issued of the Shadow Cabinet in session. Shadow Ministers, especially the Leader, have regular meetings with the Lobby Correspondents.

(b) Policy formation in Opposition

How far Oppositions are wise to formulate specific policy programmes is one of the questions politicians dispute. Surveying practice since the last war, Punnett concludes that probably the most profitable approach is for an opposition to try and create a general climate of support rather than to specify the details of intended legislation.

(i) One way in which the Press may affect this process is by virtually committing the Opposition to a policy – unintentionally or not. 'Once a spokesman has given expression to a particular point of view which attracts publicity, the Government, the Opposition's own supporters, and the electorate in general, see the Opposition as being committed to that stance.' (Punnett, p 262.) This can be embarrassing if the commitment is controversial (eg Mr Heath's undertaking in 1968 to examine the possibility of creating a Scottish Parliament) or is only an ill-considered chance remark (George Brown's '3% mortgages' in 1964, 'Bomber' Thorpe, etc).

(ii) In a simpler but crucial way the Press is indispensable to the Opposition as a source of information, both about that important abstraction 'Public Opinion' and about matters on which to challenge the Government or take up a position. In a letter to *The Times* about the House of Lords judgement in *The Sunday Times* thalidomide case (24 July 1973) Harold Wilson acknowledged plainly the importance of the Press. 'Parliament is hamstrung in its discussions of, and decisions on, matters of public importance if it cannot draw both on the facts and opinions freely published in the press . . . . For the raw material of parliamentary debate is in fact what members read in the press.' In this particular case, 'our Debates, and the ultimate outcome, were inspired and informed by the original article in *The Sunday Times*. Without that article and the facts and arguments it adduced, Parliament would have been inhibited in a way none could attempt to justify so far as the merits of the thalidomide case are concerned'. (For a full copy of the letter see Appendix VI.)

To the Opposition the Press is especially important, for policymaking and ephemeral debate alike, because it lacks the help of the civil service. Labour in 1970–74 relied on a patchwork of assistance, including six 'political Fellows' paid for by the Rowntree Trust. Shadow Ministers, 'like all MPs, can . . . obtain some information from general sources such as constituents' letters, radio and television, books, journals and the press', writes Punnett (p 280). He names Denis Healey as an example of a Shadow Minister before 1964 who kept his own files of press cuttings, in this case on defence. The resources of the House of Commons Library, which now provides much extended facilities for all Members, include a wide-ranging cuttings service.

In exceptional circumstances, newspapers are a unique source for the Opposition and the Government. John Whale has described in some detail how the Press became after the late 1960s an unwitting intermediary between the IRA and the British Government, in a situation where the two could not talk together. (*Journalism and Government*, pp 30–36.) The Opposition at Westminster was equally excluded.

(iii) *Opposition Spokesmen as 'Opinion Leaders'*. Much of a Shadow Minister's work, Punnett thinks, is public relations. 'He may be called upon to make formal statements of policy and party attitudes, and the mass media look to a spokesman for 'instant comment' about the affairs of the department that he is shadowing. In this sense the Spokesman becomes a press and television agent for his party. The news media are more likely to deal with an officially designated spokesman than with an unofficial figure, and one of the effects of the use of Spokesman's titles since 1955 (when they became formalised) has been to confer a certain status on Opposition leaders' (*op cit* p 209).

(iv) *Conclusion*. Since 1955, when Mr Attlee adopted a system of designated Shadow Ministers, the collective leadership of the Opposition has become increasingly institutionalised. Some of the reasons concern the range and complexity of postwar government. Some are to do with personalities: Herbert Morrison, a great parliamentary manager, wrote of the development with distaste in his book *Government and Parliament* (1959) (' . . . one Labour party publication went so far as to refer to the Minister of so and so in the Shadow Cabinet.'); and Harold Macmillan also expressed disapproval (*Tides of Fortune*, p 44).

A more recent generation of parliamentarians has preferred to stress the advantages; and there is no doubt that the requirements of publicity – particularly of TV, with its 'on-the-one-hand-on-the-other' obligations in political reporting – have been an important influence. Thus Punnett observes: 'The more formal the organisation of the Opposition front bench, the more publicity the arrangements are likely to be given, and thus the more easily the Opposition leaders can be identified by the electorate as a *team* of possible Ministers' (p 71). Given this emphasis on a team, it is ironic that publicity evidently tends to concentrate disproportionately on the Opposition Leader. In general, it seems that the Opposition recognises the indispensability of the Press, gears itself partly to press requirements and ends up with a somewhat different coverage from what it wants.

1.4 Private Members and Press Publicity: Two notes

The attitudes of individual backbenchers, quite separate from any particular form of parliamentary organisation and procedure, can make a great difference to their press publicity. There seems no point in going into detail here, partly because various examples are familiar to most people, and partly because an accumulation of examples is unlikely to lead to more confident or detailed generalisation.

Two notes are worth mentioning.

(a) Individual publicists. Some MPs are naturally good communicators

One national editor acknowledged a temptation to report Enoch Powell's speeches at length because they are so beautifully composed. A *Times* press gallery veteran recalled the pleasure of reporting Lord Shawcross 'because he talked prose'. Some Members are assiduous in cultivating the Press and pandering to news values: Sir Gerald Nabarro was a well known example. Some MPs are themselves occasional journalists and draw on parliamentary affairs for copy. 'I've seen MPs on both sides of the House', Lord George-Brown has claimed, 'obviously having to create a sensation on a Thursday in order to have a peg on which to hang an article for Sunday.'

Lord George-Brown is an unusual case of such occasional journalism being the critical factor enabling a man to stay in politics. After the general election of 1951 Brown met Cecil King one weekend. 'I talked about the possibility of leaving the House of Commons to return to the union [TGWU], and King asked, rather directly, if this was because I wanted to, or because I had to. I said that it was quite a bit of the former, but it didn't really matter, because I didn't see how I was going to maintain the family and keep our house and our car on what Parliament was then willing to pay MPs. King then made me what I am convinced was a wholly genuine offer of a retainer to work for the *Mirror* ... Without it, I do not see how I could have managed to stay in politics' (*In My Way*, Penguin Books edn p 58).

(b) Backbenchers, Interest Groups and the Press

These three can be an influential triad in subjects where press publicity is an effective weapon. The terms of the relationship vary. For instance an interest group may provide information, a backbencher status and a focus of attention, and the Press publicity: eg social policy questions like those espoused by the Child Poverty Action Group. Alternatively the Press may provide information as well as publicity, with the backbencher adding prestige and parliamentary pressure: eg *The Sunday Times*, Jack Ashley and thalidomide. Again, back-bencher and interest group may share the information-gathering. Between October 1970 and December 1971 MPs tabled some 1,579 Questions on matters to do with the environment, often in alliance with environmental interest groups. 'The young and extremely small population pressure group Population Stabilisation . . . received a considerable amount of press attention, when its report submitted to the Government's Population Panel was unveiled at a press conference sponsored by two MPs and chaired by Baroness Gaitskell' (S K Brookes and J J Richardson, 'The Environmental Lobby in Britain', *Parliamentary Affairs*, Summer 1975, p 321). MPs often combine to form parliamentary pressure groups on particular subjects, partly because this eases contact with Departments, Ministers and outside interest groups. An example is the 'Disablement Group' of MPs. One difficulty for such groups can arise if newspapers become actively interested in the same area: they may then 'swamp' the group. A strong parliamentary campaign about vaccine-damaged children, for example, probably suffered at first in its publicity from press preoccupation with more 'fashionable' disabilities.

The relationships between interest groups, backbenchers and newspapers would be worth detailed study. Certainly they seem a significant factor in parliamentary publicity.

1.5 Parliament and the Provincial Press

Provincial dailies are well represented in the press gallery, and much of the previous sections, particularly about parliamentary attitudes to publicity, applies to national and provincials indifferently. Provincial dailies have been studied less specifically in the past, and this section goes wider than the earlier ones as well as concentrating more on the papers themselves. The information is based mainly on visits to the following papers in Winter and Spring, 1975–76.

Title	Circulation*	Publisher
Liverpool Daily Post (Morning)	99,000	Liverpool Daily Post and Echo
Liverpool Echo (Evening)	315,000	Liverpool Daily Post and Echo
Darlington Northern Echo (Morning)	114,000	Westminster Press
Darlington Evening Despatch (Evening)	18,000	Westminster Press
Shields Evening Gazette (Evening)	37,000	Westminster Press
Newcastle Journal (Morning)	102,000	Thomson Regional Newspapers
Newcastle Evening Chronicle (Evening)	200,000	Thomson Regional Newspapers
Cleveland Evening Gazette (Evening)	107,000	Thomson Regional Newspapers
Sunderland Echo (Evening)	81,000	Portsmouth & Sunderland
Worcester-Hereford Evening News (Evening)	39,000	News International
Gloucestershire Echo (Evening)	34,000	Associated Newspapers
Gloucester Citizen (Evening)	41,000	Associated Newspapers

They cannot be regarded as 'representative', although they include the main chains apart from United Newspapers.

* The figures for circulation are for January to June 1974 (ABC).

(a) Provincial Dailies and Parliamentary Constituencies

One MP in three has a provincial daily published in his constituency or in the city of which his constituency is a part (excluding London). Many more – the number is difficult to calculate – represent constituencies in which a provincial daily reaches at least half the households although it is published elsewhere.

(The *Northern Echo*, for example, is published in Darlington but reaches over half the households in the constituencies of Bishop Auckland, Durham, and Durham North-West.) As Table 1 shows, the figure for Scottish MPs is a little more than one in three. In Wales it is less than one in four. (Northern Ireland is omitted.)

Most morning papers are published in cities also publishing an evening paper. Only one MP in eight in England and Wales has a morning paper – and all of these have an evening paper as well, except the Member for Warwick and Leamington. In Scotland the distribution of mornings and evenings is different: one MP in three has a morning and an evening.

Table II puts these figures in a party context. No less than three-quarters of Britain's provincial dailies are published in Labour constituencies – a uniform tendency across England, Scotland and Wales, and the result largely of their concentration in big cities. No provincial paper is published in a Liberal seat. In English constituencies having both a morning and an evening paper the proportion is as high as four-fifths. Figures in brackets in Table II refer to constituencies where there was a difference of less than 2% between the first two parties at the October 1974 general election. There were only nine of these – the same proportion as for the country as a whole (in which there were 24). Proportionately rather more of the Conservative than of the Labour seats were marginal.

(b) General Attitudes

In the nineteenth century provincial dailies gave considerable coverage to Parliament. With the broadening of their interests and the growth of the nationals this declined. Now only the *Yorkshire Post*, *Birmingham Post*, and *Northern Echo* have a regular report of parliamentary debates, plus *The Scotsman* and *Glasgow Herald*. Coverage in the *Yorkshire Post*, *The Scotsman* and the *Manchester Guardian* at particular points since 1900 is shown in Table III. The decline has been substantial; but while it had happened in the *Yorkshire Post* by 1948, in the other two it has happened largely thereafter.

There was little sign that the editors we interviewed felt parliamentary coverage was under pressure at the moment. One (from a rural area) clearly felt there was too much politics altogether in his paper. The *Newcastle Journal* had more space four or five years ago, and Parliament was quoted as a subject that has suffered from the shrinkage: every line has 'to earn its keep'. On a busy evening three out of five parliamentary stories might end up spiked. But this is a reflection of changing space rather than the changing salience of Parliament. The *Sunderland Echo* have a 'Last Night in Westminster' feature two or three days a week, which includes news beyond that of local MPs. Another north-eastern editor reckons he publishes more parliamentary news than five years ago: there is a greater response from readers. (His meticulous memo about budget coverage including directions about tea and sandwiches, is at Appendix VII.) In Liverpool we were told that tendencies inside local party organisations (like Mr Reg Prentice's row in Newham) had increased the attention paid by the papers' local government correspondents to MPs. Professor McQuail's content study (Cmnd 6810–4) shows that the tradition of the London Letter survives, including news of MPs – for instance in the *Eastern Daily Press*, *Western Morning News* and the *Courier*. The *Sunderland Echo* felt that local MPs get 'tremendous coverage' of their constituency activities, based more on press conferences and statements nowadays than on speeches.

(i) Leading Articles. One test of attitudes to Parliament is whether provincial editors like to use their leader columns to comment on the national political scene.

The leading article seems more entrenched in the morning than the evening papers. The Cheltenham, Gloucester and Newcastle evenings, for instance, do not have a leader every day; and the Newcastle editor places them near the stories to which they refer, rather than always using the same spot. The *Northern Echo* leader, in contrast, has the added status of being circulated round the Westminster Press Group for use by the evening papers if they wish. None of the other groups represented in our interview (Thomson Regional Newspapers, News International, Associated Newspapers and Portsmouth and Sunderland) has a group leader writing service – 'God forbid' was one comment. But at least one of them subscribes to the Westminster Press news agency and occasionally uses their leader notes as a basis for his own. Westminster Press papers are not obliged to use the group leader. One editor recalled using a group leader unchanged except for turning all the verbs into negatives.

The retirement of Mr Wilson was a fairly topical subject for asking about Leading articles. A few papers had not carried one and seemed to think that it would not have been very appropriate. The Darlington evening, for example, being a small paper (circ 18,000) very much in the shadow of the *Northern Echo* likes to stress local questions. When Mr Callaghan was eventually appointed however, it did carry a leader – a 'doctored' London one. The *Northern Echo* had leaders on both the resignation and the succession; and the other papers had leaders on one or the other. Leaders on the Budget were quite common.

This seems an area where editors' personal preferences vary widely. Some dislike leaders altogether. Some like them but beware preaching at their readers. Some take them seriously and comment frequently on national as well as local issues. The *Sunderland Echo* was pondering one on Solzhenitsyn.

(ii) Partisanship. Another possible indicator of attitudes to Parliament is partisanship. The editors were all very cautious about this. Some linked caution explicitly to their monopoly position. One said, 'You couldn't run a Conservative paper here nowadays anyway – the readership is overwhelmingly Labour'. Another (a fairly new appointment) said he supposed he would take 'a middle road'. A third thinks he is probably *too* careful about balance – 'I've spoilt 'em a bit'. Yet another is concerned that since twice as many local MPs are Labour as Conservative, the Conservatives tend to get 'too much' publicity – a 50–50 balance being common in the news columns.

One sign of caution is the universal rejection by all the editors of telling people how to vote. The editor of the *Sunderland Echo* (with the Group since 1935) recalled that in Sir Samuel Storey's day the paper used to carry a panel – 'Vote Tomorrow and Vote Right'. (Sir Samuel, the proprietor, was a Conservative MP.) Nowadays the paper's conservatism is issued-based and flexible, and there is no great round-up leader at the end of an election giving an overall view on how to vote. The two Darlington editors thought it would be 'a bit of a cheek' and 'an insult' to tell readers how to vote. The editor of the Cleveland (Middlesbrough) *Evening Gazette* will give an editorial view on any other issue but has 'a thing' about never telling readers how to vote in general elections.

This self-denial is quite recent. As well as having their roots in party politics, many of the papers had followed the practice of the *Sunderland Echo* until the 1960s. In some cases, however, the neutrality is limited and does not extend to withholding an editorial preference altogether. The *Newcastle Journal*, for instance, followed a general policy of support for Heath against the miners in the February 1974 election. The *Evening Chronicle* editor distinguished sharply between expressing the paper's *own* view and telling readers how to vote. The *Northern Echo*'s editor defines his paper's stance as 'independent Labour'. The *Liverpool Daily Post* plumped for Mr Wilson when Mr Heath won and Mr Heath when Mr Wilson won. Quite a common practice is to base comment on a comparison of sections of the party manifestos. The Darlington *Evening Despatch* lays them side by side and lets readers judge for themselves.

Papers that are careful not to express a partisan preference at all at general elections include the *Worcester/Hereford Evening News*, which doubts whether even an implicit attitude is identifiable now; the Cheltenham and Gloucester papers; and the Cleveland (Middlesbrough) *Evening Gazette*, whose editor takes care not to side with local MPs on anything within about a month of an election.

Another aspect of their caution is editors' arrangements for election coverage. The tendency in those papers most clearly eschewing editorial comment is to give candidates direct access to their columns. The arrangements at the *Gloucester Citizen*, for instance, is that all candidates in the three local constituencies (including minor parties) are offered one or two 8/900 word articles, in which 'anything goes except personalities'; plus coverage of two meetings of their choice by a reporter; plus their share of a rota of daily 'Election Platform' pieces; plus a proportionate share of the letters. The day before polling day there is no election coverage at all.

(c) Arrangements for coverage

(i) Routines. Provincial papers naturally focus mainly on their own MPs and on parliamentary concern with their own problems: nine times out of ten, said one North-East editor, his lobbyman was concerned with 'the extension of a local story to the national arena'. The number of relevant MPs varies greatly: the *Northern Echo* have some 44 and the papers in Shields and Cheltenham only two or three. MPs also vary in newsworthiness. *Worcester Evening News* have Peter Walker; Newcastle have Ted Short (and the added interest of John Ryman and Eddie Milne – though he is no longer a member); Liverpool have Eric Heffer and a generally interesting group, Cleveland have Bill Rodgers.

Among the papers we visited the commonest arrangement for Westminster coverage involved sharing the facilities of a group London office. The Gloucester and Cheltenham papers share a Northcliffe Newspapers (ie Associated Newspapers) lobbyman with a Swansea paper. The Newcastle and Cleveland papers use a Thomson lobbyman and *The Shields Evening Gazette* a Westminster Press man. Usually contact is maintained, not always daily, through the London office more than with the lobbyman direct, simply for convenience. The Shields editor could not recall ever having spoken to the lobbyman (though he had not yet been editor for a year). In a few cases, however, there is direct contact. The *Liverpool Evening Echo* lobbyman calls the office every morning at 8.30, often to discuss possible leader topics. The *Sunderland Echo* lobbyman (serving Portsmouth, Sunderland and Hartlepool) rings up in the same way ('He's not sitting up there on Mount Olympus').

Only one group – News International – does not provide a London office service; and there is no doubt that the *Worcester Evening News* misses it. Instead the paper has to rely exclusively on Press Association copy, plus a parliamentary feature produced by the Westminster Press-owned National Press Agency.

The *Northern Echo*'s exceptional status in the Westminster Press is reflected in its having a lobbyman of its own. (They had just appointed a new one – from TV – when we visited them.) He is in direct daily contact with the office. For papers that are not in a group, like the Liverpool morning and evening – each of which has its own lobbyman – this arrangement is typical. (Mr Wilson's first Downing Street PRO, it will be recalled, was the *Liverpool Daily Post*'s lobbyman.)

For most papers the PA is used as a back-up service. The *Northern Echo* uses it for its daily parliamentary report, for instance. The *Newcastle Journal* quoted major White Papers and the Budget details as other obvious examples. Nearly all the papers also subscribe to the special PA Service which provides them with coverage of their particular MPs and subjects of local interest. The one paper we visited which did not, seemed to have particularly close contact with its half-dozen local MPs, both at Westminster and at home – and also to have a very high opinion of the service provided by its group lobbyman (to whom it gives a byline).

Few papers used the PA for parliamentary features – eg a weekly commentary. Group London offices generally provided these, for editors to use if they wished. (The Cheltenham paper usually did: the nearby Gloucester paper in the same group usually did not.)

(ii) Relationships. Newspaper, London office lobbyman and MPs form a triangular relationship complicated by the MPs shuttling to and fro. Paper and MPs talk direct. Paper asks London office about MPs. London office asks paper about MPs.

The most consistent relationship (ie broadly similar on all papers) is probably between newspaper and London office. The editor who talked of the extension of a local story to the national arena could also have turned his description around. The relationship is a continual exchange, daily on the bigger papers and only once or twice a week on others (eg *Gloucestershire Echo*). Lobbymen 'chase things up' – particular topics, or comments by local MPs – at the request of their paper, and are often able to anticipate them. A recent example when we visited Sunderland had been the future of a local shipyard. The lobbyman was asked to try and find out from Fred Willey (a local MP) what were the Government's intentions. Similarly rumours in Newcastle that the Government's devolution plans might include a regional assembly for the North-East prompted the *Journal* to ask its group lobbyman to sound out Ted Short (and Lord Crowther-Hunt). Such examples were commonplace. Equally lobbymen needed briefing on local matters – like a row in Newcastle about the Tyne Metro System.

Relationships at Westminster between provincial lobbymen and local MPs are traditionally close. Again the relationship is one of exchange. In a study of *The Member of Parliament and his Information* (Allen & Unwin for PEP and the Study of Parliament Group, 1970) Anthony Barker and Michael Rush interviewed 111 MPs. They generalise about contact with lobbymen as follows: 'These journalists constantly ask the Members whose constituencies come within their papers' circulation areas for advance news and background on activities such as Questions, adjournment debates and party disputes, expecially where local affairs are involved. Although Members do give some news to lobby journalists it is usually "personal": what the Member is doing or thinking about a topic. The "public" news usually flows from the journalist, who is, as a result, a significant source for the Member. Thus a provincial newspaper's lobbyman will ring up a Member from his paper's area and say, "The Government are going to announce (or have just announced) that they will (or will not) give the much-awaited ship-building contract to a yard in your constituency's area: what do you think?" The Member then replies off the cuff. The lobbyman may well also say, "I suppose you think it quite right (or wrong) and (if wrong) that you'll be putting down a Question and even considering leading a delegation to the Minister?" One ex-lobby journalist told us that this leading of Members by journalists, based on giving MPs news, is very common among lobby journalists, especially the provincial papers' men who know "their group of MPs so much better than the national papers' correspondents can hope to know the whole House".'

Our interviews with editors were consistent with this view.

Relationships between MPs and local newspapers at the constituency level are more variable. Barker and Rush asked their sample to rank the local press as a source of information on local affairs against the constituency postbag, the local party and the local authority. Two-thirds of the seventy-one who felt the comparison practicable put local newspapers first and another quarter put them second. 'Only two Members thought them the least important . . . and one of these was moved by the political argument that the paper was so anti-Conservative as to not report his local doings, so he ignored it.' One-third of these seventy-one Members stressed further that the Press was important also because of inside and background information which they acquired by personal contact with journalists and which would not appear in the paper itself. Once again the exchange relationship appears: 'These Members felt they often told the journalists things as well as learning from them. Woven in with this "information relationship" between MP and local journalist is the "news-publicity" relationship: the Member wants publicity from the paper and the paper wants news from the Member.' Again our interviews bore out these general impressions. The editor of the *Worcester Evening News* contrasted Peter Walker's active approach to publicity with that of some other local MPs. (He felt, though, that Walker did not rely particularly on the paper for constituency news.) Mr Dodds-Parker used to look in at the *Gloucestershire Echo* every couple of months when he was a Cheltenham MP. His successor used to be Mayor and is still a Councillor, so he is about the place regularly. The editor of the Cleveland (Middlesbrough) *Evening Gazette* thought his half-dozen local MPs probably had a closer relationship with the paper's home base than at Westminster. They had close contact with the News Desk, with particular reporters (each being 'assigned' to one) and with the paper's district offices -- in addition to vicarious contact with the editor himself -- who was unusually active in civic life. The Liverpool papers, with large catchment areas including up to 35 MPs (some in North Wales) keep in touch similarly via branch offices; and some of the MPs contribute a periodic column to the *Daily Post*.

(iii) Campaigns. Sometimes the routine relationship between newspaper and MP becomes 'campaigning'. When the Green Howards' regimental band instruments were replaced after being blown up in Northern Ireland, the Regiment found they were underinsured by some £10,000. The Ministry of Defence refused to pay the difference. Local Cleveland MPs contacted the *Evening Gazette* for help in organising opinion to get the decision changed. The *Sunderland Echo* quoted the continuation of the Regional Employment Premium, the problem of ship yards closing in Hartlepool, and the growing use of drugs in the area as subjects on which the paper had pressed MPs (eg to put down Questions), sometimes at the same time as running a campaign in the paper. The *Newcastle Evening Chronicle* ran a 'Give a boy a job' campaign for school leavers in which help was requested from MPs. The *Northern Echo* circulated MPs with a reprint of an article against the proposed flooding of a local 'Daffodil valley' by the Water Authority, and their lobbyman followed up the reactions. The *Darlington Evening Despatch* started a campaign taken up by the *Daily Mail* and culminating in a successful Private Member's Bill by a local MP, to regulate doorstep selling 'on behalf of the disabled'. (Salesmen in Newton Aycliffe were giving only a minute fraction of an inflated sale price to the disabled and keeping the rest.) The *Liverpool Echo* liaised closely with MPs in a campaign to prevent the Government closing down the big Shotton Steel-works.

(iv) MPs as Columnists. The *Liverpool Daily Post* appears to be unique among provincial mornings – and possibly among evenings too – in publishing a regular column contributed by a rota of MPs. When we visited the paper late in 1975 the North Wales edition rotated a column weekly between Mr Wigley (Plaid Cymru), Mr Hooson (Liberal), Sir Anthony Meyer (Conservative) and Mr Ellis (Labour). The Merseyside editions rotated between Mr Heffer (Labour), Mr Crawshaw (Labour) and Mr Page (Conservative). Mrs Chalker (Conservative) and Mr Kilroy-Silk (Labour) had also been given a turn recently.

After the 1964 election the paper's lobbyman sounded out local MPs about the idea of a column. Only one out of thirty-five expressed interest. Now it is established, 'they fight to get a turn'. Not all contributors, naturally, have had the right touch. The most successful, partly because of his sheer originality, has been Eric Heffer. He had to give up when he became a Minister in 1974 but gladly came back after resigning office. Three other contributors were also described as 'naturals'. Once an MP from outside the area was brought in, but the experiment was not considered successful. No Liberal contributes to the Merseyside edition because there is no Liberal MP – although Liberals have been dominant in the Council. Extend the practice beyond MPs, the editor's argument runs, and where do you stop? Contributors are given a free hand, on the understanding that the column is not intended for party propaganda. Occasionally ideas may be suggested to them: for example, Mr Heffer was invited to go to Blackpool and write about the Conservative Party conference. The column ceases during general elections.

The Liverpool arrangement is worth outlining in detail because it seems to the paper to work so satisfactorily and yet all other papers we talked to were highly sceptical of the idea. It is such an obvious way of providing access and 'opening up' a paper that one might expect it to appeal to editors - especially when they stress the public responsibility that follows from their (normal) near-monopoly position in the market. Why do they dislike it? Between them the editors offered six reasons:

- MPs have 'the freedom of the letters column' and need no separate forum for their views.
- MPs get plenty of publicity already. 'Too much . . .' 'They shower you with stuff.' 'They get tremendous coverage.' 'If you offered them the chance they'd grab it.'
- MPs contribute occasional articles anyway, when there is something they can usefully say. Peter Walker has occasionally written for the Worcester Evening News. Fred Willey wrote an article for the Northern Echo about a piece of legislation when he was Minister of Land and Natural Resources. The Darlington Evening Despatch had an MP writing about the Common Market referendum.
- MPs are not often good at this sort of thing, 'They tend to write boring propaganda.'
- It would be difficult to strike a balance. 'Most of the MPs in my area are Labour.' 'You'd get grumbles about bias and balance.' 'The problem of balance makes me reject the idea on principle.'
- Where would you stop? 'It would be the thin end of the wedge.'

The editor of the Newcastle Journal used to run a regular MPs' column when on the Birmingham Post in the early 1960s. It was dropped when some of the contributors became Ministers and their successors proved less successful. Barker and Rush reported that 'some Members write regular columns or occasional articles' (p 216). Unless the evening papers we visited are untypical, these must be mainly in local weekly papers.

The idea of an opinion column as such is certainly acceptable to editors. The Northern Echo has 'Sideview', described by the editor as 'political in the broadest sense' and written by a staff man, by a right wing novelist and by a left wing school-teacher. The Gloucestershire Echo has 'Personally Speaking', written by staff members about once a month if they have something to say ('one of our men was chased by some dogs recently').

(d) A Note on Hereford Weekly Times

With a circulation of 33,000 this reaches much the same number of readers as the Worcester/Hereford Evening News (37,000) and is in the same group – Berrows, part of News International. It generally has twice the number of pages, so the difference in total weekly reading matter is 1:3, much less than 1:6 – the ratio of frequency of publication. The Times has a weekly monopoly in Hereford and a near-monopoly in the County as a whole.

For many purposes its attitudes to parliamentary coverage are obviously quite different from a daily paper, but in the area of MPs relations with their constituencies the weekly and daily papers seem more comparable. Barker and Rush evidently did not find it necessary to draw continual distinctions between the two. In the Hereford Times both local MPs write a 500-words column once a month (ie alternating fortnightly). In practice their copy is often late. For many years both have also taken advertising space to publicise their constituency surgeries. One of them is an assiduous letter writer, sending something up to three weeks out of four.

It may be that for many MPs, especially from country towns and areas, the difference between having a daily paper and just a weekly in their constituencies is less important than one might at first think.

Table I
Provincial Dailies and Parliamentary Constituencies, 1974

	Total MPs	MP has in his Constituency: Evening Paper	Morning Paper	Both	Either
England	424	141	49	48	142
(exc Greater London)		(33%)	(12%)	(11%)	(33%)
Wales	36	8	4	4	8
		(22%)	(11%)	(11%)	(22%)
Scotland	71	26	24	24	26
		(37%)	(34%)	(34%)	(37%)
Total	531	175	77	76	176
		(33%)	(15%)	(14%)	(33%)

Note: Includes all MPs who have a provincial daily paper published in their constituency *or in the city of which their constituency is a part.*

Table II
Parliamentary Constituencies with Daily Papers: Party Representation (Marginal seats in brackets), October 1974

	England Con	Lab	Wales Con	Lab	Scotland Con	Lab	SNP	Total Con	Lab	SNP	All
Morning paper only	1	–	–	–	–	–		1	–	–	1
Evening paper only	26	67	–	4	–	2	1	26	73	1	100
	(2)	(2)	–					(2)	(2)		(4)
Morning and Evening Papers	10	38	2	2	7	16	–	19	56	–	75
	(2)	(2)			(1)			(3)	(2)	–	(5)
Total	37	105	2	6	7	18	1	46	129	1	176
	(4)	(4)			(1)			(5)	(4)		(9)
Total Constituencies (exc Greater London and Liberal seats)	212	204	8	23	16	41	11	236	268	11	515

Definition of Marginal Seats: Difference of up to 2% between first two parties. Total Marginal seats (including those with daily papers): England – 24; Wales – nil; Scotland – 7.

Table III
Coverage of Parliament in three 'Regional' Dailies, 1900–1972

	Yorkshire Post Coverage as % of Total Space	Total Editorial	Manchester Guardian/ The Guardian Coverage as % of Total Space	Total Editorial	The Scotsman Coverage as % of Total Space	Total Editorial
1900	—	—	7·6	11·4	6·3	9·6
1912	5·3	6·9	8·4	12·0	6·7	10·2
1924	5·5	7·6	5·8	8·0	5·9	9·8
1936	3·8	4·7	4·1	5·2	6·2	8·0
1948	1·7	2·1	8·3	12·0	6·7	10·6
1960	2·0	3·4	3·3	5·3	3·6	5·8
1972	1·6	2·9	3·0	4·3	3·9	4·8

Sample: Ten days in each parliamentary session.
(Research supported by the Nuffield Foundation.)

1.6 Conclusions

The observations in this section stem from the previous sections and perhaps from a number of wider considerations not discussed here.

Of all our major social and political institutions, in my view, Parliament has most to gain from a strong, diverse national press. Civil servants, to judge by impressions, find the Press more useful than they used to but still find it often a nuisance. Cabinets normally seem at loggerheads with the Press. Politicians of all kinds away from Westminster seem to find advantages in broadcasting. 'The Press could get on without politics', J A Spender wrote, 'but politics could not get on without the Press.' That was before the days of TV, but Parliament's reluctance to exploit TV means that for Parliament the opinion retains much truth. Few institutions would feel themselves more impoverished than Parliament by a decline in Fleet Street. Previous sections have sought to show how Parliament depends on the Press for much of its 'agenda' (both in general and in detail) as well as, obviously, the publicity without which it is relatively powerless. A press-parliamentary alliance, as the thalidomide story dramatically shows, can be a very powerful weapon. Newspapers can be better welfare officers than MPs. They can be more resourceful researchers. They can compete even with organised Opposition in informed expertise. ('With the rise in the power of the Prime Minister and the decline of the Cabinet and the House of Commons', wrote Cecil King in 1963, 'the newspapers have really become the unofficial Opposition'.) Some of this could be said of a few provincial dailies – especially those in groups with substantial central services (it can be reassuring for a Thomson regional paper, for instance, to have the services of the Times Newspapers' legal staff). But really it is the national press of which it is mainly true and the national press which Parliament needs.

An extra gloss can be put on this argument because of the studious non-partisanship of the provincial dailies. I argue in 'National Daily Papers and the Party System' that the basis and degree of partisanship in Fleet Street have changed. But the nationals take sides in parliamentary elections in a way which the provincials do not. With fewer or even more judicious nationals, the simple expression of partisan attitudes, it seems to me, risks being unduly muffled.

Even if Fleet Street does not contract, how far is parliamentary news 'at risk'? From Parliament's viewpoint, press coverage must naturally seem inadequate and distorted. Michael Foot's criticism is understandable. How could it be otherwise in a modern newspaper? The editor of one popular national said he treats Westminster like an 'open theatre'. With the growth of TV politics – and now of radio broadcasts of Parliament – the public are tending, he thinks, to see Parliament in theatrical terms. The traditional Parliamentary sketch, therefore, has similarly changed to resemble somewhat a theatrical criticism. To deplore such tendencies, it can be argued, is to misunderstand the nature of politics. Politics is not a self-contained activity, like a game of football. Politics has no existence apart from the communications media prevalent in society. When the hustings, the country house and the political club were important places for communication, politics suited them. With mass politics and modern technology, forms of political communication have necessarily changed. TV is the prevalent medium and inevitably tends to impose its own manners on its subjects. This is not to 'distort' politics, for there have never been politics that were not conditioned by the dominant media of the day. What Michael Foot regrets, this argument runs, is not just the passing of a type of parliamentary reporting (which in principle might be reintroduced) but the passing of a type of newspaper – which could not.

On a less abstract level, Parliamentary news might be thought at risk on several grounds. It is not a subject of major audience interest. It does not earn advertising revenues. Parliament's work is diversifying – in fairly 'untheatrical' directions – and thus requires more not less resources for effective coverage. With a shift in political decision-making away from Parliament, papers have developed specialist correspondents whose subjects include political activities but in different arenas – Whitehall, Trades Unions, pressure groups. Perhaps newspapers are thus giving us a less 'Westminster view' of politics. (Recent staff changes at The Guardian, for instance, support this interpretation.)

This last development might reflect changes in British politics. The other risks would seem less defensible from Parliament's point of view. But in fact they do not seem serious at the moment. Even an operation on the scale of The Times' coverage, involving a total gallery staff of a dozen or so (much the same size throughout this century) is not especially expensive compared, say, to sports reporting. Political news in general, one Fleet Street popular editor told us brightly, is 'quite cheap all round' – even at the level of the weekly expense sheet. At present Parliament has more to lose from a contraction in Fleet Street or a decline in its own importance than from changes in newspapers' attitudes.

2 Government: The Lobby Correspondents

2.1 Background: Discussion in the 1960s

The Lobby Correspondents are the main channel of news about the political direction of British Central Government. That is one reason for studying them. Another is that they are a fairly small group for the task – well under one hundred are 'active'. While more reasonably described, in the view of Ronald Butt (an ex-member) as a 'closed' than a 'secret' society, their secretiveness has brought them notice too. The Lobby system has also proved durable – 'harder to get rid of than mice behind the skirting board' (David Wood *The Times* 13 March 1972.) Proposals for its abolition have never yet got far.

Until the 1960s the Lobby was not much discussed. In the previous twenty years governments had experimented with their own arrangements for contact with the Lobby, but practice on the journalists' side proceeded with little change, apart from an increase in members and a couple of embarrassing misunderstandings about confidentiality. The Lobby's reputation for discretion and reliability had reached new heights in the War and for the Press the system worked well. When the reform of Parliament and the power of the Prime Minister became subjects of increasing interest in the early 1960s, the Lobby was drawn in. The tribunal inquiring into the Vassall spy case in 1962 exposed some normally discreet news gathering procedures and showed just how flimsy stories based on 'Whitehall Circles' and 'reliable informants' could be. Comment on the system then had to start from scratch. 'What and where, in fact, is "The Lobby"?' asked a *Sunday Telegraph* story that went on to tell us (27 January 1963). By the mid-1970s comparable stories could assume in readers at least a vague familiarity with the system.

The early 1960s saw a number of reflective articles and broadcasts amounting almost to a dialogue, about the merits and defects of the Lobby. Mr Wilson's exceptional interest in press relations, and later his disillusion, provided a sharper and more popular concern, which was immediately renewed upon his return to office in 1974. Its culmination, even making the Lobby the page 2 lead in the *Daily Express*, was the decision in June 1975 by Mr Joe Haines, Mr Wilson's press secretary, to end the system of daily Lobby briefing from 10 Downing Street. Mr Heath in his turn had had problems: less with the Lobby than with 'communication' in the abstract, but the Lobby was inevitably under scrutiny in his efforts to solve them.

In the past ten years, then, the Lobby system has not only been discussed, as never before, as part of the machinery of British politics: it has also sometimes become, for those at the centre, virtually an issue *in* British politics. In both

117

forms the discussion to some extent simply reflects the perennial tension between press and government. Each side often portrays itself as the hapless plaything of the other. Charles Wintour, editor of the *Evening Standard*, writes about the Lobby in a chapter 'News Management' in his book *Pressures on the Press*. Marcia Williams, on the other hand, constantly stresses in her memoirs the difficulties with which Mr Wilson struggled when trying to get a fair hearing (as he saw it) from Downing Street. Mr William Deedes has seen the system from both sides: 'When I was a lobby correspondent, I imagined that there were a tremendous number of stories that I ought to get and did not know about. When I was a Minister in [Mr Macmillan's] Cabinet and had some responsibility for giving out the news, it never seemed to me possible that anything the Cabinet was doing or about to do could conceivably remain secret for more than about twelve hours. And in my view it very rarely did.' (Anthony King and Ann Sloman, *Westminster and Beyond*, Macmillan, 1973, p 88.)

Some of the less recent arguments about the Lobby do not reflect this tension so strongly. They were concerned quite simply with the system's efficiency as a piece of journalistic machinery. One of the earliest articles was by David Butler, whose criticisms were digested by Jeremy Tunstall in his sociological study of the Lobby as follows:

'1. "Scoops are surprisingly rare"
 2. "Informed atmospheric stories are also in short supply"
 3. "Then there is little in the way of Whitehall stories"
 4. "Political portraiture, too, is oddly unenterprising"
 5. "Again, there is a shortage of 'Case-study' reporting"
 6. "A final shortcoming is in the background story, the re-telling of how a situation developed".'

(*The Westminster Lobby Correspondents*, Routledge and Kegan Paul, 1970, p 21.)

Most, if not all, of these criticisms manifestly no longer apply – though not all have been met by developments within the Lobby itself. Some may never have been fair as criticisms of the Lobby alone. Other parties to the 'dialogue' (David Wood, Ian Waller, Ronald Butt) emphasised, for example, that the Lobby was not *meant* to be more than an arrangement for straightforward *news* reporting, on a 24-hour cycle; and that anyway its procedures were largely conditioned by the collective nature of cabinet government and the dynamics of the competing party, parliamentary system.

This paper concentrates, therefore, on the more recent comments on the Lobby, and especially on those made since and about the first Wilson administration.

2.2 Elements of the Lobby System

'Lobbymen are specialists who are also generalists. They are the top generalists in the trade. Politics covers the whole of human life, and they cover politics . . . They are probably the hardest-working journalists in Fleet Street.' (John Whale. *Journalism and Government*, pp 77–78).

Jeremy Tunstall collected information about 39 national Lobbymen in 1967–8 (85% of the nationals' total). Their median age was 42; they had more formal education than most journalists; their pay was better than all except Senior Foreign Correspondents, financial journalists and senior newspaper executives and was about the same as MPs'; nearly all thought their status in their organisation 'high' or 'fairly high'; their median time in the Lobby was eight years. with more than one-fifth having done over twenty years.

The basis of the lobbyman's position is privileged access:

(*a*) *to politicians*, informally at Westminster (in the Lobby, Annie's Bar, etc) and in private collective briefings. Prime Ministers vary in their direct contact with the Lobby. Their PROs normally have twice-daily briefings and are available for inquiries at all times. The Leader of the Commons and of the Opposition each have weekly briefings. Departmental ministers have briefings as appropriate.

(*b*) *to documents* – advance copies of White papers, reports, etc.

(*c*) *to information off the record* which, but for the terms of confidentiality governing its exchange, would not be so readily obtained. The three words 'on Lobby terms', 'more binding than any legal contract . . . are an essential thread of precious metal on our British Parliamentary democracy.' (Harold Wilson, 6 December 1962.)

The original privilege was access to the Members' Lobby outside the Commons, from which the general public were banned for security reasons in 1885. This was the best place for reporters to meet Ministers as well as backbenchers. A Lobby Committee was quickly set up: the Serjeant-at-Arms could more easily keep track of numbers, and its existence helped establish the reporters' good faith. By 1914 there were some thirty members. News was found by individual sleuthing, although partnerships were not uncommon.

With the growth of government activity between the Wars, the focus of attention shifted somewhat. When an official spokesman was appointed to No. 10, *collective* Lobby briefings started. The war gave these great impetus: news of Dunkirk and the preparations for D-Day was passed through the Lobby. By 1945 there was a clear distinction between the small 'inner' Lobby of national and provincial dailies, working to a 24-hour cycle, and the 'outer' Lobby, denied access to the routine briefings and consisting of Sundays, weeklies, various editors and foreigners. Many of these had one day a week tickets just for access to the Lobby itself.

Partly as the result of grumbles to the 1947 Press Commission, membership started to grow. It has continued to do so. First came the provincial evenings. Then papers started to have more than one lobbyman. About 1958 they were also permitted an 'alternate' (ie a substitute attender at briefings, not an *extra* attender). In 1961 Sunday papers won full membership. They were followed some ten years later by the weeklies. In 1965 the inner/outer distinction clearly survived, with nearly 70 in the former category out of about 120. Today it was described to me as having 'largely broken down'.

Soon after the War the growth of membership and a few misunderstandings in the new Parliament led to the 'rules' of Lobby practice being codified.

The history of the Lobby so far can thus be seen as having two 'golden ages' when the needs of politicians for publicity and of papers for news were met most smoothly: an age of *individual newsgathering* before 1914 and one of *collective newsgathering* in 1935–45. At other times, particularly the 1970s, either the government or the press – or both – have been criticised for not matching their machinery to their needs.

2.3 Comment on the Lobby

(a) Anonymity of Sources

Several linked criticisms stem from the common Lobby practice of not attributing stories to named sources. This habit is obviously not peculiar to the Lobby, but its prevalence there and the importance of their subject make it especially noticeable. It can be illustrated any day of the week but its implications may be emphasised by taking a classic story – David Wood's forecast on 1 June 1959 that Mr Macmillan planned to move Mr Selwyn Lloyd from the foreign office within a few months. The story began: 'We may safely accept that Mr Macmillan has lately taken Mr Selwyn Lloyd's arm in a paternal grip, led him to one side, and spoken from the heart . . . Mr Macmillan has let Mr Lloyd know that at the foreign office, in these troubled times, enough is enough'. What were *The Times* readers to make of it (and of its position as the paper's lead story)? Was it true or untrue? Speculation or fact? Whose speculation anyway? The explicit story reported both a kind of event ('led him to one side' etc) and the communicating of a decision. But what did the decision amount to? That 'enough is enough'. Explicitly the story said absolutely nothing. Implicitly it spoke volumes: but how many volumes and exactly what they contained required guess work or independent knowledge. The story's timing – during a Foreign Ministers' meeting in Geneva preparing for a summit conference – and its presentation as hard news rather than as a speculative column or think-piece, encouraged enormous reaction overseas, in the Commons, at Geneva and even among the Lobby hierarchy (who thought, evidently, of a disciplinary move). Sir William Haley had eventually, to write a leader called 'Back to Sense'. David Wood, describing the episode recently, indicated that his source was Harold Macmillan. Macmillan describes the article in his memoirs as 'long and somewhat patronising', and 'particularly aggravating'. He thought the effect in Geneva was 'deplorable'. (*Pointing the Way*, Macmillan, 1972, p 65.)

The basic criticism of source anonymity is therefore that *the reader does not know what to believe*. Stories may confuse and obfuscate more than they clarify. One step removed is the possibility that *guesswork may be deliberately presented as fact* – what John Whale, an ex-lobbyman – calls 'the besetting sin of the Lobby' (*Journalism and Government*, p 80): 'When I was first in the Lobby I was amazed by the omniscience of my colleagues, and despaired of ever attaining it; but then I began to notice that they were in the same places as me all day, and seemed to have few special sources of information; and the seditious thought began to dawn that these confident assertions, these detailed readings of the minds of Ministers, could not strictly be classed as more than inferences: inferences based on experience and evidence, but still not quite what they seemed.' Slightly different again is the possibility of *magnifying sources*. Anonymity enables the lobbyman, Whale suggests, 'after a conversation with one parliamentary secretary, to write: "Ministers were saying last night . . . ."' It even enables him to write the same thing after a conversation with one departmental press officer – whose ministers doubtless would have been saying the same thing if they could have been fallen in with' (*op cit* p 79). Yet again, the Lobby often report the Government's propaganda, Ian Gilmour argues; but source anonymity prevents them from saying clearly that it is the Government's propaganda. (*The Body Politic*, Hutchinson, 1969, p 416.)

A different kind of distortion follows from the fact that *some politicians more willingly talk off the record than others*. One particular version of reality may prevail, without readers being clear whose it is. Richard Crossman's diaries provide numerous examples of Cabinet leaks and counter leaks and of views attributed by him to different Ministers as to where the majority of leaks were coming from.

Source anonymity also contributes to the *air of cosiness* critics have sometimes disapproved in the Lobby. Whale claims the Lobby like the privacy of the system and the 'incidental gratifications' it offers (*op cit* p 78). Anthony Howard has teased that 'it is almost like Piccadilly before the Wolfenden Report: there stand the Lobby correspondents waiting, soliciting, for the politician to come out; they treat them as if they were their clients . . . ' (*Westminster and Beyond*, p 73). Guy Eden, an architect of the mid-century Lobby, wrote in 1948 that because of their 'special personal relationships' lobbymen 'have also to know when *not* to write, as well as what and when and how to write' (*Parliamentary Affairs*, 1948, p 26). With some members staying in the Lobby 20 years or more it is hardly surprising that, to quote David Wood again, 'political friendships, in this curious love/hate relationship between the Lobby and politicians, are very durable. It is astonishing how much stick we can take from politicians and how much they are prepared to take from us' (*Westminster and Beyond*, p 77).

The impression of cosiness may be exaggerated to the outsider by other features, such as the air of a private world. Source anonymity may create a feeling of 'knowingness' – that lobbymen are writing about a small, informed circle and for that circle, of which they, but emphatically not the reader, are a part. What the reader is told only makes him aware that other things are being withheld. He is excluded from the private world. John Whale's remarks on competition suggest a similar result: the Lobby 'will write a story which they know to be a waste of their readers' or listeners' time . . . and they will write it only because they know that their competitors will write it, and rather than offer long explanations to the news desk when the 'phone rings at home at midnight, they find it easier to write the story now' (*op cit* p 80). Whale thinks competition in this climate also reinforces the habits of guesswork and exaggeration. He argues too that the privacy protects the Lobby's status: 'If the machinery were public their job would look too easy' (*op cit* p 79). Even in this private world the opacity of stories sometimes makes them incomprehensible, if a *Times* report during the Heath administration is to be believed: 'Communication between the Government and its own servants, which has traditionally relied upon newspaper reports to a much greater extent than might be supposed is now said to be hampered. Officials claim that it is impossible any longer to distinguish between collective ministerial "lobby" briefings, authorised leaks to individual reporters, unauthorised leaks, and "imaginative reconstructions".

What may be a narrower but equally serious consequence of source anonymity was implicit in remarks of one national newspaper editor whom we interviewed. He declared himself amazed at the prevalence of *Conspiracy theories of politics* – quoting as examples the opinion in one section of the Conservative Party that his paper was part of a 'conspiracy' against them and, secondly, the belief by some Liberals that the stories about Mr Thorpe had been carefully geared to try and ditch Liberal chances in the local government elections. These were casual remarks; but certainly the opacity of some Lobby stories can hardly succeed in reducing the incidence of conspiracy theories.

One quite different and unusual criticism stemming from the source anonymity/private world character of the Lobby was advanced by Hugh Macpherson in the *Spectator* on 15 May 1976. He claims that 'some Westminster correspondents work for others besides their own papers. Often this is immediate and obvious. Equally often it is not . . . There is no reason at all why lobby correspondents should not declare their interests, like MPs, so that when they write any interested party can know the full range of their activities'. He also claims that lobbymen allegedly act 'at times, in a public relations capacity. There is seldom any proof advanced for this, and the only time that any such activity has come to light was a few years ago when a lobby correspondent for a London evening paper was found to be carrying out some PR work. He was immediately dismissed by his editor – though subsequently given a Lobby ticket in one of the freelance agencies, presumably on the recommendation, or with the acquiescence, of the Lobby Committee.'

The defence of source anonymity is in a simple paradox: upon secrecy rests openness. 'Unless news is to be reduced to a bleak and uninterpreted account of public statements, there must be a good deal of non-attributable exchanges between the press and politicians.' (Ronald Butt, *The Power of Parliament*, Constable, 1969, p 416.) ' . . . if you can get more information by not naming names then you get your information that way' (David Wood, *Westminster and Beyond*, p 83). The practice, as lobbymen point out, applies to any of the specialist correspondents – indeed to reporters in general. Occasionally critics argue that if the press took a stand against it, sources would eventually become reconciled to speaking only on the record. This argument risks confusing two points. It may well be, firstly, that information is given to the Lobby off the record which the source would have given just as freely on the record if he had to. Lobbymen complain of Ministers sometimes doing just that; giving the Lobby a story unattributably and then repeating it openly to the TV cameras soon afterwards. To acknowledge this point, however, is not inconsistent with the view that some information would never be disclosed to lobbymen if it had to be on the record. Some information is unnecessarily given off the record: other information is necessarily so. Joe Haines evidently ended collective Lobby briefings partly on the first ground: 'I used to go to Lobby meetings each morning with a list of the information that I wanted to give them – always on a non-attributable basis. When I ceased the Lobby meetings, I continued to give that, but I gave it on the record.' (*The Editors*, BBC-TV 4 July 1976.) (His disagreements with lobbymen partly turned on who was responsible for making the Lobby briefings so thin in the other sort of 'necessarily anonymous' information.)

The substantial argument about the necessity for anonymity comes round eventually to the terms of the exchange between politicians and journalists: do politicians want publicity badly enough to get it on the Lobby's terms, or on their own? It is another facet of the continuous tension between them.

(b) Lack of Expertise

The Lobby have often been criticised for their lack of specialised knowledge of important areas of government. The criticism has obvious affinities with the claim that they are liable to be 'managed' by Government.

The problem is partly structural, rather than about the qualities of particular journalists. It is put well by John Whale: many specialists 'have at least some expert knowledge to weigh what they get from the department against. Now lobbymen are just as much one-department journalists; they are in fact Downing Street correspondents. But they are not specialists; they have to cover the entire field of politics . . . they cannot possibly know enough of the detail of legislation, of Government planning, in order to check what is handed out to them from Downing Street' (*Westminster and Beyond*, p 87).

Gerald Kaufman, having observed the Lobby when working for Harold Wilson before 1970, remarks similarly: 'It really is absurd to expect one or two or three men to be able to cover a Vehicle and General Report, and a Rhodesian Report, and all these other things' (*ibid* p 86).

Lobbymen can reply that the problem is part of 'big government'; and that theirs anyway is a *political* not a *subject* expertise. But the difficulty is similar to that of the old Civil Service Administrative Class of 'generalists'. What kinds of expertise are appropriate to the generalist? Just as the case grows stronger for saying a 'generalist' civil servant might appropriately have some knowledge of, say, statistical methods or Keynesian economics – once considered 'specialist' subjects; so it could be argued that lobbymen, though 'generalists', needed comparable experience to enable them, so to speak, to 'ask the right questions'. To this extent the criticism of lack of expertise is against the lobbymen as journalists. John Beavan (Lord Ardwick) considers that 'sometimes Mr Macmillan, Mr Heath or Mr Wilson have given briefings in greater depth than could be followed *critically* by the political general practitioners of the Lobby. City editors may from time to time feel that the Lobby did not have the specialist knowledge to question a spokesman who may have discussed the economic situation with them in a mood of unwarranted optimism. Defence correspondents too have been known to complain when their subject has been uncritically handled by the general practitioner of the Lobby.' (Main evidence to the Royal Commission on the Press, Mirror Group Newspapers, Section 1, p 28.) A non-Lobby specialist asserted privately that the Department of Employment 'put things out through the Lobby not the Labour Correspondents, to hoodwink them'. Mr Heath, in Opposition, made a similar claim: the Lobby system was open to abuse – particularly when used 'to put across technical information which the average Lobby correspondent is not equipped to test and question searchingly' (speech to the Institute of Journalists, printed in *The Times*, 6 December 1968). Mr Heath quoted an example (naturally in a party context): 'When the Vote on Account was published earlier this year it showed – just over two months after the Government's so-called expenditure cuts – a £1,000m increase in Government spending. The Government spokesman – if one reads correctly between the lines – explained to the Lobby that the Vote on Account was of no importance and this year was largely meaningless. One Lobby correspondent – but one only – refused to accept this bland assertion, and it was largely due to him that this deliberate attempt to mislead the public failed.' In office Mr Heath apparently continued to feel the same. *The Times* reported his advisers as alleging that the Lobby was failing to convey 'reliable political information based on intelligent background appreciation'; and that a plan was being invoked, in effect, to downgrade the system in preference for wider use of subject specialists (*The Times*, 11 March 1972).

A response in the press to the structural criticism has been a diversification of specialists reading with politics. More documentary material, in particular, gets passed straight on from the Lobby elsewhere. City and Industrial Correspondents – at the *Daily Mirror* for example - are more closely involved with political reporting than they used to be.

The other, human, response is the *cri de coeur*, like this from David Wood: '. . . though we lead our papers every second day on average, we no more than scratch the surface of politics. With a handful of men we are trapped in a superficial routine that satisfies newsrooms yet leaves every man engaged in the operation profoundly frustrated. The test of a political reporter at Westminster today for a Fleet Street newspaper is not political acumen, good contacts, and reporting in depth. It is peasant stamina, and a mind trivial enough to know a good political cliché when he sees it.'

(c) *'The Lobby are "Managed" by the Government'*

'Politically', writes Charles Wintour matter-of-factly, 'the machine through which the news is managed is the group of political correspondents known as the Lobby'. (*Pressures on the Press*, p 45).

Obviously Governments always prefer the press to see things their way. 'If news management means that you release a piece of news which is good for you on a day when it is not in competition with some other piece of news, you do not release them all at one time so that they are crowded out of the paper', said Joe Haines in a BBC interview, 'well of course everybody does that.' (*The Editors*, 4 July 1976.) 'What I have proved is that politics is not just working out policies but putting them over' reflected Richard Crossman after getting a good press about his Rating Bill in 1966. 'I have managed to give the impression that we regard rates as a foul tax and that I am really trying to relieve domestic ratepayers of part of the burden.' (There is no reason to doubt his good faith, even though he does add: 'That should help us in the election'. *Diaries of a Cabinet Minister*, p 463.) Gerald Kaufman, asked in a radio interview whether Ministers try to create an effect in the press, replied: 'The Ministers who are brightest try very hard indeed. I am afraid, though, that on both the Labour and Conservative Parties there are not all that many Ministers who know how to go about it' (*Westminster and Beyond*, p 80). In this kind of activity newspapers may sometimes deliberately cooperate. Cecil King describes Harold Wilson in 1966 'planning to arrive at a settlement [of a rail strike], which he has already worked out, by 5 am on Sunday morning.' He told Hugh Cudlipp over lunch. 'Hugh told him that this, though dramatic, was bad timing, so the hour is to be 8 pm on Saturday to dominate the front pages of the Sunday papers!' (*The Cecil King Diary*, 1965–1970, p 57).

There is a difference between these kinds of activity and a more constructive management of the Lobby amounting to positive deception or the manipulation of news as an instrument of policy. In various forms this allegation became common about the late years of the first Wilson administration. Satisfaction with his own press relations did not prevent Richard Crossman commenting about a judicious leak that 'This is typical of Harold's handling of politics. He still thinks he can settle problems just by talking to the press' (*Diaries*, p 161). The proposals for a Commonwealth Peace Mission to Viet-Nam in 1965 was widely quoted as one example of 'just a gimmick that kept a Commonwealth conference quiet'. (Wintour, p 50; and of Crossman Diaries, pp 254–5. 'I really was anxious, Harold, that if this stunt had come off you might have been away for a whole month', Crossman said. 'Oh, I do not think it would have been a month', he reports Wilson as replying; 'at the most it would have been a fortnight'. 'And he added these significant words', Crossman notes: 'Anyway, I think we have got most of the value we can get out of it already'.) Comparable comments after the event were made about a Wilson proposal in January 1966 for a Commonwealth initiative to relieve famine in India. Alastair Hetherington quoted the Industrial Relations Bill of 1969 as an example of a measure 'presented through the Lobby in a way that favoured one faction within the Cabinet' (Lecture at Stirling University, reported in *The Guardian*, 27 February 1970). 'I can recall maybe planting one or two stories' Joe Haines has said, 'but it is not a feature of life at Downing Street' (*The Editors*, 4 July 1976).

Some of the suspicion about news management derived from an awareness of the difference between being told the truth and not being told a lie. Comments by Joe Haines bring out this difference nicely. 'Well of course, I always withhold information . . . But then so does every press secretary. Governments give the information that they want the press to have. Even the press would not expect one to turn up at a four o'clock Lobby meeting and say there was a hell of a row in Cabinet this morning. So naturally, one withheld information. But I never denied a true story. If I knew that a story was true and it was put to me, I never denied it' (*loc cit*). Much more, however, the suspicion grew from the unprecedented accessibility of Mr Wilson to the Lobby. Wilson 'sees James Margach every week', Cecil King noted in his Diary (22 September 1967), 'but all this has done is to weaken Margach's position in the *Sunday Times* office. He will be transferred elsewhere before long'. (He was not; and his own view is that 'the greatest dangers to the integrity of the Press within my experience have come when proprietors and editors became too deeply involved with Premiers'. *Sunday Times*, 9 May 1976.) Lord Ardwick comments in the Mirror Group evidence to the Press Commission: 'A feeling developed among editors and among other journalists, envious perhaps of their privileges, that the Lobby were too well in with Mr Wilson. Indeed, a year or so later, some members of the Lobby who had basked in the new intimacy had second thoughts when Mr Wilson's predictions about the economy, which they had so confidently reported, failed to be fulfilled on more than one occasion. Had they been suckers?'

One corollary of intimacy is the sanction provided by its possible withdrawal. Mr Wilson appeared to 'punish' particular journalists. For example, Crossman reports him as telling the Cabinet in 1966 that Norah Beloff of *The Observer* 'must be denied interviews by any of us' and as cutting her off from access to No 10, (*Diaries*, p 552). Similar strictures were made about Anthony Howard as *Sunday Times* 'Whitehall Correspondent'. Corporately, *The Times* was punished during the second Wilson administration by denial of certain press facilities at Downing Street.

Withdrawal seems more serious if one takes the view that Downing Street constitutes a 'single source'. When Joe Haines was himself a lobbyman 'It seemed to me that it was wrong for journalists to be getting too much of their information from a single source'; and that was 'the principal reason why eventually I cancelled the off-the-record briefings' (*The Editors*, 4 July 1976).

Whale remarks that 'Lobby Correspondents cannot have a very wide range of sources, partly because they have not very much time, and also because they have not very much freedom of movement' (*Westminster and Beyond*, p 85).

If a wider view of the Lobby's work is taken, on the other hand, David Wood's 'counteracting' point is important: 'We are dealing with a Government and an Opposition, or even if we are dealing with a party, we are dealing with the leaders of the party and their rebels. So there is the constant correction if you want it' (*Westminster and Beyond*, p 84). Ronald Butt also comments: 'At any given moment, it is likely that one or the other of the parties will consider a particular Lobby correspondent an "enemy" because he seemed unduly critical, or un-receptive to the line which the politician had wished to put over' (*The Power of Parliament*, p 417).

This 'monopoly danger' can be extended more widely. Mr Heath, in Opposition, considered 'there is a great deal to be said for the Lobby system. It is convenient alike to the politician and to the press. It provides the best-informed political commentators in the country. But it should never be the sole vehicle of political information'. (Speech to Institute of Journalists; reported in *The Times*, 6 November 1968.) In Government he felt much the same; and the idea was mooted of broadening the range of political reporters (*The Times*, 11 March 1972). One national editor (of a broadly Conservative paper) feels the range has been broadened by the development in recent years of political columnists independent of the Lobby.

(d) 'The Government is the Victim of the Lobby'

In Opposition Mr Heath saw that Governments may gull the Lobby. In Govern-ment evidently the opposite seemed true 'As its critics in Whitehall see it,' Peter Jay wrote in an 'inspired' story in *The Times* (11 March 1972), 'the Lobby system has ceased to provide a flow of broadly accurate accounts of what Ministers are thinking and what the Government is doing . . . It makes it harder for the Government to convey a clear picture to the electorate of what it is trying to do and how it sees the nation's difficulties. This, it is felt, is bad for democracy as well as an unfair handicap to Ministers trying to grapple with the real difficulties facing the country.' Lord Windlesham, Minister with special responsibility for Government information in the Heath administration, said in a Granada lecture in 1974 that complaints from his colleagues about the handling of the Government's case in the media were frequent and 'often accompanied by requests to intervene with the management concerned'. (Nine out of ten referred to broadcasts; partly, he felt, because broadcasters were much less well represented in the Lobby, with whom politicians tended to take up complaints directly.) Ian Gilmour, observing events from the backbenches and as ex-proprietor of the *Spectator* remarks that 'most politicians are sur-prisingly sensitive to criticism and surprisingly afraid of Fleet Street . . . Nearly all of them go to great lengths to avoid press criticism and to gain press praise' (*The Body Politic*, Hutchinson, 1969).

This sensitiveness is certainly one reason why politicians sometimes feel them-selves victims of the Lobby. Marcia Williams (*Inside Number 10*, Ch 9) and Joe Haines (*The Editors*, BBC-TV 4 July 1976) have both stressed how often Harold Wilson was hurt by 'the fact that people whose guests he had been, who he regarded as friends, could then go into print and print really some of the vilest things about him' (Haines). Other reasons have to do again with the basic tensions between press and politics. Marcia Williams's account of press relations in the first Wilson administration describes a constant attempt to find the most effective machinery for projecting the Government as the Prime

Minister wished. 'Harold did everything he could to give journalists greater status and respect, particularly the Lobby journalists.' 'He wanted the journalists to feel he accepted their wish that he should be accessible and he made himself so.' His initial choice of a Press Secretary – Trevor Lloyd-Hughes – was of a provincial lobbyman (*Liverpool Daily Post*) because 'to appoint a senior daily or Sunday Lobby journalist would cause offence to those who felt they might have been chosen'. By the summer of 1965 came 'the ever-increasing realisation that we needed a political Press man in Downing Street, acting separately, independently and politically with the Press on Harold's behalf'; a post filled by Gerald Kaufman. When frequent contact with the Lobby at large did not seem to be working well, the 'White Commonwealth' experiment was tried. This involved 'fortnightly evening meetings at No. 10 with senior Lobby correspondents from a number of daily and Sunday papers'. These did not last beyond 1968. Provincial papers were excluded: beyond that, the determining factor of membership seemed to be whether Mr Wilson liked a journalist – hence the group were at once privileged yet suspect. Mr Wilson wanted to run meetings 'like a seminar': the journalists wanted hard news. George Wigg, who had responsibility for co-ordination of Home Information Services for a time, remarks in his memoirs: 'I could only reflect, sardonically, that Wilson and his coterie had learned little about relationships with the press' (*George Wigg*, Michael Joseph 1972, p 354).

This experiment illustrates one other factor giving the Lobby a kind of 'hold' over Government. What the Lobby write provides a benchmark for Government to judge its own performance. Marcia Williams says Wilson 'did very much want to see the emergence of a Reston or Lippman'. The Crossman diaries provide continual illustrations of how Crossman – and Wilson – measured events against press coverage. If the Lobby provided the 'wrong sort' of coverage (as Wilson felt more than Crossman), it would be natural to feel frustrated by the system. The feeling cannot have been eased by small but symbolic factors such as the convention that Ministers address the Lobby by invitation. When Crossman wanted to have a conference about his new Rating Bill the Lobby 'which is a pretty autocratic body, decided that they were busy enough on Thursday and had not time'. (*Diaries*, p390.) Crossman had to organise briefings for individual journalists.

(e) 'I Give Guidance: You Leak'
Leaks to the Lobby are inevitably a preoccupation of politicians in a system embodying the principle of collective Cabinet responsibility and in which the Government depends upon the continuing cohesion of a parliamentary majority. Both constitutional convention and the realities of party competition are powerful pressures towards secretiveness – especially in decision-*making*, rather than in decisions themselves (for which publicity is normally desired). Equally, competition within the Cabinet – for place and financial resources – impel Ministers to feed their versions of events to the Lobby; and the same applies to intra-party rivalry. Competitive leaking from the Parliamentary Labour Party meetings became so frequent that in 1967 the practice was started of giving the Lobby an 'official' account of proceedings, so that at least the leaderships' version had an equal chance of an airing along with unofficial versions.

127

Leaking is thus built into the system by the simultaneous existence of a need for a unity against the Opposition and of argument and competition within the Government. 'Leaks' are what happens when you are the *victim* of undesired publicity. 'Guidance' is what you give in order to be the *beneficiary* of desirable publicity. The two views illustrate once more the rival arguments that Ministers are at the mercy of the Lobby and that the Lobby are managed by Ministers.

The Crossman Diaries are full of stories about leaks. The importance of secrecy/publicity as a factor in the relations within Governments and between Governments and outsiders is beautifully illustrated. George Brown and Harold Wilson grumbled about leaks before a Cabinet Housing Committee on Crossman's option mortgage scheme in June 1966. 'I wonder whether it is worth having these meetings with the kind of leaks we saw in the Sunday press', the Prime Minister says (according to Crossman). 'This took my breath away', Crossman comments, 'because, of course, I had organised the interviews with Jimmy Margach and Anthony Shrimsley and Norah Beloff, and thought they had done a first-rate job' (p 551). Earlier Crossman is 'not very happy' about Mr Benn. 'To begin with, on every single occasion when he is about to bring a plan to Cabinet a leak occurs giving the full details in advance . . .' (p 227). When Mr Wilson complains on another occasion about leaks 'this exasperated Cabinet because 99% of the so-called leaks come from No 10, or from the DEA or from the Treasury. With the Prime Minister, George [Brown] and Jim [Callaghan] leaking about each other there is no good blaming the rest of us' (p 580).

One senior ex-lobbyman whom we interviewed considered that leaking has increased enormously in the last 10 years. However, it must primarily be dependent upon the extent of divisions in the Cabinet and governing party.

(*f*) '*The Lobby has grown too Big*'
This was a common complaint by 1970, among politicians and some lobbymen alike. As the Lobby grew in numbers, Marcia Williams writes, 'the quality went down. Their own rules began often to be broken and the standards they originally imposed upon themselves not always kept' (*Inside Number 10*, p 178). George Wigg refers to standards falling 'lamentably'. 'At one time a conversation on "Lobby terms" meant that MPs and journalists could speak together in complete confidence. There are still Lobby correspondents . . . whom I would trust with my life. The Lobby, however, has grown too large and competition between newspapers too fierce for the integrity of its standards to be maintained without reform' (*George Wigg*, pp 333–4). Joe Haines quotes an example of loss of confidentiality arising at least partly, in his view, from excessive size. 'There was one instance where I had instructed my deputy to tell the Lobby something because there was a current controversy with the Conservative Party over a debate, and the Government were getting a lot of stick when in fact they were in the right. And so I told my deputy what to say. She told the Lobby. By five o'clock three Lobby correspondents had gone to the Opposition Chief Whip and told him what she had said. Now I could not carry on a system where I get complaints from our Chief Whip because three Lobby correspondents had gone to the Opposition Chief Whip naming my deputy and saying what she had said' (*The Editors*, 4 July 1976). George Brown shares the same general view – and admits to have been especially vulnerable to lapses of confidentiality, 'because I am given to being slightly uncontrolled' (*In My Way*, pp 61–2). 'Standards have declined everywhere', he writes. '. . . there is a new

generation of chaps now, and they work in tandem. If they get something off the record that they know they must not use they seem quite likely to arrange that somebody else uses it so that they can pick it up, and then they say "Well, I am awfully sorry, George, of course *I* did not break your confidence, but as *he* had got it already I could not *not* use it".' In his view, too many of the modern men do not think for themselves. 'They just walk around the Lobby or the conference, buy drinks for a certain number of chaps, and churn out a few gossip paragraphs' (*loc cit*).

The increase in size contributed both to Joe Haines's disillusion with collective Lobby briefings and to journalists' feeling that these were no longer much use. 'Long ago, every political reporter worth his salt looked elsewhere for his information about what was happening inside the Government' (*The Times*, 20 June 1975). The conferences were still useful, though, for imparting routine information.

2.4 Provincial Dailies and the Lobby

Half the Lobby correspondents represent provincial morning and evening papers. Yet much of the comment in previous sections has the national press mainly in mind. Provincial dailies seem generally satisfied with the system. Their needs are hard news stories, preferably with a local angle, on a day-to-day basis. Arguments about expertise, bureaux, 'management', etc, may be real when applied to their home town: they do not impinge much when applied to the Lobby. Provincials want a routine daily service about Government business – along the lines described in the section about Parliament – and there is no doubt that they get it. The collective briefing from the Prime Minister's PRO every morning, for example, is largely for the benefit of provincial evening papers and the news agencies.

The success of the Lobby for provincial papers possibly constitutes part of the problem for the nationals. It is reflected in the complaint about size. Part of the surge in membership came from the expansion of provincial evenings. Provincial morning papers have been members since the Lobby started: at that time (1885) the national/provincial distinction scarcely existed. But provincial evenings were excluded until after the report of the 1947 Royal Commission on the Press. Between the Wars, when the evenings were becoming more important relative to the mornings, they had quite a variety of schemes to get representation. Some had a morning 'partner' in the same ownership whose facilities they could use. Others made more devious arrangements. Portsmouth and Sunderland Newspapers, for example, had first call on the services of a lobbyman employed by the Central News Agency, which always qualified for a ticket.

After 1945 some of the bigger evening papers (eg *Manchester Evening News*, *Bristol Evening Post*) were particularly keen on getting membership and took the opportunity of complaining vigorously to the Press Commission. The Lobby establishment's resistance rested on arguments about shortage of space. The evening papers were sceptical about that, and they won their case, becoming full members in about 1949.

2.5 Reform of the Lobby

The most detailed and extensive discussion of the possibilities for reform of the Lobby is chapter 10 of Jeremy Tunstall's book *The Westminster Lobby Correspondents*. This includes size, conflicting interests within the Lobby and between different media, access to news sources and documents, and relations with other specialists. Among politicians and journalists two general ideas have prevailed, though neither has been worked out thoroughly – nor applies very widely.

Both the Wilson and Heath administrations saw advantages in trying to *diversify* political journalism, in order to counteract the tendencies in the Lobby to concentrate on short run (24 hours), hard news stories, and in order to reduce the Lobby 'monopoly'. Mr Heath experimented with massive open press conferences at Lancaster House. Mr Wilson, as we have seen, tried various experiments, none of which seems to have been happy. In particular he felt the lack, as Labour Prime Ministers usually have, of journalists somewhat distanced from the day-to-day routine of 'capitalist' journalism with whom he could share an understanding of Labour's visions and values.

Journalists, for their part, have naturally been aware that the shifting methods and priorities of politics require adjustments in their own procedures: economic and industrial matters were two mentioned often in our interviews with editors. Lobbymen themselves have tended to favour a *Bureau* development. Possibly the earliest published version was by Ian Waller (*Sunday Telegraph*) in *Encounter* (June 1965). The gist of the idea is that specialist correspondents dealing with primarily political/government subjects should operate under the control of a political editor who would himself be a member of the Lobby. Gerald Kaufman, having seen the present system from both sides, thinks the proposal sensible (*Westminster and Beyond*, p 87). David Wood links it to possible developments in the EEC and British national assemblies and hazards that any news organisation adopting it 'between now and 1985 will scoop the pool' (*Times News*, March 1976, p 5).

Lord Ardwick comments that the Bureau idea 'deserved more consideration than editors have given it' (Mirror Group evidence to the Press Commission). Certainly our own interviews with editors confirmed that the idea has not made much headway. Some clearly had given it no thought – if indeed it had impinged at all. One objected on geographical grounds. The Bureau idea works in Washington, he argued, because the *New York Times* (for example) does not have its head office there. In London, by contrast, 'natural co-ordination' can be achieved because most specialists are in the same building. Contact with lobbymen is 'a problem' because they are not in the building; but taking other specialists out and transferring them to a Lobby office would be unnatural and unpractical.

It is important, lastly, to stress the 'organic' nature of political journalism. In some respects the Lobby and other specialists undoubtedly are more co-ordinated than, say, ten years ago. On the *Daily Mirror*, for instance, industrial and political coverage seem closely involved. Economic specialists, who have developed much in recent years, may also become closely concerned with political coverage. But there is no sign of such developments being institutionalised in a political Bureau.

3 Government: Economic Policy and the Press

3.1 The Context

Press coverage of economic affairs (defined to exclude the day-to-day reporting of finance and industry – important subjects in themselves) deserves study for several reasons.

(i) Successful management of the economy is a condition of success for many other government policies, notably in the spending departments.

(ii) Governments traditionally like to stress how far success depends on the attitude of individual citizens. Spending departments seek to use the press to fight battles against each other and against the Treasury. Chancellors are more concerned (among other things, obviously) that the right notes are being struck in the mass circulation tabloids. Conservative Chancellors look carefully at the *Daily Mail* and *Daily Express*. No doubt Mr Healey and the Treasury consider themselves fortunate that the Labour Government's counter-inflation policy has had the support of the *Daily Mirror* and *The Sun*. If anything the appeal to the people has increased in the last fifteen years, with the experiments in indicative planning and voluntary incomes policies, new examples continually present themselves. 'Special importance is now attached', wrote Peter Jay of a Treasury reply to a Public Expenditure Committee report 'to educating the public to "a better appreciation of the tax implications of public expenditure", so as to create a political counter-constituency to balance the pressures for more spending' (*The Times*, 17 February 1976). Were the Chancellor's expenditure cuts and other measures announced on 22 July an attempt to take a grip on the situation? asked Hugh Stephenson, editor of *The Times* Business Press. 'What emerged has much more the feel of a soothing public relations exercise' (23 July 1976). Soothing public relations exercises may be common around Whitehall, but they are particularly appropriate to voluntary incomes policies, etc.

(iii) Governments need to impress 'opinion abroad'. This is based in part on the contents of the British Press; both directly and through the contents of countries' own papers, which often 'replay' stories from British papers. The latter habit was remarked on both by the head of the Treasury Information Division and by a member of the Foreign Office Press Department. The Treasury Information Head reckons to spend perhaps 20% of his time on the foreign press – often reading into a particular paper intensively over a short period, rather than a more evenly spread pattern.

(iv) Our interviews with provincial editors suggested that for their general attitudes to economic policy they relied on commentators like Samuel Brittan and Peter Jay more than on comparable writers in other fields. (The papers we visited mostly did not have economic correspondents of their own.) This may be a field in which the national press exercises considerable opinion leadership.

131

(v) Economic journalism has been a growth subject. In the late 1950s Andrew Shonfield was almost the only practitioner, Samuel Brittan came a little later and was subsequently joined on the nationals by the likes of Peter Jay, Nigel Lawson and Frances Cairncross. The roots of the subject were in City journalism. Samuel Brittan feels that 'it took some time to be accepted that we did not need to be authorities on the City'; though he is inclined to think now that he might have benefited from the experience.

(vi) The subject is also one around which demarcation lines have not hardened like the Lobby or industrial correspondents. Economic journalists resemble the Lobby in their preoccupation with a shifting range of topics – the variety of factors bearing on the formation of policy. 'While training in economic reasoning is still needed', wrote Lord Balogh recently, 'the complexity of factors having a potentially major influence on developments makes flair the most important qualification for economic advisers.' (*Times Literary Supplement* 9 July 1976.) 'Flair', here, is the quality covering the professional economist's familiar reservation, 'other things being equal'. The economic journalist may have to confront these 'other things', which might be a Trade Union leader or a Middle-East crisis. What the economic journalist lacks, compared with the Lobby, is the institutional focus provided by the system of Cabinet responsibility to Parliament. There is no Serjeant-at-Arms to keep his name on a list. The subsequent boundaries are therefore perhaps more flexible; it may be a more organic subject.

3.2 A soft news area

(i) *Much news about the Economy is inherently soft*. The journalist deals with trends, tendencies, forecasts and with short, medium and long terms that run into one another. He is more often discussing the prospects for the next round of the Cup than reporting the round in progress: or, if he is reporting the round in progress, it is with an eye on the lessons for the next round. Quoting round figures may actually be sensible, since precise figures have a spurious air of exactitude.

The number of organisations involved in the forecasting game has been increasing. One of the most authoritative (and watched with particular attention abroad) is the National Institute for Economic and Social Research. In several ways its operations are affected by keen press interest. The Institute's quarterly review (*National Institute Economic Review*) was started in the later 1950s on the initiative of the Treasury, which at that time felt that it lacked 'controls' for its own economic forecasts and techniques. What was intended as part of a modest, rather private, dialogue, became, to the surprise of those concerned, widely quoted at large. Now the *Review* nearly always gets editorial comment and often headlines in the heavy papers. It is made available to 'serious journalists' a few days early. It is designed so that a 'summary and appraisal' (some three pages) is printed at the front in a non-technical form suitable for press use. (Formerly a separate press statement was drafted.) When a printers' strike delayed publication in 1975 the *Review* article about the EEC referendum was mimeoed specially for distribution to the press so that its point would not be lost by appearing too late. The *Review*'s publicity not only leads to much contact with journalists at home and abroad but has also led to arguments among the staff about how far the Institute should get involved in policy issues. The present Director (since 1965) feels that to plug a particular line would be inappropriate but that taking a position on short-term problems is fair.

There is nothing directly comparable to the Institute's *Review* though other regular forecasts – for instance by the London Business School and the Cambridge Department of Applied Economics – also attract considerable press coverage.

(ii) A second form of *softness* is connected to the problem of *putting economic news in context*. 'Report any economic statistic or speech by a politician straight – ie from the handout – and you will almost certainly be perpetrating or conniving at a culpable deception of your readers . . . The latest figure in a statistical series may be up: yet its significance may be that it reveals or confirms a falling trend.' (Peter Jay, *The Listener*, 24 August 1972.) Samuel Brittan is suspicious of 'phoney figures' – superficial attempts at short term forecasting, which can be dressed up and compared with each other to give the appearance of reliable estimates. There was a stage, too, when 'the basic apparatus seemed well established' (Brittan). The Director, similarly, considers that a useful job of the Institute *Review* is to have helped develop 'a common language'. In recent years, though, arguments about interpretation have intensified. ' . . . In economic affairs every statement implies a degree of interpretation and the interpretation presupposes a comment' (Jay, *op cit*).

(iii) Economic news can also be soft because *much of it is enveloped in secretiveness*. It is a great subject for hints and non-attributed sources. Samuel Brittan describes the Treasury as obsessed with secrecy. The Director of the National Institute reads the *Financial Times* carefully for his Treasury news. The Information Division of the Treasury seems to exercise an effective monopoly in press relations: everything is channelled through it and telephone calls from journalists to officials eventually have to be reported to it. But it is arguable that the Division does not have enough muscle power to counteract unnecessary secrecy. One example quoted to me was the publication of the monthly Trade Figures. These used to come out at mid-day. The Bank of England disapproved because the markets were still open. Now they come out at 4.00 pm. The argument presumably turns on whether the reaction the following morning is significantly different from what it used to be the previous afternoon. But the change is a nuisance for the press.

A few developments have slightly reduced this secretiveness. Until about 1968 the Treasury released virtually no more information than the Chancellor made available to Parliament. Mr Jenkins started publishing details of the Financial Statement (excluding forecasts of prices, unemployment and the balance of payments). The inquiries of the Public Expenditure Committee (especially the General Sub-Committee) have added to the stock of knowledge, especially about methods. Brussels is increasingly an (unreliable) outlet of information. Most recently, the Industry Act had inserted in it on the initiative of Mr Jeremy Bray a requirement that the Treasury should publish its full model of the economy. The implications of this have not been fully worked out. (One nice detail of these developments is that the Treasury Manual which used to be given to 'bona fide users' free now has to be purchased by them.)

3.3 A Difficult Area for the Press ?
(i) Almost the first thing Samuel Brittan mentioned in our discussion was *the tyranny of the daily newspaper timetable* – to which much economic news is inappropriate. Pressures inside the office are for instant comment, though it would in theory be better often to delay a day or two. 'Of course you can always come back to the subject in next week's column, but by then people have had

enough.' The economic journalist 'exposes himself to the widest possible audience every day', writes Peter Jay, 'on the strength of the briefest possible period for reflection, composition and checking' (*op cit*). The Chancellor's July 1976 package of expenditure cuts and national insurance contributions did not reach Brittan till between 5.30 and 6.00 pm.

(ii) *The complexity of economic affairs* is a problem. Sometimes this leads to simple silly mistakes. One example quoted to us was that the Lobby correspondent of at least one heavy paper wrote a story in July 1966 saying no reflationary measures were expected, when it was blatantly obvious that they were imminent; but he could not be expected to know it, since he had little economic expertise. In another example, we were told that one serious Sunday paper had been briefed by the Chancellor on possible ideas of what the next stage of the counter-inflation policy might look like, and 'it came out garbled' – though later on 'it got straightened out all right'. More frequent than simple errors are mistakes of emphasis, wilful or unintentional misrepresentation, the highlighting of individual figures out of context and so on, especially in the popular papers. A remarkable instance of this kind of 'mistake' seems to have been the 1976 Budget. In many papers the 'missing bits', which inevitably get excluded from press coverage of even such a massive annual news story as this, contained the crucial table showing the trade-off between the pay rise norm and the tax concessions.

The journalist has a problem of how much to assume about his readers' understanding of the subject. Brittan thinks he probably assumes too much. He doubts, for instance, whether the July 1976 measures were properly understood. They were projected widely as £1,000m cuts in public expenditure; and the other half of the package – a comparable increase in employers' national insurance contributions – seemed to make less impact.

There is also the journalist's understanding of the subject. Quite apart from the expertise of other correspondents encountering economics (eg the Lobby), the economic specialists themselves may 'fail to keep up with all the developments in their discipline; and then become progressively imprisoned in the out-of-date notions and oversimplified rules of thumb which they imbibed with their undergraduate beer' (Peter Jay, *op cit*). Brittan was in one of the last generations at Cambridge to be taught that for economics you did not need to know maths. The divorce between econometricians and many writers is 'a difficult gap to bridge' (although he does not feel it causes extra difficulties in interpreting the subject to his readers). Brittan agrees that keeping up-to-date becomes more difficult; and that he is unlikely to have the feel for monetarist theory that he had for the demand management theories of the 1960s.

(iii) Economic affairs often *do not fit conventional news values*: one informant thought perhaps 'too much of an element of good news is no news' and of 'the gladiatorial contest' came across in press coverage. The subject's 'softness' and complexity both work against it. Even on the *Financial Times* Brittan sometimes wants to write on something which he thinks is interesting but the news editor finds fantastically boring. Being the *Financial Times*, it gets published, only in an inconspicuous place. The difficulty works the other way round too. Brittan may want to write a 'probability' story. He does not like putting these in his weekly column; but they are not popular with the news desk unless they are 'hardened up'. Some papers avoid this difficulty by maintaining columnists dealing in speculation distinct from advocacy (eg Peter Jenkins in *The Guardian*).

The best examples of papers whose news values work against much economic coverage are of course the populars. They are faced with the dilemma classically illustrated by Mr Wilson's remark on TV after the 1967 sterling devaluation, to the effect that 'the £ in your pocket is worth no less than yesterday'. That remark represented an attempt to explain to a nationwide audience in simple terms the significance of foreign exchange adjustments; and it was subsequently thought to have been an unhappy choice of phrase, open to misconstruction. But economic affairs in principle are a good news subject, close to jobs and shopping baskets and suchlike topics that regularly score highest in the NOP and Gallup polls of voters' chief concerns. But in practice it is difficult to translate into those terms without oversimplification and the pitfalls Mr Wilson met in 1967.

Treasury officials observing the media sometimes have a higher opinion of the economic coverage of TV and radio than of the popular press, on grounds both of their exposition of 'context' and 'background' and of a lower frequency if not absence of misleading use of figures etc. Brittan, by contrast, has a low opinion of broadcast coverage. ('Put a bomb under the news agencies and the BBC' was his immediate response to my solemn question about 'improvement of economic coverage'.) He broadened the opinion to include 'the popular media' as a whole.

The populars obviously are conscious of the difficulties of handling the subject. The editor and political editor of the *Daily Mirror* mentioned it spontaneously when we interviewed them. Their City Editor, Bob Head, is evidently involved with the political side of the paper much more than formerly. City coverage in the *Daily Mirror* started in the 'affluent society' era (investment advice for the mass readership, etc). The focus has shifted away from 'Board Room struggles' and has increasingly included the Treasury. The *Daily Mail*'s Patrick Sergeant is similarly very much more than an old-style City Editor. Their political writer Andrew Alexander also covers economic policy, and the editor reckons to 'do it through leading articles' too. The editor left the impression that economic coverage was under review, though without seeming to have any very clear intentions.

(iv) Economic journalism has been criticised by Peter Jay, in an analysis which was broadly endorsed by everyone I asked as *suffering from certain habits of newspaper organisation*. First is the distinction of journalists into feature/leader writers and reporters; second the division among reporters according to sources of information. 'Traditionalists are still suspicious of people who both report and comment. And woe betide the economic journalist who presumes that it's his job to report the unemployment figures – a time-honoured plum of the Labour correspondents – or to report a major economic speech by the Chancellor of the Exchequer – a guaranteed front page by-line for the Lobby correspondent.' Economic information is 'so bad chiefly because it is operating in the interstices between the time-honoured baronies of political and business journalism and because it is operating against the grain of Fleet Street attitudes'. (*The Listener*, 24 August 1972.) As an illustration, Jay quotes *incomes policy* (1971 style). A TUC proposal for 'threshold clauses' in pay settlements was reported by *Labour Correspondents* at a briefing with Vic Feather – at which other subjects loomed larger. The Chancellor's (Mr Barber's) reaction was brief and in a situation reported by *Lobby Correspondents* – who knew nothing of the TUC initiative. *City Editors* 'tended to reflect the publicly and privately expressed news of the Bank of England that a formal incomes policy of some kind was needed'. A subsequent CBI initiative on price restraint was in the province of *industrial correspondents*, so the pattern went on. 'Almost nobody ... followed or covered the story consistently, and almost none of those who have been involved in covering bits of it have any expertise in the subject.' In addition there were analysts and feature writers, most of whom had to rely for their information on the reports of their colleagues.

Jay moots the idea of *subject specialists* to get round this difficulty. Some subject specialists (Education? Social Services?) already tap a variety of sources. The particular problem for economic affairs seems to be the feature identified at the beginning – its potential breadth, like that of the lobby's subject matter. Brittan emphasised how far influence over economic policy had moved away recently from the academic/civil service/parliamentary political world to the big Unions. Most economic journalists, he suggested, 'are not instinctively in that world'. Those that are – columnists as well as reporters – 'are usually the first to say they are not economic analysts'. Brittan himself is less involved with news gathering than he was.

Jay's and Brittan's comments both seem consistent with the 'Bureau' proposal discussed in the section on the Lobby. That proposal would fit the idea of subject specialists – and shifts among them (no one would want an 'incomes policy correspondent' *all* the time). It might also lessen the tendency to 'baronies'. Brittan was sceptical of the proposal, however, seeing it as a 'bureaucratic device' making insufficient allowance for individuals.

(v) *Does Economic journalism suffer too much from fashions?* One informant was inclined to think that the 'good case' for 'Bennery' and for not cutting public expenditure has been inadequately covered in the press. It is not easy to get a hearing for certain views. This is claimed for classical theory too. John Low, Deputy Director of the Institute of Economic Affairs, told Ronald Butt (*The Times*, 8 January 1976) that 'What has happened has been a terrible failure of intellectual articulation of the classical argument for the market'. He used to think 'this could largely be explained by the state of the media', but recently 'quite a lot of market analysis is beginning to come through'.

Brittan mentioned the same general point spontaneously – 'the tendency to create a consensus atmosphere with which it is impossible to disagree'. The 'bounds of discourse' – for the heavy press at least – tends to be set by what Civil Servants think is politically possible. Intellectually he feels the bounds are becoming wider; but in relation to practical policy they are narrower.

4 Local Government and Provincial Dailies

4.1 Critiques of Press Coverage of Local Government

This section draws firstly on the evidence of Local Authority officers and associations to the Royal Commission on the Press; and secondly on the fairly recent academic studies of provincial newspapers and local government.

(a) Critiques by Local Government Officers and Associations
NALGO criticises press reporting of local government on several grounds. 'The system of news reporting in the context of newspaper philosophy and funding tends to militate against presenting complex situations and rounded accounts and to encourage simplification for the supposed tastes of readers.' Loaded phrases like 'spendthrift councils' and 'the big spenders' and demands for staffing levels to be 'pruned' creep into 'supposedly factual accounts' of economy measures. Local and national papers alike 'operate on the system of ferreting out the "bad" news story, usually with the Council, or, more often, the officers, as the villains'. Selection and summary are inevitable, but the tendency is that 'a political row in a council meeting will make hot news, pro-rate payers bias will appear when council expenditure is under scrutiny; editorial attitudes will be taken against provision of services'. Sensation and controversy are sought rather than papers 'reporting the bulk of the local decisions that affect the ratepayers and the public'. Some local government officers may have developed 'a general fear in talking to, or giving information to, the press. The result is, in many cases – particularly at local level – mutual mistrust and misunderstanding'. NALGO provides documentation of some of these claims in an example of *Daily Mail* coverage of local affairs.

The Association of Metropolitan Authorities' evidence to the Royal Commission suggests that 'there is only a limited number of journalists with the specialist interest and knowledge now needed to report accurately the complexities of local government affairs'; and that reporting is too often trivial, sensational and unbalanced. It considers there is a 'very definite need' for inclusion in local papers – and not as paid advertisements – of responsible information about 'important public issues'. The evidence includes no illustrations. *The Association of District Councils* takes the same view, so, at less length, does the *County Councils' Association*. The latter acknowledges the great importance of the press to local government in the county areas. The *Greater London Council* notes that in its own area 'what appears to be lacking is the more comprehensive treatment of local government and the more reflective and in-depth journalism associated with good provincial morning papers'. Like the other organisations it feels that local government complexity creates a 'barrier of incomprehension' reinforced by 'piecemeal and superficial coverage of events'.

137

(*b*) *Academic Critiques*
Ian Jackson concludes from his study of provincial evening and weekly papers
(*The Provincial Press and the Community*, Manchester UP 1971) that the four roles
of 'local watchdog, pump primer, booster and reflector' enable papers to
project themselves as 'community conscience, idealist, standard bearer of local
pride and recorder' (p 273). Despite seeing local life as 'a confrontation of the
agencies of community order and disorder', the papers present institutional
leaders 'in their normal, positive roles with much greater frequency than the
popular national dailies' (p 295). Indeed 'the local press attaches great importance to the opinion that community leaders hold of it; these leaders are important as the controllers of much community news, and as key influences of local
attitudes to the newspaper. Typically, the Press cooperates with the institutions
and feels a "sense of responsibility" towards them' (*ibid*). Jackson's content
analysis confirmed the view that 'in general, the tone of watchdog comment
addressed to local councils is equable and circumspect; sternly censorious
leaders appear to be reserved for situations where culpability is both proved
and already in the open. As a rule, editors evidently prefer correspondents to
shoulder much of the burden of direct, uncompromising criticism of the institutions; they claim that this may well be the most effective form of criticism in
any case' (pp 275–6).

Cox and Morgan reach similar conclusions in their study of six Merseyside
papers (H Cox and D Morgan, *City Politics and the Press*, Cambridge UP 1973).
Content 'was largely made up of small snippets from reports and minutes or
heavily personalised accounts of council or committee conflict. Much of it was
highly routine matter, some was essentially trivial'. Papers 'either seemed
unaware of the existence of inherent conflicts and interests between different
groups in the towns, or they chose to report politics as if these did not exist',
and to invoke 'the good of the town' as a touchstone (pp 132–3).

4.2 Local Government: The Perspective of Editors
Section II presents evidence based on interviews with the same group of pro-
vincial editors referred to in the section about the provincial press and
Parliament.

(*a*) *Editors' Attitudes to Local Government*
Provincial editors are certainly very conscious of their papers' closeness to the
local community. 'Step across to the window and we can see our readers . . .'
'We've been here a hundred years . . . reliable . . . trusted . . .' 'We're very
closely read in the community . . .'.

(i) One result of this sense of involvement is *caution*. The editors commonly
contrasted themselves with national papers: 'nationals can come in here and
stir the place up, then leave us to clear up the mess'. You have to be careful,
as 'people may be round at the back door the next day'. 'You can't just
muckrake. You've got to continue to live in the community and demonstrate
your integrity.' In Liverpool an example was quoted to us of a report about
one of the local police forces. Only three copies became available. The national
press homed in after reading a *Liverpool Daily Post* story. But because they
had not actually seen the report (unlike the *Post*) their subsequent stories,
though skilful, seemed to the *Post* irresponsible. One area we visited, the
north-east, has had recent examples of local government corruption. Newspapers picked up plenty of hints and innuendo – but very little they felt was
publishable. The Middlesbrough/Cleveland *Evening Gazette* 'worked hard

138

digging' – several Councillors were questioned by the Fraud Squad (though no charges were made). At the time of the Poulson and Cunningham affairs the Newcastle papers received libel threats. *The Journal* spent at least three months investigating one individual but could only publish four or five stories. The problem was not primarily one of resources but of proof and getting people to go on the record. Even when critical stories were published (eg about the advanced age of the members of a local public utility, alleged in effect to be placemen) no one could do anything. The *Northern Echo* put a reporter onto Cunningham for three years but never wrote anything substantial. It was obvious Cunningham was not living on his income. 'There was plenty of smoke but no fire.' Libel, inevitably, was mentioned everywhere as an inhibiting factor. One editor thought people were 'more willing to have a bash' at a provincial paper, and 'we don't have highpowered legal brains in the office'. (Group papers, however, may have the services of group lawyers.) Another editor, at present in receipt of writs from a head teacher and from a Planning Officer, commented that people in public sector authorities 'run to their professional associations and unions' when criticised.

(ii) Community involvement also encourages 'balance'. Too many provincial papers print stories that are insufficiently documented, an editor in the north-east commented; papers ought to get the views of all sides before publishing. An obvious area is industrial relations. Editors generally said that Unions managed their press relations better than management (whose views often consisted of 'no comment'). Politics is another obvious area. As in parliamentary politics, the papers we saw are reluctant to commit themselves to a party locally. (Being a local monopoly encourages this too.) One editor was worried by the fact that whichever party controlled the Council tended to get '90% of the publicity'. Others had been concerned at the recent elections simply to cope with the enormous number of nominations (435 in the *Gloucester Citizen*'s area). One 'takes note' of the fact that some parties and candidates are more articulate than others.

Caution and balance may also help to account for editors liking to channel controversy into the *correspondence columns*. A typical attitude was that people want to write feature articles but must be invited with care. Their articles are long, boring, lack spontaneity and put in 'too much political claptrap'. Commissioned articles on particular topics are not uncommon – for example by Planning Officers. But regular 'licensed access' does not exist for councillors – apart from the correspondence columns – any more than for MPs.

(iii) One more sign of papers' standing in the community is *editors' attitudes to joining things*. At least one turned down membership of the Rotary Club because there would inevitably be 'pressures'. Most had rules about not attending functions more than two or three times a week. Sometimes they preferred these to be public relations – addressing Women's Institutes, for instance; although some left this activity altogether to a colleague if they could. The big exception to this rule was the editor of the Cleveland *Evening Gazette*. He was extremely careful about maintaining political impartiality but otherwise very active in local affairs. The best example was a campaign called 'Target-Work', launched with a full page one splash in January 1972 when the area had 17,000 unemployed. A committee was set up, including the Mayor, Chairman of the Port Authority, representatives of local industry and Trade Unions. One day a special train took seventeen separate lobbies down to London. The editor

139

stood down as chairman when the initiative was clearly 'getting bigger than the paper': he did not want to risk it being thought a *Gazette* stunt. Twice in eight years, too, he was called in as an arbitrator between management and unions in industrial disputes. In the EEC referendum he organised and chaired a Town Hall Forum. An audience of 100 was expected, but the 1,400-seat hall overflowed. (Arthur Bottomley, a local MP, apparently said it was the best meeting since steel nationalisation in the late 1940s.) The editor was also trustee of a Fund for victims of the Devil's Bridge coach disaster, a road tragedy involving a group of local people.

(iv) *Interest in 'Investigation'*. A sense of responsibility is not of course incompatible with criticism. Several editors, having said they enjoyed a good relationship with local authorities, went straight on to say they were always having rows: 'we're at loggerheads . . .' 'we fight them hammer and tongs . . .'. Their critical stance is necessarily that of an organisation *within* the community. An 'alternative' newspaper in Liverpool naturally, therefore, sees its first object as criticising the Council and its second as criticising the *Daily Post* and *Echo*. Editors accept this situation, but nearly all emphasised a growing interest in 'investigative' or 'background' reporting. The *Sunderland Echo*'s editor – with the group since 1935 – called this 'the big news growth area for local papers'. The *Worcester/Hereford Evening News* editor felt that 'asking questions' is the biggest change in Local Government coverage. Papers used to be keyed in to reporting the local establishment: now they reported 'fewer speeches but more issues'. The *Liverpool Echo* has a penchant for the 'five-part series', saturating a subject (eg the threatened closure of the Shotton steel works) with a series of big features. Only one editor – though subscribing to the 'loggerheads' view – was sceptical about such activities. He thought campaigns could be counter productive; though 'we've had trouble with Planning here', and he took credit for the Council opening a public inquiry (which they thought was their own idea).

Some papers have special staffs for major or 'investigative' stories (not just in local government). On the Newcastle *Evening Chronicle*, for example, one of this team might take on a story from a local government reporter who, say, picked up a rumour; thereby saving the reporters' relationship with his sources. The *Sunderland Echo* features team spent nine months on housing questions and produced sixty or seventy articles. Two of the Features Staff are available for 'instant features' when a news story breaks. The example given to us was the research they did after a child died from glue-sniffing. Generally, however, this interest in investigative journalism seems to represent a change of attitude more than a reorganisation of resources.

The two Liverpool papers gave us a list of topics which the Executive News Editor considered illustrated well their questioning approach to local affairs, and their influence. One example was the decision to abolish the office of Lord Mayor of Liverpool: 'letters cascaded in on us, we ran a public questionnaire and received thousands of replies. Later, the decision was reversed . . .'. The 'car-parking problems are always a fairly emotive subject'. From 1970, the papers 'kept a watchful eye' on all decisions about car-parking charges and gave publicity to proposals which were subsequently reversed. The future of Liverpool airport is another, 'somewhat long-running saga'. The Liberal Council 's ability to cut a penny off the rates in 1975 was 'predicted exclusively'; 'and we have been assiduous in our efforts to keep the council spending programme under continuous scrutiny'.

140

Other examples illustrated the way that the national press follow up local paper stories; (an everyday occurrence on all provincial papers): 'National papers and television . . . followed up our disclosures on the activities of a Liberal councillor, whose activities as a landlord had attracted very adverse comment and who subsequently resigned from Liverpool Council as a result. Again the national press showed a lively interest in a report that the Chairman of the North West Water Authority has spent what we considered to be an unreasonable amount of money on the acquisition of a personalised number plate for his car. Our reports of proposals affecting the closure of certain Mersey ferry services were again followed up. . . . We were well to the fore in our disclosures of the amounts being claimed by members of various councils for expenses, and we provided detailed breakdowns relating to a number of local authorities. Again, there was substantial follow-up. . . . First ventilated in our newspapers was the case of the Kirkby ski slope – a somewhat remarkable scheme to build an artificial ski slope at Kirkby, a deprived community – which had finally to be abandoned after several large sums of public money had been spent on it.'

(b) The Local Government Context

(i) General. The work of local government has tended to ramify, and in recent years it has been complicated by the reorganisation in 1974. Apart from the Councils themselves, other public authorities may have a comparable standing from a paper's point of view. In one area we visited, for example, the local water authority was the subject of much concern because it was actually levying a higher rate than the local council. In the north-east the Coal Board and Shipping authorities loomed large in some towns. Everywhere the work of courts – also recently reorganised – has been increasing. The range of general local government subjects is extremely wide.

(ii) Open Committees. In local authorities themselves, one consequence of reorganisation has been an increase in the number of Council Committees that open their proceedings to the press. In the light of this, the findings of a study made before reorganisation – when fewer committees were open – are very interesting.

Ray Taras (Lanchester Polytechnic) sought to test whether open meetings increased press communication and would be the most effective way of providing a better-informed public. ('Communications and Press Relations in Urban Government', *Policy and Politics*, Vol 1, No 2, December 1972, pp 15–30.) The study involved a nine-months content analysis of local papers and council documents in four towns; over sixty interviews with selected council members, officers and journalists; and a postal questionnaire to all the Council members of the towns concerned (average response rate: 65%). The towns were Bolton and Ipswich, which admitted the press to meetings of most standing committees; and Preston and West Bromwich, which followed only the letter of the 'Thatcher Act' (giving the public a statutory right to attend committees consisting of all members of a Council, plus the Education Committee). Not surprisingly Taras found that 'admission of the press to most committee meetings led to a marked increase in press coverage of council business'. More significantly, open committees made a considerable difference to the *time* at which subjects were reported – and hence to the opportunities for public interest to be expressed before formal Council consideration (and virtually automatic endorsement) of committee decisions. In all the towns except Bolton 'a considerable proportion

141

of important local issues was publicised in the press only on the occasion of the monthly (or in Preston six-weekly) council meeting.... Partially – open committee meetings do not guarantee that major issues will be reported at committee stage. Only if the entire committee meeting is open to the press is it likely that substantive issues will be more public at an early stage in the decision-taking process.'

In Preston and West Bromwich, which did not open their committees, 'the press had to rely more extensively on council agendas and the actual council meetings for its information. The resulting pattern of sporadically available information meant that newspapers could not allocate suitable coverage to all the news items released within the very short time available. The consequence of not having extensive information about council activities publicised, of having substantive issues reported only at the council stage, or of having superficial coverage given to many council matters within a very short time, was that representations by affected interests were impeded.' Large majorities of the questionnaire respondents in Bolton (95%) and Ipswich (77%) agreed with the statement that 'Press attendance at committees has contributed to a greater amount of information reaching the public than before committees were more open'.

Taras' interviews and questionnaire also tested opinions about *alternative* methods of informing the public: for example, council-sponsored publications, press conferences and public meetings; or personal contact between the public and councillors or officers (including PR men). Looking at these various techniques, Taras' conclusion was that 'the most reliable source of information [for the public] remains the committee meetings. In the two authorities we examined which had admitted the press to most committee meetings, this source of information generated more press coverage than any other source, including the monthly council meetings'.

(iii) Load. However gratifying in principle, the openness of committees adds considerably to the burdens of the press – already increased by reorganisation and the load of the courts. Asked what their chief worry was at present, several editors spontaneously mentioned local government coverage. The reasons varied. One said so much of it was 'turgid'. Another has no full-time local government specialist in a town where Council stories are 'strong' (most of the housing is Council owned). But overwhelmingly the main reason was their inability to cover as much as they should. Many found the success of their pressures to get access to Council committee meetings slightly embarrassing: now they felt an obligation to cover them, but they did not really have the resources. Even so, one editor still made a point of publishing all he could about a particular District Council precisely because it continued to close its doors.

The number of possible committees to report can be enormous. The *Sunderland Echo* has to cope with over one hundred, for instance, with 24 of them in Sunderland alone. They take up a substantial part of its manpower. As to the Courts, papers acknowledge an inevitable arbitrariness about which cases end up reported, though they operate rules of thumb. The *Gloucestershire Echo* (Cheltenham) reckons that to cover the courts fully would need at least four reporters full time (its staff is thirty, including photographers). One rule is that nothing less than 'careless driving' is reported. For a company law case that had reached the committal stage a qualified High Court reporter would probably have to be brought in via the group London Office. That general position is typical. 'We carry too much court news anyway, yet it doesn't scratch the surface', said one provincial morning editor. Others said much the same. The *Hereford Weekly Times* has abandoned traffic offences. It concentrates on the Hereford Crown Court and 'dodges about' between the magistrates. It has consciously tried to get away from the old idea of reporting everything (though it does not sound as though there was much option).

Typically, then, editors used phrases like 'more and more concerned', 'more and more of a problem', to describe the scale of local government coverage. The only tendency working in the other direction in some places is the practice of Councils producing their own news sheets or paying for local paper supplements. The *Gloucester Citizen* had recently published a four-page 'annual review' paid for by the County Council. Easily the best example, however, was the monthly four-page supplement published for the local Council by the *Sunderland Echo* – 'so good that we don't always need to cover the same news separately'. The news sheet carries a tab 'Compiled by the Borough of Sunderland' but Portsmouth and Sunderland Newspapers insist on keeping ultimate editorial responsibility. It is distributed in the *Sunderland Echo* and the weekly *Washington Echo* (14,000), the group's free sheet circulating in Washington New Town. The Council distributes some separately too (eg through post offices).

(c) *Arrangements for Local Government coverage.* Some papers have reporters specialising only part-time in local government. With a staff of about thirty (including photographers) the editor of the *Shields Gazette*, not long in the job, was concerned that he did not have a full-time specialist. The *Gloucester Echo*, with a similar size staff, has reporters specialising in Planning and in Education, although doing general reporting too. The editor would like more such semi-specialists – in local authority finance, for instance. The *Gloucester Citizen* also has two part-time specialists (one of whom received a public tribute from the lately retired Chairman of the County Council).

Most of the other papers have a full-time specialist styled 'Municipal Editor' or 'Chief Municipal Correspondent', with a full-time or part-time assistant and the services of reporters out in the districts. In the details, much depends on whether a paper covers a region, like the Liverpool dailies, with their North Wales edition, and the *Newcastle Journal*; or whether circulation area is more compact, as in Cleveland and Shields. The *Worcester/Hereford Evening News* has two full timers, one in each city. In Liverpool, 'one of the key members of our news gathering operation is the Local Government Editor.' He is primarily concerned with Merseyside and has assistance. Another full-time man is based in Wallasey. 'Our local government coverage in other parts of our circulation area is the responsibility of District Staff Reporters located in all the main towns.' Part of the definition of a 'main town' is its local authority importance. There are twenty-five District reporters – covering everything in their areas, not just local government – out of a total reporting staff of sixty-five serving both the *Post* and the *Evening Echo*. In Cleveland, by contrast, the editor judged that at any time there might be about four reporters working on local government stories, of which one, the Municipal Editor (a JP and a journalist of great experience) was a full-time specialist. Similarly in Sunderland three or four reporters concentrate at a time on local government – but they rotate periodically to keep up their experience of other subjects. A separate Features Staff also takes an interest sometimes in local government subjects. In Darlington the *Northern Echo* has one local government specialist in a reporting staff of forty, only six of whom work in Darlington. The specialist is in Teesside and in other towns a reporter 'semi-specialises'.

The two Newcastle dailies, unlike the two in Liverpool, have separate reporting staffs (though they work out of the same offices). Both have Municipal Correspondents, but the *Evening Chronicle* has three (one specialising on Northumberland) to the *Journal*'s one-and-a-bit. As in Liverpool, help is given by the general reporters in District Offices – which are located partly with an eye on local authority offices.

4.3 Conclusions

(*a*) Setting the views of the local authority officers and associations beside the evidence of interviews with editors shows two widely different attitudes towards press coverage of local government. The aspirations implicit in the former seem most implausible beside the resources of the latter. If anything, the attitudes seem likely to diverge further, given the emphasis papers now place on 'investigative' work. Oversimplification and triviality may perhaps decrease, but attacks on 'spendthrift councils' will surely become if anything more frequent not less. Many of the other criticisms refer to more general aspects of the provincial press (ownership, economics) that require more than tinkering to change them.

(*b*) The interviews with editors generally confirm the findings of Jackson and Cox and Morgan about provincial papers projecting themselves as a 'conscience of the community', etc. This attitude is hardly surprising; and it should not conceal the fact that editors certainly see themselves as critics. Their papers are necessarily part of the local institutional establishment; but within their framework they are probably becoming more, not less, critical.

(*c*) Press criticism from *outside* the local establishment, can come from only two sources: '*alternative*' *newspapers*, which no doubt are partly parasitic upon the established press, and the *national newspapers*. The former presumably lack resources and tend to be influential to the extent that their stories get taken up by established papers. The latter can run 'campaigns' (eg against 'waste'), which may give the appearance of victimisation, and the inflation or distortion of issues (*cf* NALGO complaint against the *Daily Mail*); or they may zoom in on a corruption story or something more trivial. ('We're not really interested, apart from duty stories about local government reorganisation', said one senior journalist on a national tabloid, 'unless there's a "Mayor elopes" kind of story.') Nationals can co-ordinate stories too. Papers in several parts of the country clearly had their suspicions about Mr Poulson's activities; but none was in a position to realise how widespread they were.

(*d*) It is worth noting finally, that despite often being near monopolies most editors do believe they are *competing* in the areas we visited – against other morning or evening dailies, weeklies, local radio, TV, nationals – even if competitors are in the same ownership. Economic monopoly, in other words, may not be reflected in journalistic attitudes. It was interesting to learn that the two Newcastle dailies share branch offices but have different staffs in them. They used to have joint staffs, but the reporters preferred to identify with the different personality of a particular paper. In Liverpool there appeared to be no such problem, and the papers do share branch staffs; a fact which perhaps emphasises that the feeling of competition is a matter of psychology.

144

Appendix I
House of Commons' Select Committees as at 1 April 1976

Abortion
Armed Forces Bill
Chairmen's Panel
Consolidation &c, Bills (Joint Committee)
Court of Referees
Cyprus
European Secondary Legislation, &c
   Sub-Committee A
   Sub-Committee B
   Sifting Sub-Committee
Expenditure
   General Sub-Committee
   Defence and External Affairs Sub-Committee
   Environment Sub-Committee
   Trade and Industry Sub-Committee
   Education, Arts and Home Office Sub-Committee
   Social Services and Employment Sub-Committee
House of Commons (Services)
   Accommodation and Administration Sub-Committee
   Broadcasting Sub-Committee
   Catering Sub-Committee
   Library Sub-Committee
Members' Interests
Nationalised Industries
   Sub-Committee A
   Sub-Committee B
   Sub-Committee C
Overseas Development
Parliamentary Commissioner for Administration
Privileges
Public Accounts
Race Relations and Immigration
Science and Technology
   General Purposes Sub-Committee
   Energy Resources Sub-Committee
   Science Sub-Committee
Selection
Standing Orders
Statutory Instruments (Joint Committee)
Statutory Instruments
Unopposed Bills (Panel)
Violence in the Family

Appendix II
House of Commons: Committees Sitting in public: week beginning 8 March 1976

Monday:
a.m.: None
p.m.: Abortion
Science and Technology: Science Sub-Committee

Tuesday:
a.m.: Standing Committee B
Standing Committee D
Standing Committee E
Standing Committee G
Standing Committee H
p.m.: Standing Committee D (Cont)
Nationalised Industries: Sub-Committee A

Wednesday:
a.m.: Standing Committee F
Welsh Grand Committee
Northern Ireland Committee
Expenditure: Trade and Industry Sub-Committee
European Secondary Legislation: Sub-Committee A
Science and Technology: Energy Resources Sub-Committee
Armed Forces Bill
p.m.: Expenditure: Environment Sub-Committee
Science and Technology: Science Sub-Committee
Expenditure: Social Services and Employment Sub-Committee

Thursday:
a.m.: Standing Committee C
Standing Committee D
Standing Committee E
Standing Committee G
Standing Committee H
p.m.: Standing Committee D (Cont)
Race Relations and Immigration

Friday:
None

The decision of a Committee to sit in public may be rescinded without notice and Committees which sit at short notice may not be included in this list.

Appendix III
House of Commons: Select Committees Meeting in public: week beginning 5 April 1976

	Time	Room
Monday 5 April		
ABORTION Witnesses: Representatives of the Church of Scotland	4.00	6
EXPENDITURE: Education, Arts and Home Office Sub-Committee Subject: Priorities and Decision Taking in the DES Witnesses: Department of Employment	3.45	13
Wednesday 7 April		
SCIENCE AND TECHNOLOGY: Science Sub-Committee Subject: Industry and Scientific Research Witness: Lord Bowden	4.00	6
ARMED FORCES BILL Witnesses: Ministry of Defence	11.00	8
EXPENDITURE: Trade and Industry Sub-Committee Subject: Public Expenditure on Chrysler (UK) Ltd Witnesses: Central Policy Review Staff	10.30	16
NATIONALISED INDUSTRIES: Sub-Committee B Subject: British Steel Corporation and the past Witnesses: British Steel Corporation	10.45	6
EUROPEAN SECONDARY LEGISLATION ETC Subject: Hops - Common market organisation Witnesses: Ministry of Agriculture Officials	4.15	5
Thursday 8 April		
RACE RELATIONS AND IMMIGRATION Subject: The West Indian Community Witnesses:	4.00	15

General Inquiries: Committee Office, House of Commons, London SW1A 0AA.

To Secretary of Gallery and of Lobby.

Appendix II

House of Commons: Select Committees
Meeting in public week beginning 5 April
1976

	Time	Room
Monday 5 April		
ABORTION	4.00	6
Witness: Representative of the Church of Scotland		
NEW NATURE: Education, Arts and Home Office Sub-Committee	4.45	15
Subject: Policies and Decision Taking in the DES		
Witness: Department of Employment		
Wednesday 7 April		
SCIENCE AND TECHNOLOGY: Science Sub-Committee	4.00	6
Subject: Industry and Scientific Research		
Witness: Lord Bowden		
ARMED FORCES BILL	11.00	8
Witness: Ministry of Defence		
EXPENDITURE: Trade and Industry Sub-Committee	10.30	16
Subject: Public Expenditure on Chrysler (UK) Ltd		
Witness: Central Policy Review Staff		
NATIONALISED INDUSTRIES: sub-Committee B	10.45	2
Subject: British Steel Corporation and the past		
Witness: British Steel Corporation		
EUROPEAN SECONDARY LEGISLATION ETC	11.15	5
Subject: Hops ... Common market organisation ...		
Witness: Ministry of Agriculture Official		
Thursday 8 April		
RACE RELATIONS AND IMMIGRATION	4.00	15
Subject: The West Indian Community		
Witness:		

General Inquiries: Committee Office, House of Commons,
London SW1A 0AA.
To Secretary of Gallery and of Lobby.

Appendix IV
MPs 'uneasy' over abortion clinic links

By Pat Healy

Social Services Correspondent Pregnancy counselling services should be provided separately from advice services linked to abortion clinics, *two MPs suggested last night in the Commons select committee on abortion.*

Mr Leo Abse, Labour MP for Pontypool, said that disclosures of financial and other links between abortion clinics and pregnancy advisory bureaux underlined committee members' unease.

But Mr N M Hale, an under-secretary at the Department of Health and Social Security, said he did not think there was a categorical case for separating counselling from advice bureaux that had connections with clinics.

'I do not see that a clear case has been made out for saying it is not possible to provide counselling in an unbiased way', he said. 'You can never force a woman to have counselling, just as you can never persuade her to stay in a hospital.'

Sir Bernard Braine, Conservative MP for Essex South East, asked whether the fact that nine women out of ten going to advisory bureaux went on to have abortions did not suggest that the vast majority received advice that led them to have an abortion.

Mr Hale said the committee was talking about women who selected themselves because they started out with a desire for abortion and were therefore highly motivated for it. It did not surprise him that most of them did eventually have an abortion.

The department provided the committee with a paper on the links between bureaux and clinics. That showed financial interests in some cases, and that, in others, people running the advisory bureaux were married to doctors running the clinics. Mr Abse suggested that, in many cases, every time a woman saw an adviser at a bureau and did not go on to have an abortion a financial loss was involved.

Mr Hale agreed. He told the committee that the question was whether the links led to any impropriety. The department would be glad to have any evidence that a woman was being pushed towards an abortion she did not want because of those links. A few did regret having an abortion while others who continued with their pregnancies wished they had not.

Mr Abse said that every time he visited Birmingham he had complaints from the medical profession about one of the nursing homes listed. Mr Hale replied that the department had no evidence to suggest that women were being given counselling that ran counter to what they wanted to decide.

From *The Times* 18 May 1976.

Appendix V

Committee Office

House of Commons
London SW1A 0AA

01-219 3281 (Direct Line)
01-219 3000 (Switchboard)

Expenditure Committee

Environment Sub-Committee

Press release

The Environment Sub-Committee of the House of Commons Expenditure Committee has decided to carry out an enquiry into planning procedures with the following terms of reference:

'To examine, in the light of recent legislation and reports, the system of land use planning and development control in England and Wales in relation to planning applications, appeal procedures and determination, with a view to identifying reasons for delays and the resource costs that such delays create.'

The Sub-Committee will be issuing a number of specific invitations to persons and organisations to give evidence. Those wishing to make a written submission should write to the Clerk to the Environment Sub-Committee, House of Commons, London SW1. It is expected that the enquiry will last until July.

A Sandall
Clerk to the Sub-Committee

5 April 1976

Commons orders inquiry into planning procedures

By our planning reporter

Growing disenchantment with planning procedures and inordinate delays in reaching decisions have prompted the House of Commons Expenditure Committee to set up an inquiry.

Confusion over who is responsible for what, with consequent disputes between councils, is widely regarded as the biggest disadvantage of local government reorganisation. But it will be asked what the committee can hope to discover that was not already made plain in the Dobry report on development control, the main recommendations of which were rejected by the Government last November.

The specific terms of the inquiry will be 'to examine, in the light of recent legislation and reports, the system of land use planning and development control in England and Wales in relation to planning applications, appeal procedures and determination, with a view to identifying reasons for delays and the resource costs that such delays create'.

The inquiry is expected to last until July. Written submissions may be made to the Clerk to the Environment Sub-Committee, House of Commons, London SW1.

From *The Times*, 7 April 1976.

Appendix VI

Letters to the Editor
24 July 1973

Freedom of Parliament and Press

From Mr Harold Wilson, FRS, Labour MP for Huyton

Sir, In your issue of Saturday you quoted my speech at Shildon, Co Durham, on the House of Lords decision in *The Sunday Times* thalidomide case, and its inhibiting effect on the vitally important role of press freedom in matters of public concern.

I said, 'No one will presume to challenge the authority of the House of Lords in their interpretation of the law as it stands. The duty of legislators is to consider whether the law as it stands requires amendment'.

I was speaking in Durham on the issue of corruption in local government but the House of Lords decision raises another consideration, namely the effectiveness of Parliament.

Although Britain has survived for centuries without a written constitution, we have operated conventions designed to make effective and workable the demarcation of duties between the judiciary, the executive and the legislature. For example, the functioning of the courts is protected from parliamentary interference by Parliament's own *sub judice* rules, strictly enforced by the Speaker. Equally Parliament is protected by rules, and, indeed, by the Bill of Rights, ensuring that none of its proceedings can be called in question in the courts. Even the House of Commons itself appeared to be limited in its ability to discuss the thalidomide case until, following a wise ruling of the Speaker, its own select committee on procedure produced a report re-defining the *sub judice* rule so as to enable parliamentary discussion to take place in a manner which did not prejudice the functioning of the courts.

The most recent House of Lords judgment, reversing the decision of the Court of Appeal, means that the emphasis is now tilted in a way that affects, in a sense derogatory to the functioning of Parliament, the separation of powers between the judicial system on the one hand and Parliament, both in its legislative capacity and in its constitutional duty in acting as a check or a goad on the decisions of the executive.

Parliament is hamstrung in its discussions of, and decisions on, matters of public importance if it cannot draw both on the facts and opinions freely published in the press. In 1972, I stressed this argument on the operation of the Industrial Relations Act, following what I and other members of Parliament regarded as a threat to the freedom of the broadcasting authorities and press, namely the communication of warning messages to the media from officers of the National Industrial Relations Court. For the raw material of parliamentary debate is in fact what members read in the press.

The same inhibition would have applied in the thalidomide case, had not the House of Commons, following the select committee report, modified its own *sub judice* rule. In this case, the judicial process had been frozen for 11 years. During those years much has changed, including knowledge of the effects of the drug and the actions taken by other countries and governments, and there had been a significant change in public opinion on these questions, which it is Parliament's duty to reflect.

The fact is that parliamentary questions and debate forced a substantial change in the handling of the thalidomide issue. This is beyond dispute. The serious aspect of the House of Lords judicial decision in the context of the parliamentary decision is this: our debates, and, the ultimate outcome, were inspired and informed by the original article in *The Sunday Times*. Without that article and the facts and arguments it adduced, Parliament would have been inhibited in a way none could attempt to justify so far as the merits of the thalidomide cases are concerned.

The gravity of the House of Lords decision in respect of a further, and still unpublished, article lies in the fact that, had that decision been operative a year ago, *The Sunday Times* article which was published together with supporting evidence could never have appeared. The result would have been that the parliamentary debates, if they had taken place at all, would have been uninformed and lacking in decisive content, and the result which in fact flowed from those debates would never have occurred.

The issue therefore is that this decision, if it is from now on to condition public comment, will not only inhibit the freedom of press comment; it will equally inhibit Parliament in both its legislative functions and in its duty of holding the executive accountable to its authority.

I repeat that it is not for us to question the authority of the House of Lords in construing the law of contempt, or any other law. Accepting the doctrine of the separation of powers, what Parliament cannot accept is that such construction should be allowed to shift the balance of power against its own authority, and the fulfilment of its own duties.

Therefore, if the law is as the Lords have authoritatively stated, Parliament, the legislature, has not only the right but the duty to change it. That task must begin now.

Yours faithfully

Harold Wilson

House of Commons, 23 July

Appendix VII

Middlesbrough/Cleveland *Evening Gazette*

Budget

Tuesday 6 April 1976

Full Box all editions

Edition times

Late Final   (To carry Late Final and Budget seal)   4.10 p.m.
City Late Final (To carry Budget Special seal)   4.25 p.m.

Coverage

Late Final   – Chancellor's statement as lead (last copy at 3.55 p.m.). Follow
                  through with boxing.

City Late Final – Chancellor's statement updated as lead (last copy 4.10 p.m.).
                  Follow through with boxing.

Copy handling

Four copies of 'Flashes' and 'Rushes', one to each as follows:
Lead story   F Grunwell
Headlines   B Croft
Box, Middlesbrough   D Browning
Box, Branches   R Cook (Tight and numbered)
Full report to be held for checking by copy taster who will control copy.
Lead story–catchlined 'Rush'–on Late Final all copy × 2 cols em ES–18pt, 14pt,
12pt, and rest 8pt on 10pt. Crossheads 18 Sancs 1c × 2. Same style for City Late
Final, intro and headlines updated as warranted.
Heads to be sent out on boxes (No pre-set heads).
Contents bill – A Goldsmith

Pre-publicity

Budget Special trailer on Page One, First and Second editions only. Mr J Madden,
Circulation Manager, providing list of newsagents.

Seals

Late Final to carry 'Late Final and Budget' seal.
City Late Final to carry 'Budget Special' seal.
(Both in hands of Mr R Potts, Stereo)
Colour – BLUE.

Tea and sandwiches

Canteen Manageress to provide tea and sandwiches for TEN editorial staff
involved in Budget. To be ready at 3 p.m. in Subs room.

Note

Subs Room *out of bounds* to all personnel other than those directly involved.

***Racing

Boxed results on Late Final and City Late Final to be contained at foot of page.

Back page to be replated for City Late Final to take in 4 p.m., 4.05 p.m. and 4.15 p.m. races.

Ian A Nimmo
Editor

Part B   Section 3

National Daily Papers and the Party System

by Dr Colin Seymour-Ure of the University of Kent

Contents

List of tables

Author's note

This paper aims to define the 'party context' in which the press operates and to suggest why it is important to the Commission's terms of reference.

C K S-U

August 1976

1 Importance of the Party Factor

How far and in what way is party a factor governing the organisation and behaviour of the press? There are three reasons for believing it to be of fundamental importance:

(*a*) Historical connections;

(*b*) Natural affinity between the functions of party as an institution and press as a medium;

(*c*) Key concepts like 'diversity', 'independence', etc, are defined by reference to standards linked to party.

1.1 Historical connections

The press today is governed by commercial considerations. But the shape of the industry, the position of particular papers and the values that govern content are substantially a product of proprietors' attitudes to party over the years since Northcliffe founded the *Daily Mail* in 1896. Perhaps the single most important consequence of Northcliffe was that by attaching newspapers to advertising revenue – selling 'a penny newspaper for a halfpenny' – he freed them from dependence on parties. Associated developments led to the elimination of competing party papers in the provinces.

Northcliffe and Rothermere were not good party men. They did not see their papers primarily as political instruments. Rothermere diversified, and the *Daily Mail* today is therefore 'cushioned'.

Beaverbrook boasted that his papers were primarily a political instrument. He did not diversify, and the *Daily Express* is less well cushioned.

Major Astor bought *The Times* when Northcliffe died in order to protect it from party interests – and put it in the care of a group of non-party figures like the Lord Chief Justice and the President of the Royal Society. By 1967 it was no longer a secure independent economic proposition.

IPC promised on party grounds to keep the *Daily Herald* going for seven years, as a condition of purchasing Odhams in 1962. Had they not done so, there would be no *Sun* today (unless Murdoch had bought, for example, the *Daily Sketch*).

Weetman Pearson, Lord Cowdray, virtually drifted into newspapers as part of a Liberal syndicate. The position of the Westminster Press, lodged in the Cowdray empire, is thus the eventual result of a civil engineer's incidental party enthusiasms.

Wherever political parties and newspapers exist there have tended to be connections between them. The growth of competing parties in 19th century

Europe – in Britain, France, Germany, Russia and Scandinavia, for instance – was widely paralleled by the rise of newspapers supporting them. The same was true in North America. More recently papers have been extremely important to nationalist and revolutionary movements. Lenin's influence before 1917 owed much to his control of the newspaper *Iskra*. Hitler risked overstretching the Nazi party's resources in 1920 to acquire the practically bankrupt *Völkischer Beobachter*, which became the party's central organ. Mussolini's success was built on his editorship of the Socialist paper *Avanti* and his foundation of the *Popolo d'Italia* immediately he left the Socialists. Nationalism in colonial Africa owed much to the enterprise of papers like Dr Azikiwe's *West African Pilot* in Nigeria.

1.2 Affinity between party and press

These historical connections reflect the affinity between the functions of parties and the capabilities of newspapers. For a party at birth a newspaper is an obvious midwife. 'The formation of a party' wrote Lenin, ' – if this party is not properly represented by a well-known newspaper – remains to a significant degree just words.' A paper is an obvious focus of activity and instrument of education.

For established parties the affinity is as great. Parties exist when men combine to seek a common goal. Cooperation requires communication. Newspapers are a highly suitable medium. They are cheap and penetrate communities deeply. They are verbal, and politics is largely a verbal activity. They have a broad range of contents; and parties are potentially concerned (in contrast to pressure groups) with the entire range of a society's problems. The criteria by which parties and papers judge what is important tend, by virtue of their relation to society, to be similar. The same social forces that find expression in a party find expression also through the press. Parties are therefore bound almost by definition to be concerned with, and about, the press.

1.3 The link between party and key concepts like 'diversity'

The historical and natural connections between parties and newspapers mean that the two are linked in theories about the proper role of newspapers in society and in relation to Government. In Britain the view that has found widest acceptance – certainly among newspapers themselves – can be summarised as follows. Political leaders should be responsible to the electorate. Therefore, to quote the 1949 Press Commission, 'democratic society needs a clear and truthful account of events, of their background and causes; a forum for discussion and informal criticism; and a means whereby individuals and groups can express a point of view or advocate a cause'. Efficient performance of those functions requires independence from Government control. Where, then, is the safeguard for the people against irresponsibility and incompetence in the press itself? The traditional answer has been competition: 'The number and variety of papers should be such that the press as a whole gives an opportunity for all important points of view to be effectively presented in terms of the varying standards of taste, political opinion and education among the principal groups of the population' (RCP, 1949). But what on earth is an 'important point of view'? Since the bulk of political argument is carried on round the poles of the parties, any definition that is not circular almost certainly involves using parties as the main criterion of importance.

166

In the matter of public affairs, therefore, 'diversity' is normally taken to mean a range of papers at least as wide as the range of parties. The possibility that one paper might reflect the entire range is not enough. The argument's concern with 'responsibility' means that only an editorial commitment to a party can ensure confidence in that paper's treatment of the party.

While 'diversity' (and thus 'choice') have been linked to party, the customary definition of 'independence' or 'freedom' has been linked to Government. 'A free press' in the liberal democratic sense is free from Government control. Party control, in contrast, may be a positive virtue: who is more secure from Government than Opposition? What happens, however, when a paper's own party is in Government? Here the liberal democratic theory becomes self-contradictory: the virtues of 'freedom' from Government and 'loyalty' to party conflict. Party papers are often uncomfortable when their party is in power; and Governments often cavil at what they perceive as 'disloyalty' by their party papers. (Mr Macmillan's Government suffered considerable criticism from the Conservative press in the early 1960s. So did Mr Wilson's from Labour papers in the late 1960s.)

Which is more important – a 'diverse' press representing 'all important points of view', some of which will be represented in Government? Or a 'free' press, opposed to Government and thus not reflecting fully the Government party view? Those are the extremes, and opinions about the right amount of diversity veer between them. At present the tendency in the press is against close party identification and towards a persistent anti-Government stance.

There is no corpus of literature constituting a 'theory of the press' in Britain. (A reflection of the fact is the frequency with which those quotations from the 1949 Commission are invoked.) In ephemeral discussion, the theory outlined above, which is rooted in a nineteenth century liberal democratic view of the constitution, is as strong or as weak as that view itself. At the moment press 'freedom' is increasingly construed instead by reference to centres of 'real' social and economic power rather than constitutional abstractions. On the one hand the press is seen as the prisoner of capitalist conglomerates (many of them multi-nationals). On the other, it is seen as threatened by the monopoly power of organised labour – for example in the Labour Government's 'closed shop' legislation.

2 Present Connections between Press and Parties

The risk of labouring the obvious when discussing press/party connections is reduced when one considers the variety of forms connection can take. Different forms may give one a different view of 'diversity' and 'independence'. Possible forms include:

(a) Balance between the *number* of papers and the number of parties;

(b) Balance between the *total circulations* and the total vote for each party;

(c) *Ownership or control* of individual papers by parties;

(d) *Editorial loyalty* to a party's goals;

(e) *Fair and balanced reporting* of a party;

(f) *Party membership or support by journalists*;

(g) Party support by a *paper's readers*.

2.1 Balance between the number of papers and the number of parties

The Labour Party probably had this criterion in mind when it stated in its written evidence to the Royal Commission that 'Most of the national and regional and local press are well to the right' and referred to 'marked political imbalance'. The criterion is implicit also in Sir Denis Hamilton's 1976 Haldane Memorial Lecture (Report: Appendix I).

Table I shows the party support of national dailies at general elections since 1945. The obvious consistent Conservative dominance, notwithstanding the decline in the overall number of papers, requires qualification.

From 1966 fewer papers have been willing to commit themselves. Previously only *The Guardian* had ever declined to come off the fence. But from 1966 onwards *The Times* has always divided its loyalty, and in October 1974 coalition fever struck the *Daily Mail* and *The Sun*.

Divided loyalty is distinct from switching loyalty between one election and the next. Four papers have done this:

The Times: went Con in 1950, ambiguous in 1966 and Con/Lib in 1970.

The Sun: from Lab to Con in February 1974 and to all-party coalition in October 1974.

Daily Mail: from Con to Con/Lib in October 1974.

The Guardian: from Lib to Con/Lib in 1951; to Lab/Lib in 1959; to Lab in 1964; to Lab/Lib in 1966, to Con/Lab/Lib balance in February 1974; to 'more Lib influence on governing party' in October 1974. (Only twice in the last seven elections has *The Guardian* voted the same way – 1966 and 1970.)

Table I

Party Support of National Dailies: General Elections 1945–74

	1945	1950	1951	1955	1959	1964	1966	1970	1974(1)	1974(2)
Con	4 D Express D Mail D Sketch D Telegraph	5 D Express D Mail D Sketch* D Telegraph Times	5½ D Express D Mail D Sketch* D Telegraph (Guardian)	5½ D Express D Mail D Sketch D Telegraph (Guardian)	5 D Express D Mail D Sketch D Telegraph Times	5 D Express D Mail D Sketch D Telegraph Times	4 D Express D Mail D Sketch D Telegraph	4½ D Express D Mail D Sketch D Telegraph (Times)	4½ D Express D Mail — D Telegraph (Times) Sun	2½ + ½ D Express (D Mail) — D Telegraph (Times)
Lab	3 D Herald D Mirror Times	2 D Herald D Mirror	2 D Herald D Mirror	2 D Herald D Mirror	2½ D Herald D Mirror (Guardian)	3 Sun D Mirror Guardian	2½ Sun D Mirror (Guardian)	2½ Sun D Mirror (Guardian)	1 D Mirror	1 D Mirror
Lib	2 Guardian News Chronicle	2 Guardian News Chronicle	1½ (Guardian) News Chronicle	1½ (Guardian) News Chronicle	1½ (Guardian) News Chronicle	—	½ + ½ (Guardian) (Times)	½ + ½ (Guardian) (Times)	½ (Times)	½ + ½ + ½ (Guardian) (Times)
							Times preference unclear between Con & Lab		Con/Lab/Lib balance: Guardian	(D.Mail) All-Party Coalition: Sun
Comm	1 Morning Star†	1 Morning Star†	1 Morning Star†	1 Morning Star†	1 Morning Star†	1 Morning Star†	1 Morning Star†	1 Morning Star	1 Morning Star	1 Morning Star
Total	10	10	10	10	10	9	9	9	8	8

*Named *Daily Graphic* at this period. †Named *Daily Worker* until 1967.

170

Taking *switching* and *divided loyalty* together, the picture is of decreasing party commitment in the last decade. The only *consistently loyal* papers since 1945 have been:

Con: *The Daily Telegraph*
    Daily Express
    [*Daily Mail*]
Lab: *Daily Mirror*
Comm: *Morning Star*

(The *Daily Mail*'s Con/Lib stance in October 1974 was manifestly a reaction to party flux and a device to avoid a Labour Government. The loyalty of the *Daily Express*, of course, has not always been welcome to the party establishment – notably in the 1960s over Europe.)

The Liberals have not done as badly as might be supposed. Only once, in 1964, have they been without editorial support at all. Otherwise they have never had the support in whole or part of less than two papers. Their real problem is that since the death of the *News Chronicle* in 1960 they have never had the support of a popular (apart from the *Mail*'s tactical support in October 1974). A characteristic view was that of *The Sun* in February 1974: 'If it wasn't an election, we'd all vote Liberal'.

In this very general sense, then, the national dailies do 'parallel' the party system, although there are 'too many' Conservative papers.

2.2 Balance between total circulation and total vote for each party

Table II shows the total circulation and vote for the major parties in general elections since 1945, plus the circulation of papers individually. The general picture is not so much that Labour and Liberals have done extremely badly as that Conservatives do 'too well'. Moreover the imbalance has got far worse since 1959.

Labour circulation has been more than the Labour percentage of the vote only in 1970 (just). It has been close (2–5%) since 1964, apart from the coalition fever election of October 1974. The big discrepancies were in 1945 and 1951, largely because the *Daily Mirror*'s circulation was proportionately much smaller then.

Liberals, until the loss of the *News Chronicle*, had much 'too big' a circulation. Clearly very many *News Chronicle* readers cannot have been voting Liberal in the 1950s: the paper's circulation was twice the total party vote in 1951 and 1955. Between 1959 and 1974 they were badly out of line.

Conservatives have had anything like the right proportion of circulation only in 1951 and 1955. Since 1964 they have normally had one-third too much and, in February 1974, nearly three-quarters.

Although these aggregates make useful symbols and debating points (see Appendix II for a TV discussion between William Rees-Mogg and Harold Wilson), their crudity is obvious. Readers do not all support their paper's partisanship; many people read more than one paper; page traffic figures suggest that much political content is not widely read at all. Moreover the wide range between the smallest and largest newspapers makes the calculation

171

Table II

Newspaper Partisanship and Circulations, and Party Votes in General Elections, 1945–1974

Newspaper	Circulation in thousands; Party support									
	1945	1950	1951	1955	1959	1964	1966	1970	Feb 1974	Oct 1974
Daily Express …	3,300 Con	4,099 Con	4,169 Con	4,036 Con	4,053 Con	4,190 Con	3,954 Con	3,607 Con	3,227 Con	3,081 Con
Daily Herald/The Sun[1] …	1,850 Lab	2,030 Lab	2,003 Lab	1,759 Lab	1,465 Lab	1,300?* Lab	1,248 Lab	1,509 Lab	3,303 Con	3,457 All-Pty Coalition
Daily Mail …	1,704 Con	2,215 Con	2,267 Con	2,068 Con	2,071 Con	2,400 Con	2,381 Con	1,916 Con	1,768 Con	1,738 Con-Lib Coalition
Daily Mirror …	2,400 Lab	4,603 Lab	4,514 Lab	4,725 Lab	4,497 Lab	5,085 Lab	5,077 Lab	4,697 Lab	4,192 Lab	4,218 Lab
Daily Sketch/Daily Graphic[2] …	896 Con	777 Con	794 Lab	950 Con	1,156 Con	847 Con	849 Lab	839 Con	—	—
The Daily Telegraph …	813 Con	984 Con	998 Con	1,055 Con	1,181 Con	1,324 Con	1,354 Con	1,402 Con	1,427 Con	1,385 Con
The (Manchester) Guardian[3] …	83 Lib	141 Lib	139 Lib/Con	156 Lib/Con	183 Lab/Lib	278 Lab	283 Lab/Lib	303 Lab/Lib	365 Con/Lab/Lib Balance	354 More Lib Influence
News Chronicle[4] …	1,549 Lib	1,525 Lib†	1,507 Lib	1,253 Lib	1,207 Lib	—	—	—	—	—
The Times …	204 Lab	258 Con	232 Con	222 Con	254 Con	255 Con	273 ?/Lib	402 Con/Lib	351 Con/Lib	340 Con-Lib Coalition
Total circulation …	12,799	16,632	16,623	16,224	16,067	15,679	15,419	14,642	14,633	14,573
Total Conservative circulation …	6,713 (52%)	8,333 (50%)	8,599† (52%)	8,487† (52%)	8,715 (54%)	9,016 (57%)	8,538 (55%)	8,133† (55%)	10,441 (71%)	6,898† (47%)
Total Conservative vote …	9,578 (40%)	12,503 (43%)	13,718 (48%)	13,312 (50%)	13,750 (49%)	12,001 (43%)	11,418 (42%)	13,145 (46%)	11,872 (38%)	10,465 (36%)

172

Total Labour circulation...	...	4,454 (35%)	6,633 (40%)	6,517 (39%)	6,484 (40%)	6,145† (38%)	6,663 (42%)	6,608† (43%)	6,509† (44%)	4,557† (31%)	4,572† (31%)
Total Labour vote	...	11,633 (48%)	13,267 (46%)	13,949 (49%)	12,405 (46%)	12,216 (44%)	12,206 (44%)	13,065 (48%)	12,178 (43%)	11,646 (37%)	11,457 (39%)
Total Liberal circulation	...	1,632 (13%)	1,666 (10%)	1,646† (10%)	1,409† (9%)	1,390† (9%)	—	556† (4%)	705† (5%)	716† (5%)	2,432† (17%)
Total Liberal vote	...	2,197 (9%)	2,622 (9%)	731 (2%)	722 (3%)	1,639 (6%)	3,093 (11%)	2,327 (8%)	2,117 (7%)	6,059 (19%)	5,347 (18%)

[1] Name changed to *The Sun* in 1964.
[2] Named *Daily Graphic*, 1946–52.
[3] 'Manchester' dropped from title in 1959.
[4] Ceased publication in 1960.
* Figure uncertain due to relaunching at that time.
† Includes paper(s) with divided support, but omits *The Sun* in October 1974.

Source of circulation figures: 1945, 1950: Nuffield election studies; thereafter, Audit Bureau of Circulation, excepting *The Daily Telegraph* figures for 1951, 1955, 1959 (London Press Exchange). Circulation figures are for the period of the year in which the election was held.

The *Daily Worker*, the Communist daily paper, which changed its name to the *Morning Star* in 1966, is omitted: comparable circulation figures are not available. The number of Communist candidates at general elections was as often as not under fifty.

open to massive swings. *The Sun*, which has vacillated, is now sufficiently large by itself to turn a Labour 'underrepresentation' into a substantial overrepresentation, or to skew the Conservative bias still further.

2.3 Number of papers, circulation size and class of readership

Aggregate circulations and the number of papers both gain more point in a party context if account is taken of the classes of readership. Table III bears on the question 'what *effective* choice of party papers confronts the reader?' given that the class distribution of readership confirms that for most people heavy and popular papers are not real alternatives. It is important to note too – what is substantiable – that readers do not go out and look for a paper, in or out of an election campaign, in search of one supporting their views. They are loyal, rather, to a particular paper which presents them with its party opinion.

The higher you go up the socio-economic scale, Table III shows, the greater the effective range of papers available. Although two Conservative papers (*Daily Express* and *The Daily Telegraph*) between them have the ear of more than half the Registrar-General's A B classes (13% of the population aged 15+) the A B readers are quite widely spread. (As many of these 'top people', for instance, read the *Daily Mirror* as *The Times*.) The very width of spread, however, means that if you were in this category the chances of your paper putting a non-Conservative point of view in 1974 were very low. It is likely, of course, that the same factors which make most A B people vote Conservative make them tend to read Conservative papers, though there is little evidence of direct causal connection between readers' partisanship and their choice of paper. From the parties' standpoint, however, Labour has very little opportunity of reaching the A B classes through a Labour paper.

At the other end of the spectrum, the two-thirds of the electorate in the C2 DE categories have an *effective* choice of only four papers (though only about 10% in fact choose the *Daily Mail*). The circulation of the *Daily Mirror* in February 1974 was not enough to counteract the combined circulation of the papers recommending a Conservative vote. From the Labour Party standpoint again, there is a much greater chance that people in these categories will find themselves presented with a Conservative paper than a Labour one – and in a situation where the political attitude of papers is not an important factor in the competition between them. *The Conservative Party thus has much greater access to those whom Labour thinks of as its natural supporters than does Labour to the natural Conservatives.* The position is not altered by bringing the remaining category, C1 (22% of the population) into the calculation. As for Liberals, the restriction of their support in February 1974 to *The Times* and *The Guardian* – exclusive in neither case – meant that the two-thirds of the electorate for whom those papers are not really in the market had no chance at all of being exposed to a Liberal supporter.

A different view of 'diversity' is gained by separating the heavy and popular markets and looking at the papers' shares of each. One paper, the Conservative *Daily Telegraph*, dominates the heavies much more than the Labour *Daily Mirror* dominates the populars. Again, the significance of this, it may be thought, is greater if one bears in mind that *The Daily Telegraph*'s brand of conservatism is *incidental* to its readers. They do not choose the paper deliberately in order to get it.

Table III
Newspaper Readership and Social Class, 1974

% reading

	Daily Mirror	Sun	Daily Express	Daily Mail	Daily Telegraph	The Times	The Guardian	Financial Times	Total
AB (13% of population aged 15+)	12	9	23	16	30	12	10	9	121
C1 (22%)	26	23	26	17	14	4	5	3	118
C2 (33%)	42	39	21	11	4	1	1	1	120
DE (31%)	36	33	19	9	3	1	1	—	102
Heavy Papers	—	—	—	—	52	18	18	13	—
Popular Papers	34	31	22	13	—	—	—	—	—

Source: JICNARS, Jan–Dec 1974
Note: Percentages are inflated by duplicate readership.

175

All the figures in the table include *duplicate readership*: the percentages add up to as much as 121. One in five of the electorate (outside the DE category) is thus exposed to the political attitudes of at least two daily papers. JICNARS duplication tables show cross-reading not only between similar papers (nearly half *The Sun* readers also see the *Daily Mirror*) but between heavies and populars. Eighteen per cent of *Daily Telegraph* readers see the *Daily Mirror* too, and the same proportion see *The Sun*. About a quarter of *The Times* and *The Guardian* readers see the *Daily Mirror*. Ninety-two per cent of *Financial Times* readers also see another paper. Duplication is thus quite often with a paper of an alternative political colour.

Table IV considers again, in this context of stratified readership, the critical importance of big circulations and especially of the position of *The Sun*. The table shows the distribution of different classes of readers between papers supporting the various parties in February 1974. In brackets are the figures that would have applied if *The Sun* had voted Labour not Conservative. Instead of an overwhelming Conservative dominance there would have been an even greater Labour dominance for the two-thirds of the electorate in the C2DE categories. For the other third, the switch would not have involved nearly enough readers to swing the balance away from the Conservatives. The same scale of change would apply if the *Daily Mirror* switched parties. But a *Sun* switch is more likely, both because it has already vacillated and because its readership, being four-fifths lower middle and working class, makes it a 'natural' Labour paper – notwithstanding its lack of roots in the Labour movement. If *The Sun* did go reliably Labour and the *Daily Mail/Express* combined or continued to shrink, the Conservative choice among populars could become almost as small as the radical choice among heavies.

2.4 Ownership or control of papers by parties

'Party control' could mean anything from formal ownership of a paper by a party (common, for example, in Scandinavia and among Communist Parties everywhere) to informal sympathy between owners and party leaders.

The classic example of a party-owned paper in recent times was the *Daily Herald* (1912–64). George Lansbury founded it in 1912 on a capital of £300 and relied much on voluntary support. (G K Chesterton left the *Daily News* to work for it unpaid. Osbert Sitwell wrote leaders, occasionally in verse.) The paper frequently attacked the party leadership and tried to finance its own parliamentary candidates. It survived the First World War only as a weekly. In 1919 Ernest Bevin, who had been looking round for a paper and had sought unsuccessfully to acquire *The People*, became a director. He tried at first to seek regular financial support through an arrangement with the parliamentary committee of the TUC. In 1922 the National Executive Committee of the Labour Party and the TUC agreed to take the paper over officially. Sales rose steadily (from 200,000 in 1923 to 363,000 by the General Strike), but only once, in the first six months of 1924, was a profit made. By 1929 the TUC had sunk over half a million pounds into the paper, and Congress voted to enter an arrangement with J S Elias of Odhams. Odhams took 51 per cent of the shares, leaving the TUC with 49 per cent (and four directors against five).

Only for the brief period 1922–29, therefore, was the *Daily Herald* fully owned and controlled by the Labour Party. But although Elias' methods were aggressively commercial – he was the instigator of the 'free gifts' circulation war in

176

the early 'thirties – the paper did not shift far along the axis towards the pole of independence. For the TUC directors were the only ones allowed to vote on political policy. The paper's line was to be that laid down at the Annual Labour Party Conference: hence in 1931 it stuck with the Party, not with MacDonald, Thomas and Snowden. Until some years after 1945 the editor attended the regular meetings of the Parliamentary Labour Party at Westminster; and he had to answer criticisms of the paper at a private session of the Annual Conference.

The *Daily Herald* thus retained a formal organisational connection with the Labour Party. But Odhams' financial control meant that when massive losses put the paper's future in question in the early 1960s the party could do virtually nothing. Odhams was taken over by the Mirror Group in 1962. The possibility that the Conservative Roy Thomson might buy the paper – he was known to aspire to a national daily – naturally alarmed Labour leaders greatly. On the other hand it was by no means clear at first that the Mirror Group would keep the paper going – certainly for more than a year or two. Eventually, to clinch the success of their bid and secure the approval of the TUC, the *Daily Mirror* gave a public pledge never to amalgamate the *Herald* with the *Mirror*, and to run the *Herald* for a minimum of seven years. Relaunched as *The Sun* in 1964 it continued to lose heavily until sold to Rupert Murdoch in 1969.

Another paper which until its closure in 1967 was controlled by an organisation affiliated to the Labour Party was *Reynolds' News* (1850; renamed *Sunday Citizen* in 1962). This belonged for some thirty years to the Co-operative Press, which was registered as a Co-operative Society and controlled by the Co-operative movement. At the time of its closure its circulation had dropped to 220,000 (from 720,000 in 1947).

Table IV

Distribution of readers between party papers, February 1974, by Social Class (If *The Sun* were Labour, in brackets)

			Conservative papers*	Labour papers	Liberal papers*	Uncommitted
A B	...	...	...	99 (90)	12 (21)	12	10
C 1	...	...	...	87 (64)	26 (49)	4	5
C 2	...	...	...	77 (38)	42 (81)	1	1
D E	...	...	...	65 (32)	36 (69)	1	1

Source: JICNARS, January to December 1974.
*Includes papers with divided loyalties.
Includes Duplicate readership.

The only national daily now surviving with such close organisational links to a party is the *Morning Star*. This goes back to the *Sunday Worker*, founded in 1925. It was converted into a daily on 1 January 1930, partly as a protest against the 'betrayal' of the *Daily Herald* to the capitalist Odhams Group. The paper attracted little advertising and from the start called regularly on its readers for financial help. (This totalled £9,000 in the first two years.) But it achieved a circulation of 100,000 by 1939 – 150,000 on Saturdays – against a wholesalers' boycott that lasted until 1942 and made distribution difficult. I have not found the exact relationship to the Communist Party easy to discover.

177

But the editor at the start of the 1970s, George Matthews, was Assistant General Secretary of the Party before he joined the paper. The paper changed its name in 1967.

Ownership or control of papers by individual politicians has also declined. The big change is that at present controllers do not see their papers as the instrument of their own personal political advancement. No politician is rich enough to do what Lloyd George did when he felt the weakness of his party base towards the end of the First World War. He simply bought the *Daily Chronicle* – easily the largest circulation Liberal daily – and put in a reliable editor. Of the three ex-Cabinet Ministers to become editors in recent years, two – Richard Crossman and William Deedes – did so in retirement. The third, Iain Macleod, returned from the *Spectator* to the Cabinet in a new administration under the new leader. It is accidental that the heirs of Beaverbrook and Rothermere have not sought party or parliamentary careers.

If control of papers by individual party politicians has ceased, I believe it is equally true that there are no examples of papers controlled by persons supporting parties other than those supported in their papers.

The position of papers which have tried to institutionalise a political viewpoint while remaining independent of party is worth noting. *The Guardian* trust was established in 1936 to safeguard the paper against forced sale to pay off death duties or against takeover bids; and it enjoined the trustees to run the paper 'on the same lines and in the same spirit as heretofore'. *Guardian* men seem to have no difficulty in knowing what that means. After buying *The Times*, Lord Thomson retained a vestige of the Astor arrangement of five wise men by making four of the eleven directors 'national directors' charged to preserve the paper's commercial and editorial freedom. The Monopolies Commission thought this was 'window-dressing' (HC 273, 1966, pp. 39–40).

2.5 Editorial loyalty to party goals

Leader column loyalty to party is difficult to generalise about. In broad terms it has been treated in previous sections. Two further aspects are worth exploring. Firstly, *The Times* has traditionally valued principles above party – going further than *The Guardian*, whose commitment is limited to radicalism. Secondly, one may ask whether leader column loyalty has changed in ways affecting the Royal Commission's terms of reference.

'*The Times* idea', as William Rees-Mogg described it in an interview in 1969, 'is of an impartial, independent, comprehensive newspaper . . . an idea of immense value to society. [It] gives society something against which it can check what is going on, and [to] rely on.' Essential to this idea is the notion of balance. Partly this implies broad, comprehensive coverage of national and international affairs. In formal political contests, like elections and parliamentary debates, it involves an obligation to give a balanced coverage of the views and activities of all sides. It even justifies the letters column – quite literally the only forum where all branches of the social, political and economic Establishment meet. The notion of balance, further, attributes rationality to the reader and assumes it in the paper. Unless readers have an overall view of news and opinions they cannot judge events for themselves. If they adopt the paper's own judgments, it should be through force of argument not biased presentation: better that readers should disagree than reach agreement for the wrong reasons. ('I don't want to carry them along with us because we just sort of persuade them against their better judgment', said Mr Rees-Mogg.) The paper's views therefore must themselves reflect a rational process of deliberation, to which considerations of party advantage are inappropriate.

The Times has not always lived up to this ideal. The argument that for a 'real' understanding of what Britain is like historians have to turn to the popular press points up the limited 'public affairs' arena to which '*The Times* idea' applies. (Crime was one subject, for example, in which *The Times* in the 1950s was weak.) Within that arena it has had notable lapses in recent history, the best example being its attitude to appeasement. The charge in the paper's own official History is that *The Times* became too committed to appeasement; the Editor, Geoffrey Dawson, behaved like a Statesman instead of a journalist. Governments necessarily have to take account of the ballot box and there was some excuse for their feeling they could not carry the country towards war in the mid-thirties. *The Times*, however, had no excuse. It should not have cared what people thought – and it should have been better informed anyway. *The Times* History blames Dawson for not staffing the paper so that it had a 'specialist with a complete understanding of European and World politics than a Prime Minister and Foreign Secretary'. This is an extraordinary claim, if it is meant to embrace the resources of the Foreign Office too. It sees *The Times* as the only British political institution untrammelled by considerations intrinsically irrelevant to the merits of those questions the nation has to decide; and therefore uniquely qualified to point the proper path. In the 19th century, when the sphere and resources of the Government were much less, it may have made sense. How much can it make sense today?

It is worth considering '*The Times* idea' in detail because it represents the extreme case of the argument that what matters most in the press is independence from government rather than a diverse reflection of the party system. Is it still a practical idea, in point of resources, to make the paper as well informed as Government itself? Apart from that, the continuation of the idea is well illustrated in *The Times*' late preoccupation – predictably distasteful to the parties, especially Labour – with a realignment of the centre-left in British politics. No party paper could have pursued that particular logic from its premises. If Fleet Street shrinks, will it be tolerable that perhaps the only remaining heavy daily should behave like that? Or, alternatively, that it should not be able to do so?

The second question is how far leader-column loyalty in the press generally has changed in ways affecting the Royal Commission's terms of reference. This is most easily considered at the same time as the question of 'fair and balanced reporting'.

2.6 'Fair and Balanced' reporting

What is fair and balanced reporting? Papers can often meet criticism on one criterion by invoking another.

An excellent example of the range of plausible criteria was the Common Market referendum in June 1975. Most appealing to anti-Marketeers was the idea of *balance as equality* – fifty-fifty coverage. The *Daily Express* could feel virtuous in making the main element of its feature coverage six guest articles – three by Pros and three by Antis. Mr Ian Mikardo was using this criterion too when he complained that although the Referendum Act made public funds available to both umbrella organisations, the Pros would have millions of pounds extra from private contributions.

Balance could alternatively mean *coverage proportionate to the strength of the rival sides*. In this case the Pros could fairly enjoy an advantage because of the fact that Britain was already a member of the Community and the majority of well-known politicians were in favour.

A further refinement could see *balance as proportionate to the 'output' of the campaigners*. This again justified greater coverage for the pro-Marketeers. They had a large staff. 'Editors organising the reporting of the debate point nervously from a comprehensive pile of advance texts of the pros' speeches on the one hand, to a couple of pre-releases from the antis on the other.' (*Financial Times*, 30 May 1975.)

Following the earlier sections, balance could mean *the same number of papers supporting each side*. In fact, of course, only the *Morning Star* among national dailies supported the anti-Marketeers. The largest circulation anti-Market journal (certainly outside Scotland) was the TGWU *Record* (regular circulation about 300,000).

Deciding what to include in the arithmetic complicates the problem of balance further. The boundaries of the referendum, like those of an election campaign, were a matter of argument. For example the *Daily Mirror* published a series of articles three weeks before polling day that equalled all its explicit campaign features put together. Called 'Hello, Germany!', the series' aim was to 'examine life -- German style', with a look at Denmark and the low countries along the way. The material had the most tenuous connection with the pros and cons of the referendum debate. But it was presented under the question 'Will their future be our future?' and thus was arguably linked implicitly to the campaign. To an anti-Marketeer it must have seemed straight pro-Market propaganda. A pro-Marketeer might have regarded it as neutral.

To anti-Marketeers on the Left the press coverage could not be *fair* even if it was in some sense *balanced*. Newspaper proprietors, to quote Mr Benn, 'reflect the economic interests which find the Common Market attractive'. They would inevitably look at the subject through capitalist spectacles.

Unfairness might result also from *press coverage that was explicitly on one side implicitly favouring another*. In the referendum there was widespread belief, backed up by opinion poll evidence, that coverage of Mr Benn harmed his own side. In various elections, Mr Hogg and particularly Mr Powell have been considered in some quarters doubtful assets to their own party. Churchill blamed Beaverbrook's campaign efforts for the scale of the Conservative defeat in 1945.

An associated source of unfairness is in *the choices papers necessarily make about which stories to highlight*. Their priorities may not coincide with the parties'. In the referendum, for example, the Antis evidently felt that some of their biggest points – for example about the other side's attitude to political union – never got proper treatment.

Added to that is the perennial crude distinction between 'issues' and 'personalities'. Sometimes politicians want to stress the former, sometimes the latter (specially if they want a 'quiet campaign'). In the referendum, Mr Benn claimed that the press 'are seeking to make this campaign a campaign about personalities and about the Labour Party'. The Antis wanted to stress the 'issues'.

Finally there is unfairness in the sense of *wilful distortion and inaccuracy*, which is difficult to prove.

The simplest thing to measure is quantitative balance. For general elections since 1966 I have measured the contents of the national dailies according to the same criteria. The results – for *reportage* only – are summarised in Table V. *This shows that papers have consistently given more space to the party they support editorially.* The *Sun*, the only popular to shift its support significantly, switched the balance of its coverage in line with its switch of support. The *Daily Express* and *Daily Mail* gave Labour more coverage than Conservatives in October 1974, but much of it was knocking copy. On these figures the Liberals have done quite well. Even in the populars they had at least as much space as their proportion of the vote until 1974. The figures for the heavies were swollen by their practice of printing the Liberal manifesto in full. Only in *The Guardian* was the Liberal proportion of the poll in the 1974 elections equalled by the party's coverage.

There is a little evidence in Table V to suggest that papers generally tend to give more space to the Government party in elections. It was true – and would be characteristic – of *The Times* in all four elections. It was also true of the Murdoch *Sun* (ie omitting 1966). The Labour bias (in this sense) of the *Daily Mirror* was rather less in the election called by the Heath Government; and the *Daily Mail* and *Daily Express*, as has been noted, did give Labour more attention in October 1974, even if some of it was attention the party could have done without.

In this limited, quantitative context, then, coverage has not usually been balanced either in a fifty-fifty or in a proportionate sense – though there have been a few exceptions.

In an attempt to assess trends in 'qualitative' partisanship I have been back over the ten Nuffield College election studies since 1945. In a longer perspective they can be set beside the extremely thorough study by Professor Neal Blewett of the 1910 elections in his book *The Peers, the Parties and the People* (London, Macmillan, 1972). Blewett was able to line up seven metropolitan morning papers and four evenings on the Unionist side, against three mornings and two evenings for the Liberals. (The *Daily Mirror*, already with the second largest circulation – but a very different audience from today's – was Independent.) The party imbalance of numbers was reflected in total circulation: 2·3 millions for the Unionists; 1·3 millions for the Liberals. This gave the Liberals 30% of the circulation compared with 43% of the vote. These papers were not as completely national then as now: even as late as 1935 well under half the families in the North-East, for example, were yet taking a national daily. But there were still 45 provincial mornings and 15 towns with two or more mornings competing against each other, sometimes on party lines. Blewett quotes a contemporary comment on the 1910 elections: 'The daily newspapers have ceased to be retailers of news – they are merely mammoth political pamphlets of the most violent partisan type.' It would be quite wrong, however, to picture a happy coincidence of press and party strategies. Factionalism in the Unionist Party on the important question of tariff reform was reflected unevenly. Liaison between party headquarters and the Unionist press was poor. Blewett is emphatic that the press 'altered profoundly the course of the debate' rather

181

than amplifying the priorities of party leaders. This was due not least to Northcliffe, who followed a characteristically individualistic course. Most significantly, given the general partisanship, there was no paper putting the Labour case. The Movement could not manage to organise and finance a daily evening paper for so much as the four weeks of the campaign.

By 1945 the various types of party bias and unfairness had declined a lot from 1910. In the thirty years since then partisanship has continued to change in ways and for reasons that may include the following.

(a) *Increasingly sophisticated journalistic analysis* of the electoral process, with adoption of appropriate concepts – 'swing', 'marginals', 'image', etc – and fewer assumptions about the 'rational' basis of voting behaviour.

(b) *Virtual disappearance of stunts* intended to frighten voters away from a party. The classic example remains the 1924 Zinoviev Letter published by the *Daily Mail*. The best post war examples were the *Daily Mirror*'s 'Whose Finger on the Trigger?' theme in 1951, and the *Daily Express*' attacks on 'Gauleiter Laski' in 1945. ('We had an election weapon as good as the Zinoviev Letter', wrote Arthur Christiansen. ' . . . It was all-in wrestling, hand-to-hand fighting, commando stuff. . . .')

(c) *Greater willingness to play a balancing game*; a good example being the habit of inviting opposing leaders to contribute articles and interviews in the same paper. In 1945 there was only one article actually by a Conservative leader (Beaverbrook apart) even in the Conservative press. The habit was started by the *Daily Mail*, *Daily Mirror* and *News Chronicle* in 1955. Papers have more often gone through an exercise of weighing the issues before declaring their position. 'First the Inquest – Then the Verdict' was the *Daily Mirror* theme in 1966.

(d) *Decline of 'official' loyalty*. The demise of the *Daily Herald* was the key event here. Its party role is nicely symbolised by the fact that it organised a great Labour election rally in the Albert Hall (in 1945, at least; I do not know about later). The 1950 Nuffield study comments: '. . . the *Herald* judged its news by the test of whether it could help the party.' Was there any paper of which that could be said in 1974 – for any party (except, perhaps, the *Morning Star*)?

(e) *Need to come to terms with opinion polls*. Polls provided 11% of election headlines in the national dailies in 1966, 25% in 1970, 18% in February 1974, 7% in October 1974. Papers often found themselves headlining a poll showing a clear lead for a party they opposed. 'For all the good that it has done Mr Wilson's critics it seems that the General Election campaign need not have taken place' *The Daily Telegraph* commented gloomily in 1966, faced with a massive, steady Labour lead in its gallup poll. Papers had to gear their approach to independent estimates of the electorate's mood instead of to the kind of wishful thinking that lay behind the *Daily Express* Set-the-People-Free campaign in 1945.

(f) *Implications of growth in election broadcasting*. The structure of British broadcasting has continued to impose its rigorous, essentially quantitative concepts of party balance since the enormous growth of election broadcasting after 1959 (the first year when there was *any* election broadcasting apart from the parties' own broadcasts – the news included). The consequences have been

Table V

Distribution of Space between Parties in General Election, 1966–74

		Party Support	Conservative %	Col ins	Labour %	Col ins	Liberal %	Col ins
Daily Mirror	1966	Lab	33	294	59	519	8	68
	1970	Lab	35	506	58	854	7	106
	1974(1)	Lab	41	786	49	950	10	196
	1974(2)	Lab	34	442	59	776	7	91
Daily Express	1966	Con	59	775	33	431	7	96
	1970	Con	49	527	42	455	9	94
	1974(1)	Con	43	536	42	516	15	188
	1974(2)	Con	34	561	54	887	12	198
Daily Mail	1966	Con	61	528	33	287	6	53
	1970	Con	50	449	38	345	12	112
	1974(1)	Con	49	818	33	539	18	296
	1974(2)	Con/Lib coalition	39	528	54	731	8	106
The Sun	1966	Lab	44	576	42	553	13	176
	1970	Lab	37	681	47	860	16	299
	1974(1)	Con	49	870	36	641	14	248
	1974(2)	All Party coalition	39	523	53	700	8	108
Daily Sketch	1966	Con	51	434	38	321	11	95
	1970	Con	51	546	40	424	9	98
	—	—	—	—	—	—	—	—
	—	—	—	—	—	—	—	—
The Daily Telegraph	1966	Con	52	1,199	31	708	18	408
	1970	Con	53	1,000	36	688	11	200
	1974(1)	Con	54	1,131	34	725	12	249
	1974(2)	Con	49	799	40	647	11	179
The Guardian	1966	Lab/Lib	29	788	43	1,163	28	760
	1970	Lab/Lib	45	1,288	40	1,157	15	421
	1974(1)	Con/Lab/Lib balance	40	1,508	40	1,513	19	729
	1974(2)	More Lib influence	35	1,275	45	1,649	20	713
The Times	1966	Lib?	40	508	47	606	13	173
	1970	Con/Lib	42	1,233	51	1,504	6	185
	1974(1)	Con/Lib	43	1,519	39	1,370	18	629
	1974(2)	Con/Lib coalition	40	985	46	1,121	14	336

Notes:

Minor parties excluded. These never received more than 2% of total election coverage. The figures refer to reports of speeches, manifestos, press conferences, etc. They *exclude*, for example, leaders, feature articles, letters, gossip columns.

The period covered is the three weeks of each campaign, ie 18 weekdays. In 1970 a strike reduced coverage to 16 days.

Source: Data collected for Nuffield College election studies.

complex both for the style and substance of electioneering. Arguably it is a bit more difficult – or just less sensible – for papers to paint a party in lurid colours if its readers are going to see the party's leaders on TV every night. Could Bevan have been such a hate-figure to the Conservative press in a TV age? Benn and Powell have been hate-figures, so the possibility remains. But have they been such crudely depicted hate-figures?

Newspaper partisanship is also dependent on the strength of the parties' own differences. In retrospect the 1950s and 1960s may seem to have been a time when these were muted. Certainly the 1974 elections saw a more partisan approach to electioneering – for example, in the *Daily Mirror* – than in recent elections. Tabloid techniques of selection and presentation recalled the early 1950s. Apart from the absence of a paper like the *Herald* directly controlled by a party, the structural conditions for a general recurrence continue to exist. Many of the tendencies listed above are 'reversible'.

2.7 Party Support by Journalists

The most thorough attempt to measure the party support of journalists was Jeremy Tunstall's survey of 295 specialist correspondents in 1968[1]. One hundred and seventy-nine provided an estimate of their own politics in relation to the politics of their news organisation. One hundred and seventy stated their current voting intention and their vote in the 1966 election.

Tunstall felt the most important finding was that four out of five specialists were either in broad agreement with their news organisation or only 'somewhat' to the left or right. Of the remainder five times as many were 'well to the left' as 'well to the right'. On Labour papers,[2] only one respondent out of forty-eight felt himself 'well to the left' of his organisation. On Conservative papers the ratio was about one in four. Tunstall explains the avoidance of 'extreme incompatibility' by the possibility that (a) a specialist may disagree with his paper's politics but support its policy in his field (eg Football); (b) papers choose some 'deviants' in consideration of 'balance' or good relations with certain kinds of news source; (c) news values tend to override political values; (d) specialists arrive with their eyes open.

On voting intentions the specialists divided as follows:

Equally balanced (ie distributed roughly proportionate to the electoral strength of the parties): Foreign, Lobby, Aviation, Football.

Strongly Labour: Education, Labour.

Strongly Conservative: Crime, Fashion, Motoring.

Tunstall comments: 'These clear cut differences immediately point away from news organisation control and focus attention on particular fields and the relevant news sources.' The mainly trade union news sources in the Labour field, for instance, 'probably attract journalists of similar Labour Party loyalty'.[3]

Overall, Tunstall concludes: 'News organisations are not concerned to force their politics on individual specialists. The specialists in turn are able to preserve much tactical autonomy – including the production of news stories few of which are sharply in contrast with their own political views'.[4]

1 Tunstall. *Journalists at Work*, Constable 1971.
2 Defined as: *The Guardian, The Observer, Daily Mirror, The Sun, The People, Sunday Mirror, Morning Star.*
3 *Op cit* p 124.
4 *Idem* p 125.

Politics and journalism are so entwined that there have always been plenty of journalists standing for Parliament. (At the general election of 1906, to quote a random case, no less than three senior *Daily News* staff found themselves elected Liberal MPs.) Table VI shows the number of journalists standing for each major party at elections since 1945. Labour has shown no really significant shifts since 1950: the number has fluctuated between 40 and 50. Conservatives have generally fielded fewer; but there has been a consistent increase since 1951, and in both 1974 elections Conservatives in fact fielded one more than Labour.

Table VI

Journalists as Parliamentary Candidates 1945–74

Election Year				Conservative	Labour	Liberal
1945[1]	...	...	...	...	27	18	?
1950	...	...	...	...	34[2]	40	14 (475)
1951	...	...	...	...	26	50	?
1955	...	...	...	...	33	57	?
1959	...	...	...	...	33	50	20 (216)
1964	...	...	...	...	35	48	31 (365)
1966	...	...	...	...	36	43	22 (311)
1970	...	...	...	...	40	47	25 (343)
1974(1)	...	...	...	...	46	45	33 (517)
1974(2)	...	...	...	...	48	47	30 (619)

Sources: Nuffield College election studies.
Notes: Conservatives and Labour have always contested nearly all seats.
The Liberal total of candidates is given in brackets.
Nuffield data for Liberals is incomplete before 1955.
The definition of 'journalist' has been standard since 1955.
[1] 'Writers, Journalists, Authors'. Excludes women candidates.
[2] Includes five directors of newspapers.

2.8 Party support by readers

Readers generally support the same party as their newsaper. This is not surprising and is therefore not something opinion pollsters continually test. The latest data NOP could give me referred to October 1970. However, one of their associated companies, MORI, was able to show me data for October 1975. Both lots are shown in Table VII, with 1967 for comparison. Except when *The Sun* has been Conservative, no paper has had a majority of its readers supporting a party different from the paper's own preference. But only the *Financial Times* has had as many as three-quarters of its readers 'loyal'. The main difference in 1975 from 1970 is due to the increase of Liberal support. Both *The Times* and *The Guardian* had about as many Liberal as Labour readers in 1975, and *The Daily Telegraph* had substantially more. In each case Labour easily outnumbered Liberals in 1967 and 1970.

These figures are not a simple index of the popularity of party points of view, like the Top Twenty. Many readers, for instance, do not have a strong sense of the partisanship of their paper at all. In 1963 Butler and Stokes found[1] that only half their sample, if that, named the party support of their paper correctly

---

1 David Butler and Donald Stokes, *Political Change in Britain*, Macmillan 1969.

(apart from *The Daily Telegraph* and *Daily Herald* – three-quarters). Well over a third of readers thought their paper was neutral. Their evidence suggested, further, that 'newspapers often profit from, rather than shape, their readers' party ties'. People pick up partisanship from their family and match it by their choice of paper – or the family passes on 'a more general social location to which both paper and party are appropriate'. The press thus helps to conserve more than to create party alignments. Non-supporters of a paper's party, Butler and Stokes found, tended to move towards that party at a higher rate than supporters moved away from it.

Surveys of readers' interests generally rank party politics low. But the extent to which the press is seen as involved with the party system is highlighted by the contrast with TV. A survey by Jay Blumler in the October 1974 election found TV easily the 'best medium'. But whereas TV scored highest on the neutral points of 'judging what the leaders are like' and 'helping me make up my mind how to vote', the press did best relatively on the partisan points – 'To use as ammunition in argument with others' and 'To remind me of my party's strong points'. (Even on these two last points, over 50% thought TV the best medium and only about 20% preferred the press.)

Does the party skew of the press matter less because most readers do not care much about it? or more? Certainly it means that editors can present a point of view to audiences who are not particularly alert to its nuances – or, perhaps, to the assumptions on which it rests.

Table VII
Party Support of Daily Newspaper Readers: Percentages in 1975 (1970 and 1967 in brackets)

Party Support	General Labour support by paper				General Conservative support by paper				
	The Sun*	Daily Mirror	The Guardian	Daily Sketch	Daily Express	The Times	Daily Mail	The Daily Telegraph	Financial Times
Con	23 (22;8)	27 (27;28)	33 (28;30)	— (52;53)	58 (54;47)	47 (52;53)	55 (62;56)	70 (65;67)	79 (72;70)
Lab	59 (60;69)	57 (56;53)	33 (52;36)	— (36;31)	26 (33;33)	22 (22;29)	26 (28;29)	10 (20;16)	— (11;11)
Lib	13 (7;7)	12 (8;9)	29 (15;19)	— (5;7)	12 (5;10)	24 (11;8)	16 (3;8)	18 (7;10)	15 (11;9)

Source: NOP, July 1967, October 1970; MORI, September 1975.
Labour lead approx. 2% on each occasion.
* *The Sun* supported Conservatives in 1974 (Feb) and Coalition in 1974 (Oct).

3 The Historical Context

3.1 General changes in the press since 1900

The ideas discussed in Section I about the proper relationship between press, parties and government were well developed by 1896, the year of the *Daily Mail*'s foundation. Between then and 1945, by which time the present pattern of the press was settled, there were four trends with important party implications.

(a) Decline in the number of provincial mornings

Table VIII shows a drop from 53 in 1890 to 18 in 1970. Evening papers, less vulnerable to London competition, dropped only from 81 to 75. In 1900 17 towns had two or more morning papers. Already by 1930 that number was down to eight.

Table VIII

Provincial Daily Papers (England, Scotland and Wales) 1890–1970

				Morning	Evening	Towns with two or more Morning Papers
1890	...	...	...	...	53	81	?
1900	...	...	...	...	52	?	17
1910	...	...	...	...	45	?	15
1920	...	...	...	...	45	89 (?)	15
1930	...	...	...	...	32	82	8
1940	...	...	...	...	25	76	7 (1938)
1950	...	...	...	...	25	76	4 (1948)
1960	...	...	...	...	19	74	1
1970	...	...	...	...	18	75	1

Sources: RCP, 1949, 1962; Press Council Annual Reports; Butler & Freeman, *British Political Facts.*

(b) Growth of chains

This was a complicated episode, linking provincials with each other and with the nationals. In 1921 5 out of 41 provincial mornings belonged to chains. By 1939 10 out of the diminished number of 25 did so – mainly to the Berrys or the Westminster Press. Forty per cent of the provincial evenings were in chains by 1934, and half the Sundays and London mornings. The Berrys' division of family holdings in the later 1930s reduced the totals somewhat.

(c) Loss of provincial circulations (Table IX)

Figures are unreliable before 1920; and the loss since 1939 has been only relative. Between the Wars the London mornings doubled their circulation in the process of becoming national papers. By contrast the London evenings remained static and the provincials dropped. Separate figures for provincial mornings are particularly scarce. It seems probable that their total circulation

189

was at least half that of the London mornings in 1920. Twenty years later (and since) it was down to one-seventh. Individual circulations – and competition – were affected drastically by price changes. *The Daily Telegraph*, while it cost twopence, dwindled from 180,000 in 1918 to 90,000 in 1929 but then shot to 175,000 in a year upon reduction to one penny. This was not untypical.

(d) *Rapid decline of the London evening papers*

In 1900 there were almost as many of these (9) as of the morning papers (10) and they paralleled the party system exactly. When W W Astor bought the *Pall Mall Gazette* and turned it overnight from a Liberal into a Unionist paper George Newnes simply founded the *Westminster Gazette* for the displaced editor, J A Spender. By the mid-1920s only the *Star, Evening News* and *Evening Standard* remained.

Overall, the press changed from a large number of metropolitan morning and evening papers and a very large number of provincial morning and evening papers, to a small number of national morning papers and a small number of provincial morning and evening papers.

Table IX

Daily Press: Total Circulations, 1920–47

	Metropolitan		Provincial	
	Morning ('000)	Evening ('000)	Morning & Evening ('000)	Total ('000)
1920	5,430	1,940	7,300	14,670
1925	7,440	1,980	7,080	16,500
1930	8,650	2,030	7,270	17,950
1935	9,390	1,830	6,960	18,180
1939	10,570	1,900	6,990	19,460
1947	15,560	3,500	9,500	28,560

Sources: N Kaldor and R Silverman, *A Statistical Analysis of Advertising Expenditure and of the Revenue of the Press*; RCP 1949.

3.2 Reduction of 'diversity'

(a) *Party competition in the provincial press decreased.* A P Wadsworth, looking back from 1955, remarked: 'The party political spirit was less keen than it had been when every large town had to have its Tory and its Liberal papers who fought and scratched each other like the papers of Eatanswill.'

(b) There was *less scope for the expression of regional particularism.* There might be a greater choice among national dailies than there had been among provincials in a given city. But national papers were mainly interested in national politics, including at election times.

(c) At the metropolitan level the decline in numbers between the Wars *reduced the opportunity for the reflection of nuances of debate about policy and personalities within the parties.* Tables X and XI show the consolidation respectively of the Conservative evening press and the Liberal daily press. The latter, of course, represented a 'response' to the decline of the Liberal Party. It was eventually matched to some extent by the growth of the *Daily Herald* in the 1930s, by the transformation of the *Daily Mirror* after the J Walter Thomson report in 1935, and by the modest success of the *Daily Worker*. (The 'lag' in Labour press growth meant the Party's first government faced overwhelming newspaper hostility – much greater than anything since.)

3.3 Loss of party control/ownership

What did political parties do with their money – often obtained in return for Honours – before the First World War? A J P Taylor tells us Lord Beaverbrook's files reveal that one thing was to spend it on papers. 'The subsidy was disguised in the form of investment in the paper's shares by some individual, who had himself to be a man of substance so as to make the transaction plausible; and the individual usually added some genuine investment of his own.' *The Observer*, *Standard*, *Globe* and *Pall Mall Gazette* were all receiving Unionist money – 'sometimes as much as £10,000 a year'. When Beaverbrook bought the *Globe* in 1911 for £40,000, £15,000 came from his own pocket and the rest from party funds. On the Liberal side, families like the Cadburys, Rowntrees and Colmans ran papers in the party interest without regard to profitability. Weetman Pearson spent three-quarters of a million pounds keeping the *Westminster Gazette* going as a morning paper from 1921–28. By 1929 the TUC had sunk half-a-million into the *Daily Herald* and seen a profit only once, in the first six months of 1924.

Table X

Consolidation of the Conservative Metropolitan Evening Press

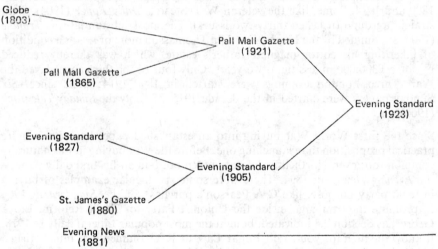

Table XI

Consolidation of the Liberal Metropolitan Press

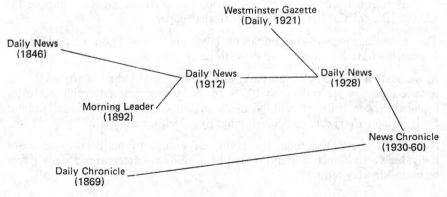

191

In the 1930s all this stopped. The *Herald* was being made profitable by J S Elias of Odhams – using aggressive salesmanship that had nothing to do with partisanship (not to mention socialism). Despite a plea to Neville Chamberlain the *Morning Post*, rescued by a Conservative syndicate in 1924, found no backers when it tottered again in 1937. (Its circulation was said to decrease each day by the number of deaths reported in its columns; and no cause was said to be entirely lost until the *Post* took it up.) No Liberals saved the *Daily Chronicle* in 1930: it merged with the *Daily News*. In 1934 the editor, Aylmer Vallance, was said to be thinking of 'a combination and understanding with the *Herald* on a progressive policy'.

Subsidy in a party interest – and particularly *by* parties, seems to have stopped by the outbreak of World War II.

3.4 Decline in 'responsiveness' of the press to changes in the party system

Apart from the *Daily Worker/Morning Star* no new national daily has been founded since 1912 – though *The Guardian* (provincial) and *Financial Times* (specialised) have turned themselves into nationals. Before 1912 new papers were commonplace. Thirteen metropolitan mornings were launched between 1890 and 1914. Some, like the veteran W T Stead's *Daily Paper* (1904), went straight aground (it lasted thirty-two issues). The most substantial was *Tribune* (1906–8), founded by the Liberal Franklin Thomasson more or less as a condition of inheriting his cotton-magnate father's estate, which was thereby reduced by some £300,000 in less than two years. Only four of the thirteen survived the War. Three London evenings were started in 1890–1914: none since. Six Sunday papers were started in the decade 1915–25: only the *Sunday Telegraph* (1961) since.

Since the First World War buying into an established paper has been a more practical proposition than launching one. Before the War buying in was naturally common too: even Northcliffe did not launch but bought his first daily paper – the *Evening News* – in 1894. There were some spectacular examples of buying in for a party purpose, like C A Pearson's purchase of the *Standard* in 1904 to promote the campaign inside the Unionist Party for Tariff Reform. Lloyd George, as Section 2.4 indicated, bought the most popular Liberal daily in 1918. 'I know the man for you', said Bonar Law to R D Blumenfeld, impoverished controller of the *Daily Express* in 1910. 'Max Aitken is enormously rich. He knows nothing about newspapers and is not interested in them. But he wants to have a big political career, and he'll be glad of a paper which will back him.' Blumenfeld dashed to Monte Carlo, where Aitken signed a cheque for £25,000, the start of his association with that paper.

The spectacular post-1945 examples of 'buying in' – Roy Thomson and Rupert Murdoch – have had nothing to do with party politics.

Movements like Mosley's New Party and the National Labour Party could not finance a daily paper in the early 1930s. Instead they promoted weeklies. Mosley founded *Action*, with Harold Nicolson in the Chair. The National Labour Party bought *Everyman*, a bookish magazine. Neither did well.

Already by the 1930s, then, the ability of groups of politicians – let alone individuals – to launch a grand design or a political career with a daily paper was considerably reduced.

3.5 Declining concern of papers with politics

To sell the *Daily Mail* Northcliffe had needed advertising revenue. He also needed profits: the paper had shareholders expecting a dividend. Competition for readers became damaging only when the market was saturated and they had to be won by poaching from other papers in the same readership group. The costs of competition then rose. The formation of the chains in some cases involved grossly inflated capitalisation: to get a return, big profits and therefore higher circulations were necessary. All these pressures tended to 'depoliticise' the popular press. Readers were won partly by a low price and partly by the extraordinary insurance and free gift wars of the late 'twenties and early 'thirties. A whole Welsh family, it was rumoured, could be clothed for the price of eight weeks reading of the *Daily Express*. At one point the *Economist* estimated that 56% of gross profits were spent on such promotions. The selling point was the free gift; the newspaper was the wrapping. Readers were also attracted by the much wider range of contents typical of the *Daily Mail*, with a premium on brightness and entertainment.

The popular press thus developed a broad social function rather than a narrowly political one. Editors became technicians like Arthur Christiansen, not trenchant political essayists. Had he and his like been put in charge of a really popular paper, the 'quality' editor J A Spender admitted in 1927, they 'could have been relied upon to kill it in about a fortnight.' 'With a few notable exceptions,' the *Economist* remarked in 1928, 'the British Press consists no longer of "organs of opinion".' 'The largest circulations develop an opportunist politics of their own which cuts across the schemes of all parties', J A Spender wrote sourly. 'Their allegiances and their loyalties are quite temporary, and the politician who claims their support is liable to a swift reminder that the newspaper has more important things to think about.'

Large circulation and wide ranging content were not necessarily incompatible with close party affiliation, as the example of the *Daily Herald* showed. But they tended to work against it. The most spontaneously successful paper in the late '30s and '40s, the *Daily Mirror*, confirmed the tendency. Its expansion into the working class, the last great market, was achieved by exactly the methods of the *Daily Mail*'s expansion into the lower middle class 40 years earlier – with the same stress on a range of values and interests geared to entertainment, but without the need for high-pressure salesmanship since it did not rely on poaching readers.

3.6 The press barons and the parties

In the 'depoliticised' papers partisanship became precarious and therefore unpredictable. To politicians and to journalists like Spender, used to a party press, the 'press barons' were irresponsible. Spender grumbled that they had 'a power which was a serious rival to Parliament, and upon which in the last resort Parliament depends' – yet for which they were responsible to no one. Lloyd George wrote of Northcliffe: 'He owed no allegiance to any party, so that every genuine party man deplored his paper. Most of them bought it and read what was in it and then damned it.' Baldwin, in the most famous jibe of all, talked of their 'power without responsibility – the prerogative of the harlot throughout the ages'. The press barons could not be bought. They were untrammelled by party machinery and the fine adjustments of concerted policy.

Not all proprietors had political ambitions – though that was disconcertingly fortuitous, from the parties' point of view. The havoc that resulted if they did is best illustrated by the initiatives of Beaverbrook and Rothermere between the Wars. Not only did they detach their papers from the established parties. They used them as the instrument of new ones, a substitute or nucleus for new party organisations. The Communist Party hoped, obviously, to grow with the *Daily Worker*, and Mosley's New Party with *Action*. But in those cases movement and paper would grow together. The press barons, in contrast, already possessed an instrument linking themselves to the millions of their readers. It had won them on a non-political basis; now it was turned to the construction of a movement like the Empire Crusade which had no spontaneity and was built from the top downwards. The barons' political style was populist. Leaders of established institutions – in Parliament, party and the old press – saw them as a threat. They had no geographical, social or economic constituency. Their constituency was a disorganised mass of readers, from whom they claimed to draw strength and legitimacy but to whom they were not really responsible at all. The definition of mass opinion was effectively the barons' own. Their leadership ignored intermediaries and was free from the restraints of collective membership. Their instrument, with its new style of journalism and wide ranging contents, was ideal for preaching a populist gospel – for assertion more than argument, for the prescription of simple, comprehensive remedies. ('I have made up my mind that I am for Empire Free Trade', wrote Beaverbrook during his Empire Crusade in 1930. 'No damned economists are going to put me off.') Even the national circulation of the papers gave their political movements an appearance of national importance. The Empire Crusade is the best illustration of Beaverbrook's and Rothermere's 'disruption' of the party system, since they sponsored parliamentary candidates against their natural allies, the Conservatives, in pursuit of the goal of the Empire as a single economic unit protected by a tariff wall. To Gwynne of the *Morning Post* Beaverbrook wrote: 'I want Empire Free Trade. I don't care if it comes from one party or another. If no party gives it, I am for trying to take it from the public.' When Baldwin remained obdurate, the barons cut loose – and Rothermere issued his tactically disastrous demand to be told the names of 8 or 10 of Baldwin's proposed colleagues in the next Ministry as a prior condition of journalistic support. An Empire candidate beat the official Conservative in one by-election but lost the key St George's, Westminster, by-election in March 1931. This was regarded as the test case of Baldwin's leadership of the Conservative Party. With the economic crisis and the National Government the movement was eclipsed.

In party terms the press barons were at best tiresome, needing to be coddled like one more interest group; at worst, a menace. Above all they were unpredictable – perhaps pursuing a principle, perhaps a personal ambition, or perhaps just existing. (John Astor was teased by his relations for owning *The Times* but not actually reading it.)

Newspaper owners are in the same position today. It is accidental that there is no Beaverbrook or Rothermere.

4 Parties and the Press: Some Implications

The present party-press position described in Section 2 has the following implications, one may argue – especially in the light of the changes sketched in Section 3.

4.1 Parties – in Opposition and in Government – can no longer 'command' any of the press. This situation poses a threat:

(*a*) *To the parties.* Newspapers used to be the clients of the parties: now parties are the clients of the press. Owners paid handsomely for peerages: now peerages are thrust upon them. (By his own account, Cecil King seems to have been offered a peerage five times during the first Wilson administration.) Parties now have to cajole and threaten where once they could be sure that at least some of the press would see things their way. Mr Attlee knew that the *Daily Herald* was preaching party orthodoxy, Albert Hall rallies and all. Mr Wilson simply had to hope that the *Daily Mirror* would. The fact that there is no simple causal connection between press partisanship and readers' voting behaviour in no way reduces party frustrations.

(*b*) *To the press.* If newspapers are not 'responsible' to parties, as Baldwin and Lloyd George would have it, their own foundations as public institutions are less secure. The narrower the diversity of papers, the more is their right to deviate from political orthodoxy open to challenge. They may defend it consistently but the premises from which they start carry less conviction. *The Times*' flirtation in recent years with a realignment of the centre-left (eg its support of Dick Taverne) is in the traditions of '*The Times* idea'. But it surely suffers from being judged in the context of the international Thomson conglomerate. The paper is not a disinterested observer but is beholden for six-figure subsidies to an organisation with direct economic interests in the outcome of policy. The crude argument that electorates are gulled by mass media gains greatly when media and the institutions of mass politics are dislocated.

(*c*) *To the Constitution.* The British Constitution depends on party for public acceptance. Through the great legitimising ritual of general elections, party determines the majority in Parliament on which the authority of the Cabinet rests. Through Ministers, the non-elected Civil Service is held formally responsible to Parliament. How well can this system survive in an age of universal suffrage if the parties do not have opportunities to project policies and leaders as they themselves wish? This is not, in my view, a question of academic interest but of basic, practical, immediate importance.

4.2 These threats seem more serious when other factors are considered

(*a*) *Parties have progressively lost control over broadcasting.* Section 2.6 mentioned briefly the growth since 1959 of political programmes beyond the control of the parties. Some Labour politicians used to take comfort in the fact that though the press might be disproportionately Conservative, at least broadcasting was balanced. This is true no longer. No doubt broadcasters are not wilfully biased. But the simple fact of deciding their own programme content allows for the possibility, in the extreme, of a projection of party policies and leaders that might run entirely counter to the parties' own views. After screening a discussion on the EEC during the 1966 election, one BBC producer explained to an observer: 'What we've achieved today is to smoke them out – to get them to participate in the programme on an issue they were unwilling to see dealt with.' For party leaders struggling to implement a campaign strategy, such freedom in the broadcasters has been a major and frustrating development in electioneering.

(b) *'Biases' implicit in news values*. The situation was difficult enough for the parties anyway. To a considerable extent the contents of the press – and now broadcasting – *are* 'the national campaign' in a general election, and they skew it in particular directions. Studying the elections since 1945, one is struck how often the Government party has wanted a 'quiet election'. Yet newspapers dislike quiet elections. Parties have sometimes wanted a 'men not measures' election. Newspapers like personalities – lively, colourful people like George Brown, Quintin Hogg, Enoch Powell, having lively, colourful arguments. But they like the arguments to be about *issues* – the clearer, simpler and fresher, the better. Above all, issues should be 'real' – ie consistent with the papers' own views of political priorities. Parties' ability to influence the choice of 'issues' has always been severely limited by the impact of chance remarks (Churchill's 'Gestapo' smear in 1945; George Brown's '3% mortgages' in 1964) and by the even less predictable connections between the election and independent, spontaneous news stories (eg about strikes).

Those tendencies are the product of media news values – they were observable in the *Daily Herald* in the heyday of its Labour loyalty. They make the projection of a party's self-image that much less controllable.

(c) *The political content of the press is 'at risk'*. Politics was the staple of many 19th century dailies. In the 'depoliticised' press, politics not only rates fairly low among readers but it is one of the subjects which surely costs much more to include than it earns.

(d) *Attacks on the 'capitalist press'*. The blurring of newspaper partisanship has paradoxically made the whole press more vulnerable to attack for being biased to 'capitalism' and the 'status quo' – especially at a time when so many papers are kept alive by the profits of other activities and when the rhetoric of party argument has shifted to the left. The argument of the official *Labour Year Book* fifty years ago has quite a modern ring: at least in pre-1914 days, a report on the press remarked in 1925, 'the falsehoods and misrepresentations of one party were promptly exposed and refuted in the national organs of another'. Now there was no such balance; and the right-wing press was not even loyally and consistently Conservative but under 'purely capitalistic control'. 'Capitalist' newspapers are not just anti-socialist, in other words: they are anti-party and unaccountable.

(e) *Development of an 'anti-Government' ethic?* The dislocation of the press and the parties is exacerbated by the spread of an anti-Government ethic – a reaction, perhaps, to 'big government', unsuccessful economic steering, demands for 'participation', the fashion for 'investigative journalism' and so on. On one line of argument developed in Section 1 this may seem splendid – the growth of a long standing tradition. But if it spreads to virtually the entire press – and it has spread to broadcasting too – it puts up yet another barrier against the party in Government conveying its perspective on events. (The 'capitalist' connection presumably increases the frustration that Labour Governments must feel.) Scrabbling at the foxholes of bureaucratic incompetence is one thing. A general assumption that Government is wrong until proved right, inept unless demonstrably efficient, perhaps threatens the system as well as particular ills.

(f) *Inadequate response?* Could a revival like the Liberals' in 1974 (20% of the vote), or the Celtic Nationalists', have taken place in 1900 without a daily paper being launched or purchased by a syndicate? Newspaper economics make it impossible now. Moreover, the fewer the surviving papers, the less likely it is that any will respond. In a diverse party press, factionalism is possible – if not unavoidable. (*The Times* Centre-Party flirtation was rather different, given '*The Times* idea'. This was not an open, dance-floor affair, a normal event at the party ball. It was the intrusion of a gatecrasher who normally claimed to dislike such things.)

4.3 Change in parties

Party itself, of course, has not been a constant during the changes since 1900. Apart from the rise and fall of particular parties, it may be that the period of mass-based party organisations is ending: one political effect of TV in many countries seems to be the elimination of intermediaries between representatives and electors. Perhaps our political system is relying more on interest groups for functions party used to perform – or perhaps those functions have lapsed altogether.

This paper is certainly not intended to imply that the press and the parties should necessarily be put back together somehow. (The idea could be explored in various ways. For example, the TGWU recommended to Lord Houghton's Committee on the financing of political parties that the Government should help the parties to run national weekly newspapers, starting with £250,000 a year; and that general and local election party broadsheets should also be publicly financed.) But the values by which the Commission's report will be judged contain a 'party element' that goes beyond mere prejudices – and that was defined when press and party system were closer than they are now. The present economic structure of the press makes it vulnerable to attack as fundamentally irresponsible, however much in its day-to-day activities it may be careful, honest and disinterested.

Appendix I
Sir D Hamilton's Haldane Lecture

(*The Times*, Wednesday, 4 February 1976)

Chairman of The Times *suggests TUC newspaper*

Left wing 'needs voice in the press'

By a Staff Reporter

Sir Denis Hamilton, chairman and Editor-in-Chief of Times Newspapers, said yesterday that the left did not have a clear enough voice in the national press. There was a gap at the point where there ought to be serious coverage of the news from a left-wing standpoint.

Giving the 1976 Haldane Memorial Lecture at Birkbeck College, London University, Sir Denis said that in political terms the ideas of the *Tribune* group did not get the sympathetic treatment that the ideas of the Monday Club did; and the lack was not entirely supplied by the readiness with which newspapers like *The Times* carried occasional signed articles by representatives of the left.

The *Daily Mirror* backed the Labour Party but did not regard itself as a vehicle for ideas; *The Guardian* and *The Observer* were not so much Labour as liberal-radical. There were left-wing papers, but for the most part weeklies such as *Tribune*, and the daily papers on that axis, the *Morning Star* and *Workers' Press* had insignificant circulations.

He asked if the TUC could try once more to run a newspaper; it might be a new one or an ailing daily or Sunday paper revived. Their experience with the *Daily Herald* was discouraging, and to some extent difficulties caused by lack of purchasing power persisted.

'But blue-collar workers have more money to spend, in real terms, than they had 20 years ago; there is printing capacity idle in both London and Manchester; the new technology of printing could reduce composing costs to a third of their present level; and costs could be further lowered by saving on some of the expensive frills of journalism: the Washington office, the daily crossword.

'Such a paper would not be competing for readers with any of the existing nationals, and its layout and tone should make that clear: it would be complying with the classic commercial maxim: find a gap in the market and fill it.'

Sir Denis, who was discussing the question 'Who is to own the British press?' spoke of the alternatives to private ownership which, he said, was inseparable from private caprice. The shade of Northcliffe could never quite be exorcised.

Political ownership narrowed the press's range of vision to the choices offered by parties or unions, and their prime interest was not the quest for truth; trust ownership in theory permitted total freedom of editorial view but in practice had shared with private ownership the disability of representing a comparatively narrow range of political views; ownership by workers, if it was a reality, was in danger of producing wrong-headed newspapers without much advancing the public good; and state ownership flouted the essential rule that newspapers should be in a position to criticise the state.

In the end, wherever ownership lay, control was with the readers: a newspaper was dead without them. 'If you run your newspaper in such a way that your readers do not like it, then it will not be saved by any amount of reflection that if they were decent people they ought to like it. Human nature is what it is.'

The chief merit of private capitalism as the least imperfect of the available systems was that it was more responsive than other systems, through the ordinary mechanisms of the market place, to the wishes of its readers. It meant that the capitalist press accurately reflected the mixture of good and bad, high-souled and fleshly, which was in human nature itself.

Imperfections included dependence on advertising, all the greater among quality papers, since they needed more money to do their work. *The Times* and *The Sunday Times* derived nearly three-quarters of their income from advertising, and for that reason good newspapers were particularly vulnerable to fluctuations in the economy.

Spending on advertising might fall for another reason, so far little attended to: nationalisation. Nationalisation of the clearing banks, for example, would make competitive advertising needless. 'Good newspapers would suffer, a consequence which might not be unwelcome to the architects of the socialist state, even though they had not planned it.'

(*The Times*, 17 October 1972)

Mr Wilson criticizes British press as overwhelmingly anti-Labour

By a Staff Reporter

The British press was criticised as 'overwhelmingly anti-Labour' by Mr Wilson, Leader of the Opposition, on the Granada Television programme *World in Action* last night.

He said the press would 'go to almost any lengths to discredit Labour's leader, whoever he is'. He thought there were 'different standards between the treatment of any Labour leader and a Conservative leader'.

Mr William Rees-Mogg, editor of *The Times*, who was appearing on the programme with Mr Wilson, replied that it was not true that the press was overwhelmingly anti-Labour.

He compared the circulation figures of national papers at the last election on the basis of which party they advised their readers to vote for and said that in the daily press there was a pro-Labour circulation of 7,250,000 and an anti-Labour circulation of just over 7,000,000. In the Sunday press, depending on how the *News of the World* was viewed politically, the pro-Labour figure was 15,900,000 and the anti-Labour circulation 6,200,000.

'The Labour Party has a pre-dominantly favourable press', he concluded.

Mr Wilson said the figures might be statistically accurate but he thought the position was now different. He did not believe that most of the press had supported the Labour Party's policy on Europe. At the start of the programme, the interviewer, Mr David Boulton, said that most of the papers were in favour of entering the EEC although public opinion leant in the opposite direction. He added that over a three-month period *The Times* had carried an average of one editorial article every three days on the subject of entry to the EEC.

Mr Wilson said it was not a question of numbers but of virulence. He added: 'The virulence with which the Labour leader is pursued by the Conservative press is out of all proportion to that against the Conservative leader.'

He compared the criticism and 'libel' to which he had been subjected over his statement about 'the pound in your pocket' when announcing devaluation to the treatment of Mr Heath over his claim to be able to reduce prices and unemployment 'at a stroke'.

Mr Rees-Mogg said *The Times* had severely criticised Conservative leaders, including Mr Harold Macmillan and Mr Selwyn Lloyd. He said he was not personally against Mr Wilson. 'I have always thought he was a very nice man.'

He had attacked Mr Wilson more recently because Mr Wilson had 'changed his mind on the European issue', and he believed it was to gain a party advantage.

Mr Wilson said: 'I do not think Mr Rees-Mogg has a vendetta against me', but he added: 'I think he wants to destroy the Labour Party'. He suggested that Mr Rees-Mogg was 'a kind of theological crusader', one of whose crusades was to change the Labour Party. 'When I was Prime Minister, I would have liked to recommend him as an archdeacon.'

He pointed out that Mr Rees-Mogg was a twice-defeated Conservative candidate. 'I do not think he is the man to decide for the Labour Party what it ought to want.'

Mr Rees-Mogg said: 'I would not dream of plotting against Mr Wilson, or anyone else. An editor of a newspaper, particularly an editor of *The Times*, who engages in plotting against a man in order to achieve personal changes would have to be out of his mind.'

Mr Wilson said: 'I don't suspect him of plotting. Anything he has to say about me he has the courage to say openly in his paper.'

Much of the discussion arose out of a recent opinion poll published in *The Times* about possible support for a new centre-left political party.

Mr Wilson said he was not contemplating any specific action from a future Labour government on the attitude of the press. It was not a matter for government but he added: 'The Press Council is a washout. It does not touch any of the basic problems.' He believed there should be more freedom for journalists and suggested that there was no freedom at present among the many *Times* journalists who were against joining the EEC.

Mr Rees-Mogg said it was the policy of *The Times* to give both sides of an argument. The newspaper had published 'a distinguished series of anti-Common Market articles'. He added: 'It is also our duty to form an opinion of our own and to let people know what that opinion is.'

Part C Section 1

Letters to the Editor

by Jeremy Tunstall of The City University

Contents

Author's note

Six provincial dailies were visited and questions were mailed to the papers in Wrexham and Bradford. In all but one case the information was supplied by the Editor.

In the case of the nationals, *The Daily Telegraph* and *The Guardian* Editors and their assistants supplied the information. *The Times* exercise is described below. In the other cases information was supplied by another executive usually the Features editor or Assistant editor (features). *The Sun* Editor, Larry Lamb, declined to provide oral answers but asked for written questions. The questions and *The Sun* answers appear in Appendices 2 and 3.

In all cases the ultimate response was warm. Only one of the people interviewed expressed a negative opinion of the Royal Commission. As anticipated, letters were in nearly all cases seen as an interesting, but unthreatening topic.

Only one publication, the *Morning Star*, failed to reply. It was consequently not included in the study.

J T
January 1976

Summary

1   For every 100 copies sold most daily papers receive about four letters a year; The Times, however, receives 25 letters a year (Chapter 1).

2   The flow of letters into a daily paper is determined mainly by the size of its circulation, and not by the proportion of letters which get published (Chapter 1).

3   The main goal of letters columns is circulation or sales revenue; there is a subsidiary goal of prestige (Chapter 2).

4   MPs, educators, Peers and Peeresses and Clergy accounted for a quarter of The Times letters in 1968 and a fifth in 1974–75 (Chapter 3).

5   Popular national dailies see letters in terms of entertainment and small cash prizes for naughty or nostalgic anecdotes (Chapter 4).

6   A typical provincial evening newspaper prints half the letters it receives; smaller provincial dailies print nearly all the letters received (Chapter 5).

7   Provincial morning letters' operations resemble those of their profitable evening stable companions (Chapter 6).

8   The *Radio Times* and *TV Times* letters pages provide the largest regular audience for public criticism of British television and radio (Chapter 7).

9   All Editors set the basic criteria for letters selection – in a way that they do not establish detailed criteria for most other areas of the paper (Chapter 8).

10   The only remaining national newspaper Readers' Service is that of the Mirror Group. It answers 70,000 letters a year; has a staff of 42 and a budget of £200,000 a year (Chapter 9).

11   Letters come mainly from the more educated and affluent (Chapter 10).

12   Insofar as Legal, Press Council and Public Relations problems exist their effect is to induce editorial caution and blandness (Chapter 12).

13   A general bias in favour of the educated, affluent and prominent does exist – but it arises from the writing of the letters, not the selection (Chapter 13).

14   Serious criticisms of major local advertisers are rarely found in provincial dailies' letters columns (Chapter 13).

15   Letters columns do not perform an effective watching – the – watchdogs function (Chapter 14).

16   Letters to the British press probably exceed two million a year. It may thus be the main form of citizen access to large audiences of fellow citizens; however only a minority of these letters are on serious topics (Chapter 15).

1   Letters: Scale and numbers

At first sight there seems to be an enormous range in the numbers of letters received by different publications. Among the national dailies the range for 'main letters sections' is between 2,500 a week (*The Sun*) and 150 a week (*Financial*

Times). If various other sorts of letters (such as once a week specialised letters columns) are included, the range is still wider among the nationals – from 3,150 (*The Sun*) to 220 (*The Guardian*).

Among provincial dailies the range again seems large – for 'main letters' it varies from nine a week (*Wrexham Evening Leader*) to 240 a week (Leeds *Evening Post*).

However, in relation to circulation there is very much greater similarity. With one exception, all of these dailies' total annual receipt of letters equals between 1·5% and 6·8% of a daily circulation. Most daily newspapers appear to receive between two and five letters a year for every 100 copies sold daily.

The Times is the solitary exception – it receives for every 100 copies a day no less than 25 letters a year.

As to letters published: the lower sale dailies – the prestige nationals and all the provincial dailies – publish around one or two letters per year per 100 daily sale. The high sale national dailies (which includes *The Daily Telegraph*) – with sales roughly ten times as high – publish about the same number of letters, that is one or two per year per thousand (not per hundred) daily sale.

The flow of letters into a daily paper is therefore determined mainly by the size of its circulation, and not by the proportion of letters which get published.

Table 1

Letters received and used, 1975[1]

	Weekly main letters Received	Printed	Weekly[2] total letters Received	Printed	Annual letters as percentage of circulation Received	Printed
Financial Times	150	40	240	60	6·7%	1·7%
The Times	1,500	60	1,550	90	24·6%	1·4%
The Guardian	200	70	220	80	3·5%	1·3%
The Daily Telegraph	800	50	800	50	3·0%	0·2%
Daily Mail	600	40	800	60	2·3%	0·17%
Daily Express	830	23[3]	830	23	1·5%	0·05%
Daily Mirror	1,500	75	2,500	100	3·6%	0·14%
The Sun	2,500	75	3,150	115	4·5%	0·17%
Bradford Telegraph & Argus	59	38	59	38	2·5%	1·6%
Derby Evening Telegraph	44	22	44	22	2·3%	1·1%
Leeds Yorkshire Post	120	35	120	35	5·4%	1·5%
Leeds Evening Post	240	75	280	80	6·8%	2·0%
Liverpool Post	75	40[4]	75	40	3·7%	2·0%
Liverpool Echo	110	50	260	62	4·1%	1·0%
Reading Evening Post	30	25	30	25	2·7%	2·3%
Wrexham Evening Leader	9	7	9	7	2·2%	1·7%
Radio Times	500	7				
TV Times	500	12				

[1] Figures for the number of letters received and printed are based in most cases on estimates provided by the letters' editors on the publications in question. This information was used to make an estimate for the whole year of 1975, and this figure was then divided by 52 to produce the weekly average figure shown above. There are in fact quite big fluctuations through the year.

[2] Unlike 'main letters' this includes various usually once a week additional letters features.

[3] London editions only. Manchester printings use separate letters both for Scotland and North of England.

[4] Lancashire editions only. Welsh editions carry separate letters.

2 The goals of letters columns

In a sense one cannot accurately describe letters columns as having specific goals. Letters columns are traditional; indeed letters to the Editor pre-date *News*papers, while 'correspondence' pre-dated journalism and subsequently gave its name to 'correspondents'.

Nevertheless in previous writings I have proposed a set of goals – circulation, advertising, non-revenue and mixed goals. And letters operations do fit quite neatly into the circulation goal; all 18 publications from which I obtained information attributed high readership to letters. There is also a cost-benefit aspect: a particular sort of content may score fairly high on readership but may also be very costly to obtain. Letters are, however, as nearly free as any content can be; an Editor can fill a whole page with letters and only use the time of a single sub-editor on handling them. There are some legal dangers. But compared with some other high readership items – such as crime and sport – letters are *relatively* safe; the competitive element exists but in a relatively passive form.

The high readership and strong reader appeal of letters are broadly confirmed in the case of the provincial press in the Royal Commission's own survey, *Attitudes to the Press* (Cmnd. 6810–3).

Asked about items which they 'always or usually' read, 50% of readers of regional mornings indicated 'readers' letters'; the proportion rose to 54% for readers of provincial evenings and 61% for local weeklies. This placed readers' letters as the sixth equal most highly read item out of seventeen specified items for regional morning readers, fourth for provincial evenings and third most popular among readers of local weeklies.

Readers' letters were especially popular with people over 45. But in local weeklies they were very popular with the 25–44 age group and with women in general.

Although *the main goal of Letters-to-the-Editor columns is circulation or audience revenue*, there is also some 'mixed goal' element. This is obvious in *The Times* and the other prestige dailies; letters in *The Times* confer prestige upon it. This prestige element in letters runs well beyond the 'prestige papers'; popular national and provincial daily newspaper Editors, almost without exception, say they would like more serious letters, and more letters from prominent people such as MPs. This is so, even though conventional wisdom among journalists views MPs as typically rather dull creatures. The note of regret recurs again and again . . . we'd like more serious letters . . . no we don't have a problem of too many prominent people. This note is especially strong in the marginally prestige oriented papers (the provincial mornings, *Daily Mail, Daily Telegraph*).

What about the advertising goal? Clearly letters columns, unlike Motoring, Fashion and similar consumer types of journalism, have little direct connection with the seeking of advertising revenue. But advertisers on the whole are more interested in women than men readers, and letters do appeal especially strongly to women. Moreover in three indirect ways letters columns are indeed edited in the interests of advertisers. These are the main ways:

1 One of the main page layout problems for a daily newspaper is that advertising not only determines from day to day the number of available pages, but the uncertain flow of advertising keeps uncertain even the amount of advertising (and hence the editorial space available) on editorial pages, including the page on which letters appear. *The Times* is a major exception to this, because its

211

main letters page never carries advertising; but even *The Times* has this problem for its Business News letters section. Given this general editorial problem letters are extremely satisfactory because they are so flexible; if an extra advertisement arrives at the last moment, the letters space can quickly be cut.

2 Letters sections can be similarly expanded if expected advertising fails to appear. It is a standard procedure to keep a surplus of letters set in print for this and other emergencies.

3 Letters columns on provincial dailies are in practice edited in such a way that offence to major advertisers is minimized. One large provincial evening paper's letters' editor operated a policy of not usually publishing letters critical of big retailers in the city (such letters are instead handled by its energetic readers' service section).

Readers' service operations undoubtedly have as one of their incidental uses the deflection of reader criticisms of advertisers. But the major purpose of these operations is to help readers – thus the goal is primarily a mixture of circulation and prestige. (See Chapter 9 below.)

One final purpose of readers' letters operations is that they can be the source of news or feature stories. Most daily papers use one or two letters a week as the basis of a news story.

3 *The Times* and the prestige dailies

A chapter of *The Times*' 150th anniversary publication, *A Newspaper History, 1785–1935* was devoted to its letters. In the very early days they were 'Letters to the Conductor' and then 'Letters to the Printer'. The leading article had its origin in letters addressed to the Editor. Throughout the Victorian period its letters played a special part in the life of *The Times* and in the political life of the country. Many of the great controversies of British public life have been fought out as much in the letters column of *The Times* as in Parliament. The State of the Navy has been a topic on which these columns have seen some particularly heavy gunfire. Lord Fisher's 'Sack the Lot' campaign began with a letter to *The Times* in May 1919; an enormous correspondence then thundered forth to which Lord Fisher himself eventually contributed no less than twenty-four letters.

The failure of a letter to appear in *The Times* has occasionally created great interest. In July 1939 nine prominent Liberals sent a letter to *The Times* advocating the inclusion of Churchill and Eden in the Cabinet. Dawson, the Editor, replied privately giving his reasons for not publishing the letter. The authors of the letter, led by Lady Violet Bonham Carter, then sent the letter to the news agencies and other newspapers with a statement that *The Times* had refused to publish it. It *was* widely covered in the national and provincial press.[1] That refusal to publish a letter could be widely regarded as an outrage indicates the position *The Times*' letters had attained.

The Times letters operations is described in more detail in Appendix 6. In addition to the high number of letters it receives, *The Times* internally gives special status to its letters. The letters have a larger space than in *The Daily Telegraph* and a more stable position than in *The Guardian*. *The Times* prints an unusually large

---

1   Colin Seymour-Ure, *The Political Impact of Mass Media*, London: Constable 1974 pp 95–6.

proportion of long letters; it is unusual in normally leaving letters free of cuts and other sub-editing. The Editor of *The Times* plays a bigger part in the letters operation than on most other national dailies – the Editor himself does the final selection.

The staff on *The Times* letters column is unusually large – three full time journalists, plus some other journalist help, plus three secretaries, plus use of the typing pool. Much of their effort goes into providing personal replies to the writers of the best rejected letters – the personal reply softens the blow of rejection and implicitly encourages the rejected writer to try again later. *The Times* letters team sub-edit and also stone-sub their own material; this is unusual (outside diary gossip columns) but follows inevitably from the rule of absolutely no cuts. 'On the stone' a whole letter often has to be dropped and one or two shorter letters substituted. Another quirk of *The Times* layout is that the letters have an irregular space on the left hand columns below the leaders.

Does *The Times* only take letters from top people? The letters staff are aware of this criticism, but believe it to be inaccurate. They quote the figures which appear in Table 2. These seem to show that MPs and Educators get the most letters into *The Times; MPs, Educators, Peers and Peeresses and the Clergy accounted for a quarter of The Times' letters in 1968, a fifth in 1974 and 1975.*

There are two ways of looking at such figures. Most of the letters do not come from these few categories. On the other hand MPs probably buy about one in every 1,000 copies of *The Times*[1] but write one in every 12 or 13 letters published. The compiler of some of the figures in Table 2 also believed them to underestimate the numbers of 'Captains of Industry' many of whom write from their home addresses; the letters staff themselves believe that many letters are from lawyers and doctors.

The letters operations of the other three prestige papers operate somewhat in the shadow of *The Times*. The Editor of *The Daily Telegraph*, William Deedes, was quite openly trying to 'improve' his letters; he thought the view that *Telegraph* letters had always come from embittered retired Colonels in Bournemouth was not entirely a caricature. He is going for letters written by 'young and prominent people, not all of them Conservatives'. *The Daily Telegraph* has a weekly letters conference chaired by the Editor which he allowed me to attend; the thrust of the meeting was to anticipate good topics for letters – flowing mainly from leaders and leader page articles. Letters are actively solicited mainly through the paper's own numerous specialist correspondents; in one case the Conservative writer of a controversial feature article was to be asked to alert his *socialist* friends to write answering letters. *The Daily Telegraph* letters operations is controlled directly by the Editor as part of the non-news side which *Telegraph* Editors traditionally control direct. The Editor wants to expand the letters space by taking the facing-leader-page page away from the news people – but has not yet succeeded.

---

1   Assuming that about half of all MPs buy *The Times*, while more read it but do not buy it.

Table 2

Letters published in *The Times*; Letter writers from certain occupations as percentages of all writers

	Whole Year 1968	January 1974	January 1975
Peers and Peeresses	3·6%	3·3%	3·5%
Members of Parliament...	7·0%	7·0%	9·2%
Parsons, Clergy, Bishops	5·1%	3·0%	3·0%
Dons and Schoolmasters	10·1%	—	—
Professors	—	6·3%	4·0%
These combined	25·8%	19·6%	19·7%
Total Number of letters published ...	4,268	434	396

Source:

For 1968 letter from James Henderson, *The Times*, 15 January 1969.
For 1974–75 letter from David Tang, *The Times*, 28 July 1975.

The Guardian letters operations is also loosely controlled by the Editor, again as in the *Telegraph* via the features editor. While *The Daily Telegraph* is trying to imitate *The Times*, the policy of *The Guardian* is to counter *The Times* by running letters from what the letters editor called the 'counter establishment'. He claimed that no paper equalled *The Guardian*'s frequency of letters from HM prisoners. Most letters to *The Guardian* are, however, from the educated and articulate. Even in the case of the recent consultants' and junior hospital doctors' disputes nearly all the letters received and published were from doctors and few were from irate patients, nurses or medical social workers.

The *Financial Times* has a quiet, almost sleepy, letters operation. The journalist in charge also writes on another subject (advertising); the main executive control lies with an assistant editor. The *Financial Times* operation has been shaped by the view of the former Editor, Sir Gordon Newton, that it should be a 'reader's forum' – no preference, it seems, was or is given to those many heads of companies on whom one might think the *Financial Times* could call for interesting letters. In this, as in other ways, the FT may be like a provincial daily – perhaps the prominent locals are so well covered in the news columns that they don't bother to write letters. Newton himself used to read every letter sent to the main letters operation – and it could be that this gave him little motive for expanding the volume of letters to unreadable numbers.

4 The *Daily Mirror* and the popular dailies

In contrast to the prestige dailies, the *popular national dailies see letters in terms of entertainment, the amusing anecdote, the nostalgic, and the naughty*. This is true even of the *Daily Mail*; here, as elsewhere, it has given up most of its pretensions of a decade ago to being a semi-serious paper. The *Mail* doesn't even have a full-time journalist in charge of letters; main control is exercised by the Features Editor. In keeping with the tabloid format and lack of space, letters are short and light. The features editor and the relevant assistant editor both lament the lack of 'serious' letters.

The *Daily Mirror* in particular, and Mirror Group newspapers in general, have a letters operation of great organisational complexity. Letters in the *Mirror* are short and breezy. The *Sunday Mirror* actually describes one of its letters sections with the revealing phrase 'Let off steam'. Even more than the *Mail*, the *Daily Mirror* has letters scattered through the paper. 'Live Letters' still supposedly run by the 'Old Codgers' is the main letters section; but there is also a second near-daily letters section (the daily equivalent to 'Let off Steam') called 'Public Opinion'. The *Mirror* has several other non-daily letters features – including sports letters, letters answered by Marjorie Proops and the *Help!* column; the latter is the main public face of a very elaborate Readers' Service operation (See Chapter 9 below).

In addition to its daily and (roughly) weekly letters operations the *Daily Mirror* also runs a large number of other letters activities which mainly take place outside the columns of the paper but also occasionally surface there. Most of these are competitions or 'offers' of something to *Mirror* readers at a special price. One circulation-promotion offer recently involved £5 worth of price reductions for specified goods at Tesco Supermarkets – and this received over 1·2 million letters. Against this must be set the very large, and very largely philanthropic readers service section. The whole letters operation at the *Mirror* has deliberately been given a kind of working-people's-club-by-correspondence atmosphere – an amalgam of beery anecdotes, jolly contests with many small prizes, money-off come-ons, letting off steam, Proops-a-Daisy naughty advice, and genuinely expert help with your real tragic life.

The *Sun* must presumably already have been described as a stripped down version of the *Daily Mirror*. This is certainly true of its letters operations – the main sections being 'Liveliest Letters' and 'Letter Box'. The *Sun* also has taken further than the *Daily Mirror* the idea of 'Five pounds for the best letters on the first time your husband kissed you'. Even more than the rest of *The Sun* its letters read as if they were sub-edited by a computer. (For further details on *The Sun* see Appendix 4).

The *Daily Express* gave (late 1975) the smallest space to letters of any national newspaper. This is odd because recently the *Daily Express* with its Action Line (see section 9) gave letters very great prominence. Action Line is now dead and *Express* letters are small in number printed, as well as in space. Since letters inevitably reflect the paper's editorial philosophy current *Express* practice with letters probably reflects wider editorial uncertainty as it finds itself in the yawning chasm between the prestige broadsheets and the pop tabloids. The *Express* treats its letters like the populars only in sharing their policy of savage cutting; it is unlike any other paper I visited in having come quite near to abolishing a letters column altogether.

5 Provincial evenings

The letters operations of the evening papers in Bradford, Derby, Leeds, Liverpool, Reading and Wrexham have much in common. They all print quite a high proportion of the letters they get. *A paper like the Derby Evening Telegraph prints half the letters it receives; of the other half a fair proportion are deemed unpublishable for one reason or another* – some are merely 'thank you' letters (eg to a hospital), some just say that the Derby County goalkeeper is wonderful, and others are obviously libellous. Such a paper is reduced to publishing letters about particular bus stops or road signs which even a local weekly might find parochial. The smaller Reading *Evening Post* with a 50,000 circulation in

Berkshire, prints almost every letter it gets. It is, then, only the very large evenings – such as those in Liverpool and Leeds – which have any significant selection problem.

These provincial evening letters operations are all like those of the prestige nationals in that they are directly controlled by the Editor. The 'log-book' of letters is a familiar piece of these Editors' daily lives. But provincial evening letters operations are in most other ways like muted, and more local, versions of the national tabloids' letters.

The largest provincial letters operation I saw was at the *Evening Post* in Leeds. The Editor is a great believer in letters. He has a main section called 'You Say'. Each day also there is one nostalgic letter under a separate heading, 'It happened to me'. A columnist also publishes occasional letters and the Saturday paper has 'TV Letters', 'Junior Post' and 'Old Yorkshire Diary'. This paper especially favours nostalgic letters on topics such as the imminent disappearance of horses from Leeds.

The 'Let off Steam' element in these letters operations is paramount. Editors spontaneously describe letters as 'airing grievances' and 'a way of drawing attention to grievances'. I didn't suggest that letters might be a way of 'throwing the rascals out' or in more English phraseology 'Finding the next generation of Poulsons'; this, very obviously indeed, was not what these Editors saw as the purpose of letters.

Established authority in the circulation areas of these provincial daily papers consists firstly of the public sector (presided over often, since these are urban areas, by a Labour Council); secondly the big commercial interests and, most importantly for Editors, the big advertisers such as department stores and estate agents.

On most provincial dailies I visited letters critical of local government or other major local interests are as a routine practice accompanied by a ' footnote ' reply from the official spokesman of the criticised organisation. As two attached examples (Appendix 1) from the Derby *Evening Telegraph* show, these replies can be longer than the original letter. This practice is, of course, defended in the interests of 'balance', 'both sides' and 'right of reply'. National paper letters editors were asked about this practice but all said their papers were against it. It runs contrary to the belief widely held by national journalists that journalists should not let the subject of the coverage see the story 'until it hits the streets'. This practice at the very least allows the criticised party to influence the date of publication – the letter not being published until the official reply has been received.

6 Provincial mornings

The *Yorkshire Post* circulates mainly outside Leeds and throughout Yorkshire; the *Liverpool Post* circulates in SW Lancashire and through the northern half of Wales. In both papers the letters operation broadly resembles that of their profitable evening stable companions.

Both Editors personally read all letters and control their selection. Both get many fewer letters than the larger evenings; both would like more, and more serious, letters. The *Yorkshire Post* allows phone-in 'letters', but it only gets

216

20 a week. Both of these papers also give public officials or large companies the 'footnote' right-of-reply facility. Nevertheless letters in these papers are a bit more weighty than those in the evenings.

7 Britain's largest magazines: *Radio Times* and *TV Times*

Both the *Radio Times* and *TV Times* receive about 500 letters a week. Thus for each issue they receive about as many as the *Daily Mirror*.

The *Radio Times* and its Editor take letters extremely seriously. The letters have high readership – 78% of readers or 8 million out of their total 11 million. *Radio Times* is unusual in several ways. In some regions which lack local radio it carries a second letter page. One of its biggest topics for letters is the appearance and layout of the paper itself; a single striking format for the paper has produced up to 2,500 letters. The *Radio Times* letters page quite often carries statements of BBC policy from senior programme executives – these appear as 'footnotes' in provincial daily style.

In contrast to some *Listener*-like overtones at the *Radio Times*, its opposite number *TV Times* is much more a showbiz weekly fleshed out with colour consumer advertising. Its Editor is one more who regrets the lack of serious letters:

'Most of our letters are requests for information (Who played the butler in last Thursday's feature film? When is Roger Moore's birthday?) . . . .'

These two magazines are important for a number of reasons. They are our largest magazines. They illustrate the important overlap of press and broadcasting; they have many fascinating production aspects – *Radio Times* has 25 regional sub-editions. The *TV Times* is unique in other obvious ways, including its regional editions, its use of colour in a 'down market' publication, and its profitability.

But apart from this general interest these programme magazines have a special significance in the field of letters. These two letters pages provide the largest regular audience for the public criticism of British television and radio.

8 Editorial control and selection

With the single exception of the *Daily Express*, the Editors of all the publications apparently took letters seriously. Letters fit more closely with journalists' conceptions of reality than do readership research studies; moreover, unlike such research studies, which are a resource primarily of commercial management and a potential threat to the Editors themselves, 'Letters to the Editor' are the Editor's own unchallenged preserve.

Even where Editors play only a minor part in the selection of letters – mainly on the popular nationals – some letters are still seen by the Editor; typically several sub-categories of letters are routed to the Editor – those which complain about named journalists on the staff, letters which have legal or Press Council implications and so on. Even the *Daily Express* Editor sees letters at the proof stage and sometimes rejects them.

All Editors set the basic criteria for letters selection – in a way that they do not establish detailed criteria for most other areas of the paper. The most common explanations for this control (either direct or indirect) by the Editor himself are:

Firstly, the Editor is responsible for the publication's relationship to its readers. Secondly, letters are the main channel for complaints against the paper and its staff. Thirdly, letters have legal implications.

What are the criteria for selection? This is always difficult to establish in any area of journalism and even more so when the Editor's personal control means that criteria for selection can remain even vaguer than elsewhere; one Editor said that he preferred himself to choose the letters, because this absolved him from having to invent any rules. I asked three questions about selection:

1   In choosing letters most Editors, or their letters staff, say that they are not especially interested in 'prominent' people. They believe that on the whole prominent people write letters of greater interest. A correspondence on housing in a provincial daily would obviously benefit from a letter by the chairman of the Council Housing Committee. All publications claim to like a fair proportion of letters from 'typical' readers.

2   As to pungency, length and style, the most common answer was that letters must be 'interesting' and must avoid excessive repetition. Most publications prefer short letters. Several provincial dailies carry in their letters column a warning that letters longer than 150 or 250 words will be cut. The prestige nationals are unusual in actually welcoming some much longer letters.

The Times takes an extreme position on cutting – the standard rule being that all letters run in full. Other prestige nationals do a little 'tidying up'. Popular nationals cut letters ruthlessly, in some cases extracting two or three sentences from a much longer letter.

Some provincial dailies – armed with Press Council disapproval of distortion – through-cutting, and also short of enough letters to fill the space – publish rambling letters in full; some journalists disapprove of this practice on the grounds that it is unfair to the reader as well as the letter writers. The number of complaints against cutting appears to be quite small. Many publications warn writers that letters will be cut; others agree major cuts with writers on the telephone. Working class letter writers quite often ask to have their letters 'improved'.

One major category of letter falls outside the control of Editors. This is the flow of letters direct to named journalists – usually specialist correspondents and columnists; these letters are mostly not intended for publication – although some columnists, such as Proops in the *Daily Mirror*, do publish some letters.

3   My previous study of specialists correspondents at the national level[1] suggested a very wide range – varying from only one or two reader letters a week received by foreign correspondents to about 70 a week received by Fashion correspondents (see Table 3).

---

1   **J** Tunstall *Journalists at Work*, Constable 1971.

Table 3

National Specialist Correspondents: letters from the public, 1968

Type of Specialist Correspondent	Number of correspondents in study	Average number of letters received per week by each correspondent	Total letters per week
Washington	18	2	36
New York	19	2	38
Bonn/Rome	18	1	18
Political Lobby	39	8	312
Aviation	11	10	110
Education	14	12	168
Labour	23	4	92
Crime	14	26	362
Football	24	19	456
Fashion	11	71	781
Motoring	16	24	384
Total letters per week =			2,757

Total = 143,000 per year

Source: Jeremy Tunstall, *Journalists at Work*, London, Constable 1971, p 252.

9   Readers' service operations

By 'Readers' Service' operation is meant a letter answering service which receives letters not primarily intended for publication and provides information and advice of various kinds. There is some overlap with the advice column which advises readers on their emotional problems; but the Readers' Service I have in mind deals mainly with social service, tax, and consumer problems.

The two most famous of these services were developed by the *News of the World* and the *Daily Mirror* and both began during the second world war. The *News of the World* service was sharply cut back in 1969 and subsequently run down by the Murdoch management. The *Daily Express'* Action Line flowered and died quickly. The *Mirror*'s service is now the only large-scale national service in operation and it serves the three weekly nationals in the Mirror Group as well.

The *News of the World*'s service was launched by John Hilton, a Professor of Industrial Relations at Cambridge and named after him. At its peak in the year 1957 it received 206,000 letters; its main emphasis was on social welfare, and it was physically separate from the editorial offices.

The *Daily Express* set up Action Line in 1968. It had a more consumer emphasis, it was part of the editorial organisation, and it used the quick phone call rather than correspondence. For a short while Action Line dealt with 6,000 letters and phone calls a week[1]. Successes were loudly proclaimed in the news columns in traditional Beaverbrook self-congratulatory style.

---

1   Tim Albert, 'Dear Reader', *New Society*, 19 July 1973.

The remaining service, Mirror Group Newspapers' Readers' Services, retains the original welfare emphasis. It operates from separate premises in Camden Town and its main purpose is to solve readers' 'serious' problems – not to give advice about personal relationships. Answers to some of the letters appear in the 'Help' columns of the *Daily Mirror* and *Reveille*, but the operation is mainly geared to providing private answers to individual letter writers.

Mirror Group Readers Services has handled about 70,000 letters in each of the last few years. The total staff including secretaries is 42 people and the present budget is about £200,000 a year. Each letter thus costs about £3 to answer. The impressive current head of Readers' Services, Mrs Duveen, is the housing specialist; there are two health and social services specialists and a tax specialist. The level of expertise is clearly extremely high.

Why does the Mirror Group bother to have such a service? In hard commercial terms the service must have some promotional value; but this cannot be measured – in contrast, for example, to promotional efforts involving free provision of the *Daily Mirror* for a week (this can be measured by interviewing the recipients subsequently to see how many have become paying subscribers). Although the Mirror Group operation appears not to be in immediate danger, a long-term argument against it is that there are now many more services available to citizens – Citizens' Advice Bureaux, the Director of Fair Trading, the Ombudsman and so on. The Mirror Group operation, however, is almost certainly unique in the combined breadth and expert depth of its advice across the whole range of social services, and beyond.

The Mirror Group service is less well known than it perhaps deserves. It is an obvious dilemma of such a service that if it were to be widely publicised it would attract extra floods of letters. It already gets problems which CABs, MPs and others have failed to solve. But if the Mirror operation is not very widely known the Readers Service operations run by provincial dailies are even less known.

Of the eight provincial dailies in my study, two have quite elaborate Readers Service operations.

Firstly the Bradford *Telegraph and Argus* answers 'up to 40 letters a week . . . on income tax problems and the like'. (This paper only receives about 60 letters-to-the-editor per week). Secondly, the *Liverpool Echo* operates a readers' service called 'Helping Hand'; this service receives about 150 phone calls and 150 letters per week – the letters alone exceeding conventional letters-to-the-editor for publication. This service used to have a 'Helping Hand' column in the *Echo* two or three times a week; now with smaller papers it is only once or twice a week. But the column is quite prominently displayed and it specialises in appeals to the public – often for out-of-touch relatives. This may account for its startling tally of 300 letters and phone calls a week. Many of the letters deal with missing persons (one I was shown was from an American lawyer hunting for possible relatives of someone who had died in the US leaving $12 million and no heirs); many ask for odd bits of information. The consumer side of this service handles complaints against department stores purely on an individual, non-published, basis. This service also gives advice on social service, welfare, and tax problems. The journalist in charge of the service, Neil Williams, is clearly a man of great energy and devotion. He has an assistant, two secretaries, and a large phone bill. The total cost of handling his 15,000 letters and calls per year could be £20,000. The *Echo* gets one or two columns a week out of him, but also a lot of local prestige. For instance the Lord Mayor regularly hands across letters which he receives from the public.

A third paper of the eight provincial dailies, the Leeds *Evening Post*, did run a readers' service operation from 1968 onwards but it was axed early in 1975 as an economy measure. It was called 'Action Desk' (presumably after the *Daily Express* operation) and it received 70 to 80 letters a week. The Editor argued that it was no longer so necessary as a result of the appearance of more advice services and agencies of redress in Leeds. This Editor now publishes once a week a long list of such agencies in Leeds.

The Mirror Group service stands out in several ways. Its air of social purpose is markedly at odds with the deliberate triviality of many letters published by the *Daily Mirror*. The service's expertise is sometimes tapped by Mirror Group journalists; the Readers' Service operation has in its field a level of knowledge not normally met in either specialist or investigative journalism. The service, however, appears not only to do something not done elsewhere in journalism, it also has a broad but integrated information and monitoring capability which neither Whitehall nor Westminster offers to citizens.

10 Letter writers: who and why?

The survey on *Attitudes to the Press*, conducted for the Royal Commission[1] indicates that only a small minority of the British public have ever written a letter to a newspaper. Only 11% of the sample claimed ever to have written such a letter; of those who had written, 52% had done so within the last five years and 17% within the last year. Thus only 2% of the sample at large had written in the last year. Since this 2% must include both the persistent letter writers and some who are contributing their lifetime's only letter, presumably the majority of the letters appearing in the press in any single year come from under 1% of the population.

Table 4 indicates how those who have written in the last two years, and those who have 'ever' written differ from the total national sample. Since the 'past two years' column is based on only 70 cases, it is probably safest to compare this and the 'ever' writing column with the sample at large. This procedure suggests that letter writers are more likely to be men than women; are fairly evenly spread by age; are more Conservative and Liberal (and less Labour) than the population at large. In terms of occupational social class the letter writers are substantially more likely to be middle class than to be in manual occupations. Amongst those who have 'ever' written the non-manual categories outnumber the manual by 41% to 24% as against the sample which contains a (small) majority of people in manual occupations.

---

1 Cmnd 6810–3.

Table 4

Characteristics of those who have written letters to newspapers, 1976

	All Writing Letters in past 2 years	All Ever Writing	Total Sample
Sample Number =	70	230	2,401
	%	%	%
Sex:			
Men	57	54	47
Women	43	46	53
Age:			
16–24	17	9	14
25–44	42	34	33
45–64	22	39	34
65 and over	18	18	18
Working status :			
In work	66	65	60
Not in work	34	35	40
Socio-economic group of employment:			
Prof/Emp/Manager	25	17	9
Junior Non-manual	13	24	19
Skilled Manual	22	15	16
Semi/Unskilled Manual	6	9	14
Forces/Unclassifiable	—	1	2
Political view:			
Conservative	39	44	36
Liberal	17	15	11
Labour	25	25	33
Nationalist	2	1	3
Other/No Party/Not stated	17	15	17
Very Strong Conservative	16	20	14
Very Strong Labour	13	11	20

Source: National Sample Survey conducted by Social and Community Planning Research, reported in *Attitudes to the Press* (Cmnd 6810–3).

The same survey confirms that writers to provincial or local newspapers are much more likely to have their letters printed. Of those who had last written to regional or local papers 66% had had the letter printed, whereas for the national papers the successful proportion was 30%. The data in Table 1 suggest that nationals print only about 6% of letters received, while provincial dailies collectively print about 35%. Since the inclusion of weeklies would probably boost this latter figure to 50% or higher the main discrepancy is in the case of the national newspapers. One cause may be that many people when writing to a national newspaper are uncertain as to whether they are submitting their letter for publication, and when it is not in fact published they subsequently do not consider this as a letter rejected for publication. Probably also many people who write to their local papers are similarly uncertain, and only when the letter in fact gets published do they acknowledge that they intended it for publication[1]. According to the national sample survey the highest proportion of letters published were those sent to regional mornings, followed by local weeklies, provincial evenings, national Sundays, and regional Sundays with national dailies the most difficult category in which to get a letter published.

The middle class bias in letter writing is, of course, easy to predict and arises primarily from the simple fact that standards of literacy and the propensity to write are less common among the less educated. Not only the ability, but also the motivation, to write letters is likely to be stronger the more education a person has. More middle class people will be orientated towards furthering their own interests and careers in this diffuse manner; more middle class people will be involved in causes.

Impressionistic evidence from this inquiry supports such an interpretation. Although some letters are handwritten – including some published in *The Times* – many are typed; some papers accept telephoned letters and the telephone is less used by working class people. Most publications have a few individual readers who send letters as often as twice a week, occasionally even two letters on separate topics in a single day; letters editors tend to say of these star producers that they write extremely good letters – and if two a week are sent, then at least one or two a month will be used. I saw a Christmas card sent to a letters editor by one such correspondent; another paper had recently carried a large feature story about its most persistent letter writer. These people seem to regard letter writing to the press as a variant on the crossword competition; and they tend to come from such occupations as schoolteaching. Probably the star performer in the land is David Holbrook, mentioned by *The Times*, *The Guardian* and the *Radio Times* as among their most frequent letter writers.

Are many letters concocted in the office? No publication admitted this, although several journalists said that it was a common practice on weekly newspapers. Most newspapers claim to be cautious about using letters from journalists on other publications. My guess would be, however, that the prestige nationals and some of the larger provincial dailies do, unwittingly, carry a fair number of letters written by journalists – especially from journalists on smaller or less well known publications. All publications want good letters by their own criteria; journalists are skilled at writing to fit set formats, and an aspiring journalist who can include in his 'cutting book' signed letters to respected papers may indeed further his chances of employment on a larger publication. Journalists, then, even more than other middle class people have both the skill and the motivation to write letters.

11 Recently popular topics

Here is an unsystematic list of topics which have attracted a lot of letters:

Financial Times: Inflation accounting, Wealth tax, Rates, Government assistance to small firms.

The Guardian: The EEC referendum, Prisons, Jill Tweedie, Doctors.

Daily Mail: Rates, Rape, Concorde (anti), Fluoride, Foxhunting.

---

1 It follows that the present writer is adopting the publication's definition of a letter intended for publication in preference to the definition used by members of the public in the SCPR national sample survey.

Yorkshire Post (Leeds): Arthur Scargill, Motorway schemes, EEC referendum, VAT and shopkeepers, Fluoride, Abortion, Hooliganism.

Evening Post (Leeds): Brewery horses, Motorways, Rates, Popular Songs.

Derby Evening Telegraph: Rolls-Royce, Unemployment, Bus fares, Peripheral roads.

I failed to ask specifically about topics which had produced few letters. One example was the British Steel Corporation's proposal to close the Shotton steel works where 6,500 men are employed; since Shotton is 18 miles from Liverpool and on the edge of its circulation area the *Liverpool Echo* ran a series of five feature articles on the subject. The *Echo* received only one letter[1] about this series, which the Editor described as 'disappointing'.

12 Perils: Legal, Press Council, Politicians, PR

Editors are concerned about legal problems in letters, although some say they are no worse here than in any other section of the paper. Libel is the biggest single problem and is one major reason for rejecting letters; it might also be used as an excuse by Editors not wishing to publish highly critical letters. Another legal problem is authenticity – is the letter really from the person it purports to be from? To combat the hoax danger many publications send acknowledgment cards and deliberately allow recipients a day or two in which to protest that 'their' letter is not authentic.

Letters constitute one of the Press Council's most active areas. Three of its main themes in this area are: Firstly, the 'right of reply'. Secondly, letters must not be cut or sub-edited in such a way as to mis-represent the correspondent's views. Thirdly, final discretion must rest with the Editor. The responses of Editors and letters editors can also be placed in three broad categories. Firstly, some publications find the Press Council's activities in the letters area to be irritating and mainly concerned with trivia. Secondly, the majority of publications express passively accepting views in this area: 'The Press Council supports what we've always done anyway'. Thirdly, a few Editors were positively enthusiastic about the Press Council; one Editor quoted Press Council rulings in support of his own rather cautious attitude to letters and his policy of giving public officials 'right of reply' in footnotes attached to critical letters.

Politicians are more of a potential than an actual threat in this area. Several provincial dailies said that they automatically printed letters from Councillors and MPs – partly because they received very few; prominent local politicians usually sent few letters, since they could get their views aired in the news columns. Most newspapers would prefer more letters from politicians. Only during election campaigns do newspapers adopt 'quota' arrangements for letters – usually on BBC lines.

'Public relations' letters are on the whole not welcome. A perfectly typed letter which mentions a commercial product is highly suspect. Slightly less well typed letters which support a cause – whether Zionism, Welsh Nationalism, the National Front or a 'social' cause – are much less suspect and are 'treated on

---

1   The Shotton Works are in Connah's Quay where 420 copies of the *Echo* are sold daily; it is 2 miles from Ellesmere Port where 24% of all households take the *Echo*. Thus probably about 1,000 of the 6,500 Shotton workers live in households which buy the *Echo* every day. Early in 1977 the Shotton Works closure was cancelled.

their merits'. Asked about letter writing 'campaigns', Editors say they are on the look-out for repeated phrases or other signs of national orchestration. Despite this, since there is no consultation between publications – and only the prestige national dailies really bother about exclusivity – a well orchestrated letter writing campaign will almost certainly be successful at placing letters (written from suitable local addresses) in numerous provincial publications. Any ex-journalist working for a PR firm could formulate the rules: Use a local address, don't type the letter too well, try to comment on a story or editorial in the publication to which you're writing, do not repeat in one letter phraseology used in a previous one, space the letters out over a period of weeks, vary the name and address of the local correspondent. Editors admit that probably a few letter writing campaigns 'do get past us, although we can spot the obvious ones very easily'.

The general impact of all these 'perils' is to induce caution. Since letters are free and libel is costly, why run the risk of publishing critical and possibly libellous letters? Since the Press Council favours the right of reply and uncut letters, why not append officials' answers to critical letters and allow letters to ramble on uncut? Since a well phrased but 'political' letter could have PR origins, perhaps it's safer to choose something duller.

13 Are letters columns biased ?

I found no evidence of any deliberate bias in the editing of letters columns. The main biases at work, as usually in journalism, are the constraints of time and space and journalists' views of what is interesting or novel. There is no bias against uneducated people as such. Popular national dailies and provincial evenings like to carry letters by extremely modest people; bad handwriting and spelling are no bar and journalists try to edit and improve letters with sympathy and without distorting what the correspondent 'wanted to say'.

There is a general bias in favour of the more educated, the more affluent and the more prominent but this lies in the writing of the letters not in the selection or editing. The propensity to write letters to the press is not evenly distributed, because literacy and education are not evenly distributed.

There is also a second form of bias which again is not deliberate bias in selection. As writers such as Jackson, Cox and Morgan, and Murphy agree, the provincial press is reluctant to criticise Authority in general – and the local authority and major advertisers in particular. This is reflected in the Letters Column. Letters critical of major department stores may be 'taken up with' the store in question – and the correspondent may indeed get the faulty goods or service replaced – but such letters seldom get published. Letters critical of the local authority tend to be referred to the departments criticised – in a manner which would not occur if for example a local footballer were being criticised; some of these letters are then seen as too dated to be used in the news columns; others are used, but only with a footnote which deploys the heavy guns of the local planning department's superior knowledge to blow the critical letter out of the water. Some such critical letters are also used unfootnoted and in their original form. Probably very few letters are deliberately suppressed. But the extremely cautious approach to such letters will in due course convey a message to potential letter writers; all letters' editors agree that letters published attract similar letters. If would-be

225

critics notice that the local evening newspaper never allows advertisers or local officials to be heavily criticised in its letters column they may send such complaints elsewhere.

It is, of course, precisely its extremely *critical* general tone – and because it creates the impression that no politician, official or company is immune from sharply worded and well argued attacks – that *The Times* letters column derives much of its authority.

14 Letters columns as watchdogs of the watchdogs

There is little evidence from this brief enquiry that letters columns act as an effective watchdog on the press itself.

Many letters criticise the publication in question for errors of fact, interpretation, or taste, but these seem nearly always to relate to particular stories. Of these letters, a fair proportion seem to fall in a grey area between being, and not being, intended for publication. Some are published, some receive personal replies and explanations. But very very few such complaints, it seems, make informed general criticisms of the overall operation of the publication, beyond details of particular news items or editorials.

I did ask whether the recent wave of underground papers implied some inadequacy in the press. In areas which had active underground papers the Editors tended to state that this did suggest some degree of failure on the part of the established press; they also recognised that fundamental criticisms of the established press were a central feature of underground papers. Little, however was suggested by Editors as to what they could do about such criticism. I asked whether they would favour an Ombudsman of the internal house-critic kind. Reaction to this suggestion was amused and negative, as it was to another suggestion about local press councils along American lines. 'No, I'm my own local press council' said one provincial evening Editor. The Editor of the *Radio Times* and the features editor of *The Guardian* were the only journalists willing seriously to consider the internal house-critic idea – although neither thought it quite suitable for his own publication!

My own view here is that letters columns could indeed be edited in such a way as to deploy sustained, reasonable and informed criticism of a newspaper in its own columns. One obvious way to do this would be to initiate a separate correspondence column once a week which would specialise in this type of letter. The editing of such a column would be a problem; this task could obviously be more easily handled if there was some kind of licensed columnist or Ombudsman who could both write criticisms and select letters for publication as part of his column. My impression also is that such an idea might be acceptable to some prestige national newspapers under fair conditions:

1 That the house critic was allowed to criticise other publications as well as his own (along *Wall Street Journal* lines).

2 If more than one national prestige paper adopted the practice at the same time.

3 That the house critic did not criticise the production unions.

4 Since firing the house critic would be a delicate (but perhaps necessary) task the best way to start would be for a house critic to be employed to write, or edit letters for a fixed number of columns or a fixed period.

15 Letters columns: Implications for press content and policy

Letters columns, even if ineffective at watching the watchdogs, are surely a major way in which individuals can put their views before large numbers of fellow citizens. An educated guess at the total numbers of letters written to the British press in one year is as follows:

National Dailies	–	500,000 letters
Provincial Dailies	–	300,000
Sunday newspapers	–	100,000
Weekly newspapers	–	200,000
Consumer magazines	–	250,000[1]
Trade/tech magazines	–	150,000
Total		1,500,000[2]

Although much of this is guesswork, the 850,000 figure for all daily newspapers plus the programme guides is unlikely to be far out.

Then there is another category of advice-seeking letters to magazine readers' service operations – some of these letters are, and some are not, intended for publication; but they would probably raise the total well above 1·5 million. There is also the category of letters written to individual named journalists – such as specialists and columnists. The 200 national specialist correspondents in my 1968 study together received some 143,000 letters a year – and those specialists at the time constituted only half of all specialists at the national level in Britain. Including provincial media and magazines such letters alone might number as many as 500,000 a year. The SCPR Survey data suggest that about 1·25 million people claim to have written to a newspaper in the last two years. But this is probably a low figure and it includes those who have written two or more times in a year.

Letters to the British press, both those intended and those not intended for publication, thus probably exceed two million a year. This must be compared with a reported figure of 350,000 letters as the total received by the BBC in a recent year; of these, 25,000 were to *Radio Times*. On the other hand one must also remember the single Tesco offer which brought the *Daily Mirror* 1·2 million letters.

Does not the press, then, provide the bulk of public access to the media? As always with press and broadcast comparisons, the answer varies greatly according to the assumptions behind the comparison. If one merely takes the BBC letters received and adds the more serious national phone-in programmes on TV and radio, then the press probably wins easily; but if one also includes more of the local radio phone-in and similar programmes the contrast is not so strong.[3] Moreover one could also argue that the many phone-in and write-in record

1 The two largest consumer magazines *Radio Times* and *TV Times* together receive 50,000 letters a year.

2 The SCPR Survey (Cmnd 6810–3) reports that, of those who say they have 'ever' written to a newspaper, 30% had last written to a national daily, 36% to a provincial daily, 10% to a national or regional Sunday and 22% to a local weekly newspaper. For reasons stated above, the present writer suspects that these figures underestimate the numbers of letters sent to national newspapers.

3 Frances J Berrigan, *Access and the Media: New Models in Europe* draft report for UNESCO 1974. 245 pp.

request programmes provide just as genuine 'access' as does the letter in *The Sun* or *Daily Mirror* on 'the first time my husband kissed me' or letter in the Leeds *Evening Post* on 'Games children played fifty years ago'.

The 2 million or so letters received by the press at least provide the *potential* for much public access. But less than 150,000 letters a year are received by the four serious national dailies and under 15,000 of these are printed. Paradoxically perhaps the most obviously serious letters operation in the popular press – the Mirror Group Readers' Services – does provide, or help to obtain, much redress but provides relatively little access to print. And the provincial daily newspapers which provide in some ways the most obvious potential for access are in many cases short of enough passable letters to publish – serious or trivial, literate or illiterate.

Appendix 1

Two examples of 'footnotes' longer than the original letter
Derby *Evening Telegraph*, 28 October and 6 November 1975

From the Derby *Evening Telegraph* 28 October 1975

On the surface, a too-severe saving

'I think Derbyshire County Council have taken their money saving efforts a little too far in one stretch of road resurfacing which they did recently, namely Cumberhills, leading from Park Nook, Quarndon, into Duffield.

The gravel has been applied so sparingly that 50 per cent of the road (spread over the full length) hasn't even been touched.

This road can be treacherous enough in winter with a normal surface, so what it will be like this winter I fail to imagine.'

W T S
Quarndon

Mr E Farrell, senior assistant county surveyor, replies: 'I am aware of the condition of Cumberhills Road and an investigation is at present being carried out into the apparent partial failure of the surface dressing which was carried out earlier this year.

Your correspondent can be assured that the correct spread of stone chippings was applied to the road but unfortunately an adhesion failure occurred over a large area of the carriageway.

In excess of 4¼ million square metres of carriageway surface dressing has been carried out by the department in the current year, but since this type of work is subject to many variables, not least the weather during and immediately following the work, such partial failures are regrettably unavoidable.'

From the Derby *Evening Telegraph* 6 November 1975

Sell-out on Spondon Buses denied

'If I may be permitted to enlighten Mrs L Cotton of Spondon (Letters, 25 October) concerning the bus service, I should like to point out that it was Councillor Christophers, chairman of Derby Borough Transport Committee, who sold her out at the last bus fare inquiry.

For the transport department now to be claiming to be championing the cause of Spondon residents is political hypocrisy when at the last inquiry the transport department spokesman did a deal with Trent in return for Trent withdrawing its appeal against Derby Borough Council's application for increased fares.

I was at the inquiry and I commented then that the department had sold the Spondon residents out to the Trent.

As chairman of the committee Mr Christophers must take full responsibility even though he failed to attend his own committee's application for the increases.

S P GIBSON

Prospective United English Nationalist candidate,
12 Langdale Drive,
Breadsall.

Councillor Christophers comments: 'Mr Gibson could be mistaken for a master of fantasy, if fantasy was not already the master of Mr Gibson. No deal was made with Trent at the Traffic Commissioners' hearing, and Derby borough has certainly not sold Spondon residents out. Legally the council is not in a position to do so.

Several Acts of Parliament, for example the 1930 Road Traffic Act, have prevented the council from providing bus services in areas like Spondon and Chellaston. These areas are legally part of the operating territory of the Trent Motor Traction Company.

Other Acts, for example the 1968 Transport Act, do allow bus companies to operate joint services, but this can only be done with the agreement of the legal operator.

Derby and Trent already operate joint services, for example Blagreaves Lane, and since 1968 have agreed co-ordination schemes involving several joint services. The Allestree scheme was introduced first.

The Mickleover and the Repton schemes will be introduced in a matter of weeks. The Spondon and the Chellaston schemes are agreed in broad principle, and negotiations are progressing at this moment. Those, Mr Gibson, are the deals that are being made.

The deals are arrived at after complex and detailed negotiations. Trent and Derby decide the bus services to be co-ordinated, and the sharing of money received from fares. The trade unions at Trent and Derby are then consulted in order to agree the scheme and the duty schedules necessary to operate it.

Derby Borough Council is most anxious to see that such negotiations are completed as quickly as possible, so that the Spondon and Chellaston schemes can be implemented without further delay. The Trent Motor Traction Company is similarly committed to the policy of co-ordination. Both operators are actively encouraged by the county council and the East Midland Traffic Commissioners.

Regarding Mr Gibson's last point, there is no requirement for a councillor to attend the Traffic Commissioners' hearing. To take time off from work, and then claim councillors' expenses for attending a meeting when I am not required, would be an irresponsible waste of ratepayers' money.'

Appendix 2

Questions asked

In three cases these questions were mailed. In all other cases they were used as a guide for oral questioning.

1 What are the overall arrangements for letters?
– A main Letters To The Editor section?
– Other letters sections, answered by a columnist, etc?
– Specialised letters, sports or business?
– Are letters changed for area editions?

2 In each category how many letters in total were received in the last seven days? And in each category how many letters were published in last seven days?

3 What are the editorial arrangements for answering letters, and for selecting and sub-editing letters for publication?

4 What are the main sorts of people who mostly write (eg advice seekers, redress seekers, views givers, prominent people, local people)?

5 In choosing letters for publication what sorts of letters are preferred (from typical readers, prominent people, spokesmen for organisations or groups)?

6 How important is the pungency, length/brevity, news value of the letter?

7 What policies do you have about cutting letters, correcting grammar, etc?

8 Do you offer prizes, or in other ways encourage readers to write letters in general or in particular?

9 In the last year have any topics attracted an especially large number of letters?

10 Are letters of public relations origin a problem? Do you suspect some letters of being part of a PR campaign?

11 When readers' letters make complaints against public officials or companies do you contact those officials or companies? If so, what do you then do about publishing replies and replying direct to the reader?

12 How often are letters used as the basis, or starting point, for subsequent editorial coverage? In news stories or in feature stories?

13 Do you have any special guidelines for handling letters from MPs, local Councillors, or foreign embassies?

14 Do you find it necessary to have any house quota rules (eg a maximum quota per individual or organisation per year)?

15 Are letters from journalists accepted? Your own or others?

16 Are any groups never allowed to have letters published? (eg National Front, Jehovah's Witnesses, Marxist groups).

17 Do you operate any special policies for letters during, or close to, Election campaigns?

18 What are the main legal problems with letters?

19 Are letters popular with readers?

20 Have any recent developments in television and radio (eg BBC Open Door, London Weekend 'Speak for Yourself', Tyne Tees 'Access', Cable TV, local radio, phone-ins) affected your letters operation?

21 Does your circulation department have much interest in letters (eg would a sales drive in a particular area be accompanied by the publication of more letters in the edition going to that area)?

22 Otherwise similar publications seem to have very different policies on letters. Any comments?

23 Do you have any comments on Press Council rulings on letters?

24 Letters seem to be relevant to 'access' (however defined) to the media, and also to the seeking of redress (either from the publication itself, or from local government etc). Any comments?

25 Do you have any comments on other possible forms of access-seeking or redress-seeking (eg Newspaper Ombudsman, *local* press councils)?

26 Do recent developments in the British press – such as free newspapers, controlled circulation magazines, underground papers – have any implications for letters operations?

27 Do you have any estimate of the number of letters per week to your publication which do not go through the formal editorial apparatus for letters? Do you have any policies for letters addressed to specialist correspondents, columnists and reporters?

28 Do you have any further comments on letters, which were not covered by any of these questions?

Jeremy Tunstall

Appendix 3

The Sun's answers

1   In *The Sun* readers' letters are published in four main areas:

(*a*) Liveliest Letters: A daily half-page plus of short, snappy letters or extracts from letters, mainly anecdotal.

(*b*) Letter Box: A column of letters with serious comments to make. This appears most days, but not necessarily every day.

(*c*) Sports Letters: An occasional feature on the sports pages.

(*d*) Claire Rayner's Column: Readers' letters with advice by Claire Rayner. This appears weekly as 'The Monday Problems Page'.

(*e*) In addition, we occasionally publish letters in the course of news stories or features, or for *Sun* promotional purposes, and a great many letters which are not published get individual replies. (We try to see that every letter sent to us elicits at least a formal acknowledgment.)

It is only rarely possible to change letter sections between editions.

2   In all categories, the numbers of letters received and published can fluctuate widely – seasonally and in line with the number and interest of talking points cropping up. To reply precisely to your question on the basis of the last 7 days could be misleading, but here is a table giving a reasonably accurate picture of an average week (6 publication days).

	No received	No published
Liveliest letters	2,500	75
Letterbox	311	23
Sports letters	100	10
Claire Rayner	250	6
Total	3,161	114

3   Letters addressed to a particular letter feature go immediately to the department responsible for that feature – Liveliest Letters to the Liveliest Letters Editor in the Feature Department, Letter Box to the Chief Leader Writer, Sports Letters to the Sports Editor and Problems to the Woman's Editor for Claire Rayner.

Letters not specifically addressed are opened in the Post Room and passed to whichever department seems most appropriate. There is regular interchange between departments so that a letter which appears to have been misdirected, either by the sender or in our Post Room, will find its way to the appropriate place.

Letters about the newspaper, but not intended for publication are passed to the editor, and where appropriate critical letters which *are* intended for publication are also shown to him by the departments to which they are directed. Where the editor does not reply personally he passes letters on either to one or other of the letter-handling departments or to an executive for reply.

Letters for publication are selected and sub-edited in the departments concerned. Those not selected get either a formal acknowledgment or an individual reply from the departments.

4 A wide spectrum of readers write to us, including all the categories mentioned in question four. The largest single contingent of letters is for Liveliest Letters, many of which come in response to invitations from us for readers to tell us their favourite personal story about some particular topic.

5 Generally we prefer the bulk of our letter space to be filled by letters from typical readers with personal views to express or stories to tell. Naturally an authoritative letter from a prominent person or spokesman with a particular point to make would be of interest; but long propagandist letters, advertising special pleading and party point-scoring are not welcome.

6 Originality is the most important consideration. (This is often allied to 'news value'.) We expect to ensure pungency and brevity in sub-editing.

7 We correct grammar, but try to retain individual style. We do not hesitate to cut letters, sometimes very severely indeed, so that as many readers as possible may make their main points, and as many contrasting points of view as possible may be reflected.

8 We pay a small fee (generally £1) for Liveliest Letters and Letter Box letters and sports letters published, with £5 for the lead Liveliest Letter. Sometimes we also offer special prizes for the best letter or letters on a topic where we have solicited letters.

9 Discounting topics where we have solicited letters, the topics which have brought the biggest postbag in the past year have been – roughly in order, but this must of course be a matter of memory:

(*a*) The Common Market Referendum. (A tremendous postbag over the period of the campaign, and a trickle before and since.)

(*b*) The Stonehouse Affair. (A steady flood. Very few published because of libel and/or contempt.)

(*c*) Postal charge increases.

10 Fairly frequently one recognises PR/pressure group letters. If a pressure group seem to have a valid point to make we would be inclined to let it take its chance among other valid points, but having made the point once we would naturally shun further letters seemingly of the same origin.

11 It is not possible to investigate every complaint. We try to investigate those that seem most serious. Otherwise we may advise a reader to write direct to the object of complaint, we may on occasion forward a reader's letter of complaint

ourselves, we may advise a reader about how to have a complaint investigated (eg by the Ombudsman, the Press Council, the Transport Users, etc).

Occasionally, where a complaint is general, we may publish a letter and await a reply from those complained of.

12   Letters are used – with the consent of the writers – as bases of news and features where this seems appropriate. It is impossible to generalise about how frequently this happens. Sometimes two or three good news stories may arise in one week in this way. At other times two or three weeks may go by without one.

13   Letters from public figures are normally treated exactly the same as letters from others readers. Obviously, though, if a correspondent has special knowledge of, or involvement in, a subject he is marginally more likely to have something worth saying about it than a general reader, or his views may at least be marginally more interesting to our readers because of his public standing.

14   We have no set quotas for letters. But one tries to avoid having the same correspondents cropping up time and again. Generally this is a matter for discretion by those who have to select letters for publication. They quickly get to know the regulars.

15   Journalists – our own and other papers' – are *Sun* readers, and as such are as much entitled to have their letters considered for publication as any other *Sun* readers are. They are considered on exactly the same basis.

16   We have no proscribed list of organisations. But see answer 10 above, about Pressure groups and PR.

17   During election campaigns we try to keep approximate parity between letters supporting the two main parties and to see that smaller parties also get reasonable representation. We feel it right to give, if anything, rather more letters opposed to our own editorial policy than in support of it. However, we try to avoid stultifying rigidity and set rules in this matter.

18   Readers who do not understand the laws of libel, contempt of court, etc cannot understand why we are 'censoring' their 'reasonable' letters.

19   Letters feature very high indeed in the lists of what they like about *The Sun* that readers help us with from time to time. They do not feature at all in the comparable lists of what they dislike about *The Sun*.

20   We do not think that television and radio have had an appreciable effect on our postbag. There has been some falling off in numbers of letters received but this has coincided with increases in postal rates rather than broadcasting developments.

21   Our circulation department has no influence on policy so far as letters published are concerned. Naturally unpublished letters which seem likely to be helpful to them in assessing readers' demands are copied to the circulation department.

22   *Chacun à son goût.*

23   We have not been directly affected by Press Council rulings on letters, which mostly concern cutting. Perhaps both our correspondents and the Press Council recognise that our letters columns are heavily edited and that those who submit letters to us accept that these letters will be edited.

In cases where the Press Council would be likely to uphold a correspondent's rights of reply we would normally wish to afford that whether there was a Press Council or not.

In the broader field, though, we feel that there is a discrepancy between the Press Council's contention that an editor has complete discretion as to what letters should or should not be published and their further contention that, if he does publish, he should not abridge letters without reference back to the correspondent.

24 We agree that letters are a vital element in general public access to the Press and in seeking redress. Even unpublished letters have their part to play as opinions and complaints are noted and considered.

25 We feel that there is probably adequate access to our paper at present, though we would resist any attempt, from Parliament the NUJ or anywhere else to diminish it. Redress is also available either directly or through the courts or through the Press Council. We do not believe that a newspaper ombudsman would be likely to achieve much more than the Press Council. Local Press Councils would, in our opinion, tend to a proliferation of largely trivial cases and vast uncertainty from area to area about what is or is not acceptable.

26 Apart from affording more outlets for chronic letter writers, we do not fee. that new developments in the Press have materially affected our letters operationl

27 We estimate that, apart from letters channelled through the four lanes listed at 1 and 2 above, we receive an average of 800 letters a week, but the figure varies widely from week to week.

Letters to particular members of the staff go to those members and are normally answered by them. Such letters are not, therefore, included in the 800. In some cases a letter to a staff member which seems suitable for publication and/or news or features follow-up will be passed back into the main channels.

28 Letters are the most important single feed-back we have from our readers. We take them very seriously indeed (even the silly ones!) as an indication of who our customers are and what they are thinking.

Appendix 4

Answers from Editor of the Bradford *Telegraph and Argus,* **Arnold Hadwin**
(This is a Westminster Press evening paper with a 110,000 sale, mainly in Bradford itself.)

1   It is usual from Mondays to Fridays to have a page or part of a page devoted to letters, varying from two columns to about $3\frac{1}{2}$ columns. In addition, we sometimes have a few important letters on the leader page, with a cross reference to the main letters page. We do not have letters answered by a columnist, but on very rare occasions when matters of fact are in dispute there is sometimes a comment by the Editor. We also spread specialised letters throughout the paper, primarily letters about sport (which do not introduce topics of general interest) and letters referring to Women's Page features which can be conveniently handled on the Women's Page. Letters are carried through all editions.

2   In the past seven days 59 letters were received: 38 were published as letters; 16 were followed up as news stories; and five were rejected – three on grounds of anonymity and two because they were solely abusive, containing no argument (we do not use letters with noms de plume and we have a 250-word limit on each letter).

3   Letters are generally handled by myself, my Deputy or my Assistant.

4   We have a very wide variety of letters in all of the categories mentioned.

5   In choosing letters we start from the assumption that the letter ought to be published unless it contains a libel or is plainly abusive or is a repetition of a previous letter from the same correspondent. We prefer letters that are topical, have something new to say and add to the general understanding of a problem. We would give preference to letters from people who have not previously written to the paper. We are not particularly concerned about prominent people writing to us, rather that a very wide cross-section of opinion should appear in the letters column.

6   We do have a 250-word limit, as already mentioned, so that more letters can be used. If the letter is much longer than that and comes, say, from an organisation or from an office holder, we can often turn it into a statement and use it in the news columns with the approval of the person concerned. News value is certainly important in the sense that such letters tend to get our bigger headlines.

7   Where we need to cut a letter, we would normally consult the writer, although quite often on the stone a decision has to be taken to cut a few words here and there. We would aim to make the cut in a way that does not affect

the argument of the letter or interfere with the style in which it is written. We would certainly correct grammar: indeed, many of our correspondents ask us to do just that where they themselves are not particularly literate.

8   We do not offer prizes for letters, but we certainly encourage readers to express their views in general, and on odd occasions ask them to express their views on a particular subject.

9   In the past year the Common Market attracted an especially large number of letters. So, too, did the proposed new motorway in the Aire Valley, rate rises and general problems of inflation. But by far the largest number of letters come from people who are concerned about things that are going wrong on their particular patch.

10   Letters of public relations origin do not present a problem. Over the years we have learned to spot them.

11   Every complaint made against public officials or companies is followed up. The individuals concerned are contacted immediately and their replies are published with the letter. Quite often, because of the two or three days' delay in assembling letter and reply (especially in local government affairs), by the time the letter is published the grievance has been put right. We have found this to be a very effective way of getting things done and have innumerable letters to support the point.

12   A high proportion of our letters are used as the starting point for subsequent editorial coverage. Sometimes when several letters are used on the same subject we turn them into a feature story, using the views expressed as the main content of the story. Readers have got into the habit of airing their grievances in the *Telegraph and Argus* and as a result some excellent news stories start with a letter to the Editor.

13   No, we do not have special guidelines for handling letters from MPs, local councillors or foreign embassies – they take their place with all the other letters received from our readers.

14   We do not have a house quota rule. Where individuals keep bombarding us with letters, I return some, saying that the individual must understand that the paper cannot become a personal platform, but if he has something new to say on a new subject then his letter will be considered. The same applies to any over-enthusiastic organisation.

15   Letters from journalists, my own and others, are accepted by the paper.

16   We have no ban on any groups.

17   Certainly during an election campaign we have a special policy. We have a special Election Forum section for political letters and try to keep a fairly strict balance in terms of column inches devoted to parties and candidates, giving the main headline to a different party each day. Two days before the election we bring this feature to a close, with the proviso that no new material can be introduced on the day before the election, although factual inaccuracies can be put right. All the parties locally know this arrangement and it works well.

18   There are no specially difficult legal problems related to letters that do not relate to other news stories. We discourage readers from merely getting into slanging matches and would draw attention to any possible libels, asking

correspondents either to delete the offending passage from the letter or to re-word it so that it is not libellous. There is a minor problem of some correspondents signing with other people's names. Where we have doubts, we would send a postcard to the name and address on the letter asking if the letter had indeed originated there or, in some instances, 'phone the person who was supposed to have written the letter.

19 All evidence suggests that the letters columns are very popular with readers.

20 Recent developments in television and radio have not affected in any way how we handle our letters.

21 Our publication of letters has nothing to do with any district sales drive. If there is a page of letters on a very topical subject, we would sometimes put out a bill advertising the fact, but the bill is a result of the letters, not vice versa.

22 Several newspapers have different ways of handling letters. It is often a question of individual judgment. For our part, we think the letter-writer should always be named, that they should be restricted to 250 words to allow more correspondence to get into the paper, and that they should cover a wide cross-section of opinion. It is one way of encouraging readers to participate in the paper. It is often the only way in which an individual can get his views aired. It is a way of drawing attention to grievances and if the newspaper is doing its job correctly it will attempt to get those grievances put right. There are papers who merely want to make superficial capital out of letters. We are not such a paper.

23 By and large, the Press Council rulings on letters have contained much sense.

24 Letters, indeed, are a very important way of airing grievances and seeking redress. It is part of the philosophy of this newspaper that the paper should serve the community, canalising its aspirations and making more articulate its demands, and the letters column is certainly part of this process.

25 I have no particular comments to make in this section.

26 The development of underground newspapers and the like obviously means that newspapers are not meeting all the demands placed upon them. It would be very strange indeed if they were. Community newspapers and underground papers perform a slightly different function. We are aware of their existence and often follow up some of their leads, but here readers have easy access to the letters column and the existence of such newspapers has not affected our Letters operation.

27 Where letters are addressed to special correspondents, columnists or reporters, they are usually brought to my attention, but it is not a significant part of our operation. We do have a readers' advice service, in addition to our Letters to the Editor, which produces up to 40 letters a week asking for specific advice on income tax problems and the like. These are dealt with by an Inquiry Bureau and we constantly get letters of thanks from readers who have been so helped. We also get innumerable letters on gardening topics which are answered directly by Bill Sowerbutts and we get a cross-section of replies into our gardening page.

28   We look upon the Letters section of the paper as being an extremely important section, not merely because it is well-read but it gives readers the feeling that they have at least one platform for their views and they know that they can criticise the newspaper freely. For instance, the *Telegraph and Argus*, although editorially very much in favour of Britain staying in the Common Market, printed a higher percentage of anti-Common Market letters than any other newspaper in the country. It is not unusual for considerable prominence to be given to letters which oppose the editorial viewpoint. But by and large the majority of our letters are concerned with the improvement of the community and encouragingly, there is a great deal of evidence to suggest that they do this effectively.

Appendix 5

The Times Letters : A visit

A   General organisation of The Times' letters

I spent 7 hours from 12.00 am to 7.00 pm at The Times letter operation on the 19 November 1975. The Times letters' operation is under the control of Geoffrey Woolley and two other journalists work with him; Norman Grenyer is another very experienced Times journalist in his 50s. Thirdly there is Nicholas Keith, aged in his late 20s. This 3 journalist team is supported by 3 secretaries and they also have access to a typing pool.

In the big mid-week days all 3 journalists are on together; on Sunday only one journalist is on and there is nobody on on Saturday. A former night editor of The Times helps with the sub-editing for about 2 hours a day. The staff start arriving at 10.00 am; there is always someone on for stone-subbing at about 7.30 to 8.00 in the evening. The letters operation controls its entire output including its own sub-editing and right through to subbing on the stone.

All letters which are genuinely letters to the editor are logged. Letters which are intended for the advertising, or some other, department are routed there. Woolley himself sees all the incoming letters and divides them up into 5 categories. All letters that involve complaints against members of The Times staff are seen by the Editor. Some letters are confidential and not intended for publication, either so marked or so categorised by Woolley; some of these go on to the Editor. Woolley also divides up the letters roughly into those which are possibles for immediate publication, those which are very unlikely for publication and also ones which need to go to 'experts'. A lot of letters are routed to specialist correspondents or 'experts'. Letters about grammar, the use of English, American usages and so on go to a sub-editor who specialises in them. Other people on the staff answer letters about religion, particular foreign languages, and so forth.

Unlike most other letters' operations there is no immediate acknowledgment of the letter. As with other letters operations, they have several standard replies. Reject replies are done in the typing pool; more gentle let-down letters are dictated by the journalist members of the letters' team – usually only of four or five lines but thanking the person specifically and sometimes making a brief comment on the subject matter. In other cases a letter of 10 or so lines is based on comments received from a specialist within the office.

There is one other specialised letters' operation in The Times Business News. Some letters are routed from the main letters operation because they are to do with business; some letters are addressed direct to Business News. Letters which go to specialists for comment always come back to the letters' operation. The letters desk itself deals only with executives – a letter in the area of a news specialist would go to the Home News Editor. Standard replies are normally as from the Editor but a more detailed reply is signed by the journalist who handles it. There are no separate sports letters, no changes between area editions. Of the 250 letters a day about 30 a day are routed to Business News.

The letters operation reports direct to the Editor, William Rees-Mogg. Only two other areas report direct to the Editor – the Leader Writers and the Obituaries. One other person seems to report direct to the Editor which is Bernard Levin, who has an office which he shares with the Editor's secretaries. The letter journalists prepare letters for printing and, if the letter is typed, subbing is done straight onto the original letter. Handwritten letters – and there are some such selected for publication – are typed before being prepared for the printer. The Times' policy is that if letters are used they are used in their entirety. Occasionally letters are returned to the writer for cuts. In other cases small changes to a particular sentence for grammatical or legal reasons will be agreed over the telephone. The layout has to be arranged around the length of the letters which are chosen as lead letters. Small spaces are left at the bottom of the page and, since letters are not cut, those which go into these small spaces have to be selected to a large extent on the single criterion of their size. This makes slightly unpredictable what the final mix of letters will be. Occasionally, Woolley says, they have a very good small letter and then they try to make the page up from the bottom. In mid-afternoon he starts sketching layouts.

Woolley says the numbers of letters has increased considerably since he was first involved with letters in the 1950s; it now must be roughly double what it was then. There has been a big increase in letters coming from the education world, and from trade union leaders. There are fewer letters now from 'Proconsuls'. He thinks the biggest categories of people writing letters are professional people such as doctors, lawyers and people from the education world.

B The selection of letters

On criteria of selection, he believes that pungency is especially important. Length is not necessarily against a letter since The Times normally prints two or three long letters each day. Changes to grammar are minimal – unless it looks like a typing mistake. To some extent letter writers are allowed to make their own grammatical rules.

They always insist on letters being exclusive and sometimes check this with the writer on the telephone. Letters in carbon are always suspect, while handwritten letters are not. They normally keep about five columns worth of letters set in proof – slightly more letters than you need for a single day. This is a check against minor strikes or a hold-up in the post or something of that kind. Woolley himself looks at The Daily Telegraph and The Guardian every day but apparently not the Financial Times.

Woolley worked very briefly on The Times before 1939. When he came back in 1946 he worked on the letters column for two years. At that stage the letters were run by Derek Hudson and Woolley was the only other member of the letter staff. He went to The Times Washington Office for five years, 1948 to 1953, and he has been on the letters' column since 1953 – for 22 years.

Some of the expert advisers used by the letters' column are not staff specialists but journalists on retainers. One example is their medical expert who comes in with a comment on some letters about induced childbirth – a correspondence which was running in *The Times* a few days ago. He is the Editor of the *British Medical Journal*. One of the biggest stirrers-up of letters is Bernard Levin. Levin always sees letters that relate to his column. *The Times* carries very few appeal letters but it does happen to be carrying one today – the appeal for the journalist William Hardcastle who died recently. The story which appeared in *The Sunday Times* last Sunday mentioned, in describing the Hardcastle appeal, that it would be kicked off by a letter in *The Times* during the following week; Woolley says they do not like any statement to the effect that a letter will appear in *The Times*.

No prizes are ever offered. They seldom use the kind of letter which calls for people to write in about a particular subject. Very occasionally they will take a letter from a body like a Royal Commission asking for evidence.

They never accept letters from Press Attachés – only from Ambassadors; this came about because on one occasion an Arab Ambassador wrote a letter and when the Israelis produced their reply it came only from the Press Attaché. Something relatively new is that British Cabinet ministers now write in their own names, whereas previously the letter would have come from a PRO. The person who began this was George Brown. They never accept letters from the chief PRO of an organisation. If the letter is interesting they would 'phone back and say that they will accept the letter if it is signed by a director or the head of the organisation. They are on the look-out for letters which might be of public relations origin. Occasionally a phrase appears in a letter which you have also seen in another letter recently: you would normally reject such a letter automatically.

Letters are seldom used as the basis for editorial coverage. *The Times* regards its letters' column as important in its own right, and sees no need to expand upon a letter. Very occasionally, only once every 2 or 3 years, several letters will be used as the basis of a feature article. Letters would never be circulated to a specialist for information previous to their being used in the letters column. (This seems another example of the rather privileged position which the letters column has in *The Times*.)

They receive quite a lot of letters from MPs and, as with all categories of letters, they do not use the majority. Today is the opening day of the session, the day of the Queen's Speech. Relatively few MPs write between parliamentary sessions but when sessions begin the number of letters from MPs increases. There are on this day 5 letters from MPs, none of which is being used. They dislike using a letter which is something that the MP could say in the House. They prefer MPs to be commenting on something which has appeared in the newspaper. They would normally not use more than 2 letters from political figures on any one day. They do give a lot of space to Liberals, and I ask if there is any criterion behind this. Could it be that he is thinking of the size of the Liberal vote or the number of Liberals among the readership of *The Times*? He says the latter is probably the case.

There is no house quota for individuals or organisations. They would not necessarily be against accepting another letter from someone who had a letter published only a few days ago. They don't want to bore the readers, nor do they wish to damage the person who writes the letter. My impression is that although no numerical count is kept, of MPs or others – Woolley inevitably keeps in his head a rough score of how many letters he has had from particular categories of people in the last week or two, and in practice he tries to balance Labour and Conservatives letters, Arabs and Israeli and so on. This also follows from the way in which the Editor chooses letters for publication.

Only occasionally do they accept letters from journalists on their own staff. If a letter had been published criticising a staff journalist he might be allowed to reply. In some circumstances they willingly accept letters from journalists on other papers.

A lot of letters, including some of the best, are delivered by messenger. I suggest that they have the advantage of speed, but Woolley says this is not necessarily so – sometimes a letter arriving a day or two later fits into a correspondence better. (Nevertheless, I suspect that slightly more attention is paid to hand delivered letters and they do get some benefit from speed.)

Telephone conversations with letter writers and potential writers are common – a dozen or so such conversations take place during the day. The first telephone call is from Lord Hailsham, who has noticed a mistake in his lead letter published this morning. He dictates on the 'phone a very brief letter of amendment. They only accept such dictated letters in exceptional cases. A sizeable minority of all published letters have been shortened by the author. When the letter writer has been asked to shorten the letter, it will normally be used, but unforeseen circumstances may prevent this.

They accept letters from organisations such as the National Front, although obviously with caution. They published the first letter from the Palestine Liberation Organisation. A subject like fluoridation makes you cautious; such a letter will probably lead to many other letters on the same topic. During election campaigns there are no special rules and no quota system. They do use a lot of political letters immediately before general elections. At the second election of 1974 they had a particularly large number of letters, although the two previous elections brought fewer. The biggest legal problem is libel; another is sub-judice. A lawyer sees all proofs of the paper, and additional legal advice is available from the group legal advisers to Times Newspapers; the latter deal with special cases and with any legal cases currently in the pipeline. A particular eye from the libel point of view is always kept on letters from MPs and QCs, who are used to privileged communication in Parliament and the courts. *The Times* never accepts the legal advice of a letter writer, for instance if somebody says he has already cleared the letter with his own lawyers.

The popularity of letters with readers is high. Woolley doesn't think broadcast access programmes have had any impact. They have no connection with *The Times'* circulation drives and their only connection with advertising is that some complaints about advertising come to them, and are then channelled to the advertising department.

The idea of a newspaper Ombudsman does not appeal to Woolley. There are letters addressed to specialists, to the news editor, to Bernard Levin and so forth, but he has no idea how many such letters there are. Levin certainly gets a lot of letters and has a full-time secretary who answers them.

C The Press Council

I have a short session with John Grant, the managing editor of *The Times* and formerly the defence correspondent. He always deals with the Press Council. Roughly what happens is that *The Times* receives about 25 complaints per year dealing with letters – complaints that the person concerned will go to the Press Council. In about half of these cases, about 12 a year, the Press Council tells *The Times* that it has initiated a preliminary enquiry. In about four cases a year the Press Council goes through its full procedure of enquiry with *The Times* letter case, and gives its judgment. In all cases so far the Press Council has found in favour of *The Times* and against the complaint from the letter writer. A high proportion of the cases in which *The Times* is involved with the Press Council do concern letters. John Grant himself has never appeared personally in front of the Press Council. The situation is fairly standard – the complainant says the right of reply has been denied by *The Times*. He shows me examples of correspondence and some seem trivial. In some cases when a letter is turned down the person who receives the rejection letter complains direct to the Press Council without even saying to *The Times* that they would like the decision to be reconsidered. He personally thinks that the Press Council takes up some rather trivial cases. He thinks that the Press Council in general is embarrassed by finding in favour of the newspapers too often – so in order to try and balance things up they tend to find one small point of criticism of the paper. Then they find in favour of the paper but for that point. He thinks this is outside their terms of reference; they are supposed to give an adjudication, not some sort of balanced judgment of right and wrong. He appears to think the Press Council fairly unimportant, but he certainly thinks that Editors would take very seriously any critical finding against them by the Press Council.

D *The Times* Business News Letters

The man in charge of business letters is Dennis Topping, deputy editor of *The Times* Business News. They receive about 30 letters a day of which about 20 come through the main letters operation and about 10 come to Business News itself. The general impression created by Topping is that the Business News finds it relatively difficult to attract letters and lives very much in the shadow of the main letters column. Topping says on several times that they are never short of enough letters to publish. But this clearly is partly because they are fed letters from the main letters column – with only the letters that go direct to Business News they would scarcely have enough letters which they would want to publish.

They send acknowledgments before they print a letter – mainly as an anti-hoax device. There is a tendency for letters to log-jam – partly because of layout problems. Unlike the main letters column which always has four columns down the right-hand side of the page, the Business News letters column has a very variable space. It always has three columns at the top of the page but the distance down the page the letters run is uncertain and is dependent on advertising. They also have the policy of using letters in full and a fairly limited space, which is uncertain even earlier in the day. On this particular day Topping is using two very long letters which will take up nearly all of the space. The maximum amount of space that they can have in a week is 15 columns – because the letters do not appear on Saturday, but usually the space in a week is well below 15 columns, something like 10 – depending on advertising.

They normally reject any kind of Public Relations letter; they quite often get letters signed by chief PROs and send them back asking for them to be signed by a director. They have recently received many letters complaining about the service provided by the Post Office and the gas service. They receive many letters about consumer problems or consumer aspects of business, rather than about the production end of business.

The letters column in the Business News began in 1968 at Dennis Topping's own insistence; at first they printed a few letters and then later, when they had set a letter space, they attracted more letters. Space attracts letters – the more letters you print, the more letters you attract. If they did expand the letters space they would certainly get more good letters to put into the space.

All letters are routinely read for legal advice. They go to special legal advice perhaps once a fortnight. Letters are popular but apparently there is no special readership research which he has seen for Business News letters. They never change letters between editions and they also have a rule that they only carry exclusive letters.

He does not regard himself as having any very serious competition. *The Daily Telegraph* business section carries only a very few letters on Monday. He thinks the *Financial Times* letters are rather overshadowed by the main letters in *The Times* itself. They keep a small stock-pile of letters against breakdowns in the postal services. Recently the internal mail people in Times Newspapers were on strike which meant that incoming mail did not reach them.

Some letters even to Business News come in handwriting and they certainly use such letters. The number of letters currently is relatively stable – the amount of space given to letters has recently been reduced because of the general pressure on space in *The Times*.

They like the idea of printing letters which will attract further letters of disagreement. Sometimes they print a |letter which they know to be inaccurate because they think this may represent a false idea held by other people and they do this in the expectation that some correction will come from an authoritative source.

E   Day's drama: The missing LSO letter

Woolley tells me they have a policy of not using anonymous letters. However, as with most of their rules, they are willing to make occasional exceptions. They did recently run an anonymous letter by a girl who had been raped.

During the day, there is a minor drama connected with a letter from the manager of the London Symphony Orchestra. This morning a large interview has appeared in *The Guardian* with the LSO manager in which he is saying that members of the Orchestra drink too much and so forth. This interview took place on the way back from a tour in Japan. The manager rings *The Times* while I am there and talks to Woolley; it is 2 pm. He has written a letter replying to *The Guardian* article and it is being delivered. Will it be published? Woolley replies that they will be very interested to see the letter but can't guarantee to publish it. It seems that subsequently the manager when replying to other enquiries from Fleet Street says that *The Times* will be carrying his letter next morning. Later in the afternoon there are 'phone calls from other papers including *The Guardian*, the *Daily Mirror* and the *Daily Mail*. Woolley tells them that the letter has not arrived, which it has not. A reporter from *The Guardian* comes into the office asking for the letter.

He says isn't it amazing that a man has written to *The Times* when all the fuss is about an article published in *The Guardian*. Woolley says contentedly that this is always happening. Eventually, the letter arrives in the office at 5.00 pm and is immediately shown to the libel lawyer. He says it does make libel problems and the decision is taken not to use the letter this evening – partly because its author is now out of his home and thus unavailable to agree changes by 'phone.

I go along with Woolley to hear a discussion between him and the libel lawyer – a young Mr Hogg, son of Lord Hailsham. The lawyer points out that the letter contains statements which might be held to libel the journalist. Woolley and Hogg go through the letter, toning down the points which raise such problems. The LSO manager is still not to be found on the telephone to agree the cuts. He will now be offered the revised non-libellous version on the telephone in the morning and, if he agrees, the letter will then probably be used, but not necessarily. During this session Charles Douglas-Home, assistant editor in charge of Home News, is present.

F   The Editor selects

In mid-afternoon I see the meeting between Woolley, the letters' editor, and William Rees-Mogg the Editor. This session occurs daily at 3.00 pm and usually lasts half-an-hour. Rees-Mogg is 15 minutes late today. He sits on the sofa besides Woolley. Woolley hands Rees-Mogg one-by-one the letters which he has selected as the most publishable. Rees-Mogg looks at each letter, reads it very quickly and gives an opinion, 'Yes' or 'No'. Rees-Mogg selects, out of the pile of some 30 letters, six which are all on the same subject – 'Is Zionism Racialist?' – sparked by a recent *Times* leader. Rees-Mogg comments that this will make an interesting debate. Although Rees-Mogg gives no reason in most cases for saying yes or no, it is quickly evident to Woolley what Rees-Mogg is choosing as the lead topic. Another long letter is also chosen on the subject of pay in the Civil Service, a topic which has been running for some days in *The Times*. Sensing that these are going to be the two major topics, Woolley shuffles away some other longish letters for which there will not be adequate space to-day, and he starts serving up shorter letters—these are letters destined for the bottom of the page. As the session proceeds more of Rees-Mogg's verdicts are No. He accepts the first four or five of the heavyweight letters that Woolley has offered but by the time they are down to about the 20th letter being offered Rees-Mogg is saying no much more often than yes. When 15 or so letters have been chosen the process stops, and Rees-Mogg picks up the pile of accepted letters again and glances through them. He indicates which of the letters on the racialist Zionism issue he wishes to be the lead letter. He also designates the Civil Service letter as the right hand top. He says to put the Zionist correspondence across three columns. Then a few lighter remarks are exchanged including a joke about a funny letter which Bernard Levin offered Woolley as he was waiting for Rees-Mogg to appear; this is a two-line letter on the subject of cats. Of the total wordage which Woolley has offered, Rees-Mogg accepts about two-thirds and rejects about one-third.

After we get back to the letters office, I ask Woolley how typical this operation has been and he says fairly representative. He points out again that Rees-Mogg is a very fast reader. I say to him that some outsiders might be surprised by the lack of discussion, but he says that since this is a daily operation and time is short there is really no need for, or time for, much discussion. As the letters operation in the late afternoon moves towards the production process the decisions which the Editor has taken play a very important part. He has decided the strategic shape of the layout and he has decided certain letters as 'must' letters. These obviously are the two lead letters in the two main correspondences and one or two lower letters are also 'must' ones – for example the Hardcastle appeal letter. These decisions limit the layout possibilities and there is not room for all of the Zionism letters; of the six to which Rees-Mogg said yes, only four in fact are run in the paper today although some of them may be used the next day.

G Editorial conference

At 4.15 pm I go to the late afternoon editorial conference. This occurs in Rees-Mogg's office and all the executives are present. It takes the usual form of a catalogue of the main stories, with the foreign editor, home news editor, sports editor, etc, running down their lists. The letters constitute one such list and one decision is made at the conference. The foreign news editor reports that Franco may very well die this evening and Woolley, as letters' editor, says that in this case a letter which they still have set in print from the previous day, which deals with Franco, will therefore not be used. The editorial conference breaks up very quickly.

H Closing comments

Some letters reach the proof stage but are subsequently not used. There is the practice of sending the proofs of these letters to their authors; this happens at the rate of about two letters a day.

Other impression of *The Times* Letters' operation: All three journalists in charge of the operation eat sandwiches on this particular day.

I am surprised by the number of letters which come in handwriting and some of which are used. Lord Hailsham apparently always writes his letters in extremely readable handwriting. The lead letter of the day on the Zionist question is typed not very well on both sides of the paper.

When Woolley discovers that they will not be running the letter from the LSO manager, he 'phones up the newsdesks of the 3 papers which have enquired - the *Daily Mail*, *The Guardian*, and the *Daily Mirror*. He says this is slightly, but not very, unusual because it is quite common for *The Times* Letters to feature as news stories in other papers. They are perfectly happy for this to happen – the normal arrangement is that other papers see the letter in the first edition at 10.00 pm and then put it into their columns. *The Times* is perfectly happy with this if there is a mention that the story is based on a letter in *The Times*.

There are several indications that the letters' operation is a special élite part of *The Times*. There is a clear connection with foreign correspondence. Woolley himself has been a foreign correspondent. Working on the letters' column is a very good job for a young journalist because it brings you into direct contact with the Editor and also with all the senior executives on the paper. The normal practice is to keep the junior person in the letters' operation for about 2 years before promoting him to something else. And the policy is also to have 2 senior experienced journalists in main charge of the operation.

'Editorial Sovereignty' in the British Press: its past and present

by Jeremy Tunstall of The City University

"Editorial Sovereignty" in the British Press: its past and present

Contents

Contents

Author's note

1   The information on which this paper is based was gathered in the course of personal interviews over a number of years. While doing research for *Journalists at Work* (Constable 1971) in 1966–68, I interviewed 10 provincial daily editors, 15 editors of national daily and Sunday newspapers, 10 editorial directors, ex-editors or deputy editors and several magazine editors. In preparing the paper on 'Letters to the Editor' another seven editors were interviewed. In the preparation of this paper, I interviewed a further 10 provincial daily editors, 10 provincial weekly editors and four national daily editors in 1976. Of these latter, the interviews with provincial editors averaged about two hours and those with national editors a little less.

2   Some of these interviews were conducted jointly with Dr Colin Seymour-Ure who also provided some of the material in the opening historical sections. I am especially indebted to him for the passages which deal with C P Scott, H A Gwynne and Geoffrey Dawson. I would also like to thank Colin Seymour-Ure, Terry Dignan and Alan J Lee for commenting on this report in draft.

J T

December 1976

Summary

A The history of 'editorial sovereignty'

1 The sovereign editor

1.1 *The Editor as opinionated, partisan and competitive: Assumption and paradox.* The Sovereign Editor idea assumes an Editor who is opinionated, partisan and competitive. These assumptions were somewhat unreal even before 1855.

1.2 *The Times and its Editor before 1885.* John Delane, the famous mid-century Editor – often thought of as *the* Sovereign Editor – had less autonomy than his predecessor. Delane himself was nearly sacked at one point and John Walter III limited his sovereignty to politics and opinion. The manager played a substantial editorial role and appointed foreign correspondents; nor did the Editor have much control in production. *The Times* before 1855 was an 8-page paper, with a sizeable staff of notetaking reporters and an élite of Oxford educated leader writers presided over by the Editor.

1.3 *Provincial newspapers and their Editors before 1855.* Presiding over a small expensive weekly sheet the Editor was still not completely separate from the printer.

1.4 *The Manchester Guardian and the provincial Sovereign Editor tradition.* C P Scott was a sovereign Editor but in later years he was also the owner of the *Manchester Guardian*, as well as its Editor and night-editor. Other prestige provincial mornings had similar high-minded and educated Editors, but their sovereignty depended upon continued proprietorial support or upon membership of the owning family.

2 Around 1900

2.1 *The Sovereign Editor in commercial decline.* The Sovereign Editor idea flowered briefly at the end of the century, but quickly withered. It was getting too expensive.

2.2 *The commercial popular revolution.* The late Victorian press had fallen into a state of sloth and inefficiency; the new proprietors wanted to sweep all this away including sovereign editorships.

2.3 *The Proprietor-editor.* The *Daily Telegraph,* the most successful of Victorian dailies, was always owned and edited by one man – a dual role Northcliffe also performed in the spectacular early days of the *Daily Mail.* Pearson did likewise with the *Daily Express.*

2.4   Co-existence: Commerce and Editorial Sovereignty, Editor and Proprietor.
Editorial sovereignty continued into the twentieth century, partly because with partisan provincial daily competition, neutrality did not yet spell profit.

2.5   Editors and journalists. Journalists in the increasingly commercial conditions found themselves sinking into genteel poverty. The result was the NUJ, modelled on the teachers' union.

3   Structural change and Editors

3.1   The popular national press. With the enormously larger scale of operations the sovereign Editor was a needless luxury.

3.2   The provincial press: Chains and the decline of partisanship and competition. Massive commercial changes and the move towards monopoly in the provincial press removed the last traces of Editorial sovereignty.

3.3   The Labour press and the Liberal press. The Daily Herald Editor had to serve three different masters; the Liberal press faded with Editors subordinate to proprietors.

3.4   The eccentric Press Lords were politically unreliable in party terms but utterly dominated their Editors. The Daily Mirror was built around a marketing plan, with the Editor a relatively minor functionary.

3.5   The unionisation of journalists proceeded gradually. Recruitment was mainly through the small local papers.

3.6   Geoffrey Dawson: the most sovereign Editor. Dawson, during his second term as The Times' Editor (1922–41) secured a legal contract which made him a truly Sovereign Editor.

B   Editors in recent times (1950–76)

Introduction: Scale, complexity and the importance of financial indicators have increased enormously since 1950.

4   Some 1960s examples

This chapter gives impressionistic sketches of a number of different Editorial styles and arrangements, in the 1966–8 period:

5 The Editor as departmental manager

5.1 *The Editor as strategically dependent.* Few Editors are directors; the history of the publication and its stable-mates constitute constraints. Editorial space varies with advertising space, and circulation losses are constraining. Production arrangements must also be accepted. Managers appoint Editors, and regard them in effect as middle management.

5.2 *The Editor as autonomous departmental manager?* How autonomous an Editor will feel depends upon how much he accepts the strategic guidelines. Editors have little choice but to pursue commercial goals; conflict over advertising or circulation is usually minimal. Most attempts at editorial innovation have financial implications and require senior management approval.

5.3 *The competitive situation* lays down powerful strategic guidelines. So does a monopoly situation – plus higher profit targets.

5.4 *Editor's routine and editorial style.* These vary considerably. But most Editors are over-worked – in terms of total hours, the speed and pressure of work, the wide range of tasks and lack of relaxation.

5.5 *The Editor as presider over opinion.* This is still important on morning newspapers but elsewhere opinion as such is often minimal.

5.6 *The Editor as personnel manager.* Control over hiring of journalists is the Editor's key prerogative.

6 Editorship as occupation

6.1 *Image presenter.* Being a suitable seeming public face and voice for his publication is one of the Editor's many duties.

6.2 *Career patterns.* National Editors tend to have rapid maverick careers and to be slightly risky choices; other Editors tend to have more steady careers and are safe choices. Educational levels are low.

6.3 *Groups, pay and security.* Editors' pay is low. There is considerable security in the sense of complete sacking being unusual; there is major dis-satisfaction with pay, a strong sense of dependence – both of which contrast with the very considerable creative satisfaction of the job.

6.4 *Ideology, mystique and doctrine.* Editors may be unusual in the width of the gap between their prevailing ideology and their everyday behaviour. The NUJ stoppage is a particularly good opportunity to narrow this gap.

6.5 *Association: The GBNE.* Comments of Editors relate mainly to the GBNE's close connection with the Newspaper Society. The GBNE reflects the segmentation and polarisation of the British press.

6.6 *Editor as recruiter: The professional prerogative with the trade union consequence.* The proportion of graduate recruits is rising slowly, but among non-graduates – on present trends likely to be the majority of journalists for the rest of this century – the occupational *malaise* may be increasing. The local Editor recruits lowly paid, lowly educated young people into an occupation which offers decreasing opportunities for advancement. At the local Technical College white collar unionism is rife and seems applicable to the dead-end job of local journalism. The system of recruitment satisfies editorial prerogative but also encourages white collar unionism.

7 Possible changes

7.1 Polarisation, false dichotomies, short-sightedness

7.2 Altering titles and functions

7.3 Groups and London Management

7.4 Pay, status, training, education and security

7.5 The professionalisation of journalism?

7.6 Finance

Part A   The History of 'Editorial Sovereignty'

Introduction

'How can the editor, with responsibility for editorial content only – no responsibility for getting advertising, circulation management, buying newsprint and making deals – rate ahead of the manager? . . . The editor is no longer the top man in any viable newspaper. That is an old concept'.[1] Lord Thomson in 1967.

It may be an old concept, but was this ever the predominant – or even common – pattern? Since so many present day beliefs and statements about editorship involve assumptions about the past this paper begins with an historical survey. The influence of the past is everywhere to be seen in the British Press, and nowhere more than in the case of editorship. The prestige national newspaper field is still dominated by papers which date back to 1855; most of the leading provincials date back to the 1870s or so, and the national popular press is dominated by papers launched around 1900.

Many of the leading newspapers of today thus have their own long traditions of editorship. On the whole, leading British papers have either longer or less chequered histories than those of the USA; and in contrast to most of western Europe and Japan, Britain's press did not have the experience of being 'born again' around 1945.

Historical writing on the British press consists largely of biographies of individuals (often Editors), and histories of individual publications. Much historical material is thus available on editorship. However almost all of this material is anecdotal and lacking in hard detail – for example financial detail. These circumstances may have led to two related 'misunderstandings'. Firstly, the general impression of a tradition of Sovereign Editorship may lack historical substance. Secondly, we may in Britain have evolved a present day conception of editorship which is not held in other countries and which itself contains a logical flaw. This is the notion of the Editor separate from the commercial side of the publication but sovereign within the editorial department.

The best international comparison in this field is Colin Seymour-Ure's 100-page essay on political policy-making in mainly prestige newspapers from Britain, Australia, USA, France, Canada, Japan, Turkey, West Germany, Switzerland South Africa.[2] This essay strongly conveys the impression that even on most prestige newspapers the Editor reports either to an individual (such as an editor-in-chief or publisher) who has responsibility beyond the editorial, or a committee responsible for the strategy of editorial policy.

1   *UK Press Gazette*, 4 September 1967.
2   Colin Seymour-Ure 'Policy-Making in the Press' *Government and Opposition* 4, Autumn 1969, pp 426–525.

One of the themes of this report is that personal impressions of Editors and editorship may often be misleading. At various periods of British Press history it has been thought that the great days of editorship are recently over and that belief perhaps still persists today. My suggestion here is that Sovereign Editorship never existed except in exceptional circumstances. The most striking examples in the last hundred years are C P Scott, who in his later period also owned the *Manchester Guardian*, and Geoffrey Dawson who used his exceptional contractual sovereignty at *The Times* to pursue a policy of appeasement.

In view of the great tradition of the British Press and the vigour of historical scholarship in Britain, it is surprising that serious British Press historical research is in its infancy. Over the next decade much serious historical work on the British Press will be published; one consequence of this, I suspect, will be an increasing awareness that Britain has a tradition of Proprietor-Editors (represented by such leading late Victorian newspapers as *The Daily Telegraph* and *Daily Chronicle*), a tradition which is every bit as honourable as, and somewhat more real than, the Sovereign Editor tradition.

After a lengthy historical section this report focuses on the late 1960s – using interview and other material which I (and in some cases Oliver Boyd-Barrett) collected at the time, mainly about national Editors.

The final passages deal with 1975 and 1976. I have used data collected from Editors and journalists in mail surveys conducted for the Royal Commission on the Press. In addition, I conducted on behalf of the Royal Commission interviews with a number of Editors in 1975–76[1]. My sincere thanks go to these Editors.

Some may think this a pessimistic and negative report. In a sense it does have those intentions. In my view the Sovereign Editor is a myth rather than a tradition with real substance. In my view it should be buried, because Editors and journalists – of all people – must try to see the world as it is, and as it was. This does not mean that the present position of Editors is fixed and unalterable. On the contrary, editorship is probably entering a period of rapid change. Possibilities for the future will be better understood if past and present myths can be discarded.

---

1   For details of the interviews carried out by the author see the Author's Note.

1 The Sovereign Editor

1.1 The Editor as Opinionated, Partisan and Competitive: Assumption and Paradox

R D Blumenfeld, looking back from his long stint as Editor of the *Daily Express* in the early twentieth century, pin-pointed the partisan character of newspaper editorship in the mid-nineteenth century:

'The newspapers of those days were conducted as political organs and nothing else . . . . Each newspaper depended for its circulation on the small but solid and educated body of readers whose political opinions it represented, and who looked to it for authoritative guidance on the important questions of the day. Editors were the official links between the Party leaders and their supporters in the country. It was generally believed that the leading articles were inspired or even written by prominent politicians.'[1]

The Daily Telegraph after 1855 was based on a different assumption. But at least until 1900 many Editors were of the opinionated and partisan sort. This approach also assured *competition* – one partisan paper competed with other partisan papers; most commonly papers were either Liberal or Conservative. The business of the press was politics, partisanship and opinion, and consequently the Editor was normally a man of opinion. The Editor's special area of concern was the leader columns; much of the remainder of the paper was also political opinion, in the form of speeches. But whereas these opinions were taken down by shorthand notetaking 'reporters', the Editor was a maker and propounder of opinions. As chief propounder of opinion in a partisan-opinion newspaper, he was likely to be an important figure. Since the Editor spoke not merely to his own party or faction but against his opponents, the Editor was himself in the forefront of *competition*. A prominent Editor was thought of as a great competitive asset to a newspaper; Editors and newspapers were as much in business to *attack* their political enemies as to defend their own views.

Paradoxically, however, these assumptions of opinion, partisanship and competition contained the seeds of their own destruction. And even in *The Times*, the publication which above all acted on such assumptions, the actual basis of operation was rather different, if not the precise reverse. Before 1855 *The Times* was in effect a government protected *monopoly* rather than an equal competitor; while it was partisan, much of its appeal derived not from its partisanship but from its independence of party and its closeness to government. While it was opinionated, much of its appeal was based not on opinion but on

---

1   R D Blumenfeld *The Press in my Time*, London: Rich and Cowan, 1933 p 53.

news – and the strength of its opinions was that they tended to be based on superior information. Moreover, the anonymous journalism which *The Times* practised, and the concern of politicians with *The Times*' changing political views led to a widespread assumption that an Editor who seemed so influential in the world of politics outside the newspaper must be all-powerful inside the newspaper.

These paradoxes – present even before 1855 – are prominent in the entire history of editorship up to and including the present time. The Editor, originally conceived as an individual presider-over-opinion has become a corporate manager of news. The Editor, originally a partisan, now stresses above all his detachment from party. The Editor, originally a competitor, now knows in most cases, outside the national press, that he presides over a monopoly. Moreover where the competitive Editor still exists – in Fleet Street – the competition has long taken on forms over which Editors only have rather limited control.

1.2 *The Times* and its Editor before 1855

The removal of the most important of the 'taxes on knowledge' occurred in 1855; it brought to an end the near monopoly of *The Times* in the daily newspaper field nationally, and it produced a rash of new daily newspapers outside London where until 1855 there were (with a few brief exceptions) only weeklies or bi-weeklies.

The Times' reporting of the Crimean war illustrated the enormous political power of the paper; but it also illustrated that foreign news was expensive to gather. Another event of 1855 – an agreement between *The Times* and the Exchange Telegraph gave the Extel agency access to *The Times*' supplies of foreign news. Provincial weeklies and bi-weeklies had previously pirated *The Times*' foreign news, whereas now they would have to pay Extel (and indirectly *The Times*) for it. In effect *The Times* had in return for its tax-assisted semi-monopoly been acting as an unpaid news agency to the rest of the British press. The absence up to 1855 of effective competition – either from other newspapers or from news agencies – had encouraged *The Times* to evolve the notion of a politically sovereign and independent Editor.

So central was the concept of the Editor in the reputation of *The Times*, and so dominant was this newspaper that the notion of the Editor in Britain has been permanently influenced by *The Times*' example. However, *The Times*' concept of Editor was largely based on pre-1855 assumptions which did not fully obtain after 1855. Moreover the actual practice within *The Times*, even as it had existed before 1855, was not widely understood, partly because it was deliberately and consistently hidden behind an iron curtain of anonymity and mystery.

Up to 1855 the entire British press was extremely small. Even the larger provincial newspapers had a sale of around 2,000 copies once or twice a week; these were all four-page newspapers – with the more successful papers typically giving two of the four pages to advertising. Costs were dominated by taxation and revenue was dominated by advertising.

The number of journalists was very small. In 1851 there were only 2,751 'authors, editors, writers and other literary persons' in the whole country. Probably about 100 of these worked for *The Times* on a full-time or part-time basis. And since even the more prosperous provincial newspapers only had a staff of two or three journalists, the borderline between Editor and journalist was not clear; nor was the borderline between journalist and author, nor the borderline between journalist and compositor. Some individuals were compositors, reporters, editors, and authors on different days of the week. In such circumstances the reputation of the mighty Editor of The Times shone all the more brightly.

John Delane was the Editor of The Times from 1841 until 1877. In his person the conception of the Editor was thus carried across the great divide of 1855. But the original definition of the Editor of The Times occurred during the tenure of Thomas Barnes in the 1820s and 1830s, and John Delane never achieved within The Times the same supremacy as did Barnes. Barnes was given a free hand by the proprietor, John Walter II, to an extent which John Delane never was.

Delane became Editor in 1841 at the age of 23, when his entire experience of journalism was confined to less than one year on the staff of The Times:

'From the death of Barnes until the death of Walter II in 1847 Delane exercised only a delegated authority. His position during those years was not comparable with that of Barnes, upon whose death Walter returned to take an active, though not a public, control of the paper.'[1]

Six years later, in 1847, Delane was in danger of losing the editorship as John Walter II slowly died of cancer. John Walter III continued as a fairly active proprietor – more in the style of his father's later and activist phase than of his early passive proprietorship.

The formal power structure of The Times after 1847 involved three men – John Walter III, the Proprietor; John Delane, the Editor; and thirdly Mowbray Morris, the Manager. This ruling triumvirate were all of similar social backgrounds, all had Oxbridge educations, and all were within two years of each other in age. They worked smoothly, but somewhat distantly, together. Behind their cool, but colleaguely, working relationship was an element of tension and hostility. John Walter III was the key man in the triumvirate because he was the chief owner in two separate businesses – the newspaper business and the printing business. The Editor, the Manager and the Printer all reported direct to him, usually by letter and messenger, since he largely exercised his power from his country house outside London. Walter III also kept unclear the precise division of responsibilities between the Manager and the Editor.

The Manager, Mowbray Morris, combined what today would be the jobs of the advertising director and the circulation or marketing director. Morris was in charge of all expenditure including the pay and employment of journalists. He not only handled the special arrangements for speeding foreign news – on which The Times prided itself and which included the hiring of special couriers, special cross-channel boats, and special trains – but he actually hired and fired foreign correspondents. The Manager also played a part in City of London financial news, although precisely what part may have been left deliberately unclear by Walter III. The Manager's job had in Barnes' day been conducted by two senior men, Thomas Alsager and John Delane's father, William Delane. John Delane's supremacy was confined very much to the editorial output of

---

1 *History of The Times* Vol 2, p 2.

journalists (rather than the management of them) and his unchallenged area of authority lay in the news coverage of domestic politics and the political policies of *The Times*.

The Times in the 1840s was normally an eight page newspaper, with only four or five pages filled with non-advertising text. It was printed on equipment which

Chart I
Organisation of *The Times* in the 1840s

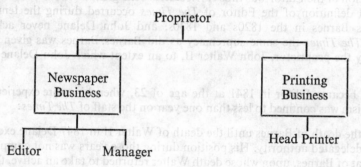

was extremely advanced by prevailing standards. Pages were still being printed at four am because the 'edition time' was geared to the London market only, with copies arriving up to two or three days late elsewhere, according to distance and the development of the railways in the precise time and place.

The Times in the 1840s and 1850s was a profitable, as well as a powerful, concern. John Delane knew that the political influence of *The Times* rested on the semi-monopoly position and the profitability which it had achieved. John Walter III in 1847 acquired only two of the 16 shares, but the rest belonged mainly to other Walters. These shares, plus the control of the printing business, were enough to enable Walter III to rebuild on a much grander scale his father's house. Although John Delane had no ownership interest in the business (apart from 1841–46), he received a generous salary. The newspaper's success in the mid-nineteenth century was closely linked to the growth of other mid-Victorian businesses, and to the growth of advertising and government.

But the notion of the politically Sovereign Editor was ultimately based on an assumption of commercial profitability which was to some extent self-disproving. Profitability led to an overall editorial concept which was doomed to unprofitability.

John Delane's central editorial interest was clearly with the news coverage of domestic politics and the formulation of opinions about politics. This was done in three main ways:

1   *The Times* carried a lengthy summary of *Parliamentary Debates* – up to half of its entire editorial space being given to these on big occasions. There was also heavy coverage of speeches in the country. The Parliamentary staff consisted of some 18 men, whose main task was shorthand note taking.

2   *Direct Contact with Leading Politicians.* Delane was a great political diner out. He corresponded with senior politicians, and he frequented Westminster a fair amount, becoming in effect the first lobby correspondent.

3   *The Leading Articles* were written by a team of some six leader writers. These were among the senior people on the staff, and when Delane first became

Editor it was these leader writers who introduced him to prominent politicians. In some respects Delane was almost the specialised editor-of-the-editorial-page in the modern American manner, but these leaders also resembled Washington columns in that they often contained exclusive information. Delane typically directed the leader writer to tomorrow's topic – often with a scribbled note on a today's news story proof; this instruction usually went by messenger in the middle of the day, and Delane saw and amended the wording at night.

The only other detailed area of control for Delane was the Letters. According to *The Times'* historian[1] letters intended for publication averaged 200 a day – a truly mammoth number, making a total annual mailbag larger in the 1840s than the annual sale. The letters occupied Delane for up to three hours a day. This was an important fraction of the Editor's total time – and was probably the main source of Delane's proverbial sensitivity to the changing opinions of his readers. In addition, came other letters not intended for publication.

In some other areas of the paper Delane also took a strong interest. Foreign news was one; Delane corresponded frequently with the staff foreign correspondents and often visited them, especially the Paris man. He visited his war correspondent in 1854 in Constantinople. Delane saw foreign news as an extension of British domestic politics – and to be covered in the same active manner.

Finally Delane exercised an overall control of editorial content by reading *all* editorial copy in proof. He did this on most nights – and made detailed changes in longhand on the proofs. His strategy here was an attempt to align the entire editorial content of *The Times* into a single whole – with an overall tone and style laid down by the Editor and exhibited most clearly in the pungently written leaders.

Delane clearly got through an immense workload. He was Political Editor, Chief Leader Writer and Night Editor all in one – although the paper appears to have had relatively little sub-editing. While Delane's editing style was enormously detailed, it left out several things which a modern Editor would do. Up to 1855 there was no use of agency copy.

There was still relatively little active gathering of 'news' of any kind by modern standards. Most coverage was of the passive gallery kind – Parliamentary Debates, Court Reports and Stock Market prices. Oddly for an Editor who prided himself so much on his (or rather his writers') vigorous prose style, there was little coverage of literature. Only a few novels a year were reviewed; several famous early Victorian novels were completely ignored by *The Times* when first published.

One could argue on the basis of the various accounts of Delane's editorship that the style was either individual or collective. He was on extremely warm terms with his official deputy Dasent (Walter III did not trust Dasent, however, and always kept a close eye on him when Delane was away). Delane worked closely with his leader writers – the name of an individual specialist leader writer was often bracketed with Delane's own by the political cognoscenti as the joint author of *The Times'* latest policies.

---

1 *Op cit*, Vol 2, p 68.

The great personal force of Delane's leadership, plus the equally remarkable gaps in the most elementary areas of editorial control, both derived from the prevalent definition of serious journalism as a *writing* activity. Despite some active news *gathering* by Delane and other senior journalists, journalism was not seen as it is today – a series of specialised operations through which copy flows or information is processed. The notion that journalism consists only of writing is today a naive idea. Then, however, journalists were a special kind of writer. Barnes had himself been an essayist of ability. Delane was seen, and even more saw himself, as the chief writer or author of *The Times*. He no more hired and fired his journalists than one author would hire or fire another author.

That at least is one explanation for the Editor's lack of power to hire or fire his own senior correspondents. Thus Mowbray Morris, the Manager, sets off in 1848 to fire the Paris correspondent and while there decides to summon the Madrid man to take over in Paris. Delane does not argue[1]. An alternative explanation is that the Proprietor wants the change and the businesslike Mowbray Morris has had these powers written into his contract.

Delane wrote everything in longhand – he did not dictate; thus detailed contact with individual correspondents beyond his leader writers would have turned him into an editorial manager rather than a chief author. Transmission problems were central at this time of rapidly changing technology; the new forms of transmission were expensive even within Britain – and abroad there were often complicated sequences to be co-ordinated. Some important stories came to Marseilles by ship, by special courier to Paris, by pigeon to Calais, and then by special steamer to Dover. Both trains and the telegraph were unpredictable in their early days. Thus handling a team of correspondents both abroad and within Britain was defined on *The Times* as a business, financial and management problem. There was none of today's routine morning phone call or Telex to the foreign correspondent.

The Times basically had two sorts of journalists. The shorthand notetakers covered Parliament, the Law Courts and other set pieces; a few sub-editors were also in this routine mould. Then there were the educated gentlemen, the journalists with whom Delane himself dealt – especially the leader writers, but also the leading foreign correspondents and a few others.

There were no clearly established journalist 'executive' positions, nor the modern notion of 'desks' each in charge of its own journalists and pages. The main heavyweight fields lacked an executive journalist boss. Delane and his leader writers ran politics; but the modern jobs of Foreign editor and Financial editor were both done by Mowbray Morris, at least in their more strategic aspects. There must also inevitably have been a 'senior reporter' phenomenon (for instance among the Westminster and police court reporters) of the senior man who divides up tasks and takes one for himself. Some of this lack of structure, of course, was made possible by the lack of hard edition times (and trains to catch), the relative lack of sub-editing, the total lack of page layout as a concern or activity for journalists, and also the night-by-night presence of an Editor presiding personally over a 'slot' of only about four editorial pages.

But the educated gentlemen/shorthand notetaker divide had further aspects. The educated gentlemen had in virtually all cases been to Oxford or Cambridge.

---

1 *History of The Times* Vol 2, p 139.

At least half of them wandered into *The Times* rather than practise as barristers Their education had been classical, theological and literary. The educated gentlemen journalists of *The Times* also represented a sharp break with the notion of the journalist as political hack. These men had to show that they were incorruptible, and this meant politically incorruptible – they showed this by refusing to accept political direction or political bribes.

These political journalists were accepted, in this sense, as politically incorruptible. Most were sons of the gentry or of colonial grandee planters; they were capable of dining out with aristocratic politicians. In order to emphasise their gentlemanly incorruptibility Delane and his educated journalists may also have deliberately feigned a lack of concern with money, business, and the mechanical production of newspapers. This may have made them welcome the Manager's responsibility for Financial news and the expensive transmission problems of foreign correspondents.

These journalists were not quite so incorruptible as journalists are expected to be today. They engaged in what would be seen as nepotism and shady deals by today's standards. Delane was connected by marriage to both his deputy, Dasent, and the Manager, Mowbray Morris. Delane's elder brother was one of *The Times*' paper suppliers – a contract first obtained by their father. Delane made an exception to his normal rule when he sought a political favour – promotion for a civil servant brother. He also obtained his deputy Dasent a University Professorship by exerting influence. Journalism (as an extension of printing) was a family business – and various non-journalists, including military officers, were used as correspondents.

The most obvious area for possible financial corruption lay in *The Times*' Financial coverage. Since Delane had nearly lost the editorship over this connection (see below) he may have been happy to see financial journalism combined with advertising under the Manager's direction. The need to be seen to be politically incorruptible was thus solved by having shorthand notetakers who were not much exposed to temptation and educated gentlemen who were well paid and capable of resisting temptation. Here also are at least some of the origins of the British distinction between news (what notetakers take down) and comment (the uncorrupted views of gentlemen).

This gentlemanly incorruptible, writing and commenting, definition of serious journalism and serious editorship was not well suited to the technical revolution which was transforming the gathering of news. There was no recognition that in its pursuit of fast news, and the earliest foreign intelligence, *The Times* had entered a race which others must ultimately win. The startling political inside scoop (collected by the Editor) or the afternoon 'special' edition with dramatic news from abroad (whose exclusivity was bought with monopoly profits) was whetting the public appetite for wider and more interesting news on a daily basis.

Delane took no part at all in advertising, and in this area *The Times* was only modestly highminded. In the great railway boom *The Times* did warn editorially against the inevitable crash, but it also contentedly profited from enormous quantities of extra advertising.

In the whole production area *The Times*' Editor had a remarkable lack of interest. Printing was actually done by a separate company. The layout of pages was left entirely to the compositors; Delane sometimes complained about the mayhem wrought by the compositors[1] but only in the way one complains about the disastrous weather. Layout was on the other side of several dividing lines from Delane; it was not writing, it was not gentlemanly, and it was literally not his business. The material continued to be placed into the columns, devoid of layout and almost devoid of headings – and this practice continued even after Delane went in 1877. Allen Hutt in *The Changing Newspaper* shows the complete lack of change in *The Times'* appearance between 1848 and 1907.

In the field of circulation, Delane had no direct responsibility. Nevertheless like any Editor he was aware of the significance of circulation, indeed the prevailing policy of political independence was conceived largely in circulation terms. *The Times* must be able to respond to changing public opinion (among its upper middle class readership) and the policy was 'to anticipate if possible' the trend of opinion. Delane's 200 letters a day were probably the most scientific audience barometer then available, especially since new editorial policies were often introduced gradually over a period of weeks – allowing time for feedback. However this response to the audience had severe limitations – the response was confined largely to political partisanship and was oriented mainly to satisfying the existing audience, not towards getting new readers.

Many readers, Delane knew, were bored by lengthy reports of Parliament; but he believed these must be carried. His idea of light relief was more interesting foreign stories. Here he may have been misled by his correspondents 'to the editor' whose interests were probably more serious than those of the average purchaser, let alone the dozen or so probable readers per copy. Apart from moments of special political excitement at home or abroad, to many of its readers *The Times* must often have seemed a rather dull Gazette aimed mainly at Westminster and the Stock market.

The strongest audience appeal probably lay in criminal and other Court cases. Certainly the courts were heavily culled by the self-styled blood-and-thunder Sundays and after 1855 *The Daily Telegraph* developed with great effect its still current policy of providing lengthy accounts of spicy court cases. *The Times* staff of some 14 police court reporters before 1855 virtually admitted as much. It was typical of the Delane concept of the Editor that he took little interest in this area.

In 1855 *The Times* found itself at last confronted by serious competition, especially from *The Daily Telegraph*. *The Times* response was a deliberate avoidance of any attempt to compete with *The Daily Telegraph*, which quickly became the new circulation leader. There were several strategies which *The Times* could have pursued:

1 Some popularisation, or some price competition – keeping all its serious features but also going some way with *The Daily Telegraph* in expanding circulation and advertising.

2 More local London news so as to consolidate itself in the most affluent market.

3 New kinds of political and financial coverage to consolidate its position there.

Instead *The Times* tried to continue a strategy which was viable in its monopoly days but which was viable no longer. It continued to cultivate foreign news,

1 *History of The Times* Vol 2, p 59.

although Mowbray Morris' antagonism towards Reuters suggests his suspicion that Reuters must become the predominant foreign news organisation. *The Times* squandered its revenue on a battle with Reuters which it could not win and did not need to win; *The Times* failed to do battle in the domestic fields where it might have won with a viable strategy. From 1855 the story of *The Times* was a slow slide into insolvency, a state from which despite three rescues (Northcliffe, Astor, Thomson) – all of them based on North American ideas and/or money – it has not in the last century more than temporarily escaped.

The pre-1855 concept of editorial supremacy has always since been regarded as the cornerstone of *The Times*. This concept has been real enough to introduce a chronic rigidity and weakness into *The Times'* operations. In long-term strategy the traditional *Times* conception is of an Editor who has responsibility but lacks power. The fatal decision not to compete with the penny papers after 1855 was not taken by John Delane – it was taken by Walter III and Mowbray Morris.

Who appoints Editors and who fires them? In the case of *The Times* it was clearly the Walters. This is illustrated by the melodrama surrounding John Walter II's deathbed in 1847. The young John Delane had at Walter II's death been Editor of *The Times* for six years but at one stage he was convinced he would be sacked. He even started to 'eat dinners' so that he could practise as a barrister. John Walter II's antagonism at the end of his life focused not on John Delane, but upon John's father, William Delane. The dispute originated in the railway boom and the subsequent decline in advertising revenue. The managerial and also financial news operations were being handled for Walter II by Alsager and Delane senior. Suspicion arose of an accounting malpractice for which Walter II fired Alsager. Delane senior was more difficult to fire because he held shares in the printing business. Walter II wanted Delane senior to sell him the shares; Delane senior refused. Walter II had throat cancer and his life was ebbing rapidly as Delane senior still refused to concede.

It was clearly possible that Walter II would fire the Editor, Delane junior; another possibility was that Walter II would die and that a disputed will would bring down *The Times* itself. Eventually Delane senior relented, and sold his shares to Walter II, who made a new will which effectively handed complete control to Walter III. This happened only a few days before Walter II's death. When Walter III inherited *The Times* he had already for some months been exercising considerable managerial control. He confirmed John Delane in the editorship, but at first on a temporary basis. When Walter III largely withdrew to his country house, he created the new post of Manager in such a form as to cut back permanently the real editorial sovereignty which Barnes had enjoyed.

This proprietorial handover illustrates some general aspects of *The Times'* editorship:

– The characteristic mixture of genuine high mindedness with business cunning and family ties and feuds.
– The principle of anonymity was maintained. Barnes' name never appeared in *The Times* in his life and many people – including such a celebrated antagonist as William Cobbett – did not even know that Barnes was the Editor. The principle of anonymity was continued, but it was partly a deliberate device both to shield where the power lay and to increase the power of the most powerful.

269

- Walter III's response to the deathbed power struggle was to set up a powerful Manager alongside the Editor and to leave the detailed delineation of responsibility in his own hands. This introduced a lack of communication within *The Times* senior management and a lack of clarity in goals.
- One consequence was a failure to work out a long-term business-cum-editorial strategy.
- Editorial supremacy was raised into a prime article of faith, a myth, and a fatal encumbrance to planning for a viable future.

The Times Editor was before 1855 sometimes said to be the most powerful man in England; but he was not the most powerful man in *The Times*. *The Times* editorship was based on a kind of institutionalised high-mindedness, but before 1855 it was – in that time of Marx and Engels – also based on monopoly profit. Even the title, Editor, was an odd one. *The Times* Editor was indeed an editor in the eighteenth century sense of cobbling together other men's work. However he was different from eighteenth century, and also from most other mid-nineteenth century, Editors in that all of his material was original *Times* material. Moreover in some senses the Editor did not actively edit anything except the paper's opinions.

Table 1.1

Stamps issued for leading circulation newspapers in selected British cities in 1845

	Total Stamps Annual	Average per Issue
London Dailies		
The Times	8,100,000	25,878
Morning Chronicle	1,628,000	5,201
Morning Herald	1,608,070	5,137
Glasgow		
Glasgow Herald (Mon & Fri)	380,000	3,654
Saturday Post (Sat)	207,250	3,986
National Advertiser (Sat, free)	175,000	3,365
Edinburgh		
The North British Advertiser (weekly, free)	608,500	11,702
Witness (Wed & Sat)	270,000	2,596
Scotsman (Wed & Sat)	248,025	2,385
Manchester		
Manchester Guardian	967,000	
Manchester Times	149,800	
Manchester Courier	280,000	

Sources:

Alexander Sinclair, *Fifty Years of Newspaper Life*.
Donald Read, *Press and People*.

1.3 Provincial newspapers and their editors before 1855

Provincial newspapers were very much smaller than *The Times* on every possible dimension. *The Times* had about 100 journalists to produce about 24 pages of editorial per week. The provincial four-page weekly would have only two editorial pages (or perhaps four or five for a bi-weekly) and a rough ratio of one journalist per page. With a much less favourable ratio of journalists to pages, the provincial paper pirated much more material out of other papers, especially the London dailies.

The task of the Editor on such a paper was clearly quite different from Delane's. It also varied enormously between different provincials – according to their circulation and prosperity and as to whether the Editor was owner, partner, or in effect a fairly junior sub-editor. One of the most common arrangements involved the kind of small staff the *Manchester Guardian* had in the 1820s, but which most provincials still had up to 1855. This consisted of a proprietor who typically owned the press; he was most often a printer or bookseller in origin. Next in the hierarchy came the editor; then there was one reporter – who also did sub-editing. Next was the overseer or head printer; then a few compositors; then some pressmen and errand boys. In 1845 the *Glasgow Herald*, a fairly large provincial bi-weekly, had an editorial department of two.

On the eve of publication day the entire staff – Editor included – usually stayed up all night, getting the paper hand set. Many journalists started as compositors and, as late as 1840, provincial journalists would describe themselves as 'printer' or 'editor' interchangeably. Some reporters would take down a speech in short-hand and compose straight from shorthand into type with no written stage intervening. A common career was that of the young compositor who taught himself shorthand or was taught it by the Editor to whom he was apprenticed. Then he would become a reporter or sub-editor, then the Editor of a weekly paper, then perhaps a junior partner and ultimately the chief owner of a paper. Because of the growth in the number and circulations of papers a substantial proportion of all journalists at the time probably went through some such upward career sequence.

Many provincial papers in the 1840s had close ties with a political party; the Editors of such papers were usually true believers, however, so they did not necessarily suffer undue constraint. The situation of the local Tory sheet and the Liberal sheet blasting away at each other was common; in the larger towns there might be more than one paper of the same political persuasion and here competition could be fiercest. Exeter was an example of a town with a long-drawn-out battle between the local newspaper Editor and the local Bishop, the one thundering in his paper, the other from his pulpit.

Not all local papers even had editorials, however, and the deliberate policy of causing minimum offence was already quite common. The main political news consisted of speeches made at local public meetings, plus filchings from London papers; big speeches were lifted wholesale, while summaries were also made of stories from *The Times* and others. Occasional letters from neighbouring towns about markets, prices, meetings, and dramatic court cases were common. 'Correspondence' also came, as it had in the eighteenth century, from abroad. A usual source of such letters were local businessmen engaged in exporting or importing. Local newspapers cheerfully pirated from papers sophisticated enough to have such interest. The other main sources of foreign news were ships arriving in local ports.

Sometimes dramatic local stories commanded attention. The 1830s saw many turbulent political meetings, by-elections and dramatic murders. In some cases the local Editor was compelled to cover local markets of special interest to his middle class readership. But there was probably also quite a wide range of discretion.

Many local Editors acquired a personal reputation, although the Editor of the *Manchester Chronicle* who challenged the Chief Constable to a duel in 1839 – a common American journalist's practice of the time – was unusual in England.

271

Some papers were bought mainly for their advertising, and some were extremely poorly written. A lively local Editor with prejudices not too much in conflict with his readers probably had a substantial amount of autonomy – although much of this would be expressed merely in his choice of material to filch.

Many young reporters and sub-editors were apprenticed. The most sought-after quality in a reporter was first class shorthand. Shorthand in the 1840s seems still to have been regarded by the public as a special magic skill. If a reporter was a good shorthand writer and could sub-edit speeches, if he could turn his hand to other tasks around the office, then he was an asset to his Editor. Senior reporters were often made partners in the business to stop them moving to rival publications. By the 1840s a distinct breed of Editors – separate from printers – had emerged in most of the cities and larger towns of Britain. Nevertheless many Editors went on to own the printing business or at least to become senior partners. In most cases in the 1840s these businesses were small and the Editor and printer (if there was one) worked closely together.

Unlike Delane on *The Times*, the local Editor was not fenced off from the business transactions of the paper. These Editors cannot have failed to notice that advertising was the life blood of the press – indeed free advertising sheets were already prominent. The greatest quantity of advertising usually went to the most widely read papers and these trumpeted abroad their sales figures – or rather their purchase of stamps.

Since Editors were also so close to the printing and sale of copies they could not fail to notice which stories sold papers. Local papers were sold mainly by the paper's own local casual work-force – often in the 1840s elderly 'Waterloo' pensioners. Editors also cheerfully made room for late advertising if it appeared. Since the stamp arrangements in practice limited local papers to four pages, the solution was to remove editorial or to squeeze it into smaller and smaller print. The next stage, if the advertising boom continued, was to print another edition on another day of the week.

Probably the bulk of Editors had a direct financial stake in the commercial success of the paper – either through shareholding or salary bonuses or both. This again was a different conception from *The Times*' view of the Editor, although a commercially perhaps more successful one.

Firing of Editors was quite common and could occur for reasons of incompetence, personality clashes or divergencies of political opinion. It was not unusual for fired Editors to be hired by the local opposition across the street and local press competition was often given an added touch of personal venom as a fired Editor tried to kill his former employer's paper.

The best known local Editors built up their own reputations and were in little danger of being fired. Some successful papers like the *Glasgow Herald*, *The Scotsman*, *Manchester Guardian* and *Leeds Mercury* had well before 1855 already established a tradition of long serving Editors. Some of these men inevitably modelled themselves in part on Delane of *The Times* whose offerings they routinely pirated. Such editorships were typically found in highly profitable papers, which usually had the largest circulation and advertising revenue in the local market.

1.4 The Manchester Guardian and the provincial sovereign editor tradition

Apart from Delane of *The Times*, the other most frequently quoted example of a sovereign editor is C P Scott of the *Manchester Guardian*. The latter paper belonged in the nineteenth century to the Taylor family, who intermarried with the Scotts. David Ayerst say C P Scott (Editor, 1871–1929) had no problems about his 'Sovereignty': Mr and Mrs Taylor both suffered from poor health and spent much of the year abroad – in days when there was no international telephone system; and he and Taylor saw eye to eye on everything except female suffrage, proportional representation and temperance, on all of which Taylor was generally content for Scott simply to refrain from flatly contradicting his view. (Even so, Ayerst shows that on these subjects Taylor did seek to influence Scott's leading articles.)

After Taylor's death Scott secured the paper in 1907 for his own immediate family. For twenty years, therefore, the *Guardian* was owned by its Editor. Ayerst says the word 'monarchical' was applied to Scott even beforehand. One of Scott's sons, John, became manager. Another, Edward, became Editor when C P retired in 1929. On holiday in 1932 Edward drowned in Lake Windermere. John Scott appointed the news editor, W P Crozier, as Editor in his place (1932–44) and as a member of the Board. John Scott always kept out of editorial questions 'because he believed that the editor of the *Manchester Guardian*, just because it was the *Manchester Guardian*, must be as free editorially as if he were proprietor'.[1]

Scott's editorship like Delane's straddled a great divide – in Scott's case the 'Northcliffe Revolution' around 1900. Scott's editorship also – like Delane's – depended upon accidents of circumstance. With Scott's editorship the general impression of absolute authority is slightly misleading – or rather in Scott's case the most quoted examples relate to the later period when he was also the owner. W P Crozier, one of his successors, recalls the editorial style:

'No interruption, no visitor, no office conference was allowed to delay the sacred task of fixing for the night the subject of "the Long". This was the long Leader, prime instrument of policy, the voice, persuasive and protestant, for whose utterance, more than for any other single purpose, he believed the paper to exist . . . .

He held the strictest views about the functions of editor. For him the editor was the personality, controlling, directing and harmonising, which gave unity of purpose and of character to the paper . . . He felt so strongly that the organism, if it was to be a consistent whole, must reflect a single personality, that he objected not only to the existence of self-sufficing departments but also the conferment of the title of "Editor" either by day or by night, on anybody charged with a feature or a department. "Night-editor?" he said wonderingly, having at that time himself been night-editor as well as Editor for nearly fifty years . . . There is only one God, and Allah is his prophet. C P's idea of an editor was that he had both functions.'[2]

C P Scott, then, was a licensed despot – not only owner and Editor, but in effect sole executive within the editorial department. This sovereignty or despotism relied in part also on the *Manchester Evening News*, launched as

---

1   David Ayerst *Guardian: Biography of a Newspaper*. London: Collins 1971 p 495.
2   W P Crozier 'CPS in the Office' in *C P Scott 1846–1932*. London: Muller, 1946, pp 91, 104.

an election paper in 1868 and acquired in the same year as a stablemate for the *Manchester Guardian*. Throughout the period 1890–1910 the *Manchester Evening News* had a sale over 125,000 and in 1900 the Boer war further raised its sales[1] – thus helping to cushion the expensive principles of its morning stablemate.

Was the *Manchester Guardian* completely atypical? No, it was only an extreme case of a more general phenomenon found in all the main provincial cities in the late nineteenth century – the prestige provincial morning paper. These papers were partisan, opinionated and competitive – the typical large provincial daily had either one or two morning rivals. Many of these papers had their equivalents of C P Scott – Alexander Russel edited *The Scotsman* for 28 years, while Edward Russell edited the *Liverpool Daily Post* for 51 years.

Simonis[2], in his review of Editors and newspapers at the turn of the century, finds C P Scott to be no more remarkable than a number of other provincial Editors. Like Scott a number of these eminent Editors also had an ownership interest. The *family* element in both the ownership and editorship of these provincial dailies was marked. The Editor was often a son or nephew of a previous Editor or owner.

Sir Frederick Wilson, for example, was chief owner of the Ipswich *East Anglian Daily Times* and edited the paper for over 40 years. He was an MP for 10 years and – like C P Scott, who was also an MP for a similar period – he apparently continued his editorship. Since the purpose of these papers was largely political the process of becoming an MP and becoming an Editor was not very different. Nor was the dividing line between editorship and ownership very sharp. Daily papers were often launched by a family or a group of politically minded businessmen, one of whom would then take on the editing. In other cases a trusted Editor would become one of the major owners.

Nor was the *Manchester Guardian* unique among provincial dailies in employing Oxford graduates as journalists and Editors. *The Yorkshire Post*, when it was set up in 1866 as a Conservative daily to compete with the 'radical' *Leeds Mercury*, had as its first Editor John Ralph, who had been President of the Union at Oxford and had practised as a barrister before entering journalism.[3]

Many other daily Editors were not university graduates but were self-taught or night-school intellectuals. W T Stead, who was made Editor of the Darlington *Northern Echo* when aged 22, was an example – his father was a Congregational Minister.

A somewhat more typical Victorian Editor, because less famous than Stead, was his friend James Annand. The son of a Scottish small-farmer and blacksmith, Annand, after stints of blacksmithing and school teaching, edited a weekly paper in Peterhead. Trying his luck in London he met Joseph Cowen who appointed him in 1871 leader writer on the *Newcastle Daily Chronicle*. In 1874 Cowen was elected to Parliament and gave up the editorship. Annand then became Editor of the same paper, but resigned the editorship in 1878

1   A P Wadsworth *Newspaper Circulations*, 1800–1954, Manchester Statistical Society, 1954, p 40.

2   H Simonis, *The Street of Ink*. London: Cassell, 1917.

3   Mildred Gibb and Frank Beckwith, *The Yorkshire Post: Two Centuries*, Leeds: The Yorkshire Conservative Newspaper Company, 1954, p 35.

because of a disagreement with Cowen over the Bulgarian question. Annand subsequently edited papers in Brighton and South Shields and also edited the *Newcastle Daily Leader* from its launch in 1885. While Editor he was an unsuccessful Liberal candidate in Tyneside. He subsequently bought and edited a weekly paper in Ripon and eventually himself became a Liberal MP. James Annand – despite his belief in the Editor's obligation forcefully to express his views – believed that he could not have long remained as Editor of the *Newcastle Daily Chronicle* and continued to state in the leader column views which sharply differed from those which the paper's MP owner was expressing in the London letter:

'Mr Annand always opposed the idea that his resignation of the editorship of the *Chronicle* was in any sense a sort of martyrdom for conscience sake. Mr Cowen, he maintained, was perfectly justified in getting rid of an editor whose views were so widely opposed to his own . . .'[1].

1   George B Hodgson, *From Smithy to Senate: The Life Story of James Annand*, London: Cassell, 1908, p 74.

2 Around 1900

2.1 The Sovereign Editor in commercial decline

The conception of the politically opinionated Editor was in commercial decline well before the *Daily Mail* was launched in 1896. This was especially evident in *The Times* itself, but the decline in the provincial dailies was not yet fully obvious. The period around 1900 indeed saw the full flowering of the sovereign Editor notion – in editorial opposition to the Boer war and in the famous London clubland evenings. But the flower grew in soil which increasingly lacked commercial nutriment.

Buckle's editorship of *The Times* from 1884 to 1912 was little more than a caricature of the sovereign Editor idea. Buckle was yet one more bright young man recently down from Oxford. He went on from Winchester to New College as a scholar and took a degree in classical and mathematical moderations. He was a struggling barrister when at 25 he was offered the post of assistant editor of *The Times*; at 29 he was appointed Editor. But it was the Manager, Moberly Bell, who was the dominant personality in the long and losing battle to maintain the independence of *The Times*.

The layout and appearance of *The Times* were unchanged. *The Times* appeared in two parts – the Inner Sheets containing the leaders and such late news as the paper offered. The Outer Sheets contained a jumble of advertising and held-over stories, some set as much as a week earlier. The congested and dated content, like *The Times*' other difficulties, derived from the straitjacket of John Walter's will. The two sets of proprietors – the paper and the printing business – drew further apart. *The Times* was out of touch even with such developments as had occurred in the sluggish life of Fleet Street.

The Times 'had lost almost everything except a high sense of superiority'.[1] Neither the Editor nor the Manager had experience of newspapers outside *The Times*. Linotypes and other new technology common in New York in the early, and in London in the late, 1890s had still not reached *The Times* in 1908. Moberly Bell did not manage the printing office, and the man who did thought change impossible.

Buckle presided over the leaders and the political opinion and the 'foreign policy' of the paper in the traditional manner. But the paper was increasingly, if not unreadable, at least unread. Regular readers could not expect to find regular features in the same place. *The Times* was thrown together by the foreman in the caseroom. Both the manager and the Editor were helpless to intervene.

---

1 F Harcourt Kitchin, *Moberly Bell and his Times*, London: Philip Allan, 1925, p 35.

In the 1890s *The Times'* circulation was behind that not only of its main London competitors but also behind such provincial mornings as the *Manchester Guardian, Yorkshire Post*, and *Glasgow Herald*.[1] Buckle continued to edit the letters with loving care of a kind not bestowed on production, advertising sales, or circulation; but, although a quick and able Editor he was also a recluse – remote from readers and journalists alike.

Elsewhere sovereign, or at least powerful, Editors, presided in various highly individual styles. Byron Curtis, Editor of the *Morning Standard*,

'used to come down to the Shoe Lane office after lunch and sit in his heavily guarded sanctum, write a few letters in his own hand to Cabinet Ministers and Bishops (the *Standard* was largely read by the clergy) and then go off to his Club in Pall Mall for tea . . . In the evenings after dinner he came down, talked to his leader writers, waited to see the proofs of the leaders and took the 12.20 train from Blackfriars'.[2]

But A G Gardiner[3], Sir Edward Cook[4], J A Spender[5] and H W Massingham[6] edited both national morning papers and clubland evenings with great verve and individuality of style – which Garvin[7] later also exhibited on *The Observer*. These Editors lost money for their papers and ultimately their jobs as well. But even most London daily papers in 1900 were still small enough in terms of personnel and pages for one energetic Editor to stamp his personality across the whole – small enough also for the losses to be in thousands of pounds rather than the millions of today. Nevertheless these highly opinionated Editors not only lacked support from readers, most of them fell out also with the owners.

The 'Sovereign Editors' of the provinces tended to be supported by the success of their evening stable companions. The 'sovereign' provincial Editors were almost invariably in charge of mornings; most successful provincial mornings had launched evenings in the 1870s or 1880s and by 1900 the evening was typically the profit maker. The owners usually, then, were indulging their political prejudices in the morning – while the evening dealt with such other matters as murder, racing results and profit.

The Boer war struck a heavy blow at the Sovereign Editor idea. Few editors came out against the war and most of those who did – like Massingham at the *Daily Chronicle* in 1899 – had to vacate their editorial chairs. C P Scott at the *Manchester Guardian* was the major exception – an Editor ready and willing to hazard the ship if need be.

2.2 The commercial popular revolution

The so-called Northcliffe Revolution can be seen in many lights. The least ambiguous evidence lies in the circulations. The *Daily Mail*, launched in 1896, very quickly reached a mammoth circulation – and towered over all other daily papers and cut sharply into their sales.

1 A P Wadsworth, *op cit*, p 25.
2 R D Blumenfeld, *op cit*, pp 73–4.
3 Stephen E Koss, *Fleet Street Radical*, London: Allen Lane, Penguin Press, 1973.
4 Wilson Harris, *J A Spender*, London: Cassell, 1946.
5 J Saxon Mills, *Sir Edward Cook*, London: Constable, 1921.
6 Alfred F Havighurst, *Radical Journalist: H W Massingham*, London: Cambridge University Press 1974.
7 Alfred A Gollin, *The Observer and J L Garvin, 1908–1914*, London: Oxford University Press, 1960.

Newnes, Pearson and Northcliffe – like so many newspaper innovators – came from outside newspapers. They all started in the world of light entertainment magazines and children's publications – not the natural habitat of the Sovereign Editor. The part played by advertising has probably been exaggerated – one key to the first successful *halfpenny* national morning lay in Northcliffe's luck in having hit on the all-time low point in the price of newsprint. Nevertheless advertising was important – both as an earner of revenue and, perhaps even more importantly, as a means of promoting the *Daily Mail*. Again not an Editor's job.

Then the characteristic business management practices of this period were new to Britain. Newspaper management both in London and the provinces had often been chaotic in the extreme.[1] There was emphasis on accountancy and on audited circulation figures publicly announced. The new press barons were professional press managers, not businessmen from other fields who happened to own newspapers. There was also the characteristic British mixture of the family managed business within the corporate form of a joint stock company. Thus there was a continuous urge towards profitability – not merely tomorrow but today. There was the innovation of the diversified press company – first magazines and comics, then the *Evening News*, then the *Daily Mail*, then other papers. The *Evening News* could be and was used as a testbed and free publicity machine for a *Daily Mail* whose sale at first was concentrated in London itself. Next came Manchester printing – first the *Mail*, then others – and soon the provincial mornings were under threat. Finally there was a revolution in what today would be called marketing. Until 1896 a retail cartel, led by W H Smith, had quite simply disapproved of halfpenny morning papers. Northcliffe as the owner of eminently respectable children's papers (highly profitable both for himself and the distribution trade) and of the *Evening News* (as a local London paper less vulnerable to distribution boycott) was a difficult man to resist; and the distribution trade did not resist the *Daily Mail* (although its traditional views on the sabbath scuppered the attempted Sunday edition).

The key point about all of these innovations from an editorial sovereignty point of view was that all of them were *business* innovations with editorial consequences – not the other way about.

Northcliffe deliberately dressed up his young wolf in old sheep's clothing – conservative appearance, advertisements on the front page. But he was trying to get away from most of the traditions of the British press – not least the sovereign Editor tradition. The first news editor on the *Daily Mail*, R D Blumenfeld recalls: 'When I first came into Fleet Street in 1887 the morning papers were great heavy-sided blanket sheets full of dull advertisements and duller news announcements . . .

The Times was pontifical; the *Morning Post* snobbish, with information about duchesses and advertisements about butlers; the *Standard* was commercial; the *Daily News* purely literary and what is now called 'high brow'; and the *Daily Telegraph* just a trifle vulgar because it printed things which others would not . . .

---

1 H Yeo in his book *Newspaper Management* (London: John Heywood, 1891) lays the blame largely on ignorant directors who appoint both unsuitable editors and unsuitable managers. According to Yeo, at this time many press managements had little idea of their true circulation or revenue.

The editors sat in their water-tight compartments resolutely refusing to see and be seen. The reporters were strange, weird people in frockcoats with note books and utterly devoid of originality and enterprise . . .'[1]

It was against this background that Northcliffe decided not only to abolish the sovereign Editor but to crown himself as sovereign proprietor-editor. For the first three years he edited the *Daily Mail* himself.

2.3 The proprietor Editor

The late Victorian Editor-proprietor tended to be an Editor first, and a – or the – proprietor only second. But Harmsworth was a proprietor first and an Editor second. Joseph Pulitzer and William Randolph Hearst were performing just this dual role in New York and Fleet Street watched with fascination and horror.

Northcliffe (like Hearst in his early San Francisco days) actually presided over the *Daily Mail* each night in the opening months. The precise date at which Marlowe was officially designated Editor of the *Mail* is disputed, although it seems to have been in 1899. Northcliffe's attention tended to switch towards his latest acquisition but he still dominated the *Mail* and dictated policy. Marlowe on one occasion in 1914 refused to accept a Northcliffe leader on British participation in France – but this is the celebrated exception to the general pattern. Marlowe was one of a small group of trusted Northcliffe aides or editorial hatchet men – Kennedy Jones and Tom Clarke were others; Northcliffe had a few other trusted managers and his Harmsworth brothers. But Northcliffe dominated this small 'management team' or group of henchmen. And he demonstrated that it is possible to control the contents of a paper without editing the paper each night – through volleys of memos, 'phone calls and summonses for the 'Editor' to hurry to the country house outside London. Terse instructions to fire this man, hire that man or run this or that story kept not only Editors but whole editorial staffs in a state of continuous fear and anxiety – as many memoires of the period recall.

Northcliffe was, however, only the most flamboyant and self-publicising exponent of a proprietor-editor style adopted by others. When Arthur Pearson launched the *Daily Express* in 1900 its front page not only contained news (the first morning paper in London to do this) but the front page also carried a leader over Pearson's initials setting forward the paper's characteristic policy:

'It will be the organ of no political party nor the instrument of any social clique . . . Its editorial policy will be that of an honest Cabinet Minister . . . Our policy is patriotic; our policy is the British Empire.'

Pearson himself was the first Editor of the *Daily Express*, just as he had been after the launch of *Pearson's Weekly*.[2]

But another paper, *The Daily Telegraph*, had almost from its birth in 1855 been controlled by a proprietor-editor. The real Editor for the first 50 years was Edward (Levy) Lawson, Lord Burnham. His father, J M Levy, was the printer who had taken over the paper after its first unsuccessful few weeks in 1855. The young Lawson was 22 at this time and soon became the Editor of his father's paper. In 1900 he was aged 67 and still going strong. The *Telegraph*

1 R D Blumenfeld, *op cit*, pp 32–4.
2 Sidney Dark, *The Life of Sir Arthur Pearson*, London: Hodder and Stoughton, 1923, pp 88–9.

emphasised news and tried to make news interesting. It was the daily circulation leader for almost all of the period 1855–96. Lawson was the effective Editor throughout this entire period. There was a separate officially designated 'Editor' but no news editor or general manager.

Lawson had served an apprenticeship in the composing room. Others – his father over the early years – handled the political coverage. But Lawson was himself an MP for 17 years. There was a big gap between the business and editorial departments and at times significant fissures within the editorial department. But in contrast to *The Times*, the whole was firmly held together by one man, who also dominated the editorial side. If the approved history of *The Daily Telegraph*[1] was a less modest or better known book, the strength and length of the British proprietor-editor tradition might be better understood.

Nor was *The Daily Telegraph* the only major newspaper with a proprietor-editor tradition. The *Daily Chronicle* was another. The *Daily Chronicle* was a leading Liberal paper from 1876 until its merger with the *Daily News* in 1930. There are perhaps three reasons why the importance of the *Daily Chronicle*'s proprietor-editor tradition is not fully grasped today. One reason is perhaps that there is less interest in now defunct papers than in the histories of those which survive. Secondly the *Daily Chronicle* after 1890 was associated with Sovereign Editorship and indeed was edited by some of the most famous 'Sovereigns' – such as H W Massingham and Robert Donald, each of whom was ultimately sacked for his opinions.

A third reason is that the proprietor-editor of the *Daily Chronicle* in its formative years was Edward Lloyd, whose name is now more often associated with the popular Sunday paper which bore his name and was the first British newspaper to sell one million copies. Incidentally the most successful early editor of *Lloyd's Weekly Newspaper* was Douglas Jerrold, who had himself been a proprietor previously[2]. The *Daily Chronicle* began life as a halfpenny weekly in London, called the *Clerkenwell News*. It became a daily in 1866 and Edward Lloyd bought it in 1876. By then Edward Lloyd was already sixty. Until his death in 1890, he seems to have dominated the *Daily Chronicle*, competing successfully with the *Daily News* and even *The Daily Telegraph*.[3] Thus in the 1880s two of the three most commercially successful national morning papers – the *Telegraph* and the *Chronicle* – were run by proprietor-editors.

2.4 Co-existence: Commerce and Editorial Sovereignty, Editor and Proprietor

The period around 1900 was still a period of co-existence. Commerce and editorial sovereignty could co-exist because it was not yet evident that editorial sovereignty was commercially disastrous. Prestige national journals of opinion were eagerly sought after by Northcliffe and Newnes, partly for personal glory but also because it was not absurd to think that such papers could be turned into profit-makers. Some of the papers – especially provincial mornings – also kept printing presses busy. Agency news cut costs; papers were still thin; and if comment was not quite free (in C P Scott's phrase) the great turn-of-the-century opinionated Editors themselves thundered out their own thousand-words-an-hour night after night.

1 Lord Burnham, *Peterborough Court: The Story of The Daily Telegraph*, London: Cassell, 1955.
2 Harold Herd, *The March of Journalism*, London: Allen and Unwin, 1952, pp 184–5.
3 See Alan J Lee, *The Origins of the Popular Press*, London: Croom Helm, 1976. I am also indebted to Dr Lee for his suggestion that the *Daily Chronicle* case should be included here.

Even though the opinionated London evenings especially, and opinion journalism in general, tended to be unprofitable, the reverse had not yet become an established principle. Neutrality did not yet spell profit. The press still was opinionated. And in the typical large provincial city where rival Liberal and Conservative papers thundered against each other each morning and to a lesser extent each evening, attempts at neutrality still tended to fail.

The new press barons on the national scene proclaimed themselves as non-partisan but not as neutral. Moreover as time passed, the new barons tended to become more opinionated, more partisan, and more politically eccentric. Most press barons were interested in politics and either entered Parliament or tried to. But their interest in detailed policy was episodic and eccentric. Thus some room was left for opinionated editorship. The typical press baron could afford the luxury of licensing at least one Sovereign Editor. Northcliffe subsidised Garvin at *The Observer* and Newnes dabbled in several prestige ventures including the *Review of Reviews* with W T Stead. Arthur Pearson for some years owned the prestige *Standard*, whose Editor, H A Gwynne, later edited the *Morning Post*.

Just as a national press baron could dominate a popular national daily and license an opinionated sovereign Editor, so also more traditional provincial proprietors often co-existed both with an opinionated morning Editor and a much less sovereign evening Editor. Both proprietors and Editors were often public personalities – nationally or locally. And the relationship between Editor and proprietor was a *personal* one. The surrounding management and corporate structure was still minimal; the roles of proprietor and Editor were still not sharply demarcated. Other basic dividing lines in the press were also not sharply drawn. News and opinion were formally separated but much 'news' was opinion in the form of speeches. The dividing line between advertising and editorial had long existed, but it also was less clearly drawn than today. One of Northcliffe's innovations was an attempt to draw this line more sharply and to purge the editorial columns of puffery; but the columns of many weaker papers were almost certainly for sale in various forms.

2.5 Editors and journalists

The Editor's role was sharply demarcated from that of other journalists. The Editor was the man of opinion – the paper, in W T Stead's words, was his pulpit. The Editor's major function, especially on the more serious papers, was leader-writing and thus the leader writers were his special assistants. They were the élite – more highly paid and more highly educated than the remainder of the small staff.

The typical journalist was a notetaking reporter whose main skill was shorthand; there were few sub-editors – since the re-writing of material was only in its infancy. Journalists were often casually employed and there were many freelance contributions. Small staffs required few journalist executives. Often a daily paper would have only a managing editor or deputy editor, while the news editor was still a 'chief reporter'; the other most senior people were the leader-writers – the men of opinion and usually the most educated on the paper. The much complained about 'remoteness' of Editors from their journalists resulted from this fundamental division of labour and prestige. The Editor as a propounder of opinion felt no need to converse with his staff of notetakers, sports reporters, and rather unskilled sub-editors.

This hierarchy was steepest in London but was expanded also in Manchester when the London papers started to print there. And it was in Manchester that the National Union of Journalists began. The conditions which the NUJ sought to ameliorate were Dickensian. The frock-coated occupation of journalism was expanding fast around 1900; hours were often extremely long and 30 shillings a week was a common wage for a provincial reporter in 1910.[1] Many local papers were being flooded with young apprentices. When Linton Andrews (later Editor of the *Yorkshire Post*) joined the Hull *Eastern Morning News* its office was in a single dwelling house whose bedrooms were used by young reporters to sober up after public dinners before transcribing their shorthand notes. At sixteen Andrews reported the deliberations of the City Council for the Hull evening paper and at the same age reported a famous Hull murder, including being with the wife at the time her husband was executed. Not surprisingly ambitious young journalists like Andrews[2] joined the National Union of Journalists – an eminently respectable organisation modelled on the Teachers' Union and led in its early days mainly by *Manchester Guardian* and *Manchester Evening News* men and other established members of a deferential occupation.

The gap between Editors and reporters was probably as great in pay as in prestige. Thus there was no reason for Editors to join a Union – the NUJ's early leaders included many men who subsequently became Editors but who at the time were still aspirants. Editors, if they belonged to any organisation, belonged to the Institute of Journalists – as, of course, did many proprietor-editors. One of the main complaints against the IOJ was that a journalist attending an IOJ branch often found the meeting chaired by his employer-editor.

---

1 F J Mansfield, *'Gentlemen, the Press!'*, London: W H Allen, 1944.
2 Linton Andrews, *The Autobiography of a Journalist*, London: Ernest Benn, 1964, pp 25–33.

3 1900 – 1950: Structural change and editors

3.1 The popular national press

There was an enormous increase in scale between 1900 and 1950. Blumenfeld wrote even in 1933:

'When I began the editing of the *Daily Express* some thirty-two years ago, the entire roster of employees of all descriptions was about 350, all housed comfortably in nice little cubicle rooms in Tudor Street. Today the organisation has on its pay list over 3,000 people in London, Manchester and Glasgow, all engaged in the same triplicate issue.'[1]

And thinking perhaps of the Beaverbrook régime on the paper which he had edited until 1929, Blumenfeld continued:

'At the editorial head of each of the great papers stands the Editor, who, rightly or wrongly, is supposed to be responsible for all that appears or does not appear in his paper. There may be behind him a proprietor or a group of owners who themselves lay down the policy to which he must rigidly conform and even give him his line of country day by day.'[2]

In 1933 the increase in scale was being accelerated by the outbreak of sales wars – and the practice of buying readers with free insurance, sets of Dickens or other objects.

This period saw the triumph of news over both editorial opinion and opinion in the form of long reports of speeches. 'News' was a commodity of many facets and many definitions but it certainly accompanied mammoth increases in sales, in numbers of journalists, in the whole scale and complexity of operations. The Editor ceased merely to preside over a small group of leader-writers and now presided over a news gathering and news processing bureaucracy.

The period 1900 to 1950 in Britain is also the great era of the popular national press. In 1900 newspapers were scarcely popular either in intent, or in size of audience, but by 1950 they were both. The great sales increases went above all to the popular papers – the popular dailies and Sundays triumphed in Fleet Street and in the provinces, where the evenings also greatly outpaced their more sober morning stable companions. This was the era of the *national* press. In 1900 national daily sales were about *equal* to provincials, but by 1950 national sales were about double those of provincials. The consumer magazines reflected, and probably fed, the same tendency. The women's magazines, whose great growth came in the second quarter of the century, exhibited in extreme form tendencies found also in national newspapers.

---

1 R D Blumenfeld, *op cit*, pp 69–70.
2 Ibid, p 71.

Politically predictable papers declined, while the politically unpredictable or neutral triumphed. The owners of such publications did not want men of opinion as their Editors.

3.2 The provincial press: Chains, and the decline of partisanship and competition

The relative stability in the total sales of provincial dailies between 1900 and 1950 concealed very big changes. Among provincial *mornings* there was a big reduction in numbers. Whereas in 1900 the situation faced by the typical provincial morning was head-on competition with another morning in the same city, by 1950 the typical situation was of a 'solus' or monopoly morning.

The total number of provincial *evenings* remained remarkably stable at around 80 throughout the period. Whereas in 1900 the majority of evenings had competition, the majority were monopolies by 1950 although the larger provincial cities still retained evening competition. But evenings had become an extremely profitable field – not only did monopoly situations emerge as typical but the loss of merged titles was roughly matched by the launch of new evening titles, especially in the 1920s and 1930s.

The decline in the provincial mornings and the expansion of the monopoly evenings was accompanied by the emergence of and partly carried out by, London-based newspaper chains. This momentous development in the history of the British press still lacks any serious analysis. One important factor may have been the reluctance of the owners of loss-making provincial dailies to sell them to their successful competitors. Clearly rivalries both between and within the Harmsworth and Berry families played a large part. Whether the economies of scale available from chain ownership were ever very great is unclear; nor is it obvious that chain *management* skills were superior. The more detached *ownership* approach, which comes from owning dailies in several cities, may have been more important.

Editors played little part in these changes, which inevitably had enormous consequences for editorship. There was clearly a decline in the old pattern of Liberal versus Conservative partisanship between competing dailies. As monopoly papers came to prevail there were more obvious advantages in neutrality. If a somewhat muted partisanship remained – as it often did – the partisan line was now more likely to be supplied from London. Even in those many provincial dailies which remained outside chains, the commercial dangers of the old opinionated style of editorship were now evident. The predominant political stance was neutral or independent Conservative – but the broad lines were laid down by a chain owner in London, by a local proprietor, or by tradition. The Editor had become largely a technician and manager.

Apart from the special case of the *Manchester Guardian*, the *Yorkshire Post* was the paper which had the highest reputation for editorial independence throughout this period – and especially in the 1930s. Yet the most famous of its Editors, Arthur Mann, and his successor Linton Andrews were both appointed by Rupert Beckett (chairman of the *Yorkshire Post* for 30 years), and these Editors were interpreters of an independent Conservatism laid down by Beckett and his fellow directors. Both Editors left good middle class educations to enter provincial journalism in their teens. Neither was the social or the intellectual equal of Rupert Beckett who was educated at Eton and Cambridge and who belonged to a prominent Yorkshire political family.[1]

The Yorkshire Post's ability to take such independent lines on appeasement, the abdication and other issues was based at least partly on its purchase of the rival *Leeds Mercury* in 1923 and the strength of its evening stable companion.

Linton Andrews' reputation as an Editor was recognised when he became chairman of the Press Council. He was clearly a journalist of all round ability and energy, who believed broadly in the policies he pursued. Andrews has written one of the best of all journalists' autobiographies and his *Problems of an Editor* is the standard work on the subject. In these two books, however, Andrews realistically presents himself as an efficient manager of the editorial department and not as a sovereign shaper of opinion.

The 1947–49 Royal Commission spent a lot of time investigating the second world war practice of writing leaders in London for transmission to chain provincial dailies. But their handling of this issue – like their handling of press policy-making generally – was curiously obtuse. By this time the notion that an Editor might resign over a policy issue of any kind, let alone the Bulgarian question as Annand did, had become increasingly improbable.

There were important changes also in the weekly newspaper fields with the emergence of Westminster Press as a major weekly chain owner. In a weekly chain economies of scale did exist – in group advertising rates,[2] in the fuller use of expensive presses and in editorial content and personnel. Very little systematic information exists about weekly Editors, but it is safe to assume that the typical scale of operations increased greatly from 1900 to 1950.

3.3 The Labour press and the Liberal press

No significant Labour provincial press appeared. Such a press might have been expected in certain Labour urban areas, had political affiliation still been the key to newspaper success. But the rise of the Labour party accompanied the decline of the Liberal provincial press and of the orthodox partisan press in general. This failure of a Labour provincial press to match the continuing existence of Conservative provincial papers did, however, facilitate the emergence of a *national* Labour oriented press.

Throughout the late nineteenth century the blood-and-thunder Sundays had had far the biggest circulations and had pursued vaguely populist policies.[3] This Sunday phenomenon continued. But the *Daily Herald* marked a quite new departure in British political journalism and in editorship. In line with common European practice the *Daily Herald*'s policies were laid down by the Labour party. The *Daily Herald* was the first British daily to sell two million copies, but it soon lost the national sales lead to the *Daily Express*. Nevertheless the

---

1 Mildred A Gibb and Frank Beckwith, *op cit*.

2 Political and Economic Planning, *Report on the British Press*, London: PEP, 1938, p 57.

3 Virginia Berridge 'Popular Sunday Papers and Mid-Victorian Society' in James Curran, George Boyce and Pauline Wingate (Eds), *Newspaper History: Studies in the Evolution of the British Press*, London: Constable (forthcoming).

Daily Herald up to 1950 continued to sell two million copies a day. The *Herald*'s Editor had three different masters to serve – the Labour party annual conference on politics, the TUC on industrial affairs and Lord Southwood on the business running of the paper. In adding to the editorial variety available to readers (and other journalists) the *Daily Herald* rejected editorial sovereignty.[1]

In contrast to the brief rise and fall of the official Labour press, the non-official Liberal press declined steadily from 1900 to 1950. One of the last great Editors of the Liberal press was A G Gardiner who edited the *Daily News* from 1902 to 1919. He was appointed from the provinces as a gamble by George Cadbury. Cadbury had joined a syndicate organised by Lloyd George to rescue the paper from financial difficulties and provide a counterweight to the imperialist wing of the party during the Boer war. E T Cook, then Editor, could not stomach the anti-war policy and resigned. His successor was R C Lehmann, who was also a shareholder but resigned from the Board on becoming Editor. He gave up after nine months, having fallen out with the manager, David Edwards. Edwards himself was appointed Editor, but the Directors disliked his policies. Cadbury was more willing than others in the syndicate to carry on the paper with little or no profit and pursue the unpopular anti-imperialist line, so he bought the rest out. In this period (a couple of years) Editors clearly had little sovereignty.

Gardiner was a great success as a writing Editor and, initially at least, in redesigning the paper for Cadbury. He gradually acquired fairly complete editorial control. His biographer, Stephen Koss, says that he was 'required to justify his policies to the Cadburys, who were occasionally known to counter-mand his instructions and engage personnel without consultation'.[2] He did not become a member of the Board (contrast Crozier). Mrs Cadbury used to send notes of criticism ('Mr Cadbury says you are a member of the Church of England; I wish the writer of the Religious Column were! It is trash!'). One of George Cadbury's sons, Henry, became general manager, with his (the son's) brother-in-law as an assistant. Gardiner was squeezed out after eighteen years (at the age of 54) after exasperating the Cadburys too much with his opinions of Lloyd George and the Versailles Peace Treaty – and at a time of falling circulation. C P Scott's comment when Henry Cadbury tried to hire Crozier as a replacement was that Gardiner had been 'only a "political" editor and that is what Cadbury wants. Crozier would not take that'; he would demand nothing less than 'a full editorship with general control'.[3]

The circulation losses of the *Daily News* between 1917 and 1920 occurred when *Daily Mail* and *Daily Express* sales were booming. This was in the long run the story of the Liberal press. From 1930 onwards the final Liberal amalgam, the *News Chronicle*, was in relative decline (alongside the *Daily Herald*) in contrast especially to the *Daily Express* and *Daily Mirror*. The longest lasting *News Chronicle* Editor during this period of decline was Gerald Barry, the prime author of the classic PEP *Report on the British Press* (1938). On this and other evidence Barry was a formidably perceptive observer of the press; the PEP report can be read as the lament for a dying species, the Liberal Editor.

---

1 *Reynold's News* had a somewhat similar relationship with the Co-operative world.
2 Stephen Koss, *op cit*, p 63.
3 Ibid, p 269.

3.4 The eccentric press Lords

The PEP report comments on the twentieth century press Lords:

'Northcliffe . . . was a very exceptional man, who was able to mould his news-papers in accordance with his will and personality . . . . Lord Beaverbrook usually keeps in close touch with the treatment of political news in his papers, and certainly implants his personality on them to a considerable extent. Lord Rothermere issues general instructions to his editors, and gives occasional broadsides in the form of articles in the *Daily Mail*, which are duly reproduced in the other papers in the group.'

These press Lords tended to be professional newspaper owners; they were also themselves interested not only in political careers but in ministerial, or other, senior office. They were unreliable in party terms; thus they not only infuriated the Conservative party and the other parties but their very eccentricity meant that their Editors always required fresh inputs of eccentric direction. These proprietors were also interested in power in a much more diffuse sense, as Alan Wood points out in his biography of Beaverbrook:

'But if you are a millionaire newspaper owner your editors will ask your opinion on every issue of the day . . . You have unlimited powers of patronage -- what friend of yours will not enjoy seeing his name in the paper? A respectful report of a speech, if he is a politician, a flattering review of a book, if he is an author; praise after a first night, if she is an actress . . . . And who has not wanted at some time or another to write for the papers?'[1]

Such proprietors took care of the opinion aspect of editorship themselves -- including the generous spread of their own opinions in the news columns. To control their day-to-day production of the paper they wanted technician Editors and a team of executives. The most representative figure of this kind was Arthur Christiansen, Editor of the *Daily Express* 1933–57, but there were others before him including his own predecessor Beverley Baxter. The whole operation was heavily geared to the presentation and marketing aspects of news. Christiansen, as he relates in embarrassing detail in his autobiography,[2] was the humble, dutiful, all-suffering and perpetually anxious servant of Beaverbrook. Christiansen was a modest man, with few discernible views on politics, who had a gift for processing news and presenting it in attractive-looking forms. His attitude to Beaverbrook seems to have consisted about equally of admiration and fear, and Christiansen in turn was perhaps regarded in the same way by his journalists.

In this marketing and presentation of news by technician Editors the influence of advertising was powerful. Editors wanted to attract advertising; but in searching for new ways of drawing the readers' attention they borrowed many techniques from advertising agencies -- which had gone further and faster in the marriage of words and pictures. The *Daily Mirror*, when it was re-launched and began its spectacular sales climb in 1933, was very heavily influenced by New York advertising techniques. Cecil King, the advertisement director who himself played a large part in this re-launch recalls:

---

1 Alan Wood, *The True History of Lord Beaverbrook*, London: Heinemann, 1965, p 132.
2 Arthur Christiansen, *Headlines all my Life*, London: Heinemann, 1961.

'So in 1933 we thought it might be wise to seek inspiration from the *Daily News* [New York]. We also thought the American advertising agencies with their copy in strip form had lessons to teach us . . .'[1]

The J Walter Thompson advertising agency was active in the re-launch and several of the key personnel (including Cassandra and the cartoonist Zec) came from advertising. It was decided that the best gap in the market was the young working class – which meant dropping the *Daily Mirror*'s previous mission of being a second paper with Conservative politics. It was to be a first paper of vaguely Labour politics.

Even if the numerous retrospective accounts of the *Daily Mirror*'s re-launch exaggerate the element of rational calculation, this was still the first case of a British national daily being more or less re-designed and 'positioned in the market' on the basis of market research evidence (now becoming increasingly common) and advertising agency participation. In this process the political policy *followed* the marketing plan – and so did the Editor. The *Daily Mirror*'s Editor from 1934 to 1948 was Cecil Thomas. The circulation more than trebled in this period (from well under one million to over 3·5 million in 1948) making Cecil Thomas' in circulation terms apparently one of the most successful editorships in world press history. This would have been the case had Thomas in any meaningful sense been in charge of the *Daily Mirror* – but quite clearly he was not. Bartholomew, the Editorial Director, deliberately humiliated Cecil Thomas in front of visitors – for example by hitting him over the head with a plank of wood, which visitors at the time did not realise was balsa wood.[2] Several somewhat conflicting accounts of the *Daily Mirror*'s history are agreed that, whatever the paper's success may have been due to, it was not in any positive sense due to the Editor. Negatively the fact that in the old sense there simply was no Editor may have played its part.

The real creators of the *Mirror* were Guy Bartholomew, a collection of other men with art and/or advertising backgrounds, plus Cecil King (advertisement director, and in the 1930s the only one who knew or cared anything about politics) and Hugh Cudlipp. Cudlipp, who left school at 14 and was Editor of the *Sunday Pictorial* at the age of 24, sees himself as the *editorial* architect of the *Daily Mirror* – and significantly he was never formally Editor of the paper. Even an editorial technician did not have actually to be the Editor in order to dominate its editorial.

3.5 The unionisation of journalists

One of the biggest changes between 1900 and 1950 was the appearance of the NUJ. In 1938 of some 10,000 journalists in Britain two-thirds belonged to the NUJ and one-quarter belonged to the IOJ; since many of the IOJ members were overseas (presumably working on papers in India and elsewhere in the Empire)[3] and some of them also belonged to the NUJ, a sizeable minority of journalists probably still belonged to no Union. The NUJ was extremely effective at negotiating conditions and minimum pay rates but not at much else. There was not much conflict between Editors and journalists. Most conflicts occurred either within or between the NUJ and IOJ.

---

1   Cecil King, *Strictly Personal*, London: Weidenfeld and Nicolson, 1969, p 101.
2   Hugh Cudlipp, *Walking on the Water*, London: Bodley Head, 1976, p 53.
3   Political and Economic Planning, *op cit*, p 84.

Most journalists, throughout the period, entered journalism on small provincial papers; there was no formal training scheme and many journalists had left school at 14 or 15. A trickle of University graduates continued to enter Fleet Street direct. But in 1937 even 'the national dailies have few, if any, sub-editors or reporters with a university degree on their staff'.[1] The proportion of graduates in British journalism between 1900 and 1950 may well have fallen – with the decline in relative importance of leader-writing, newspapers of opinion, and the old concept of the Editor.

Editors collectively took little interest. Individually Editors, especially of the smaller newspapers, were the main recruiting agents for the provinces and Fleet Street. Arthur Christiansen was typical – he began on a small weekly paper near Liverpool. The majority of both national and local Editors apparently accepted this. From time to time proprietors expressed anxiety about the National Union of Journalists but not with great conviction, and praise was more common. From time to time someone suggested a training scheme; Linton Andrews told Northcliffe in 1919 that the *Daily Mail* should have its own staff college for training young journalists. Northcliffe said he could get his pick of the best young journalists although Andrews thought (but did not say) that even the *Daily Mail* was always short of good sub-editors and employed some astonishingly ignorant journalists.[2] Andrews himself when he became a provincial Editor took on practical training as one of his tasks; like many others he was reconciled to the idea that a provincial Editor must be 'a schoolmaster to the staff'.[3]

Most other groups in the press were organised. The print workers, the journalists and the owners all had their organisations. The middle level managers and the Editors were the least organised.

3.6 Geoffrey Dawson: The most sovereign Editor

In this period there is one remarkable exception to the general rule of non-sovereign Editors. Geoffrey Dawson was the only Editor of *The Times* to hold the job twice – 1912–19 and 1922–41.

Northcliffe groomed Dawson for the editorship in 1911 and made him Editor, aged 38, in 1912. No one could be 'sovereign' who worked for Northcliffe, and Dawson resigned over a policy issue in 1919.

That first term was important because it coloured Dawson's view of the conditions he should set for accepting John Astor's invitation to return after Northcliffe's death in 1922. The wishes both of Editor and of new proprietor combined to produce a situation in which Dawson came probably closer to total responsibility for everything than any Editor apart from C P Scott after assuming ownership of *The Guardian*. Astor's aim in buying *The Times* was to restore it to 'steadier' traditions and prevent it becoming again the tool of an ambitious proprietor like Northcliffe. Hence he cemented the original Walter connection as well as taking the obvious step of sounding out Dawson to come back.

Dawson set out strong and explicit conditions in a memorandum of some 1,500 words. Astor and Walter agreed to them. Dawson demanded complete control

---

1 Ibid, p 89.
2 Linton Andrews, *The Autobiography of a Journalist*, London: Ernest Benn, 1964, p 109.
3 Linton Andrews, *Problems of an Editor*, London: Oxford University Press, 1962, pp 68–102.

over the policy *and staffing* of *The Times* and its sister publications. He recognised that the Manager (subject to the proprietors) must 'say what the paper can afford in staff and salaries' – but that was as far as the Manager should go. 'I regard the complete equality of status, in their respective spheres, of the Manager or Managing Director on the one hand and of the Editor on the other hand, as a fundamental condition'. Since *The Times* in Dawson's period was profitable, this division worked well – and in marked contrast to the periods of Moberley Bell's management and Northcliffe's proprietorship when staffing arrangements were not under the Editor's control. Dawson then won a 'free hand' (his phrase) over all his side of the paper (including the right to strike out advertisements). He became in the words of *The Times* History 'an autocrat over the whole of the editorial content . . . .'[1]

Dawson imprinted his ideas firmly on the editorial columns regardless of disagreement. Sir Colin Coote (Editor of *The Daily Telegraph,* 1950–64) describes leader-writing under him thus: 'You wrote your leader, left it for typing with the editor's secretary, and had no right to resent anything subsequently done to it'. With some fundamental policies – notably *The Times'* support for Appeasement – significant numbers of the staff were in disagreement. The importance of Dawson's power over staffing is reflected in the *History's* criticism of him for failing to appoint a new Foreign Editor when the incumbent Harold Williams died in 1928. Dawson acted as his own Foreign Editor and, it is argued, failed properly to understand the dangerous trends of European politics.

Various interpretations can be, and have been, attached to Geoffrey Dawson's sovereignty in his second term as Editor, when the conduct of *The Times,* if not the conduct of certain politicians, was once again powerfully influenced by a legally binding agreement. But the Dawson case is (with C P Scott) an exception which proves the rule of non-sovereignty in twentieth century editorship.

1 *History of The Times* Vol 4, p 781.

Part B Editors in recent times: 1950-1976

Introduction

The structural changes have been very considerable since 1950. Despite the appearance of television, the number of press journalists has greatly increased – perhaps even doubled since 1950. Many Editors now find themselves with much fatter publications – but there is also much bigger variation. The most specialised parts of the magazine field have expanded the fastest – and the whole new sector of controlled circulation publications has arisen.

The more varied sorts of Editors now typically find themselves responsible to a management structure within a diversified organisation rather than to an individual manager or to a single owner in a much smaller organisation. IPC did not exist in 1950 – it was made up later of three large press organisations. Now IPC itself is a subsidiary. Kemsley has grown into the much larger Thomson Organisation. Westminster Press and the *Financial Times* have both grown greatly and been re-organised into the Pearson management structure.

Size is only one aspect of this. Revenue is now pursued in a much more systematic way than previously. While new management categories have appeared – classified advertising executives, marketing men, in-house market researchers, sales-force experts – existing management skills such as accounting have expanded. Most of these changes are connected in some way with television which competes – and is seen by Editors to compete – for advertising, sales revenue, audience interest and time, journalists, prestige.

Editors have been encouraged by management to identify with management objectives. Documents like the Economist Intelligence Unit report on the *National Newspaper Industry* and much other material which reaches Editors through the structure of their own organisation encourages them to think of themselves as *managers* of the editorial department.

Within his editorial department the Editor is encouraged now to be the chief processor of news – but also the manager of newsgathering. Both sides have become more sophisticated and specialised. Newsgathering has grown enormously more specialised since 1950 – most specialist fields and most specialist newsgathering jobs did not yet exist in 1950. This development is especially associated with the prestige papers, with the now much fatter publications, and with attempts to do what TV cannot do. Both newsprocessing and newsgathering have led to a much elaborated executive and 'desk' structure within news departments. Editors now in general deal much less with raw news or with individual journalists – and much more with executive journalists in charge of pages, functions and teams of staff.

Table 4.1

Journalist staff of a national daily and a provincial daily newspaper in 1968

	National Daily No.	Provincial Daily No.	National Daily %	Provincial Daily %
Executives/Deskmen				
General executive	11	4	4	7
Assistants	8	1	3	2
Gathering executives	4	1	1	2
Assistants	12	1	4	2
Processing executives	3	1	1	2
Assistants	13	2	4	3
TOTAL	51	10	17	17
Gatherers				
Foreign correspondents	8	0	3	0
Financial specialists	8	0	3	0
Other News specialists	21	2	7	3
Sports specialists	8	0	3	0
General Sports reporter	7	3	2	5
Photographers	27	5	9	8
Leader writers	4	0	1	0
Columnists, Cartoonists	4	0	1	0
Feature writers, Critics	18	4	6	7
General reporters	30	10	10	17
Regional Sports, News reporters	18	17*	6	28
TOTAL	153	41	52	68
Processors				
News and specialist subs	60	9	20	15
Sports sub-editors	20	0	7	0
Features sub-editors	10	0	3	0
	90	9	31	15
TOTAL	294	60	100	100

*In the case of a paper sharing branch office staff with a partner daily paper, half the numbers were included.

Source: J Tunstall, *Journalists at Work*, Constable. 1971. p 15.

Editors also find themselves in a world which is pre-programmed by quantitative indicators in a way which was unknown in 1950. Editors (like most people) are extremely sceptical about any particular piece of research; but they work on publications which increasingly run on tramlines built out of such quantified material. Even simple circulation trends are now analysed with vastly increased sophistication; Editors are encouraged to be money conscious. In detail, of course, they are told that circulation and advertising revenue vary for reasons other than editorial performance; nevertheless it is widely agreed that in the long run superior editorial performance must be recognisable in some quantified indicator – market share, attention value, appreciation index, home delivery rate and so on.

The ambiguity of such indicators makes the prevailing ones no less compelling to Editors and their staffs. After the Thomson takeover *The Times* was geared to a rapid sales expansion and editorial effort played its part in achieving a very big increase; but because the larger sale did not bring profitability, everything – including editorial performance – then pursued a new goal of lower sales.

The provincial press has since 1950 marched steadily down the same road as before. Head-on competition has been largely eliminated, non-partisanship has become more common and classified advertising has increased enormously in importance. Since 1950 the main purpose of provincial journalism has been less and less to sway votes – and has ever more explicitly been oriented towards increasing advertising revenue and profit. Journalists have become ever more obviously, in the advertising man's phrase, 'people who write on the backs of advertisements' and Editors have become people who get given pages to edit in a strict ratio to the advertisements. These trends can be regarded as pressures, as guidelines, or as neutral facts. But they inevitably encourage Editors to make rough calculations about the costs and benefits of covering particular types of stories.

The NUJ has grown enormously. The NUJ in 1976 had roughly four times its 1937 membership; even since 1966 its membership has increased by 50%. Some of this increase results from organising new areas such as magazines, some from the increase in numbers of press journalists, and some from the NUJ's recruitment in broadcasting, commercial and public sector public relations and book editing. The NUJ has followed the general industrial pattern of diversification.

But while ownership/management on the one side, and the journalist's main trade union on the other, have grown bigger and stronger, Editors have not followed suit. Editors have collectively remained weak and have probably decreased in numbers. Moreover while both press management and the journalists' union have increasingly stressed similar goals for themselves – primarily money and security – Editors have developed few recognisable goals except the maintenance of an Editorial Sovereignty which is not well founded either in historical or present day reality.

Chart II News Organisation chart: national daily newspaper 1968

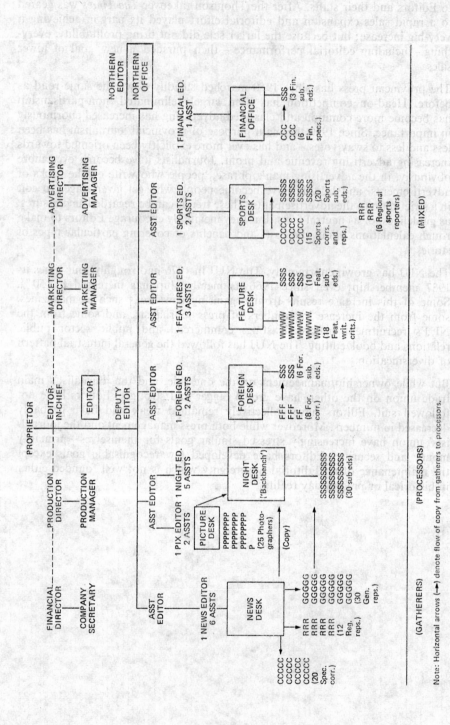

Source: Jeremy Tunstall, *Journalists at Work*. London: Constable, 1971. p 29.

4 Some 1960s examples

This section focuses mainly on editorship in the late 1960s. It is based primarily on interviews and direct observation sessions conducted by the author (and in a few cases by Oliver Boyd-Barrett) between 1965 and 1968.

4.1 Associated Newspapers

Associated Newspapers throughout the 1960s were conservative both in politics and in journalism. Lord Rothermere told the Shawcross Commission how Editors were chosen:

'Mr John Thomson generally comes to me and says he thinks the best man to succeed somebody is so-and-so, and then he brings him up and we have a chat; if I like him he gets appointed.'

Mr Thomson said:

'You appoint an editor of a provincial paper because of his technical ability· He may be a Socialist, but I assume he would carry on the paper in the old tradition.'[1]

Throughout the 1960s Associated provincial dailies did well, while the *Daily Sketch*, *Daily Mail* and *Evening News* all tended to lose money. The *News Chronicle* was merged with the *Daily Mail*.

Colin Valdar, Editor of the *Daily Sketch* for three years in the early 1960s, said he regarded his main accomplishments when Editor as cutting editorial costs and getting the paper printed on the *Evening News* presses. Valdar was convinced that his editorial attack on the Conservative 'racialist' immigration bill had led to Lord Rothermere sacking him.

William Hardcastle, Editor of the *Daily Mail* at the same period, also said that he had been well to the left of the *Daily Mail* itself. Hardcastle was one of the seven Editors of the *Daily Mail* between 1947 and 1967. Like some of the other Editors, he was not a production man – but a former foreign correspondent.

In early 1966 the *Daily Mail* was voted by 'What the Papers Say' as the Newspaper of the Year; the Editor responsible – Michael Randall – was sacked later in the same year. The *Daily Mail* at this time was widely admired for its 'investigations' and attractive layout – but the circulation continued to fall.

Deputy editor under both Randall and his successor Arthur Brittenden was the Australian, Bruce Rothwell. Rothwell was an ex-*News Chronicle* foreign correspondent in Bonn and Washington and a more intellectual man than most

---

1 (Shawcross,) *Royal Commission on the Press* (Cmnd 1812), Oral Evidence, Vol 1, pp 409–10.

popular newspaper executives. Rothwell was extremely critical of the *Daily Mail* management. Randall was in his view a scapegoat for circulation losses incurred when the *Daily Mail* had at first held its price down while the others put their's up and had then put its price up unilaterally. In addition to Randall, several assistant editors were sacked. Rothwell believed that the Board were so ignorant and archaic that they wasted half the Editor's time with needless details and queries. Rothwell himself was not well briefed about the age composition of the *Daily Mail*'s then readership – he only vaguely grasped the implications of the elderly age profile which, he said, one of the circulation managers had explained to him. In Rothwell's view the only practical way to run a newspaper 'is to assume that the editor is a genius'.

Arthur Brittenden, appointed *Daily Mail* Editor in 1966, was another ex-foreign correspondent with plenty of popular newspaper experience but little experience in production. He seemed a less forceful person than Rothwell – who may have been more important during this period than either Randall or Brittenden. In retrospect these *Daily Mail* Editors might seem to have been unsuitable for a popular newspaper – they were, however, part of a 'quality-pop' strategy which was unsuccessfully pursued in the 1960s by the *Daily Mail* management.

Yet another ex-foreign correspondent was John Gold, appointed *Evening News* Editor in 1967. John Gold had been the *Evening News* man in New York for many years. A popular journalist, Gold had worked closely with the *Daily News* while in New York and specialised in show business stories. Certainly in his early days Gold did not take a very active part in production in the style of some popular Editors. According to the Chief sub-editor, in July 1967 Gold only appeared at the 'back-bench' to see proofs of the front page.

Two examples were observed of how dailies within Associated Newspapers worked together. When the *Daily Mail* newsdesk received information at 1.30 pm of a major London bus crash (in August 1967) one of the news editor's first actions was to 'phone his opposite number on the *Evening News*. During the interview with Arthur Brittenden he spoke on the 'phone to the then *Daily Sketch* Editor, Howard French – about bidding for the exclusive rights to the story of recently arrived sextuplets.[1]

4.2 IPC newspapers

In talking to IPC Editors the atmosphere was quite different from Associated. Where Associated was sacking Editors, IPC was taking in ex-Editors; at IPC also there was an air of confidence – in retrospect, perhaps of false confidence. IPC Editors sat back rather comfortably in their standard IPC Editor's issue office – each complete with similar carpet, sofa and chairs, potted plants and television set. Only at *The Sun* was the atmosphere pessimistic.

Lee Howard, Editor of the *Daily Mirror* since 1960, was a large friendly man who, even more than the other Editors, seemed to personify the 1960s *Daily Mirror*. The paper was still selling 5 million copies a day. Howard's style was

---

1 Information for Associated Newspapers based on interviews with Colin Valdar, Herbert Pack (news editor of the *Daily Sketch*), Bruce Rothwell (on three occasions), William Hardcastle, Arthur Brittenden and observation sessions by Oliver Boyd-Barrett – two days each at *Daily Mail* and *Evening News*.

one of delegation – during a 12 to 12 day of observation my impression was of a paper put together by the news editor, the night editor and a few stars. Marjorie Proops, one of the stars, even attended the afternoon editorial conference.

Off the newsroom at the *Daily Mirror* was John Beavan (ex-editor of the *Daily Herald*) and the *Daily Mirror*'s senior envoy to Westminster. Another ex-editor (*Daily Express* 1957–62) was Edward Pickering, the editorial-director. Pickering in 1967 was a director not only of Daily Mirror Newspapers, but also of IPC itself (while Howard was on neither board); on the main IPC board Hugh Cudlipp was at that time Deputy Chairman. The *Daily Mirror* was also well supplied with other senior executives who relieved the Editor of many administrative chores.

Alex Little, Editor of IPC's *Daily Record* in Glasgow was engaged in a fierce sales war with the Glasgow edition of the *Daily Express*. Little's pungently worded view was that competitive life was a lot fiercer in Glasgow than in London – he thought that Cecil King and Hugh Cudlipp were out of touch with Scottish reality. Little was opposed to graduates and also to the ordinary training scheme as a tendency to educate journalists away from audiences. At that time (1966) the *Record* was still behind the *Express* in sales and the *Daily Mail* was still printed in Edinburgh.

At *The Sun* the atmosphere was very different – the IPC re-launch clearly had not worked well and there was a sense of isolation from the rest of the IPC. Although *The People* was in *The Sun* building, its Editor, Bob Edwards, was positively buoyant. Having achieved the unique distinction of being fired by Beaverbrook from the *Daily Express* editorship not once but twice, Edwards had landed on his feet – and reminisced happily about the *Express*. Despite his earlier editorship of *Tribune* he had never been left wing. He was most interested in political and foreign news – writing the *Sunday People*'s leaders himself – and especially happy with Terence Lancaster (a former foreign correspondent) as his lobby man. Edwards expressed mild astonishment at the low level of taste of some *People* readers.

Another interesting pop-intellectual was the *Sunday Mirror* Editor, Michael Christiansen (son of Arthur Christiansen of the *Daily Express*). Christiansen tried to convey what he evidently believed to be a new approach to popular Sunday journalism; this approach was well exemplified, he thought, by his purchase of serial rights of Desmond Morris' *The Naked Ape* for only £10,000. The 'people upstairs' thought he was crazy, but the circulation rose noticeably. Respectable striptease was on its way – and Christiansen was the only IPC newspaper Editor who had noticed.

IPC's management structure and the Editors' place in it was praised in the EIU report. In retrospect two oddities of many can be mentioned. Firstly the *Daily Mirror* in 1968 had 440 journalists[1]; secondly, it was not clear what some of them – including the Editor – did. In talking to Lee Howard's editorial superiors and to some of his immediate lieutenants, and to Mr Howard himself,[2] no precise impression was conveyed as to what the Editor's distinctive contribution was supposed to be.

---

1 J Tunstall, *Journalists at Work*, London: Constable, 1971, p 14.
2 Based on interviews with Lee Howard, John Beavan, Edward Pickering (twice), Kenneth Hord (*Daily Mirror* editorial manager), Alex Little, A J Boram (*The Sun*'s managing editor), Robert Edwards and Michael Christiansen, plus one day of observation at *The Sun* and one at the *Daily Mirror*.

4.3 IPC magazines

In 1966 IPC senior management was running its magazines deliberately in competition with each other. In the many cases where IPC owned two or more leading magazines in a single field, these were placed in different subsidiaries. For example *Autocar* and *Flight International* were in Kelley-Iliffe, whereas their competitors *Motor* and *Aeroplane* were within another IPC subsidiary, National Trade Press.

The Editors interviewed in 1966 were just getting used to this and claimed to think it was working. The larger technical magazines had a dozen journalists or so; a small magazine like *Football Monthly*, selling about 200,000 copies to teenagers, had three journalists. These publications drew most of their journalist staff from the area in question – although the Editor, or one of the senior journalists, tended to be a professional. These Editors regarded themselves as remote from Fleet Street and mainly involved in their subject area.

Clive Irving was 'editorial director' of IPC magazines – pushed by Hugh Cudlipp into a new senior job. Irving, suspended above the magazine subsidiaries, was having considerable difficulty in exerting any real influence on any particular magazine. His early efforts were being directed mainly at *The Statist, Nova* and *Woman's Mirror*. He had deliberately chosen weak publications on which to experrment (and all three magazines subsequently failed).

Monopoly was obviously both IPC's greatest asset and greatest problem. The enormous magazine fleet could be arranged on a competitive or (as subsequently) a co-operative basis; titles could be merged and others launched. But Editors in any case lived in specialised worlds; their main connections with IPC were in terms of budgets (including staff size), advertising and circulation, and some specialised editorial services such as pictures. Editors seemed to be aware of the somewhat arbitrary nature of these guidelines. For instance, the Editor of *Flight International* had a list of well-rehearsed arguments as to why he and his staff of nine needed, and were allowed to have, their own aeroplane.

4.4 Beaverbrook newspapers

By the late 1960's the pendulum had swung away from the technician-Editor pattern of Beaverbrook's mature proprietorship and had reverted to the earlier *Daily Express* pattern of the opinionated, or at least political, Editor.

John Junor and Charles Wintour had become Editors of the *Sunday Express* and *Evening Standard* in 1954 and 1959 respectively. Junor was a former lobby correspondent. Charles Wintour had been briefly political editor of the *Evening Standard*. Wintour was perhaps the most literary and artistically inclined of all the national Editors of this period. They were transitional figures from the later Beaverbrook period – when he no longer wished to exercise day-to-day political dominance himself and wanted men of political knowledge.

Derek Marks, who became Editor of the *Daily Express* in 1965, was another man of moderate (Conservative) opinion – but also a man of vigorous political conviction. Marks had not merely been a Lobby correspondent, but an outstandingly successful one. He was promoted by Sir Max Aitken who perhaps felt the need for someone in broad sympathy with his views, but who would take the lead politically.

All three Editors were basically of a writing, rather than sub-editing background; all three were men of obvious intellect. And all three were directors on the main board of Beaverbrook newspapers. Even if this board seldom met, and even though they were not Sovereign Editors, Junor, Wintour and Marks were deeply entrenched. Yet the subsequent losses of these papers must raise a question. Does the main board of a sizeable public company require no less than three journalist directors, whose collective experience is so heavily slanted towards political journalism?

4.5 The *Daily* and *Sunday Telegraph*[1]

The Daily Telegraph was maintaining its century-long tradition of the Proprietor as also being Editor-in-Chief. *The Daily Telegraph* organisation chart (overleaf) was supplied in 1968 but had originally been drawn up a few years earlier when Sir Colin Coote was still Editor.

The pattern described by Coote in his book *Editorial* was continued with his successor Maurice Green. Green was from *The Times* and before that had edited the old *Financial News*. He had taken first class honours in Greats at Oxford and was 57 when appointed Editor in 1964. When interviewed in 1968 Mr Green was accompanied by S R Pawley who answered most of our questions, which were mainly about specialists.

Pawley as 'Managing Editor, News and Production' was in charge of the main news gathering and news processing operations – the great bulk of the journalist staff. This included not only the large team of reporters and specialists, but *The Daily Telegraph*'s 27 foreign correspondents (in 1968 it had five in New York, three each in Washington, Paris and Bonn, two in the middle East and one each in Vienna, Rome, Brussels, Moscow, Geneva, South Africa, Salisbury, New Delhi, Singapore, Hong-Kong and Stockholm). In addition, Mr Pawley was in charge of sport, the City coverage and the entire Night desk and sub-editing operation. The Editor was in charge of the leaders, the rest of the leader page, and features – especially arts and women's features. The Editor also had his team of leader-writers and his own daily leader conference. Fairly clearly one of the Editor's main tasks was to be the public editorial face of the paper. However there was little doubt that Lord Hartwell was the senior figure on the editorial side or that Mr Pawley was in complete charge under him of the news operation. Nor was it completely true to say that Maurice Green as Editor was in total charge of the *political* side of the paper – since the Lobby correspondents and the foreign editor were firmly on the news side.

Other evidence of Lord Hartwell's dominance was accidentally supplied in an interview with Donald McLachlan, Editor of the *Sunday Telegraph* for its first five years, 1961–66. McLachlan was also from *The Times* (and *The Economist*) – an intellectual journalist primarily interested in political, foreign and financial news, defence and Germany. Interviewed in January 1966 McLachlan said that it must be unusual to talk to an Editor the day after he has 'resigned' his post. The answer to what it feels like, he said, is that 'The editor is sniffing' (he had a heavy cold at the time). He had been offered the job for five years and Lord Hartwell had just decided not to renew the contract. McLachlan was thus enabled to announce that he was resigning as planned,

---

1 Based on interviews with Maurice Green and S R Pawley, Donald McLachlan, Brian Roberts and Eric Marsh (*Daily Telegraph* foreign editor).

Chart III
Organisation of *The Daily Telegraph*
Circa 1965

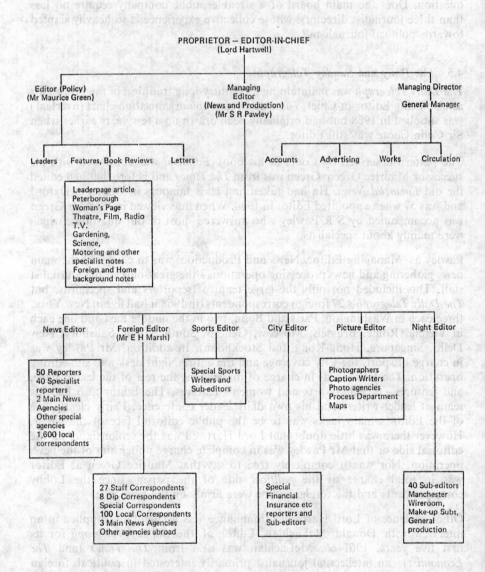

PROPRIETOR — EDITOR-IN-CHIEF
(Lord Hartwell)

Editor (Policy)
(Mr Maurice Green)

Managing
Editor
(News and Production)
(Mr S R Pawley)

Managing Director
General Manager

Leaders | Features, Book Reviews | Letters

Accounts | Advertising | Works | Circulation

Leaderpage article
Peterborough
Woman's Page
Theatre, Film, Radio
T.V.
Gardening,
Science,
Motoring and other
specialist notes
Foreign and Home
background notes

News Editor | Foreign Editor (Mr E H Marsh) | Sports Editor | City Editor | Picture Editor | Night Editor

50 Reporters
40 Specialist
reporters
2 Main News
Agencies
Other special
agencies
1,600 local
correspondents

Special Sports
Writers and
Sub-editors

Photographers
Caption Writers
Photo agencies
Process Department
Maps

27 Staff Correspondents
8 Dip Correspondents
Special Correspondents
100 Local Correspondents
3 Main News Agencies
Other agencies abroad

Special
Financial
Insurance etc
reporters and
Sub-editors

40 Sub-editors
Manchester
Wireroom,
Make-up Subs,
General
production

but he made little effort in this interview to hide his shock and surprise. Several times he mentioned his long-term plans for the *Sunday Telegraph* and sadly commented that now he would not be able to carry them out. He admitted that the *Sunday Telegraph* had in its first five years consistently lost money, but claimed that this had been anticipated. McLachlan 'retired' gracefully to write, and indeed wrote a remarkable book on wartime naval intelligence;[1] he was perhaps a little too intellectual for the Editor's job.

Brian Roberts, his successor as *Sunday Telegraph* Editor, had a stronger popular journalism and sub-editing background – he had once been *Daily Mail* night editor. He was also an Oxford graduate. He was 59 when appointed in 1966. When interviewed, Brian Roberts made it clear that he was directly responsible for both the news and processing sides of the paper – the Sunday paper had no managing editor.

Thus the *Sunday Telegraph* Editor was more directly in control of his own staff. But since the paper was losing money this must have reduced his autonomy. Clearly Lord Hartwell was in overall control – not only in strategic decisions such as launching the colour magazine in the daily (not the Sunday) paper, but also in some matters of detail. Lord Hartwell's memos were often mentioned by particular *Daily Telegraph* specialists – his proprietorial spotlight focused on one area of the paper at a time, announced to the journalists in question by a sudden flurry of detailed memos. This is, of course, the traditional method of the editorially active proprietors such as Hearst and Northcliffe – and on *The Daily Telegraph* itself. Lord Hartwell's pattern of control was also evident in his distinct preference for Editors themselves well advanced in years and with experience on *The Times* and the *Telegraph*.

4.6 The *Financial Times*

Gordon Newton had been Editor of the *Financial Times* since 1950 and had thus presided over an enormous increase in its circulation, in its number of pages, and in its general reputation. In the late 1960s, however, Newton still edited the paper in rather the same style as in the earlier and much smaller days.

Both senior and middle level journalists on the paper confirmed,[2] that the Editor tended to dominate all areas of the paper and to deal individually with a wide range of journalists. For example one feature writer on the paper said that in practice he worked as much directly to the Editor as to his formal boss, the features editor. This unusual degree of editorial dominance had a number of related aspects:

(*a*) The 'executive' structure of the paper was less developed than on most other dailies.

(*b*) The Editor seemed to devote nearly all his time to dealing with journalists and their writing – he did no writing at all himself.

(*c*) There tended to be more rapid movement of senior personnel on the *Financial Times* than on other national papers. Some movement was due to the

---

1 Donald McLachlan, *Room 39: Naval Intelligence in Action 1939–45*, London: Weidenfeld and Nicolson, 1968.

2 Most of this section on the *Financial Times* is based on interviews in 1966–8 with senior journalists other than the Editor. However, Sir Gordon Newton, the then Editor, was also interviewed in 1968.

boom in financial journalism, some because certain specialists (such as the Lex column staff) tended to leave journalism for City jobs; but some of it seems to have been due to the Editor's policy of moving people every few years – with the possible exception of the Lobby staff.

(*d*) Despite the large number of pages, the number of journalists employed was small. In 1968 the *Financial Times* had only 140 journalists, about half the number of most other national dailies.[1] Journalists on this paper filled roughly twice as much editorial space as those on any other paper and five or more times as much as popular daily journalists.[2] Newton himself said that 60% of his journalist staff were engaged in relatively routine tasks – such as market prices; in other words only 50 or 60 of his journalists were doing non-routine tasks. These 50 or 60 he himself largely directed. Another aspect of this style of control may have been the relative absence of sub-editing (or the concentration of sub-editing on market prices) – leaving the non-routine journalists to a large extent sub-editing their own material and responsible to the Editor.

(*e*) There were of course journalists in 'executive' jobs but some were relatively young and inexperienced and with demanding detailed responsibilities for large areas of the paper.

(*f*) The *Financial Times* had an unusual board with a strong representation of big businessmen plus the unique figure of Lord Robbins, an academic economist and businessman. Confronted with an extremely successful paper and an experienced Editor, the board may have been willing to allow the Editor an unusually high degree of autonomy.

(*g*) An experienced and respected Editor of the *Financial Times* inevitably acquires a reputation in the City of London which gives him a secure career alternative of a kind which does not become open to Editors of other papers. To what extent Sir Gordon Newton's style of editorship grew out of the *Financial Times* and to what extent he shaped the paper to fit his own preferred style of editing it is impossible to say. But in 1968 he was clearly one of Fleet Street's two most sovereign non-proprietor Editors.

4.7 The Guardian

The only Fleet Street Editor possibly more sovereign than Newton was Alastair Hetherington of *The Guardian*. Hetherington had one power which even Newton probably lacked – the power to hazard the ship and if need be to take it under for reasons of editorial policy.

Hetherington's early days as *The Guardian*'s Editor have often been described by himself and by others; these events were then followed by the move to London – making in total for a unique opening period of editorship. Hetherington in 1956 within a very short time of becoming Editor, committed the *Manchester Guardian* against the Eden invasion of Suez. In line with *Guardian* tradition he received proprietorial support; Manchester readers left in droves, but new ones were gained – especially in London and the South and this, accidentally, assisted the already planned London printing. Hetherington continued to edit

1 J Tunstall, *op cit*, p 14.
2 Economist Intelligence Unit, *The National Newspaper Industry*, London: EIU, 1966, p 67.

the paper from Manchester but he later moved to London. By the late 1960s *The Guardian* was a London newspaper with a Manchester print, and Hetherington had become a London Editor in every sense.

The move to London was badly handled, but these were management responsibilities. Hetherington in the 1960s had a special prestige, confidence and authority – he had been through the storm of Suez and survived. He had moved the paper to London and survived. He also played an active part in preventing the paper being merged with *The Times* (see below). Having hazarded the ship over Suez and even kept it afloat against proprietorial wishes, he was an Editor sovereign in the Dawson sense – not with proprietorial control, but with an editorial control so strong that it could over-ride, indeed act entirely counter to, proprietorial planning.

The *Manchester Guardian* had in 1956 been a small paper in pages and staff. Hetherington was modest in demeanour but enormously self-assured both as an intellectual and as a journalist. His interest in politics, in defence and in foreign affairs had a distinctly academic tone. His father was Vice-Chancellor of Glasgow University; Hetherington liked surrounding himself with stimulating journalist-academics – such as Leonard Beaton, Victor Zorza, David Marquand and Richard Gott. But Hetherington also had a gift for production and layout. In his early days in Manchester he dominated the paper probably even more than Newton did the *Financial Times*: he himself largely handled the main specialist correspondents.

By the late 'sixties Hetherington was still dominating the newsgathering and was also staying late at night (his London night editor, John Putz, had joined the *Manchester Guardian* in 1929). Hetherington was putting in 12-hour stints but only editing the paper about three or four nights a week. The 'Duty Editor' on the other nights was either Harford Thomas (then deputy editor), or the northern editor Brian Redhead, or even the foreign editor. Even by late 1965, however, John Cole while only 'London news editor' was clearly a powerful man on the paper. Harford Thomas (a former *Oxford Mail* Editor) was clearly no threat to Hetherington.[1] There were still some extremely formidable members of the staff but they tended to be in remote places – Alastair Cooke in New York for example; Hetherington towered over his London staff in every sense and in terms of editorial authority over his proprietor. Although Laurence Scott was clearly a powerful figure, his London management was still only just undergoing a managerial revolution.

The weak financial underpinnings of this Dawson-like sovereignty were illustrated in the great Fleet Street crisis of 1966. Laurence Scott announced that either the London or Manchester printing might have to be suspended. One in four of all *The Guardian*'s journalists must go.[2]

4.8 The Observer

Since David Astor was both chairman and Editor of *The Observer*, there was even less ambiguity than in the case of *The Daily Telegraph*. Oliver Boyd-Barrett spent a full week at *The Observer* in 1967 and he interviewed most of the senior people there. One senior man described David Astor's style as that

---

1 Based on interviews with Alastair Hetherington, Harford Thomas, John Cole, Brian Redhead, Harry Whewell, John Putz and Richard Gott.
2 *UK Press Gazette*, 12 December 1966.

of the enlightened despot – but one who liked his employees to agree with him, which resulted in much discussion. A number of journalists, including Anthony Bambridge (the City editor) had stories of Astor's being willing to allow journalists to lose advertising. Audrey Powell, the property correspondent, admitted that property coverage was there to gain advertising, but thought she was relatively free of detailed pressure. Astor himself discussed advertising at some length. In some fields – such as fashion – Astor found advertisers surprisingly willing to accept criticism; but motor industry advertisers did not 'allow' criticism – he then corrected himself and said 'like' criticism.

Internally the organisation of *The Observer* seemed more like a series of circles than a hierarchy. The innermost circle included veterans and friends of Astor such as Nora Beloff, Ivan Yates, Robert Stephens, Colin Legum and Patrick O'Donovan. Then there was a more detached category of executives such as K P Obank (managing editor), Nigel Lloyd (production editor) and Michael Davie (deputy editor). Another outer ring of important journalists included Rudolf Klein (leader writer) and some interesting personalities among the reporters like Peter Deeley, Eric Clarke and Colin McGlashan. Some senior people such as Anthony Bambridge had little contact with the Editor, although in 1968 Astor emphasised the importance of business coverage and was planning to increase it.

Interviewing Astor in 1968, it was easy to discover what he was against. He was extremely unhappy at what he regarded as the creeping commercialisation of the press represented by Lord Thomson – but Astor expressed a liking for Thomson as a man, and thought that he had been badly treated over the famous issue of the printing of *The Sunday Times* on the *Telegraph* presses, and the sudden notice of termination of the contract in order to launch the *Sunday Telegraph*. Astor believed in 1968 that *The Times* was going to seriously damage *The Daily Telegraph* and that the *Sunday Telegraph* would eventually be closed.

Astor gave little indication of what he thought to be distinctive about *The Observer* apart from liberal integrity and a less strong commercial element. His discussion of editorial-and-business strategy implied mainly reacting to the moves of his competitors. Nor did any very distinctive picture emerge from the journalists on the paper. On one point Editor and staff seemed in strong agreement – it was a good place to work.[1]

4.9 The Sunday Times and The Times

Both William Rees-Mogg and Harold Evans were aged 38 when they were appointed Editors of *The Times* and *The Sunday Times* respectively in 1967. The person who appointed them was Denis Hamilton. Denis Hamilton had himself been Editor of *The Sunday Times* since 1961, but before that he had been editorial director of the Kemsley provincial newspapers.[2] Hamilton is an interesting example of an Editor who did not so much work his way up into the editorial chair, but rather worked his way down into it. For some time after the Thomson takeover Hamilton remained editorial director of the provincial papers and he appears never to have edited in the usual day-to-day sense.

1 Based on Oliver Boyd-Barrett's notes on five days at *The Observer*, and author's interview with David Astor.
2 Harold Hobson, Phillip Knightley and Leonard Russell, *The Pearl of Days: An Intimate History of the Sunday Times, 1822–1972*, London: Hamish Hamilton, 1972, pp 345–430.

The present author spent seven days in *The Sunday Times* office during the General Election of March 1966 – most of the time with the 'Insight' team which was expanded for the election coverage. Denis Hamilton played a background role – even on Saturday, the big production day. On Saturday the men in charge of producing the paper were James Dow (production) and Michael Cudlipp. The person most obviously in charge of the political policy side of *The Sunday Times* was William Rees-Mogg. On Saturday, 19 March 1966 Rees-Mogg demonstrated this by changing the front page lead. In the first edition the lead story was that Harold Wilson was going to swing the Labour party towards Europe; earlier in the week Richard Crossman had told the paper about this and some feature coverage on Labour and Europe was accordingly prepared. However Harold Wilson's Saturday speech went less far than Crossman had seemed to indicate – this became progressively apparent with an advance briefing whose report was 'phoned back by a journalist covering the Bristol meeting, then the release of the text from Smith Square, and then the speech itself. Rees-Mogg consulted with Michael Cudlipp – who was performing the chief processor role, which a night editor does on a daily. Rees-Mogg's view was that even a Prime Ministerial initiative of this magnitude, because it was not 'on the record', was not worth the splash in the middle of an election campaign. Rees-Mogg also spoke to the Lobby and industrial correspondents; he then consulted Denis Hamilton and returned to say that the Wilson story would be demoted down the front page for the second edition.

Harold Evans, soon to be Editor, was already at *The Sunday Times* and temporarily presiding over the sports sub-editors as part of his first task of re-designing the sports pages. Evans had been interviewed previously in Darlington – indeed on the very day (10 December 1965) on which he was telling his staff on the *Northern Echo* that he would be leaving to join *The Sunday Times* in London. Harold Evans was popular with his staff in the North East; his biggest contribution to the *Northern Echo* was to redesign it to look much more like a national broadsheet popular. He was known nationally as a broadcaster on 'What the Papers Say' and had also campaigned for an inquiry into the execution of Timothy Evans (no relation!). Another campaign was about runaway lorries. He had not, however, engaged in exposé journalism against local government corruption, which we now know was rife in this area of England at the time.

Harold Evans had a difficult early period as Editor of *The Sunday Times* partly because he was appointed in the Fleet Street crisis winter of 1966–67, when *The Sunday Times* suffered commercial set-backs for the first time for some years. Interviewed in 1968, when he had been Editor for about a year, Evans seemed to lack his usual ebullience. He had clearly established a much more activist and conventional style of editing than Hamilton – whose main contributions, according to the approved history, were in successful delegation and in buying books for serialisation and sales increases.

As laid down in the Thomson-Hamilton plan, *The Times* had recently massively increased its sales and its losses.[1] Rees-Mogg appeared to be taking a middle line as Editor – controlling the opinion side and strongly influencing the news. Many of the changes on *The Times*, however, had been initiated partly or wholly by Denis Hamilton, although the key new personnel tended to be former colleagues of Rees-Mogg from *The Sunday Times*. Rees-Mogg thought that an

1 Based on interviews with Harold Evans (in Darlington and in London) and William Rees-Mogg, and seven days of observation at *The Sunday Times* in 1966.

Editor did not need to have production experience, and he was relying here no Michael Cudlipp who had come with him to *The Times*. A bigger detraction from autonomy may have been *The Times* Business News, currently running as a separate section under Anthony Vice – with its own staff and its own leaders. Moreover Rees-Mogg was the first Editor of *The Times* to work under an Editor-in-Chief. At this stage Sir William Haley (the previous Editor) was also chairman of the board. Compared with his predecessor, then, Rees-Mogg was clearly less autonomous – especially since when Haley took over the editorship in 1952 he came from a more important job, Director-General of the BBC.

4.10 Regional Daily Editors

A number of regional Editors were interviewed in a rather unsystematic way.

Eric Dobson, Editor of the Newcastle *Evening Chronicle* gave the impression of a man who was adjusting rather slowly to the new managerial guidelines of Thomson; several journalists on the paper were critical of Thomson along the lines of excessive advertising and profits with too little money spent on editorial. John Sayers, Editor of the Belfast *Evening Telegraph* gave the impression of being left very much alone by Thomson; he was much more concerned with a sectarian murder the day before (26 June 1966). Both his father and grandfather had edited the paper. At this time the Thomson regionals each had their own London correspondent in the London Office.

Mr J Williamson, managing editor of the Press Association, said that the PA really ran on its sports news.

The Birmingham Post Editor, David Hopkinson, had earned the reputation in Sheffield of being the most courageous provincial Editor in Britain; he was mainly concerned with strengthening the community appeal and serious news of the *Post* – but it was obvious that the *Post* was awkwardly placed between the nationals and its profitable evening stable companion, the Birmingham *Evening Mail*. Hopkinson was also pressing for more foreign coverage but had no money for it – having to rely on free exchanges and 'facility trips'. These free air trips both here and elsewhere seemed to be a major perk of provincial journalism.

Keith Whetstone, the Editor of the *Cambridge News* and John Leese of the Coventry *Evening Telegraph* were also Iliffe Editors. Whetstone in 1966 had just taken on the first graduate ever employed by the *Cambridge News* to his knowledge; only recently acquired by Iliffe, the paper was expanding its sales and spreading its branch offices farther out from Cambridge. Whetstone was worried about the shortage of money with which to reward and keep his key men; he was deliberately concentrating available money on just a few young journalists whom he wanted to keep. It was noticeable that Iliffe tended to promote its Editors within the group – Hopkinson was the exception, having come from Sheffield.

Mr K Lister was Editor of the *Sunderland Echo*, with a Tory MP (and deputy speaker) as his proprietor; communication was mainly by memo. Alf Jenner was Editor-in-Chief of the Eastern Counties group in Norwich which then comprised two dailies, a farming paper and 12 weeklies; Mr Jenner modestly expressed surprise at having got the job. The modesty of many provincial Editors was also noticeable at a national meeting of the Guild of British Newspaper Editors in Edinburgh. The meeting was intended to be half work and half social; wives attended the sessions.

Claud Morris, author of *I Bought A Newspaper* had set up a newspaper in South Wales and then a series of local magazines called *The Voice of Humber Industry* etc. He complained that local journalists refused to criticise major businessmen because they believed that their own Editors or managers would not support them. Morris thought that local Editors were also much more timid than they needed to be. (Windsor Clarke speaking at the GBNE made the same point on libel and Editors.)

4.11 Footnote: *The Guardian – Times* merger vetoed

It was widely known in Fleet Street in late 1966 that at one stage Laurence Scott favoured merging *The Guardian* with *The Times*. This proposal was put to the Scott Trust, but was voted down by the journalist members who included Alastair Hetherington and Richard Scott (*The Guardian*'s then Washington Correspondent). The reasons for these actions were discussed by Alastair Hetherington in a speech at the International Press Institute meeting in Geneva the following June:

1 Why, last autumn, did the *Guardian* choose *the austerity of independence*, rather than some form of commercially comfortable merger?

2 How have we succeeded in putting the independent *Guardian* back on the road to *economic recovery* to paying its own way?

Why stay independent?

Last summer and autumn, *The Times* and *The Guardian* found themselves in remarkably similar situations.

Both had a rising sale: both had declining revenues.

The Guardian had increased by 50% in the previous 6 years.

The Times after a long static period, had just increased its sales by about 20% in the previous 4 months.

Both were near the 300,000 mark.

But both were losing large sums of money.

They were already losing before last summer: because their advertisement revenues were too small.

Television had bitten into the advertising cake;

so had colour magazines;

and national newspapers depend on national, not local advertising.

Then, from last August, the losses of *both* papers grew quickly – frighteningly so – because the British Government's policy of financial restriction caused many advertisers to cut their advertising.

We had, then a *choice* in the autumn:

do we look for salvation through a merger with *The Times* or do we keep going on our own?

A merger with *The Times might* have been brought about in any one of a number of ways.

– We could have come to a direct arrangement with the Astors, leading to publication of a *Times-Guardian* as a single newspaper: that was, in fact, discussed both before and during the Astor talks with Thomson, but the discussions came to nothing (fortunately, I think).

– Or we could have done a deal with Roy Thomson: he would have been glad to take us over, probably as part of a *Times-Guardian*.

– Or there were other possible ways.

Now we on *The Guardian* in the end *rejected* all these: rightly, in my view.

We rejected them because we believe that, in any merger, The Guardian's *voice would be silenced: or would be so muted that it might as well be silent.*

We took the view that our first duty was to keep *The Guardian* going as an independent newspaper, by whatever means we could.

Commercially, a merger was attractive. The *Times-Guardian* would have been a rich and powerful paper. It would have been highly attractive to advertisers. It could have had probably the best news service in the world.

But it would have had no soul. It would have had a hybrid character, and no clear point of view.

That was, for us, a fatal defect. You see, to succeed, the *Times-Guardian* had to hold the politically Conservative readers of *The Times*, stuffy people, for the most part, who don't want the world to change.

If the paper did not please them they would go in droves to *The Daily Telegraph*. But the *left*-of-centre readers would have had nowhere else to go. There is no alternative on the left; no alternative paper with a questioning point of view. So there would have been a tendency all the time for the merged newspaper to move to the Right: or simply to be cautious.

That would have been wholly *alien to The Guardian's tradition*.

Here, then, we have an Editor (via the Scott Trust and with the assistance of journalist colleagues) proclaiming his reasons for vetoing what would have been the biggest prestige paper merger in British press history. Whether it was wise, and whether *The Guardian* will not eventually have to make this same merger on less favourable terms, we cannot yet know. Whether Editors and journalists should be allowed actually to determine multi-million pound mergers is a matter of opinion. What is less a matter of opinion is that this was an example of editorial sovereignty.

5 Today's editor as departmental manager

5.1 The Editor as strategically dependent

In tactical terms the Editor is relatively autonomous. Normally nobody tells him what to put in a particular number; he is the manager of the editorial department. But this department invariably exists within a larger organisation – encompassing the production, advertising and circulation departments at least, and usually other publications and editorial departments too. Within this larger organisation the Editor is strategically dependent. If his is the sole or major publication, his editorial department is consequently important; if his publication is merely a weekly newspaper or magazine in a large group he may not even be a departmental manager. But as a general statement Editors are middle level managers, although some are in upper-middle or even senior, and some quite definitely only in junior, management.

Editors are strategically dependent in a number of ways. Most Editors are not directors; the broad history and group function of the publication is a given factor. The amount of editorial space available to an Editor is determined by the amount of advertising. Circulation determines revenue and hence editorial finance. The production arrangements for printing the publication shape all other aspects of the editorial operation. Finally, all Editors in Britain are appointed by managers and most Editors are encouraged to think of themselves as part of management.

Table 5.1

Editors as Directors, 1976

	National Newspaper	Provincial Morning	Provincial Evening	Weekly Newspaper	Magazine	All Editors
	%	%	%	%	%	%
Director, Main Board	26	0	8	11	9	10
Director, Subsidiary Board	35	14	21	11	7	10
Not Director	38	86	74	79	81	79
Total	100	100	100	100	100	100
Number (unweighted)	10	9	38	103	163	330

Source: SCPR Editors' Survey.[1]

1 Social and Community Planning Research: *Attitudes to the Press*, Cmnd 6810–3. References in the text are to tables in this volume.

Eight out of 10 Editors, as Table 5.1 shows, are not directors. Only one in 10 is on a main board, and nearly all of these belong to 'non-group' publications. Some groups believe in Editors being directors on subsidiary boards. But this view is not shared by other major groups; Editors of daily newspapers owned by Thomson or Westminster are not directors even of the local subsidiary company which manages the printing plant on which their paper is produced.

Secondly, the history of the publication before the Editor arrived typically shapes much of its continuing general character. If the paper is an evening in an industrial city, or if it is a weekly in a rural area – this will largely determine its general editorial nature. The market position of the paper may result from recent mergers (and sometimes launches), the availability of advertising in the particular market and so on. In some cases (such as Thomson Regional Newspapers) the broad character and goals of the publication are formally written down and formally agreed by the Editor.

Thirdly, most publications have stable mates. Even the smallest independent firms typically own two or three weeklies or magazines, or a small evening plus one or two weeklies. If an Editor is in charge of only one of these, he will be given some particular editorial goal different from that of the other publications in the stable. For example a weekly paper Editor will be expected not to compete head-on with the company's evening in the same area; on the other hand it may be expected that some of the same material will be used but at different length. Many weekly-and-daily teams replay each others' stories at shorter length. Since all morning papers always follow up evenings' stories and vice versa, where there are morning and evening stable companions they tend – especially in their first editions – to repeat each others' stories. In many cases also journalist staff work on two publications edited by different Editors. This may include all branch offices, but more often only some; or it may be confined to a team of sub-editors who sub-edit an entire 'series' of weekly papers, or it may be merely the sharing of photographers. Or it may consist only of sharing expensive foreign correspondents (as both *The Times* and *The Daily Telegraph* do with their Sundays). All such devices take some strategic control out of the Editor's hands.

Fourthly, the amount of space available is always laid down on the basis of a management formula, over whose setting the Editor typically has little or no say. As the Denis McQuail content analysis indicates[1], there is much variation in these formulae. In national newspapers the ratios contain higher proportions of editorial, and competition ensures a relatively high minimum number of editorial pages; an extreme case is *The Times* which sticks to 17 editorial pages regardless of advertising ratios. In the provinces both dailies and weeklies (except for some which are unusually weak and/or in highly competitive situations) aim for roughly 60% advertising and 40% editorial. There is less advertising than this in provincial mornings and more in the biggest evenings and weeklies. But what a content analysis figure averaged over the year cannot show is the enormous variation on a single publication within the year, and for a daily on different days of the week. So heavily does advertising in some provincial evenings concentrate on Thursday and Friday that an Editor may have a 30-page paper on Friday, but only a 10-page paper on Monday. Lack of competition and the fact that most copies are subscribed allow management to do this. The 10-page paper may contain only five pages of advertising (50:50), while the 30-page paper has 21 pages of advertising (70:30). This means Thursday

1   Cmnd 6810–4.

carries four times as much advertising as Monday, but the number of editorial pages also can vary from five on Monday to nine on Thursday. The proportion of five-page and nine-page days can vary unpredictably at quite short notice – which is a constant reminder to the Editor that he cannot make realistic plans since he has no way of knowing how much space he has to fill even a few weeks ahead.

Circulation considerations are even more strategic, because circulation losses bring not only sales, but also in due course advertising, losses too. If these occur, editorial budgets will be held down. So Editors are extremely sensitive to circulation changes, even though they themselves typically have little say over the biggest single factor affecting circulations – namely price increases. Editors are particularly sensitive about the *timing* of price increases in relation to those of immediate competitors.

Sixthly, production arrangements determine editorial possibilities in many ways; as the major capital investment item it is one in which Editors have little say. Most publications share printing presses with other publications and this shapes their pattern of use. Magazines may be kept in existence primarily to use plant capacity. Weekly papers are often printed on a press which also prints one or two daily papers; such weekly papers get given a production schedule which uses up the blank spaces in the daily production schedule – for instance the late afternoons. This requires a flow of copy to be available several days before the final printing date, which in turn shapes the entire editorial enterprise – one obvious consequence is the concern of many weekly newspapers with feature stories and very local items (too local for daily interest) at the expense of ' hard news ' stories. Magazines have even longer production schedules in many cases, with even greater consequences.

'New technology' is the biggest example in this area and it creates new editorial opportunities, such as greater setting capacity, better picture reproduction and new layout possibilities. Some provincial Editors welcome these, but perhaps an equal number regard such innovations as providing only superficial editorial benefits, while reducing speed and flexibility near the final deadline. Especially on provincial newspapers it does not escape the Editors that the major benefit of greater setting capacity most assists in setting advertising – of which, on the prosperous papers embracing new technology, there is more than of editorial.

Seventh, whatever autonomy Editors may have they are appointed by management and they can be removed by management. Editors these days – except perhaps in magazines – are not often fired outright, but they can be moved upwards, sideways or downwards into other publications or other jobs. Most groups are known to have some broad policy about this. Thomson Regional Newspapers seem to believe in a policy of job moves for Editors every three or four years.

An eighth form of dependence is the fairly transparent management belief that the average Editor cannot expect promotion much beyond middle management. Most of the large press groups in Britain proclaim their belief in management training. But 77 % of Editors in the SCPR survey (p 311) had had no management training at all. Even Thomson Regional Newspapers, which is an unusually strong believer in such things, makes clear in its written evidence to the Royal Commission that most management training courses are of a very low-level nature. British Editors who have been on a *senior* management course are rare birds indeed.

313

The SCPR survey (Table 3.035) reports the kinds of undesirable pressure to which Editors feel themselves personally exposed. Pressure from journalists, although quoted, is much less salient than the recent 'Press Freedom' debate might suggest. Among national newspaper Editors, journalists rate fifth equal as a source of pressure; among provincial morning Editors fourth; for provincial evening Editors fifth; for weekly Editors fifth; and for magazine Editors ninth as a source of pressure. Magazine Editors regard management as a more severe source of pressure. But perhaps more remarkable is that neither journalists nor managers are thought of by many Editors as a source of pressure. The main pressures are seen as being economic, advertising, production, union, governmental, and legal ones. Daily Editors are especially concerned with legal pressures, while both weekly and magazine Editors complain of pressure from advertisers.

Table 5.2 shows how Editors' replies about threats to the Freedom of the Press in general (not to their own) compare with those of senior journalists and also 'local influentials'. More Editors see threats from the Government, whereas more journalists are worried about proprietors, owners, managers and advertisers. Journalists also stress legal threats more than do the Editors. A somewhat similar pattern emerges for the ' Biggest Threat'. But the strongest contrast is between the local influentials, who see relatively few threats to Press Freedom as compared with both Editors and journalists who see more.

Table 5.2

Threats to press freedom

	Percentage saying 'any threat'		
	Editors	Journalists	Local influentials
Costs/Inflation	59	56	27
Printing/Production Workforce ...	52	55	40
The Government	47	38	25
Libel Laws	39	45	6
Advertisers	32	45	9
Political Parties	30	29	19
Proprietors/Owners	26	44	18
Journalists	25	20	12
The Management	20	36	6
Official Secrets Act/ D Notices ...	19	40	10
Public Relations People	11	16	N/A

	Percentage saying 'biggest threat'		
	Editors	Journalists	Local influentials
The Government	23	11	10
Costs/Inflation	20	20	10
Printing/Production Workforce ...	10	13	16
Political Parties	7	5	4
Libel Laws	5	10	1
Advertisers	4	5	1
Journalists	3	1	1
Proprietors/Owners	2	9	4
The Management	2	5	0
Public Relations People	1	0	N/A
Official Secrets Act/ D Notices ...	0	2	1

5.2 The Editor as autonomous departmental manager?

Whereas the Editor is strategically dependent in several commercial ways, he might still be autonomous within his editorial department. How much an Editor feels autonomous, and how much he may seem autonomous to an outsider will depend upon the weight he gives to tactical autonomy, how much significance he attaches to intra-departmental areas which do not require extra-departmental senior management sanction, and how much he feels constrained by the strategic guidelines laid down by senior management.

There are two obvious sources for disagreement on the extent of Editorial autonomy. Firstly quite different weights can be attached to relative strategic dependence and to relative tactical autonomy. Secondly, very different readings of extent of editorial autonomy will result, depending on the *expectations* of an Editor and the extent to which he agrees with the strategic guidelines.

The Editor in practice is encouraged to identify himself with the strategic guidelines, and is encouraged also to believe that by pursuing strategic managerial goals (such as profit) he will also be able to acquire greater tactical autonomy (for instance in a higher editorial budget).

A fairly commonly drawn conclusion is that *caution* is in general spheres preferable to adventure. Especially in difficult economic times, an Editor can lose both advertising and circulation more quickly than he can increase either. Caution in these two areas will tend to favour only mild forms of innovation; and the financial character of strategic guidelines favours the news story which costs the minimum to get in terms of time, money and risk, but which has the maximum appeal in terms of readership.[1]

How much money is an Editor allowed to lose? The easiest way of losing money is to upset major advertisers or to refuse certain advertising. This famous issue is much less delicate than is often thought and the following generalisations are not very controversial:

1 On news stories which are obviously big ones for the Editor in question, and especially on stories which have already seen, or will soon see, the light of day elsewhere little or no quarter is given to advertisers. Because national newspapers are more competitive, most of the stories which interest them the most will appear elsewhere, so most national advertisers have few sanctions. On provincial papers, however, many more big stories are ones which surface more or less by themselves – for instance in courts and councils.

2 In certain consumer areas – fashion, home furnishing, cars and so on – all publications tend to be gentle on advertisers. Because this kind of story potentially looms larger for provincial Editors, and because provincial papers typically have a small number of key advertisers, advertisers in general and key advertisers such as the largest department stores,[2] are gently treated.

3 Editors like to think of themselves as having some integrity in this area and they do not easily give in to threats. Several Editors said that a request to keep something out, whether from an advertiser or from anyone else, is the best way

---

1 David Murphy, *The Silent Watchdog*, London: Constable, 1976.
2 The large department stores or large estate agents also have the important sanction that they could – and occasionally do – bypass the local newspaper and put all their advertising into their own free 'newspaper'.

315

of ensuring that it goes in. Most Editors quoted examples of advertisers they had criticised recently; the majority of these were in the public sector – Co-ops being the most often quoted example, followed by bus companies. Most Editors also claim to have refused advertising recently (cinema advertisements on grounds of sex, and high pressure selling ads on grounds of legality were the most quoted).

4   Supplements are another area with major editorial implications. Only one provincial Editor quoted an example of a supplement he had vetoed (losing two pages of advertising). In general Editors accept advertising supplements and the only contested area is who shall write the editorial – most, but not all, Editors, want their own journalists to do this.

5   In general, however, there is relatively little difference of opinion over advertising. Any dubious advertisement which the Editor would want to reject, the advertising manager would probably also wish to reject. The doctrine that Editors are responsible for advertising has only a little reality, and most Editors do not see most advertising before it appears.

The basic reason for lack of conflict is that Editors in general favour more advertising and know that only with more advertising will they get more editorial space.

Similarly there appears usually to be relatively little conflict over circulation. Editors are in frequent touch with circulation managers; the latter in some cases attend every editorial meeting, in other cases they attend sometimes or there is a special weekly meeting. Editors are supplied with the latest circulation figures – weekly Editors get these once a week; on national dailies Editors are especially aware of the circulation effects of a series – such as book serialisation. Editors wish to boost sales and their most common criticism of circulation managers is not of their excessive, but of their inadequate, interest in editorial content. Weekly paper Editors especially are inclined to complain that they themselves have to initiate and plan sales promotions.

An important aspect of the Editor's tactical autonomy is the budget under which he operates. Most Editors have budgets, but some do not. Thomson Regional Newspapers are the extreme believers in set budgets. But at least in present times – since budgets now are usually the same as last year plus an inflation factor and journalist staffs are being held steady – it probably makes little difference whether an Editor has a formal budget or not. Apart from the main item of salaries, provincial budgets focus on expenses and 'acquired' material, agency and freelance. National newspaper budgets include contingency funds for various items. The Editor we met who had the greatest budgetary flexibility was David English of the *Daily Mail*; in his case he was certainly free to save money on not filling a journalist vacancy and to spend the money elsewhere. But another national Editor would seek approval for any expenditure of £1,000 or more from the proprietor (which would include anything like a book serialisation). One provincial daily Editor had to refer to his London Chairman for sums over £100.

Provincial evening Editors are here, as usual, a fairly representative middle case. The survey data (Table 3.010) show that half of these Editors say they have 'some responsibility in consultation with management' for setting the editorial budget;

10% say they have 'complete' and 30% 'little or no' such responsibility. Perhaps more revealing is that only half the provincial evening Editors say they have 'complete responsibility' for *spending* their editorial budget.

The ways in which strategic guidelines impinge on tactical Editorial autonomy vary considerably. In the Westminster Press, financial guidelines from London seem less strong than editorial guidelines; for example, WP supplies London-written leaders (which an Editor is free to reject but typically does use quite often) and it has rules – such as that any Editor reported to the Press Council must tell the London office. Thomson Regional Newspapers, on the other hand, has less editorial guidelines, but exerts stronger managerial-financial guidelines – with written budgets, and descriptions both of the Editor's functions and the publication's goals.

For the individual Editor, the managerial structure may impinge mainly via one individual or through a broader structure, and it may impinge via a manager down the corridor or from a remote manager in a regional or London head office. On national dailies effective responsibility to a single Chairman of the Board is more common and this is true also of small provincial press groups. For newspaper Editors (and probably even more for magazine Editors) in large groups, responsibility is to several different people. The Editor of a small weekly may be responsible to three people – a local manager in his own office, a regional managing director where the paper is printed (on a daily paper press) and an editorial director in London.

5.3 The competitive situation

Its competitive or monopoly situation influences every aspect of a publication, including the person who is appointed as Editor. For instance one weekly Editor, who had an obviously competitive personality, was also editing a weekly paper which had an unusually large amount of competition – being at the crossroads of three strong local weekly groups.

Editors in exceptionally competitive situations seem to make commercial concessions which one might not otherwise expect and in Britain this means London newspapers especially. Thus Charles Wintour on the basis of London evening newspaper competition wrote in his *Pressures on the Press* (1972, p 39):

'Is it wrong to give some degree of preference to stores which advertise? Not at all, provided that their products are good – and they are unlikely to waste money advertising unless they are'.

Even the *Daily Mirror* which for long was able to afford to be independent of any kind of commercial-advertising involvement, and which has long charged needlessly low advertising rates, now engages in promotions with Tesco Supermarkets. The Editor, Michael Molloy, defends this on the ground that it helps the *Daily Mirror* in its sales war with *The Sun*.

Most provincial papers are, of course, monopolies to a greater or lesser extent. Editors are often willing to put a percentage figure to this – a weekly Editor will admit to being the monopoly paper in 60% of his circulation area, an evening Editor may quote 80%. But the monopoly situation is not without its own editorial implications. Being a monopoly makes a paper vulnerable to the charge of 'monopoly press' – and is quoted by Editors as compelling political neutrality. Editors can still be partisan on particular causes, but most safely on causes which involve supporting the locality against distant authority. Thus

317

monopoly leads to an increased emphasis on the local boosterism which is in any case traditional in local papers and favoured by general commercial and profit considerations. The Editor finds himself in editorial charge of a potential political instrument which is too powerful to use.

Moreover, since in the press monopoly usually spells profit, monopoly papers in any group will in general be given higher profit targets and will carry higher ratios of advertising.

5.4 Editor's routine and editorial style

'Without standardisation, without stereotypes, without routine judgments, without a fairly ruthless disregard of subtlety, the editor would soon die of excitement.'

Walter Lippmann, *Public Opinion* (1922) p 222.

Even though they do have routines and do not die of excitement, most Editors engage in a phrenetic series of meetings, conversations, writing, inspecting, and making snap decisions. Even at home they remain news-fixated, reading newspapers endlessly. Average figures from the SCPR Survey (Table 3.014) are:

National newspaper Editors	58 hours a week
Provincial morning Editors	55 hours a week
Provincial evening Editors	52 hours a week
Weekly paper Editors	49 hours a week
Magazine Editors	47 hours a week

Quite apart from reading done at home which these figures probably exclude, Editors must also work at speed – when talking, reading and writing. Telephone conversations often last only two or three sentences. Editors learn to read fast and many provincial Editors can write a leader on a complex topic in under an hour. The pace is kept up against not one, but several deadlines, and the variety of tasks to which the same mind must be applied is large.

The SCPR survey (Table 3.012) shows that *writing* is actually only the third most time consuming activity of Editors. This is true of all categories of Editors, and especially of national Editors – who write little. Two other activities – *editing* and *administration* take up the bulk of Editors' time. Editing (defined to include sub-editing, layout and commissioning articles) takes up two-thirds of the time of weekly Editors – who in fact operate rather like night-editor-cum-chief-sub-editor in daily paper terms.

The low proportion of time devoted to *editing* by provincial morning Editors is at first surprising. But this is probably due to the heavy reliance of these papers on Press Association and other outside material which is regarded as fairly routine and not requiring the Editor's attention. Both national and evening Editors do a lot of *editing*.

Administration (defined to include personnel, financial and budgetary planning) consumes about half the working time of daily paper Editors taken together – illustrating the extent to which Editors engage in managerial functions in general and probably personnel management in particular.

Editors spend the bulk of their time in the office building, although about a fifth on average is spent outside. Editors' time is structured by a series of deadlines and meetings. A common *daily* Editor's routine involves two main meetings – one primarily for *newsgathering* in which the news editor is the

318

key figure, and a later *newsprocessing* conference in which the night Editor is the key figure. Then there are usually two other regular small meetings – an early one for leaders and/or features and a late one to choose the front page lead story and picture. Daily Editors have a series of people whom they see at least once a day – the advertising manager (who provides a page layout showing the spaces already taken by advertising), the circulation manager, the chairman or general manager, the letters editor or sub-editor, the cartoonist if there is one, and each of the other main executives.

Some provincial daily Editors have a set time of the day for writing a leader, and also join the chief processor on the 'back bench' for some of the main selection decisions. Editors vary as to how much copy they attempt to read – in general tabloid Editors try to read all the main stories either in carbon or proof while broadsheet Editors do not.

William Rees-Mogg at *The Times* had one of the shortest office days we discovered – 11 am to 7.30 pm five days a week. The longest days seem to be worked by two provincial morning Editors – each worked about 13 hours 5 days a week. One of the most phrenetic workers we encountered was David English of the *Daily Mail*. He was, however, also the Editor most insistent that he worked these very long hours only about four nights a week and also had eight weeks holiday a year. He pointed out that his deputy edited the paper nearly half the nights of the year.

Weekly Editors, and apparently magazine ones too, work under less pressure. But some (Table 3.003) edit more than one paper, going to press on more than one day of the week – and usually have slabs of copy due for the compositors on most days of the week.

Two other things are clear: few Editors give themselves much time for contemplation – since they tend to go out to lunches and dinners as well. Secondly, there is a wide range in editorial styles; some Editors concentrate on opinion, others on news, others again on presentation.

5.5 The Editor as presider over opinion

The Delane style of the Editor presiding over political opinion is still pursued at *The Times*, but it has a more pronounced expression at *The Daily Telegraph*. The traditional *Telegraph* arrangements continue, by which a managing editor presides over home news, foreign news, and the financial pages and is also the immediate boss of the night editor. The *Telegraph* Editor, William Deedes, presides in some detail over two foreign leader writers, four domestic ones and two more who double as Westminster sketch writers. Secondly, he runs the letters, of which *The Daily Telegraph* has a lot. Thirdly, he controls all of the features, including women's and arts features. Fourthly, he controls directly the obituaries, the Peterborough diary, the Peter Simple column and the cartoonist, Garland. In addition Deedes is in charge of direct contact with the political world which, as with other Fleet Street Editors, involves seeing something of national politicians. He chooses the front page lead and picture but otherwise his involvement in the news pages is minimal.

William Rees-Mogg at *The Times* has a similar direct control of leaders and writes about two a month himself. He controls the letters, and to a lesser extent the Obituaries. In contrast to Deedes, however, Rees-Mogg does not get involved in the detail of features, whereas he does exercise a broad oversight over all the news pages. His concern is very much concentrated on news *gathering*, although he does take all three main editorial conferences of the day including the last one (which Deedes does not).

Table 5.3

How Editors (and journalists) voted in three general elections

Percentages of Editors voted as follows

(Percentages of journalists' voting in brackets)

	1970	1974 (Feb)	1974 (Oct)
Conservative	53 (39)	50 (36)	52 (34)
Labour	27 (43)	25 (40)	27 (38)
Liberal	20 (14)	22 (20)	20 (25)
Other	— (2)	2 (2)	1 (3)
Can't remember	— (1)	— (1)	— (—)

Source: SCPR Survey, p 342 and Table 3.052.

Table 5.3 shows how Editors (and journalists) voted at the recent General Elections. Among Editors, Conservative voters outnumbered Labour voters by two to one, fairly consistently in all three elections; the Liberals also consistently received the votes of a fifth of Editors. The contrast with journalists is quite sharp – among them there is an equally consistent but much smaller Labour majority and, on this evidence, an increasing Liberal vote.

Quite common is the situation of an Editor who has political views but is prevented from giving them editorial expression by the company policy of political neutrality. Some Editors say they accept this with regret: 'A newspaper ought to have a voice'. In some cases there are no, or few, leaders; other Editors write many leaders about local topics and national politics, but without taking a clear party line. Which of these solutions to adopt – within the broad company policy – is a genuine Editor's prerogative. He also has the power to give editorial support to any non-political cause which he favours.

As to the use of news stories to exert pointed criticism, most Editors of provincial papers seem cautious. They are quite prepared to relay Council debates or political speeches. But they admit to doing very little tough investigative digging. They are usually in favour of such reporting in theory, but claim that in practice they are inhibited by not having enough journalists or enough high powered and immediately available legal back-up.

5.6 The Editor as personnel manager

The Editor's control of both gathering and processing gives him considerable powers over his journalists – powers which potentially can be exercised on a daily basis and in a matter of seconds. He can allocate people to stories and stories to people; he chooses front page headlines and often page leads. Control over the content of the paper is also control over the journalists who produce the contents.

Hiring, firing, and promotion are probably the key traditional prerogatives of the Editor. Editors of national and of provincial dailies in the SCPR survey almost all claim to possess full hiring powers and nearly as many claim firing powers. However, with weekly and magazine Editors the proportion claiming hiring powers is lower, and lower still for firing. (Table 3.009).

Firing people has become less easy in any occupation recently. Consequently the key prerogative is *hiring*. And even though an Editor may have all sorts of strategic and tactical limitations over his actions in both the short and medium-term, in the long run – if he stays Editor long enough – he can appoint most of his staff; moreover since appointments cause promotions and other changes, he can gradually deploy his entire staff to suit his own wishes.

It is precisely because *hiring* is the key editorial prerogative that recent incursions into this area by the NUJ are so resented by Editors. There are even in these areas some existing constraints over an Editor's powers. Editors do not usually have complete control over the most senior appointments, such as their own deputy and the third man in line. *The Times* Editor lacks these powers – they belong to the Editor-in-Chief[1]. Elsewhere editorial directors or chief executives have similar powers.

Personnel management is time-consuming and wearying for Editors. In journalism the hierarchy is shallow and unclear; many job moves are ambiguous in terms of hierarchy and prestige. The continuous re-shuffles which occur in any organisation, probably in journalism lead to an unusually high degree of insecurity. After switching one person, the Editor may find he has a lot of other people to reassure. One Editor had recently appointed a new Features Editor, but this had involved his seeing individually – mostly after the move – another 20 people, some of whom were in a highly emotional state.

---

1   This is the position to which the Monopolies Commission agreed in 1966: 'We were also told that the role of the editor-in-chief would be to allocate the editorial budget; to organise such joint projects, joint services and cross postings of staff as he might decide; to make senior staff appointments, and to recommend to the board the appointment of two individual editors "and then in the words of Bagehot to advise, encourage and perhaps warn them".'—The Monopolies Commission, *The Times Newspaper and the Sunday Times Newspaper* (1966), p 18.

6 Editorship as Occupation

6.1 Image presenter

One of the Editor's many tasks is to be a public relations officer. In addition to the other skills required of him – writing, editing, managerial, political, legal and so on – the Editor is expected to be able to speak. After dinner speeches to social and artistic gatherings, luncheon speeches at jamborees put on by the advertising department, prize givings connected with circulation promotion, farewell words to departing employees – all these have long been, and are still, required of Editors. A more recent duty of the Editor is to get his talking head on to television with the name of his publication printed underneath.

In gatherings where the basic object is to sell advertising or copies the Editor's words add a needed non-commercial note. When the Editor speaks in public he does not deliberately deceive anyone into thinking that he is really the top man in his organisation – he claims no more than to be the top man on the editorial side. Nevertheless, by being the main public spokesman of his publication he does deliberately create an impression which is somewhat less than the whole truth.

Not all of the Editor's outside speaking engagements are simply occasions for image presentation. In some cases the Editor uses his high (external) status to meet senior politicians or other people important to his publication – and these occasions may produce news stories, or lead later to news stories. Invitations abound – getting a prominent Editor to lunch is a PR man's triumph. One daily Editor said he rationed himself to two lunches and two evening invitations a week.

Some weekly and evening paper Editors accept many invitations to speak to local groups of all kinds – usually speaking and answering questions about their own publication. One famous question is: Should the Editor belong to the Rotary Club? Most say no, but tend to belong to one or two blander things such as the local Museum committee. One seaside Editor claimed to be a regular judge at seafront 'dolly bird competitions'.

Undoubtedly, senior management choose Editors who will look and sound the part for the particular publication. The Editor of one weekly in a Cathedral city might himself have passed as a vicar. Even the age of the Editor may be part of the intended image. The *Daily Mirror*, long proud of its young readers and now needing them more than ever, has the youngest Editor in Fleet Street. Several other Fleet Street Editors seem as individual personalities to fit extremely closely the newspaper they edit. It is difficult to imagine a better fit than that between David English and the *Daily Mail*. The only Editor I met whose personality jarred with his paper was in charge of a provincial morning. A waitress asked him how she could get her picture in the paper. 'Undress dear', he advised; but even this breeziness was in line with this particular provincial morning's pursuit of a more 'lively' image.

6.2 Career patterns

The SCPR survey (Table 3.001) shows that the average age for all main categories of Editor is in the forties – with the exception of provincial morning Editors, where it is in the fifties. The typical 1976 Editor was born in 1929.

As with ages, there is a biggish spread in social class origins (Table 3.023) with the skilled manual social class of fathers providing 32% of all Editors. Taking the usual non-manual/manual divide, 51% of Editors are of middle class origin and 38% working class. Weekly Editors are the most working class, provincial daily Editors are intermediate, and those of national newspapers and magazines most middle class.

Clearly, then, many Editors have achieved a higher occupational level than their fathers. But (Table 3.020) education did not play a very marked part in this process. The proportion of Editors with degrees is lower than the proportion whose fathers were in the top occupational category. While 38% of Editors come from working class backgrounds, 57% finished full-time education with nothing above an O Level. The typical 1976 Editor left school in 1944 or 1945.

The not very enthusiastic general attitude towards education is further illustrated by the low proportions earning qualifications after finishing full-time education. But a further 3% earned degrees and 5% A Levels. Thus eventually 20% had degrees. The additional degrees were *all* earned by magazine Editors and most of the A Levels by weekly Editors.

Among the provincial evening Editors, the low level of education remains – none with degrees, and only 30% with A Levels. These data give the impression that when these Editors were entering journalism formal educational qualifications – with the possible exception of O Levels – were regarded as irrelevant both by recruiters and recruits.

Most Editors entered journalism aged either 16–17 or in their twenties (Table 3.022); military service interrupted many of these careers and several Editors seem to have got their flying start in journalism by earning a commission in the Army. But 80% of newspaper Editors had no previous paid employment before journalism, whereas the majority of magazine Editors had done other work first. Not surprisingly there are other major differences in the careers of Editors according to type of publication:

National Editors have the most rapid careers, starting latest and getting furthest. Although half began on weeklies, the other half began on dailies. Upon becoming seniors almost all were already out of reporting – the normal induction job – and on to other things, especially sub-editing or working on a desk (Table 3.024 and 3.027).

Provincial Daily Editors were most likely to have started on weeklies (in contrast to national Editors) and their first senior job was in general reporting. The majority have never been on a national newspaper even in a provincial office of one (although half the morning Editors and a quarter of the more numerous evening ones have).

Weekly Editors – 81% of them started on a weekly or a local news agency (Table 3.024) and on becoming seniors they were nearly all still on weeklies. Few weekly Editors have worked on a national newspaper, and only about half appear ever to have worked on a daily.

Magazine Editors clearly are quite different, although collectively they vary. 11% are women. Magazine Editors have often moved from non-journalist beginnings straight onto a magazine; few began on weeklies. For most the first 'senior' job was executive, desk or subbing. More than any other category, magazine Editors have never worked on any other type of publication.

How does a journalist become an Editor? As the evidence given by the larger companies indicates, there is no big mystery. Editors typically have a wide range of relevant experience; they often have somewhat maverick careers – such as very early executive experience or some rather exotic leap between apparently unrelated jobs.

Nearly all Editors have some sub-editing experience; one man, who was being considered for the editorship, was surprised to be removed from his job as industrial correspondent and put onto sub-editing – although he must have guessed promotion was in the wind. Virtually all daily newspaper Editors have previously done one of the senior executive jobs – and national Editors have done one of the jobs (Foreign, Features or Financial Editor) which involves presiding over both reporters and sub-editors. Most Editors have previously done the job on a stand-in, perhaps once-a-week, basis as number two or three in command. There is obvious truth, then, in the groups' evidence that people chosen as Editors evolve into the job, are known quantities and do not suddenly fall from heaven.[1]

Although appointments often involve the deputy editor just moving up a step, *most* seem not to. The chosen man may indeed be a deputy editor, but often of another publication in the group; or he may be a number three, or a more senior man being in effect demoted; and a fair proportion of Editors are hired completely from outside. The impression created by some of the evidence that the choice is seldom *very* surprising might be misleading, in that the choice often is – to the other journalists involved – at least somewhat surprising, and sometimes very surprising indeed. The real field of choice in many cases is closer to a dozen than to two. So what are the criteria and who operates them?

As various pieces of evidence indicate, the things looked for obviously include broad competence in relevant areas, especially technical-production-layout competence. But I believe there is a fundamentally different approach especially according to the competitive position of the publication. Thus on national newspapers – and perhaps on magazines in competitive situations – the tendency is to ignore the safe choice, and to favour the more exciting, risky, competitive, extreme and perhaps maverick choice. The risk is evidently regarded as worth taking – and on a national newspaper, if need be, the Editor can be sacked or pensioned off if the risk is thought not to have worked. The national Editors who get appointed have highly individual personalities – but they all tend to exude charm, self-confidence and an aggressive opinionated rapid-fire commentary on journalism, politics and personalities.

Provincial daily Editors (and weekly ones even more so) are very different. There is a strong impression that this man is regarded as a safe choice, a cautious predictable individual. Provincial daily Editors are also not without charm, but it is much quieter, more modest, buttoned-up. Provincial Editors weigh their answers carefully, are much less opinionated and do not express views on party political issues or on personalities. National Editors tend to be ebullient personifications of their papers, with slightly exaggerated personas somewhat

---

1 Groups such as Thomson Regional Newspapers also use annual appraisal interviews, resulting presumably in files of annual appraisals for any candidate for an Editor's job.

in the style of actors or politicians. But provincial Editors are much more interchangeable, middle-aged, middle class individuals; collectively provincial Editors are reminiscent not of actors nor of politicians but of the managers of branch banks – cautious reassuring men who doubtless know more of local scandals and personalities than they reveal.

Who, then, makes the choice? As the formal evidence reports, where there is an editorial director the appointment of Editors is normally his task; elsewhere the task belongs to a managing director, chairman or other Chief Executive. Where there is an editorial director – as evidence also indicates – he would be likely to consult his Chief Executive; the latter's veto, even if seldom exercised, is thus a factor. There is in a large group another veto, at the local level. This belongs to the local manager. For example the then Editor of one weekly newspaper explained how his successor was being chosen. The editorial director of the group chose two candidates, both of whom were then taken to meet the local *manager*; only after the local manager had been given an opportunity to veto the appointment was it finally decided.

In smaller groups the decision seems to rest invariably with the Chief Executive. But the most important question is not who makes the decision, but what are the criteria? A broad image of competence, a certain age bracket and personality suitable for the particular publication; in many cases the candidate's suitability, not merely for this publication but for a possible succession of Editorships within a group, will be considered. There is also no doubt at all that the candidate's political views will be considered. There is not necessarily anything sinister in this. Of those who are thought suitable on other grounds probably the majority anyway lack strong political views. And in many this lack is what is sought; but some publications also require political judgements. In some cases (such as provincial mornings) Conservative views may be required, whereas in others (evenings) they could be a hindrance.

What happens after the Editor is appointed:

'Some of his older rivals for the job will be still there in senior positions; the Editor's most important decisions in his first few years may be filling the gaps left by his own elevation, and subsequent moves (and resignations). After this first shuffle round he must sit out a trial period. A new Editor will often be appointed as one of a collection of measures designed to pursue some new business objective – a young Editor may be appointed as part of a revenue policy of attracting a younger audience. For his first years an Editor may find himself committed to a basic strategy devised by others.'[1]

Probably most people who find themselves for the first time in a fairly senior job have some feelings of inadequacy. This response may be especially common among Editors for three reasons: The range of duties is very wide, formal preparation for the task is negligible, and the appointment – like much else in journalism – is often sudden. One Editor was quite bitter about the way in which twelve years earlier he was appointed to his first editorship. He felt that he had been especially unprepared for such duties as negotiating with the NUJ, but he also complained of a more general lack of preparation. This was a man who was now responsible editorially for some 80 journalists in several offices, and who among many other things wrote five leaders a week; he had left school at fifteen.

---

1 Jeremy Tunstall, op cit, p 48.

During the early months an Editor knows that he is on trial. Yet the circumstances are difficult. Apart from the recent personnel changes and the still bruised egos, the new strategy of which his appointment is a part may not work well – meaning that he might be allotted the role of scapegoat. He lacks not only experience but also the supports which come with success. Even companies which believe in making Editors directors usually only do so after an interval; the Guild of British Newspaper Editors does not allow a man to join until he has been in the job a year. In his year of greatest need he is, then, most dependent upon management. With some Editors this dependence and many of the habits acquired in the first insecure year, probably persist. It is in this year, also, that many Editors first acquire their perpetual motion style of editorship.

6.3 Groups, pay and security

The SCPR survey (Table 3.017) shows the rather low state of Editorial salaries. The means for those who answered the question (87%) are roughly as follows:

Weekly newspaper Editors	£4,250 pa
Magazine	£5,500
Provincial evening	£6,500
Provincial morning	£7,500
National newspaper	£10,000 plus
ALL EDITORS	£5,000

These figures are for 1975–76.

Some Editors expressed considerable resentment about their salaries. One Editor pointed out that the Chief PRO in the local authority earned £8,250, whereas he himself – Editor of a 100,000 circulation daily employing 70 journalists – was earning less. In relation to profitability the evening paper Editors are perhaps the worst paid. Several evening paper Editors earned under £4,000. And four-fifths of weekly Editors who answered earned under £5,000.

Few Editors earn anything substantial beyond their salary; two-thirds earned under £100 extra and only a tenth as much as £1,000 (Table 3.017). Nor does it make much difference whether an Editor works for a group, although there is a slight tendency for 'non-group' Editors to have more of the very highest and the very lowest salaries.

There is, however, a difference between the career patterns of Editors in the groups and those outside them. Group Editors are heavily bunched into the middle years, whereas outside the groups there are more Editors either below age 30 or above 60. The larger groups all clearly do offer a career ladder moving from smaller to larger papers, possibly ending with pre-retirement in a smaller paper again. The groups all now have a policy of choosing Editors from within the group if possible. Provincial daily and weekly newspaper Editors had been with their present employer an average of about 17 years. The typical provincial newspaper Editor had worked about twelve years for the company before acquiring his present Editorship (Table 3.007). While it is common to meet an Editor who has previously edited another publication, this has usually been within the same company.

In small groups there is a similar, but shorter, career ladder involving perhaps two or three dailies and some weeklies, and here again there is a strong preference for hiring Editors from within the group. These career patterns mean that both managers and Editors 'know our own people', while an element of security and predictability is maintained.

More strategic consequences of these in-group career ladders are that Editors have typically gained most of their experience in a single company. We did meet one Editor who had switched from a big group to edit a single evening paper in another company. But this kind of move is uncommon. This is obviously a phenomenon common beyond the press. But it may contribute to the pervasive fragmentation, segmentation and general short-sightedness which is common in the press.

These editorial career ladders have two apparently contradictory consequences for Editors. On the one hand most Editors are not frightened of being sacked; the worst that is likely to happen is demotion to edit a smaller publication, probably at the same salary, or to be kicked upstairs – as 'director' of something rather vague.

But whereas Editors, both in large provincial groups and in small weekly series, do not fear the sack, they nevertheless do feel extremely dependent on their employers and they feel uneasy about their future in a general way. Even a relatively young, say 45-year-old, Editor has little chance of escape. Because of the in-group promotion policies elsewhere, he is wedded to his current employers and to the rather low pay they offer; poorly educated as he is (at least in formal terms) he has little chance of moving to an even moderately good job elsewhere, except in public relations. Not that Editors in general are very dissatisfied with their jobs; morale in general is high with the following aspects of journalism (Table 3.029) being the most liked by Editors:

1   Creativity and scope for initiative (38%)
2   Variety and interest (36%)
3   Satisfaction of producing finished product (24%)
4   Meeting the public (19%)
5   Able to influence events (18%)
6   Socially useful (14%)

These very strongly supported likes are gained at the expense of less strongly supported dislikes, in the following order:

1   Poor pay (14%)
2   Unsocial hours (10%)
3   Time pressures (7%)
3   Administration (7%)
3   Unions (7%)
6   Poor quality staff (6%)
7   Advertising pressure (5%)

The Editors were also asked: 'Compared with other professions, in general how would you rate journalism as a career on each of the criteria listed below?' Taking the percentages of Editors who *thought journalism either 'poor' or 'very poor' compared with 'other professions'*, here are the main areas of complaint (Table 31):

50% – for ease of movement to alternative occupations
46% – for starting salary
45% – for long-term salary prospects
35% – for security of employment

There is, then, a high level of satisfaction with the creativity, responsibility, interest and power of the job. This accompanies a substantial level of dissatisfaction with being locked into a badly paid job.

The great majority of Editors have a three to six-month contract. Especially likely to have short contracts are weekly and magazine Editors. Somewhat longer contracts are indicated for national newspaper Editors – although we found more than one national Editor uncertain as to his contract. One national Editor had no contract, while another had negotiated for himself an eight-year contract – three years plus a five-year rolling clause – when he first took on the job. One reason for the national newspaper Editor's vagueness is the well-known Fleet Street tradition of giving any sacked Editor a fairly generous golden handshake; there are several compelling arguments for managements wanting to do this – not least being the potential cost in bad publicity of an aggrieved Editor publicising his views.

Recently there have been changes in the length of contracts for some Editors. The Newspaper Society has recommended a 12-month contract and groups such as Westminster Press quickly complied. Almost all daily Editors and four-fifths of weekly and magazine Editors belong to a company pension scheme – and these normally specify 65 as the compulsory retirement age.

One other career point is worth mentioning. A still fair proportion of senior press managers are ex-Editors. This is equally true in IPC, both newspapers and magazines, and in some of the smaller provincial companies. In the past, then, two career possibilities have been for an Editor to move up into senior management, or to move up into a job combining general management and editorial direction – such as 'Managing-Director and Editor-in-Chief'. But Editors see these possibilities as being closed off by the trend towards more 'professional' management in the last two decades. The general management posts go to advertising, circulation men – and, in family firms, family members – as in the past. But accountants and other 'outsiders' have moved on to the general management career ladder, while Editors have largely moved off. Editors have a steadily declining prospect either of becoming general managers or of becoming 'Publishers' in the mixed management and editorial sense.

It was noticeable that two daily Editors we interviewed were especially vocal, and especially resentful, about such trends. These two Editors together combined more than any other pair of Editors we met these qualities: youth; technical expertise in new technology; a concern with efficient management and a desire to be thought of as efficient managers; a clearly articulated style of editorship; a willingness to think quantitatively both about stories in the news and about newspaper management; general intelligence and breadth of reading – both, for example, read a wide range of national mornings and provincial dailies and both were unusual among provincial Editors in reading *The Economist*. Both of these Editors seemed less inclined than most others to phrenetic non-stop activity. Both made clear their professional interest in newspaper management; and both said that if they became general managers they would like to retain the editorship as well. Both believed that the general status of Editors had declined and was declining. They instanced their own salary level. Both believed that the doctrine of the separate-but-autonomous-Editor must inevitably result in the subordination of the Editor, since strategic editorial decisions in practice tended to be taken by top management.

Few Editors expressed their dissatisfactions so clearly or so sharply as did this unusually articulate pair. But there was a strong sense from all the Editors that their strategic dependence, low pay, and low mobility prospects – our 'grace and favour' position as one put it – detracted seriously from the enormous satisfaction, fascination, and excitement of editorship.

6.4 Ideology, mystique and doctrine

The doctrine, or mystique, or ideology of editorial autonomy, or whatever else is claimed to characterise editorship, is as unclearly stated as it has been recently passionately debated. There are structural reasons why such fuzziness exists in Britain. A doctrine of editorial sovereignty can probably only persist if neither its past nor its present reality is too closely inspected.

But how does an Editor explain to himself a doctrine of editorial autonomy which his everyday experience supports so incompletely? Members of all occupations are of course aware that occupational reality and ideology do not make a perfect fit. Editors are not unusual in having a gap between daily routine and occupational ideology; they are probably unusual only in having such a wide gap.

Editors have to perform many other gravity-defying balancing acts. One, these days, is the task faced by Editors who still write leaders – of being opinionated in the leader column, while neutral in the publication overall. This is not necessarily an impossible task, but it may encourage a tendency to place different ideas and approaches into different corners of one's mind.

Editors ideally require a forbidding range of skills, not all of which always occur in a single person. For instance, *legal* acumen and *writing* talent might occur in one person; but how many such individuals also have the strong *visual* sense required for layout and picture selection as well as the ability to think *quantitatively* which is needed to assess political-economic stories, and to grasp newspaper finances, pay policies and salary profiles? How many also have the inter-personal skills to deal with journalists, senior managers and prominent news sources? How many are also good public speakers? In practice most Editors probably just have to admit to themselves that they are colour blind on one or two such particular abilities.

All Editors work hard and some are work obsessed. At home they read more and more journalism. Their work, both at the office and outside, gives them little time – and most of them not a lot of money – with which to get much of an outside perspective on their work. Most Editors also have fairly limited education and no training in detached analysis.

Where outside criteria are brought to play on the Editor's job these tend to lack abstract or general principles as opposed to 'case law'. The main such discipline is law, and the adjudications of the Press Council adopt a case law model. The Press Council – with its predominantly industry membership – has incorporated the journalists' myth that it is very difficult for outsiders to understand journalism. That journalists – who believe any competent journalist capable of quickly getting to the root of anyone else's work – should make such an assumption, is one more example of the tendency to file away apparently incompatible beliefs in different corners of the mind.

Editors tend to feel threatened on all sides – and not without reason. Anyone who subscribes even passively to the notion of editorial autonomy, and who then works as an Editor, must be aware of many pressures which severely constrain his autonomy. Editors also are inevitably aware that with these pressures often goes a related stereotype of Editors. In the eyes of some journalists the Editor is clearly a management stooge, entirely dependent upon management and yet proclaiming that he is autonomous. A manager's stereotype presents the Editor as an artistic maverick who is always making demands which threaten operating efficiency, and possibly advertising revenue as well.

330

Editors, like other journalists, have a romantic or sentimental streak: 'It's better than working', the exposure tradition, the tribune of the people. Such notions are reflected more or less in Editors' values. But these 'traditional', even if not always historically common, values look different when seen from the Editor's chair. The history of journalism as represented in the available books[1] casts Editors in the role of superstars.

Nevertheless there are often impressive grounds for an Editor to regard himself as some kind of last bastion. One local weekly Editor, in a town which had been incorporated for local government purposes into a larger city a few miles away, argued that his paper was 'fanning the last flames of local democracy'. Most Editors can also quote specific examples of manifest wrongs they have publicly righted.

Editors, like journalists generally, are often of a literary turn of mind which may lend further stress to the standard news value concern with personality. The tendency to see the social world in terms of dominant personalities may be further encouraged by the somewhat unusual and ambiguous relationship which any Editor has with his immediate managerial boss. Some ambiguity must arise from editorial autonomy being a doctrine both men subscribe to, while structural reality puts the Editor into the role of subordinate. In the Editor's own mind the particular personality of his boss may loom larger than the structural and doctrinal incongruity which underlies this ambiguity.

Editors do meet other Editors – although less often than might be supposed. Editors also read about each other in the press. A common story in recent years has concerned the embattled Editor whose journalists have been on strike and who is himself bringing out the paper with the aid of one or two senior colleagues.

Most of the Editors we interviewed had had short NUJ strikes or go-slows or other industrial action. Several Editors had brought the paper out themselves. There certainly is some element of play-acting on these occasions, since as some Editors pointed out, the journalists often hope that the paper will continue to come out in reduced form and some journalists, before stopping work, prepare extra material in advance. But there is also an element of real conflict and deep antagonism.

It is not surprising that most Editors keep working and it is obvious that they manage to do this largely by heavy use of agency and other outside material. What in some ways is more surprising is that the Editor seems so seldom to side with journalists. After all would it not make editorial autonomy seem more convincing if, say, one time in four an Editor sided with the journalists against management? Part of the answer may lie in a deeply held belief shared by all Editors that this is a uniquely challenging 'crisis' situation where Editors are tested – in terms of individual courage, personality and also competence in journalism. 'I brought the paper out with my deputy' is par for the course, and few Editors it seems – despite reservations they may have about management and its remuneration for journalists – can resist the challenge. The show must

---

1 Only two general histories of the British press have been written since 1950 – by Harold Herd and Francis Williams; both have an Editor's eye view of press history as does the *History of The Times*, throughout its five volumes. A large quantity of serious historical research – which will eventually correct the present historically false view of the Editor is under way. See Alan J Lee, *The Origins of the Popular Press 1855–1914*, London: Croom Helm, 1976.

go on. The paper must come out. The Editor must edit. It is one of those deeply ingrained, but largely unexamined, traditions. It is also a rare chance to bring editorial behaviour and editorial ideology into line. It is a dramatic opportunity to make a demonstration of the Editor's prowess for which even Sovereignty may seem an understatement.

6.5 Association: The GBNE

Since the Guild of British Newspaper Editors has given evidence to the Royal Commission of its views on a wide range of topics perhaps the most useful thing here is to report the views of some Editors on the Guild:[1]

'He believes the Newspaper Society has turned down the GBNE's demand for a three-year rolling contract. He thinks it should be five years.'

'He has belonged to the GBNE since being an Editor but is pretty non-active. He calls the Guild "a creature of the Newspaper Society".'

'He is very critical of the Guild along the lines that it is dominated by the Newspaper Society. Until very recently it has been no more than a social body, and only the militancy of the NUJ has made the Guild consider being anything else.'

'He belongs to the GBNE but is sceptical of it. He thinks the Guild is really controlled by, and partly financed by, the Newspaper Society. It would be impossible for it – with only 400 members – to be effective without a massive increase in the level of subscription. He also believes that the Guild represents too great a diversity – the scale of publications its members edit – the Editor of *The Birmingham Post* and the Editor of a weekly with two or three staff.'

'He belongs to the GBNE and has been President for the region. He thinks the Guild is "the best we have at the moment", but he would prefer it to be independent of the Newspaper Society. He also thinks that ideally it should be opened to Editors of papers outside the Newspaper Society. The only possibility of transforming the GBNE would be a big increase in subscriptions.'

'He is a member of the GBNE and has been a council representative in the region. The problem is that "the Guild is limited in bite". But he thinks that during 1975–76 it has been much more effective.'

One impression from these interviews was that the GBNE means more to *weekly* than to *daily* Editors.

The Guild's rules make clear that the provincial newspaper trade association, the Newspaper Society, does indeed still provide 'financial and administrative help'. All newspaper Editors are now eligible to join and weekly Editors predominate in numbers. Magazine Editors are not eligible.

The Guild's activities appear to be quite well reflected in its evidence – it is especially active on the legal aspects of editorship and in making submissions to official Committees and similar bodies. Its recent negotiations over Editors' contracts may or may not indicate a new departure; but the broad thrust of the GBNE to date has been neither a Trade Union one (in the sense of improving pay and conditions) nor a Professional one (in the classic sense of controlling standards and qualifications). Perhaps a useful analogy would be between the GBNE and those several staff associations catering to senior white collar and civil service workers some of which have subsequently followed a Trade Union, some a professional path, and some a mixture of the two.

---

1 From notes taken down at the interview and dictated onto tape later the same day.

An obvious contrast could be made with the position of producers and directors in both the BBC and IBA broadcasting. Producers, the rough equivalent of Editors, mostly belong to either the ABS or ACTT – one an ex staff association, one a mainly Technicians' Union – both of them much more 'radical' than the GBNE. In news broadcasting, of course, many senior people belong to the NUJ.

In the press the GBNE is not very unusual in being relatively weak and also in lacking a clearly trade union or clearly professional orientation. The Institute of Journalists, to which 8% of Editors belong (Table 3.019), is also fairly weak and also has long had a substantial minority of members favouring a trade union orientation. The NUJ similarly is still a weak union – certainly compared with other unions in the press industry – and it also has long had a substantial 'deviant' minority which favours a professional orientation.[1]

Nor is it entirely true that the GBNE lacks effective power. In training and recruitment the GBNE's members do hold crucial powers, although at the national level the GBNE chooses to exercise these powers in concert with the NUJ and not against it. What does the character of the GBNE itself tell us about the British press and the part Editors play therein?

1 The great grey area of Editors' autonomy receives no clear expression in the main organisation catering for Editors.

2 The GBNE reflects the familiar polarisation of the British press. National Editors play little part and until recently were not eligible to belong. The magazine Editors are still not eligible to join, even though their problems in many ways resemble those of the weekly Editors who are the GBNE's main membership.

3 Like the rest of British journalism, the GBNE suffers not only from segmentation and fragmentation but is extremely inward looking. There is little involvement with other countries – an involvement which elsewhere is part of the conventional professional as well as the conventional trade union orientation. This lack contrasts also with the fact that British newspapers, at least since the eighteenth century, have carried much news about other aspects of foreign countries.

4 The GBNE, like some other segments in the press, includes members who do have very real powers, especially in recruitment. And like others in the press, the GBNE members – while they cling to the powers in question – fail to examine what the longer term consequences of the exercise of these powers may be.

6.6 Editor as recruiter: The professional prerogative with the Trade Union – unjustified consequence

'The majority of candidates presenting themselves to us as trained journalists have been recruited initially by weekly and smaller evening newspapers. Many of them have minimal qualifications, appear to have received poor training and are of indifferent potential. It is surprising that, while the number of young people wishing to enter journalism is high, the quality of so many potential recruits is low.'

Liverpool Daily Post and Echo, Written Evidence, p 64.

---

1 Harry Christian, 'Professional Man or Wage Earner', *Journalism Studies Review* (Cardiff), June 1976, pp 18–22.

The inadequacies of the way in which British journalists have long been recruited and trained are documented in some detail in the SCPR survey, *The Recruitment and Training of Journalists*.[1]

These inadequacies are intimately connected with the position of local Editors in general and the notion of Editorial Sovereignty in particular. Editorial autonomy in many respects is a myth. Yet it is not entirely a myth. In one area – recruitment of the labour force – an area of overriding importance in any occupation, profession or trade, the power does lie in the hands of local Editors. It is presumably because they recognise it as their one major strategic power that local Editors cling to this one so fiercely. What are the consequences of the local Editor being the prime recruiting sergeant for all British journalism?

Recruitment into newspaper journalism is still overwhelmingly into weeklies. Although the typical entrant now has at least an A level in English[2] people with only O levels are still being recruited and indeed these entrants seem to get in the most easily (p 153). The majority of juniors think on-the-job training is 'not good' and 'too little' (p 154). Job training is largely confined to reporting, although almost all recruits would like instruction in printing technology and layout (p 155). Dissatisfaction with the formal teaching is quite marked and the strongest complaints among block-release students are 'teaching inadequate' and 'more teaching needed in other subjects' (p 157).

After a somewhat skimpy training as juniors, most senior journalists have not been on any subsequent course – and of the minority who have most have only been on a brief sub-editing conversion course (p 159). Seventy-five per cent of senior journalists, however, felt the need for such courses.

Despite the modest increment in formal qualifications, 45% of Editors thought the calibre of people entering journalism had declined in recent years; only 20% thought the standard had improved.

One obvious explanation for such gloomy findings lies in the low pay offered to recruits, and this is still a major complaint. The biggest single complaint from juniors about journalism is the low starting salary compared with other jobs. The next strongest complaints are about long-term salary prospects, insecurity of employment, and low status.

The gloom also seems to arise from non-graduate recruits believing that in the future graduates will have a much better chance of getting the best jobs in journalism (p 160). This is all the more striking when the proportion of graduates entering magazine journalism is 53% against only 28% entering newspapers.

It is not certain that the proportion of graduates in British journalism is as high today as it was in either 1850 or 1900 (see above). Nor is it certain that the proportion of graduates among all British press journalists is increasing. Graduates seem to have made up roughly a quarter of journalism recruits for some years now. But there are several major unknowns. We do not know about the trend in *magazine* entry, and we know almost nothing about *exit* patterns from press journalism and even less about the characteristics of those who exit.

---

1   This passage is based on the full SCPR survey. Page references refer to the summary of the survey which appears in, *Royal Commission on the Press, Final Report, Appendices* Cmnd 6810–1.
2   The preference for English as an A level subject is itself harmless, but may contribute to the low standard of numeracy in the occupation.

It may well be that graduate journalists are disproportionately represented among those making exits to television, radio, public relations, motherhood, and other occupations. But if one assumes that graduates are not disproportionately prone to exit then the overall pattern is of a very slow increase in the *proportion* of graduates in the occupation.

At first glance the 50% of graduates now found among magazine entrants might seem to indicate that journalism is becoming a mainly graduate occupation. But this is not the case. If the present trend of a slow increase in numbers of graduates continues and reaches 50% of all entrants in say 1985, it would still be many years later until 50% of all journalists were graduates. If the proportion were to rise to 50% of entrants in 1985 and then stay constant, it would presumably not be for another forty years – around AD 2025 – until 50% of all journalists are graduates. Or in terms of policy: *If you want the proportion of all journalists who are graduates to rise to a certain figure at a certain date, the proportion of graduates in your annual intake has to be much higher.* Even if you now instituted a 100% graduate intake you would probably not have reached 50% of graduates in the occupation until about 1990.

There are signs from the SCPR survey that uncertainty over this question of graduate intake leads to some of the current *malaise* in journalism generally. If with even a roughly one-quarter graduate intake, non-graduate recruits are pessimistic about career advance, this may explain the *overall decline* (whether absolute or relative to other occupations) in standards which some Editors claim to observe; presumably non-graduate recruits, pessimistic about promotion, now look more closely at conditions on small provincial papers. The low pay and prospects there give an increasingly dead-end appearance to the entire occupation of journalism – as seen by these potential non-graduate recruits.

What part do Editors play in this overall picture? Local Editors on weeklies, smaller evenings and magazines do the bulk of the recruiting, and the rest of Editors have to accept the consequences. The Editors of national newspapers play almost no part in the proceedings. Nor do the Editors of the largest provincial dailies play a big part – firstly because the most prestigious provincials do little initial recruiting but sift through people selected originally lower down the line. Secondly, the larger provincial groups do their recruiting on a group basis, although individual Editors participate in various ways.

The main front-line recruiters are the Editors of the smaller publications. These Editors themselves were recruited in the same way – four-fifths of present weekly Editors themselves began on weeklies or in local news agencies (SCPR Survey Table 3.024), most got the job either by personal contact or by writing to the Editor and most were recruited on the basis of an interview without any written test. Since this process marked the beginning of their own rise to present editorship, it is hardly surprising if the system seems reasonable to them.

How autonomous is the local weekly Editor in his choice? He is absolutely free to choose anyone who presents himself or herself. The supply, as we know, is not all that strong. Why? The pay is low, the publication itself is not glamorous and many Editors give preference to recruits who live in the locality – this ensures 'local knowledge', and perhaps parental support. For the recruit – who has often already failed to get into higher education – it often presents the unglamorous prospect of living at home with the parents. Another disadvantage is that the prospects are uncertain – the Editor can hold out no certainty of the recruit ever reaching a larger paper.

The rates of pay are all agreed between management and the NUJ, so there is little the individual Editor can do. Nor does he think it remarkable that he has to run a school as well as a newspaper – since this has always been the case. Indeed in the very recent past this has become less marked anyway – as a result of depression and lower intake.

What about the NUJ? Most weekly Editors, like most daily Editors, report that all or almost all of their journalists are in the NUJ. Editors typically are somewhat worried by the NUJ nationally but proclaim that their personal relations with the NUJ are good. While some weekly Editors have had NUJ difficulties, the fiercest conflicts seem to focus on the provincial daily papers.

On a weekly paper the Editor typically presides over two main sorts of journalists – raw recruits on the one hand and experienced 'seniors' on the other; some of the latter are destined for weekly editorships and/or have left daily papers for the quieter weekly life. This combination does not make for stirring conflicts – moreover with a small staff the direct influence of the Editor's own often very pleasant personality is strongly felt.

How many young journalists become 'radicalised'? Some Editors made dark hints that 'the NUJ gets at them in the training centres', and this was even mentioned as a reason for running an in-group training scheme. But there should be no mystery about what happens in and around the Technical Colleges where the block release and pre-entry courses occur. One thing which obviously happens is that journalism as a career gets a 'Tech' image. Emphasis on this kind of training must be a main factor repelling some recruits. For instance the Editor of an extremely fat and obviously profitable weekly paper in a farming area complained that he could not recruit onto his paper any farmers' sons, even small farmers' sons. One obvious reason may be that the Technical College ranks behind Agricultural College in status.

When journalism recruits get to the Technical College they find themselves amongst the recruits of all those occupations which are now dedicated to radical white collar unionism – ASTMS, NALGO, NUPE, DATA and the like. Moreover when they go out on stories they may well find themselves covering industrial action by nurses, junior doctors, civil servants, bank clerks, social workers and so on. What the NUJ stands for may not seem radical, so much as rather restrained, compared with the rhetoric of some of these other white collar unions.

Moreover what the NUJ says – that journalists are white collar workers who must organise, must apply the quick stoppage tactics of the manual unions, and above all must control entry – may square with what many young journalists perceive during their occupational initiation.

Paradoxically, then, the Editor's autonomy in the field of recruiting is exercised in such a way as unintentionally, but forcibly, to encourage a white collar trade union orientation in those recruited.

7 Possible changes

7.1 Polarisation, false dichotomies, short-sightedness

The false notion behind the vague idea of Editorial Sovereignty is that editorship can be separated and sharply demarcated from management. An industry which talks so much about management should be able to recognise that the Editor is a manager.

National versus Provincial splits bedevil British journalism in many ways, including all aspects of editorship. This distinction, added to the previous one, means that national Editors have little interest in, or contact with, provincial Editors and no involvement at all in initial recruitment. At the management level the provincial groups are nationally linked and indeed based in London. But old traditions – plus new fears of being accused of monopoly – make for an editorial divorce even between publications which in some cases subsidise each other.

An unhelpful distinction is made between newspapers and magazines. Although most of the most important innovations in newspapers have always come from magazines and although there is much common ownership, in terms of editorship, magazines are kept artificially separate.

Another weakness is that an industry so influenced by the past and which reveres so many traditions has such a weak knowledge of what actually happened in the past.[1] Editorship is very much a case in point, and this ignorance of the past seriously inhibits understanding of the present.

There is also a lack of realisation of the consequences of being in an industry which can structure the public view not only of other industries, but of itself. In other words, the press beyond perhaps all other industries is vulnerable to the danger of believing its own mythology. Editorial Sovereignty is a central part of this mythology.

For at least two decades we have been told how efficient much of the press now at last is, compared with the recent past when, alas, it was still being mismanaged. At any point in the last twenty years it would have been wise to disbelieve the industry's own rhetoric about its newfound managerial efficiency. Managements for which 'efficiency' was claimed often subsequently produced performances which were unimpressive in terms of both profit and editorial

---

1 Compared with France, West Germany and the United States serious press history in Britain is still in its infancy.

output.[1] If several different wings of the industry – say the main trade associations, the NUJ, the IOJ and the GBNE – agree about something, there is a strong probability that this makes sense as a lowest common denominator of self-perceived interest, but otherwise makes nonsense. Editorial Sovereignty is again a relevant example.

7.2 Altering titles and functions

If there is a central fault in the supposed divorce between editorship and management, the solution is to combine the two. This is not a new idea. The BBC did this in the 1960s when it decisively rejected the old Reithian notion that management and programmes were or could be fundamentally separate. The idea is a lot older in the press. Certain organisations like *The Daily Telegraph* have for over a century continued a proprietor-editor tradition. In America this person is called the 'Publisher'. The most successful British newspaper manager of recent times – Rupert Murdock – is in the same mould.

I would suggest the following:

The Publisher should be the person in both managerial and editorial control of a paper. Lord Hartwell, Vere Harmsworth and the IPC magazine 'publishers' already do this. So do some smaller provincial groups. Where Editorial Directors and Editors-in-Chief exist, in this view, they should be renamed 'Publisher' and explicitly given both managerial and editorial supremacy. The publisher should carry legal responsibility for advertising.

The Editor would be recognised as having an editorial-cum-business superior, but would carry legal responsibility for editorial only on the occasions when he actually edited.

Managing Editor would be a person who sometimes does the Editor's job – a national daily might have two of these. He would carry legal responsibility on the days when he edited.

The suggestion is that these titles would be introduced with some new practices. It would be recognised that Editors of major publications and other senior journalists should receive senior management training, while men with an editorial background should become Publishers in many cases.

Editors should be encouraged to hand over more duties to managing editors; they should be discouraged from working such long hours. There should be some form of sabbatical leave for Editors.

7.3 Groups and London management

If the large provincial groups are to continue, neither business nor editorial effectiveness seems to require that they be so dominated by London management guidelines. The argument that central management in London provides efficiency – either in terms of profit or editorial performance – should be considered dubious unless proved otherwise. The major provincial groups were set up for political purposes originally and have been expanded by purchase. Companies like the Liverpool Daily Post and Echo give the impression of being better managed than the national groups, as well as being more profitable and better editorially (although still capable of improvement).

---

1   For example: 'Daily Mirror Newspapers Ltd . . . must be considered a successful company by any yardstick . . . . There is a determination to produce the best newspaper of its type, but this is balanced by a desire for efficient operation.' Economist Intelligence Unit, *The National Newspaper Industry* (1966), p 10.

Like so many conventional wisdoms in the press, the 'efficiency' of London management is very probably untrue. What exactly is the point of four Thomson daily papers in Scotland being run from London? What is the purpose of the large board of highly experienced and highly paid TRN directors?[1] It certainly is not necessary for news purposes, nor for advertising – only a fraction of provincial newspaper advertising goes through London advertising agencies. The big advertising agencies are rapidly setting up provincial branches because that is where the growth in business now is.

Why not split the groups down into regional sub-groups, since they tend anyhow to own adjacent dailies? Then:

Thomson would have one group of four Scottish dailies, three in the North-East, three to the West of London etc.

Associated/Northcliffe would have one Humberside group of 3 dailies, a group of 3 in the South-West, a Derby-Stoke-Leicester group and a West and Wales group and so on.

This proposal would be opposed on various grounds but the real worries might be three:

1 That some central directors would lose their jobs.

2 That this local grouping would look like a *regional* monopoly.

3 That this decentralisation might lead to complete divestiture.

All good arguments in their way, but not good for readers, Editors or journalists and probably not for profits either.

Each group of 3 or 4 dailies could have a publisher in charge.

7.4 Pay, status, training, education and security

In my view the Editor of a paper which makes £500,000 profit should have a salary of more than £6,500. Much higher pay for Editors would be one big improvement.

Neither graduates nor non-graduates necessarily make better Editors. But it is strange that only 2 out of 47 provincial daily Editors in the SCPR survey have degrees; most of these Editors incidentally favour graduate journalists and want their own children to have degrees. The range of expected competences in an Editor is so vast that nobody can have them all; on the whole graduates may be more likely to be able to be lawyer, politician, businessman, schoolteacher, entertainer, personnel manager, PRO and Union negotiator. Nor should we forget that, as Lippmann said, these are the people we expect to preside over the difficult and sometimes dangerous task of telling the truth about public events.

Nor should any increase in the proportion of graduates be confined to dailies. If graduates can successfully edit women's magazines and other light magazines they can certainly edit weekly newspapers.

One senior Editor complained that 'there are still very few journalists who can explain what the Town Hall is doing with its money'. How many Editors can honestly be fully satisfied even with their own competence in this direction?

---

1 In 1975 TRN had 12 directors, only three of whom had responsibilities in specific geographical regions.

If daily Editors need training courses – and few Editors would deny it – they need the kind of training good financial journalists and perhaps the odd national Editor could offer. Incidentally national Editors could learn a lot from provincial ones about what happens beyond the green belt.

7.5 The professionalisation of journalism ?

One aspect of Newspaper Society, GBNE, national Editors' and managers' statements about 'editorial freedom' and 'NUJ radicalism' is that while they praise (but do not specify) the former, they denigrate, but offer no alternative to, the latter.

There is no point in expecting 'NUJ radicalism' to go away by itself. If you want it to go away you have to put something in its place. Looking at other occupations in Britain, and at journalism in other countries, there seems to be only one realistic alternative as a general direction – some kind of limited professionalisation for some kinds of journalist.

What precise form this professionalisation might take is less clear. But obvious possibilities include:

- Some kind of career structure, perhaps including all categories of publications and also radio (especially local radio) and television.
- Some kind of 'professional' journalism training such as occurs now in virtually every industrialised nation in the world.
- Some kind of re-training, sabbaticals and the like.
- Higher pay and status for all journalists.
- Presumably also one or more 'professional' organisations with a genuinely independent existence – perhaps a Guild of British Press Executives involving 2,000 Editors and managing editors of all publications including magazines.
- More training for journalists in advertising and sales and in management.
- Perhaps some kind of entry quota scheme – such as 50% with degrees and 50% with *three A levels* – which would still leave the half graduate occupation many years away.

If some moves in the 'professional' directions are to occur, Editors will have to play a central part. One of the first things they will need is a recognition that editorial autonomy is a grand idea which has limited reality. The more significant and meaningful questions concern the autonomy of journalism as an occupation. A slightly less grand, but more realistic, kind of autonomy than Editorial Sovereignty is needed. Some should probably rest with publishers – on the grounds of laying the editorial responsibility where the editorial power is; some can remain with 'Editors' and some should spread among other journalists (whether all journalists, or only senior ones, can be debated).

It seems to me that the whole issue of the 'Editor's right to Edit' breaks down into five main questions:

1 What relative weight in editorial decisions and practice should rest with management and with journalists or others?

2 How important should be the role of the small number of Editors (and others) who are both managers and journalists? Do we need to 'unpack' the notion of editorship into several pieces (for example on the United States model)?

3   What is to be the future of journalism? What proportion of graduates are wanted in the occupation overall in 10 and 20 years' time? (When this is agreed, and only then, can sensible recruitment quotas be fixed.) But perhaps more important are two other questions. What is to be offered to the majority of non-graduates now in the occupation? How will non-graduates be recruited, motivated and rewarded in the future?

4   In terms of *educating* journalists is it better to put the main emphasis on pre-entry or on post-entry education?

5   What is to be the balance between commercial competition and Government regulation?

7.6   Finance

In my personal view the most important changes might well be in pay – firstly for Editors, secondly for all press journalists. Pay should be comparable to pay in television and radio. If this means fewer, but higher paid, journalists then so be it.

Training and education cost money. The industry may complain about the PPITB levy and so on. But we should remember that:

– The press is a billion-pound-a-year-revenue industry.

– The press is the main beneficiary of a very special flow of revenue – advertising – which, in contrast to some other countries, suffers no special taxes in Britain.

– The press contains many monopoly situations, which in some cases are rather ruthlessly milked for profit by companies with very large interests in other industries – including banking and oil.

– The press is zero-rated for VAT.

In short the press can afford to pay Editors and journalists more. It is in the interests of the press that it should improve its *quality* of performance. This means that both Editors and journalists must be better equipped for their unique task.

Part C   Section 3

The problem of Industrial Relations news in the Press

by Jeremy Tunstall of The City University

Contents

Author's notes

1 Unions and Balance of Payments

A fundamental difficulty in discussing the problem of industrial relations news is the lack of consensus as to the nature of Britain's industrial relations problem or indeed on whether there is an industrial relations problem of national dimensions.

W A P Manser, for example, in *Britain in Balance* (published in 1971 in association with the Institute of Economic Affairs) argued that Trade Union intransigence was one cause falsely attributed to Britain's economic weakness and balance of payments difficulties. Manser argued that Britain had no basic balance of payments difficulties of a long-term nature (although it did have a problem of excessive overseas government expenditure). In Manser's view there was no basic weakness in the British economy (apart from bi-partisan government mismanagement). While Manser thought British trade unionism was indeed in need of reform he was sceptical of any assertion that British industrial relations were especially bad, or that Britain had an unusually high strike record.[1] In this view, then, one problem of industrial relations news would be that the media exaggerate the importance of industrial relations; but more importantly, in Manser's view, the press has accepted a false post-1945 orthodoxy of Britain having a long-term balance of payments problem.

2 Trade Unions and General Elections

In contrast to Western Europe in general, Britain is somewhat unusual in the extent to which its Trade Unions are associated with a *single* political party – the Labour Party – and this might contribute to the Unions acquiring especial salience in British politics and in the press coverage of British politics. The February 1974 election was to a large extent precipitated by a conflict between the Miners' Union, the NUM, and a Conservative Government led by Edward Heath. Nor was this the only General Election campaign in which Trade Unions featured prominently. Another recent example was 1966. During the early days of this Election a so-called 'Noose Trial' dominated the national newspapers[2] front page headlines:

'The "Noose Trial" in 1966 was the name given to an incident in which eight factory hands in the BMC works at Cowley were "tried" before several hundred colleagues and fined £3 each for failing to join an unofficial strike. During the trial a noose was dangling in the background. The press seized on this as an excellent story, and it dominated the headlines in the first week of the campaign. Leaders in both parties commented at length on its implications, and some Conservative papers (chiefly *The Daily Telegraph*) squeezed the last ounce of advantage out of it'[3]

While the amount of coverage given to the 'Noose Trial' in 1966 may in retrospect seem excessive, it was a topic upon which the national party leaders (in fact

---

1 W A P Manser, *Britain in Balance*, 1971, pp 108–9.
2 For four weekdays in succession (March 12, 14, 15, 16, 1966) over half of all the national newspaper lead stories were devoted to the 'Noose Trial'. See D E Butler and Anthony King (Eds) *The British General Election of 1966*, London: Macmillan, 1966, pp 152–3.
3 Colin Seymour-Ure, *The Political Impact of Mass Media*, London: Constable, 1974, pp 225–6.

Callaghan and Heath) made repeated comments at their morning news conferences.[1] And in 1973–74 the press could hardly have failed to give large coverage to the NUM. These two examples of Trade Unions being involved in election coverage illustrate characteristic features of the problem. Much coverage of Trade Unions in Britain is of Unions in a governmental context, and because of the special connection with the Labour Party there are thus always party and partisan overtones. This prominence of Unions at some recent elections might also explain why many people seem to think that Unions receive more press coverage than content analysis actually reveals. But such events are highly ambiguous from a news coverage viewpoint. Even if the 1966 coverage was 'excessive' and the February 1974 coverage justified, the Conservative Party still lost both Elections.

3   Trade Unions as less legitimate than management?

Another quite separate strategic view of the industrial relations news sees Trade Unions as being presented in the press as less 'legitimate' than management. Paul Hartmann, a leading proponent of this view, argues:

'We saw that the actions and statements of employers or managements seldom formed the basis of industrial relations news . . . . Industrial relations situations came to be seen as resulting mainly from the actions of unions . . . . These patterns of coverage convey the implication that the activities of unions warrant closer scrutiny than those of employers, *because their legitimacy is suspect*[2] . . . . Because the legitimacy of union activity is suspect, the unions are more frequently called upon by the media to account for their actions or feel obliged to make statements in their own justification. It would seem that employers, assured in their legitimacy, seldom feel this need and that the media accept this situation as normal.

. . . While workers and unions had adjectives applied to them, employers and government almost never had. In other words, the media frequently found it necessary to indicate to people what they should think about workers and unions, while employers and government were characteristically presented in unqualified terms . . . . There is an ambiguity . . . in a given situation which the media clarify with descriptions like "low-paid" (you can feel some sympathy with them), "militant" (you should disapprove of them), "divided" (they cannot win), or "angry" (they are ruled by emotion). On the other hand, the legitimacy of employers' actions is so seldom in question that qualification is unnecessary.

Whoever heard of a militant employer, or of division in the CBI?[3]'

Hartmann's study is unusual in that it combines content analysis with a survey in which members of the public were asked for their views on industrial relations and its news coverage. Hartmann found some (but not a very great deal of) difference in the way working class and middle class respondents saw industrial

---

1   The present author attended all these morning press conferences.
2   Emphasis in original.
3   Paul Hartmann, *The Media and Industrial Relations*, University of Leicester: unpublished report, December 1976, pp 2–46 to 2–48.

relations. Asked about the causes of strikes, blue collar respondents were especially likely to emphasise the 'need for money' and 'the rising cost of living'. White collar respondents placed heavier emphasis than blue collar respondents on 'greed for money', 'lack of co-operation, bloody-mindedness', political motivation and 'bad communication'. Hartmann then goes on to conclude that the view of industrial relations presented in the press conforms much more closely to the views held by middle class people than to those held by working class people.[1]

Clearly this 'lower legitimacy' argument is not entirely without its own difficulties. For example: In view of the general belief – accepted by most trade union spokesmen – that it is the duty of management to manage, can the media be expected to present unions and management as equally authoritative?

One other point from Hartmann's study is worth mentioning in this Introduction. Hartmann asked his respondents about their sources of 'Information and ideas about trade unions and industrial relations'. Among both white collar and blue collar respondents more people found both television and newspapers either 'very important' or 'fairly important' as a source of information than mentioned 'own Union' or 'family and relatives' or 'friends and acquaintances'. More blue collar people (80%) mentioned television while more white collar people (78%) mentioned newspapers.[2] Incidentally, this survey was confined to the industrial city of Coventry where one might have expected people to rely on personal contacts for industrial relations information to a greater extent than in Britain at large.

4 The media as problem definers, agenda setters and legitimacy conferrers

The three quite different arguments so far discussed illustrate some of the many dimensions of, and views upon, the strategic problem or problems of industrial relations news.

Behind these – and other – conflicting views lie a number of core assumptions. The media define certain things as *problematical*; these particular things (such as strikes) may be chosen by both journalists and politicians not because they are necessarily seen as the most important problem confronting Britain, but at least partly because they are problems which can easily be *presented* to newspaper readers and voters as interesting, or persuasive, or newsworthy.

A different assumption is that the media are, to a greater or lesser extent, able to set the national political agenda. If an issue appears often enough in the newspapers' front page headlines, it will get on to the Cabinet agenda, and it will appear in the pronouncements of leading politicians.

The press and other media are also assumed by some critics to be conferrers of legitimacy. While the press gives much coverage to trade unions and their leaders, this coverage at the same time questions their legitimacy. So goes a third assumption.

Not all critics of, or defenders of, the press coverage of industrial relations would accept these core assumptions. That in itself is part of the problem of agreeing what the problem is. Nevertheless behind nearly (though not quite)

---

1 Ibid, pp 5–10 and 5–24.
2 Ibid, p 5–26.

all arguments on this topic there is at least one common assumption. This is the assumption that the way in which the press and media cover industrial relations does matter because it affects outcomes – whether in terms of the national economy, or the pattern of negotiations, or the take home pay of a particular group of workers.

I am extremely grateful to Paul Hartmann and Robert Houlton for reading and commenting on this paper.

J T

December 1976

Summary

1 Press and industrial relations in Britain

1.1 A classic problem: Industrial relations is too complex to be newsworthy, said Walter Lippmann, until some unusual event happens. The most common unusual thing is a dispute and the subsequent disruption which can fit a pre-existing stereotype.

1.2 London and local level in press and industrial relations. A primarily national press has special difficulties with the informal and local character of much of industrial relations. National press coverage of national union leadership can be misleading.

1.3 The weakness of the press in relation to the Unions. 'Neutral', 'objective' or 'two sides' canons of news reporting are difficult to operate in such a complex field as industrial relations.

1.4 The weakness of the unions in relation to the press. Most Unions, especially the large General ones, have little PR staff. Top Union leaders tend to be their own PROs, often winning the publicity battles but perhaps at cost of losing the publicity wars.

1.5 Bias, conflict, neutrality and social class. It is difficult to prove that bias exists or to deny that conflict has reader appeal.

2 Industrial relations news: content and correspondents

2.1 The content of press and broadcast industrial relations news. Newspapers give only 2 to 3% of editorial space to industrial relations and only a minority even of this space deals with strikes. Television and radio carry more industrial relations and strike news. Press coverage does concentrate on a few industries and does give much less space to settlements than disputes – but both of these emphases are defensible. Union leaders figure most prominently in the coverage. Industrial relations news is, in the more serious papers, dwarfed in extent by financial/economic news.

2.2 Major strikes and the role of the press. Studies of particular strikes suggest that the press coverage is very important; the strikers themselves get much of their information on the strike from the press and it is through the press that much of the negotiation effectively takes place.

2.3 Labour correspondents. Detailed evidence about national Labour correspondents (in 1968) is provided. Probably there is an unusually high consensus

351

in story choice amongst this group of specialists – in response to other uncertainties of the field – which leads to news values being held with great unanimity across all national media and all national Labour correspondents.

3 Uses of, and attitudes towards, industrial relations news

3.1 The general public is not very interested in industrial relations news and does not think the press is anti-Union.

3.2 Community Influentials, however, do not agree and collectively think trade union coverage the weakest area of provincial press performance. The criticism is not of strike coverage, but of inadequate coverage of union affairs in general; this criticism is made by senior local government officials and by a sample of managing directors. Local union officials also make the criticism, but their own relations with the press are relatively passive and unprotesting.

3.3 Trade Union officials and members. Trade Union members – and their shop stewards and branch officials – all mainly follow popular media, which they do not think anti-union apart from excessive strike coverage. But full-time union officials, who are much more likely to read those serious papers often said to be most 'fair' to the unions, are much more critical, especially in claiming the press to be indeed anti-Union. It may be their reading of the financial pages which makes them think this.

4 Differing diagnoses and solutions

4.1 National – local and other paradoxes. Since the provincial press is now probably doing more industrial relations coverage, in some ways local informal reality is being better covered.

The national union leaders' criticism of excessive coverage of industrial relations in general and of strikes in particular is misdirected and perhaps results from the 'excessive' coverage some Union leaders receive, although this latter is largely of their own choosing. But nor is the CBI case valid.

4.2 Overseas repercussions of industrial relations coverage. There is no available evidence as to whether Britain is portrayed as 'strike prone' in the foreign press. Foreign correspondents based in London may – because of the dominant national press – be less aware of provincial reality (through reading provincial papers) than would be true of foreign correspondents stationed in most comparable countries.

4.3 Union diagnoses and dilemmas. Some kind of 'sheltered' media access, either through its own major publications, or for example, through specially provided advertising, must be attractive to Unions. Better PR arrangements both collectively and by separate Unions could help, but would also carry some penalties.

4.4 Management and business. Local managing directors think the Unions receive inadequate local press coverage; if management thinks this undesirable or that it leads to too many ultra-left 'underground' publications the answer is to accord special legitimacy to the Unions as a unique interest comparable to politics, the courts, or business, and then to consider how this can be given press expression.

4.5 Journalism, the press and industrial relations. On the press side one obvious policy is that the Unions would feel still further aggrieved if a paper such as *The Guardian* disappeared. More positively it would be possible to combat a lack of industrial experience and the purely financial view of industry on the part of many London-based journalists especially; job exchanges and some basic industrial relations training for all journalists would be such measures.

4.6 Lack of a public debate on the media. The lack of a serious running debate on the British media or press – and the lack of such middle-brow publications as *Columbia Journalism Review* or *Presse-Actualité* means that the press currently has no way of discussing complex topics such as the one in hand, and no way of evolving its own solutions to them.

4.7 Conclusions. Although no particular piece of press performance is very anti-Union, the overall mosaic of Union coverage is unfair especially in contrast to the coverage of finance and business.

1 Press and Industrial Relations in Britain

1.1 A classic problem

In his book, *Public Opinion*, published in 1922, Walter Lippmann made what is still the classic statement of the dilemmas posed by press coverage of industrial relations:

'Now in labor disputes, which are probably the chief item in the charges against newspapers, the right to strike, like the right to vote, is simple enough. But the causes and objects of a particular strike are, like the causes and objects of the women's movement, extremely subtle.

Let us suppose the conditions leading to a strike are bad. What is the measure of evil? . . . The standard is at best a vague measure. However, we shall assume that the conditions are below par, as par is understood by the editor. Occasionally without waiting for the workers to threaten, but prompted say by a social worker, he will send reporters to investigate, and will call attention to bad conditions. Necessarily he cannot do that often. For these investigations cost time, money, special talent, and a lot of space. To make plausible a report that conditions are bad, you need a good many columns of print . . ..

The bad conditions as such are not news, because in all but exceptional cases, journalism is not a first hand report of the raw material. It is a report of that material after it has been stylised. Thus bad conditions might become news if the Board of Health reported an unusually high death rate in an industrial area. Failing an intervention of this sort, the facts do not become news, until the workers organize and make a demand upon their employers . . . But if industrial relations collapse into a strike or lockout the news value increases. If the stoppage involves a service on which the readers of the newspapers immediately depend, or if it involves a breach of order, the news value is greater. . . . since all the immediate realities lie outside the direct experience both of the reporter, and of the special public by which most newspapers are supported, they have normally to wait for a signal in the shape of an overt act. When that signal comes, say through a walkout of the men or a summons for the police, it calls into play the stereotypes people have about strikes and disorders . . . obviously this is a very different experience from that which the strikers have. They feel, let us say, the temper of the foreman, the nerve-racking monotony of the machine . . . The slogans of the strike are invested with these feelings. But the reporter and reader see at first only a strike and some catchwords. They invest these with their feelings. Their feelings may be that their jobs are insecure because the strikes are stopping goods they need in their work, that there will be shortage, and higher prices, that it is all devilishly inconvenient. These, too, are realities. And when they give color to the abstract news that a strike has been called, it is in the nature of things that the workers are at a disadvantage . . ..

A great deal, I think myself the crucial part, of what looks to the worker and the reformer as a deliberate misrepresentation on the part of newspapers, is the direct outcome of a practical difficulty in uncovering the news, and the emotional difficulty of making distant facts interesting . . ..

If you study the way many a strike is reported in the press, you will find, very often, that the issues are rarely in the headlines, barely in the leading paragraphs, and sometimes not even mentioned anywhere . . .. It comes from the economy of noting only the stereotyped phase of a situation . . . It comes from the economic necessity of interesting the reader quickly . . . All these difficulties combined make for uncertainty in the editor . . . The indisputable fact and the easy interest are the strike itself and the reader's inconvenience.

All the subtler and deeper truths are in the present organisation of industry very unreliable truths. They involve judgements about standards of living, productivity, human rights that are endlessly debatable in the absence of exact record and quantitative analysis. And as long as these do not exist in industry, the run of news about it will tend, as Emerson said, quoting Isocrates "to make of moles mountains, and of mountains moles" . . . And so to try disputes by an appeal through the newspapers puts a burden upon newspapers and readers which they cannot and ought not to carry. As long as real law and order do not exist, the bulk of the news will, unless consciously and courageously corrected, work against those who have no lawful and orderly method of asserting themselves. The bulletins from the scene of action will note the trouble that arose from the assertion, rather than the reasons which led to it. The reasons are intangible.'[1]

Although Lippmann was writing about American Trade Unions in a relatively early phase of their growth, and while the element of 'exact record' in labour disputes has increased since that time, the basic situation more than fifty years later – even with radio and television and more sophisticated newspapers – is still remarkably similar.

As Walter Lippmann himself indicated, one difficulty in attempting to answer the question of press coverage of industrial relations is to decide what precisely the question is. The evidence put to the Royal Commission suggests several quite different sorts of problems:

– The press gives 'too much' coverage to industrial relations.
– The press gives too much coverage of strikes and not enough to 'positive' activities of Trade Unions.
– The press reports industrial relations reasonably fairly but it should take more account of the fact that British press reports are quoted in foreign newspapers, contributing to a picture of 'strike prone Britain' and thus to damaging the British economy.
– Journalists subscribe to typical middle class stereotyped beliefs about Trade Unionists and consequently seek out stories which confirm such prejudices.
– The press owners as capitalists are hostile to Unions and see that they are unfairly treated.

---

1 Walter Lippmann, *Public Opinion*, 1922, pp 219–22.

– Labour correspondents are favourably disposed to the Trade Unions and tend to produce accurate stories but these are distorted by owners, sub-editors and headlines.

Many such assertions are extremely vague. Some do not differentiate between particular Unions and fail to specify which level of a Union is being discussed. The media on the other side of the equation are, if not as complex as the Unions, certainly quite complex. Many statements fail to differentiate between broadcast and press media; even more assertions fail to differentiate between the national and provincial press.

Any broad question about the performance of the British press tends to cover at least three strategic dimensions: a. The connection between national and regional press. b. The connection between press and broadcast media. c. A contrast or comparison between British media and those in one or more other countries.

(a) Since strikes and Trade Union members are geographically spread, whereas the British media are heavily focused on London, the mechanism by which stories move between London and the provinces must be vital. This suggests that the Press Association, regional correspondents of nationals, and monitoring of nationals by provincials and vice-versa are vital. It focuses special attention on the London offices of provincial chains. Clearly also if Britain moves over to the European pattern of a mainly provincial press our whole pattern of industrial relations news may change fairly radically.

(b) Many assertions about *press* coverage of industrial relations appear to be partly about the *broadcast* media. As in other fields of news, press and broadcast media influence each other in many ways and cannot realistically be considered separately.

(c) Any assertions as to the deviance or irrationality of British press coverage implicitly make comparisons with other countries. To test such questions there is no substitute for *detailed* systematic comparison with what happens in selected other countries. Similarly the assertions as to the inaccurate portrayal abroad of 'strike prone Britain' cannot be seriously considered without an investigation of the particular media in the particular countries about which the assertions are made.

A more appropriate body to have looked into some of these questions might have been the Donovan, *Royal Commission on Trade Unions and Employers' Associations 1965–68*. Donovan paid very little attention to media coverage of industrial relations despite his heavy emphasis upon the *imagery* of industrial relations (often contrasted with the 'reality') and despite the presence on the Commission of two journalists knowledgeable about Trade Unions (Andrew Shonfield formerly of *The Observer*, and Eric Whigham then senior labour correspondent of *The Times*).

1.2 London and other levels in press and industrial relations

One much quoted, and subsequently much disputed, generalisation of the Donovan Commission is germane to press coverage:

'We now compare the two systems of industrial relations. The formal system assumes industry-wide organisations capable of imposing their decisions on

357

their members. The informal system rests on the wide autonomy of managers in individual companies and factories, and the power of industrial work groups. The formal system assumes that most if not all matters appropriate to collective bargaining can be covered in industry-wide agreements. In the informal system bargaining in the factory is of equal or greater importance . . .. What is of crucial importance is that the practices of the formal system have become increasingly empty, while the practices of the informal system have come to exert an ever greater influence on the conduct of industrial relations throughout the country; that the two systems conflict; and that the informal system cannot be forced to comply with the formal system.'[1]

But this passage itself is an oversimplification. Industrial relations is a multi-level phenomenon. Trade Unions exist at national, regional, branch and plant level.

What do we find in terms of industrial relations coverage by the British media? The most obvious point is that the media in Britain are heavily *national*. National press and broadcasting have the bulk of the audience and even local media are heavily London controlled and dependent on London for news; but the media also exist on more than just two levels. They also exist nationally, regionally, locally and at factory or office level.

The key group of journalists in this field are London-based labour correspondents, who work not only for the national dailies but for PA, the London offices of the provincial newspapers, for BBC and ITN. These journalists primarily cover what Donovan calls the *formal system* of industrial relations in which the chief protagonists are the national leaders of the major unions. It is left to provincially based journalists to cover what Donovan describes as the *informal system* of industrial relations – in which the chief protagonists are very often not even local union officials, but shop stewards. The latter are ordinary workers elected by their mates; not surprisingly, and as the research programme of Donovan and much other research confirms, the shop stewards are the people whose views correspond most closely to those of the union members.

Does this then mean that national industrial relations coverage focuses upon a myth, whereas only regional and local coverage focus upon reality? That would be going too far. Trade Unions at the national level are much more than a myth especially perhaps in the public sector. But they do have many weaknesses. For example Donovan found that there were only 3,000 full-time trade union officials in Britain, with one union official to 3,800 workers – a very much higher number of members-per-official than in other large West European countries.[2] But in Britain many branch officials and conveners of shop stewards are *de facto* full-time trade union workers, although management pays them as if they were ordinary employees.

It is not at all clear, then, how a *national* press should cover a system of industrial relations much of which is *non-national*. The solution in effect chosen by the British national press is to cover those aspects of industrial relations which are clearly national – but a problem here is that the more clearly national these things are the more they tend to be about politics, or national economic planning, and the less about industrial relations as such. The national press

---

1 Donovan *Report*, Cmnd 3623, 1968, pp 36–7.
2 Ibid, p 188.

also attempts to match local 'reality' by covering some of the more seemingly nationally important local events – which tend to be disputes in a few major industries. They concentrate on certain leading Union personalities both on the national scene and when these personalities 'intervene' in local disputes.

Certainly if, and when, Britain acquires a primarily *provincial* daily press, the press overall will be more easily able to cover industrial relations in a manner which fits comfortably with the strongly local character of much industrial conflict.

It could be argued that the present dislocation between primarily national media and primarily local industrial relations leads to two related myths – the myth of the General Secretary of the big Union as a dominant figure (the personality news canon operating in the national media) and the second myth of strike-torn Britain (the search for possibly nationally significant events leading in effect to a search for local stoppages which can be portrayed as threatening *nationally* spread disruption). But neither of these is unambiguously a myth. Certain trade union leaders are powerful figures, because they tend to have life-long tenure, the block vote system within the TUC and the Labour Party, because of the internal hierarchical structure of some Unions, and because politicians act as if these leaders were important, incorporating them into national planning and political decision making.

Moreover it is not clear that the media portrayal of strikes in the car manufacturing industry is entirely mythical. But such coverage may emphasise certain kinds of stoppages, such as ones caused by unofficial strikes rather than ones caused by materials shortages and it may stress the *failures* of car manufacture rather than the successes of commercial vehicle and tractor production.

In comparison with the rest of Western Europe the *national* and *non-sectarian* character of the British press makes its coverage of industrial relations seem rather un-European. In Europe the press is less national. But in Europe also both press and unions are more sectarian. Just as most West European countries have Catholic, Conservative, Socialist and Communist daily newspapers, they also have Catholic (or in Scandinavia Protestant), Conservative, Socialist and Communist trade unions. Both Press and Unions are closely interlinked with party and/or religion. Thus in much of Europe the question 'Is the press fair to your Union?' has rather different implications.

Both the 'European' and the British pattern of industrial relations media coverage doubtless contain many dilemmas and paradoxes. Two British paradoxes are as follows:

– Much British industrial relations coverage implies that the large Unions and their national leaders are extremely powerful; but much other news is of 'unofficial' strikes and in this coverage the large Unions and their leaders are often portrayed as fairly helpless.

– In European eyes a key peculiarity of the British media is that they have been almost entirely detached from political control. We have adopted the United States pattern of commercially owned newspapers, in which partisanship is muted and prevalent doctrine stresses 'neutral' news values applied by 'professional' journalists to a succession of 'events'. Yet this deliberately (and in some European ideas mythically) a-political non-partisan approach results in the industrial relations field in coverage much of which is not about industrial relations at all but is about national *politics*.

1.3 The weakness of the press in relation to the unions

British 'Neutral' news values were invented by United States news agencies which had to operate across a continent of daily newspapers and within a loose *two*-party political system. These neutral values have increasingly during the twentieth century been adopted in Britain, another country with a predominantly two-party tradition. 'Telling both sides', and 'playing it down middle' are American phrases which find easy British applications.[1] They have been canonised in Britain by the Press Association (and other agencies) and more recently by the BBC – whose news operations, as Asa Briggs' volumes make clear, were modelled on, and for some years consisted of, news agency reports. These 'two-sides' approaches are indeed applicable (if not always applied) to such events as Parliamentary debates, General Elections, and sporting encounters. But not all issues have two obvious sides and in some fields one of the two sides is 'more equal' than the other. In politics governments get more coverage than oppositions – broadly because governments can provide 'events', whereas opposition leaders can only provide talk.

How does the industrial relations field shape up in terms of 'two sides' reporting and neutral news values? In some ways it shapes up rather well; there are two main sides – employees and employers. But even within these two there are problems, especially on the employee side. There may be several unions involved in a particular dispute. At the local level there are multi-union bodies – the union side of the official negotiating machinery – and these may be at odds with national leadership. There may also be unofficial leaders quite apart even from the shop stewards.

Outside the immediate employees and employers there are other umbrella bodies – such as the TUC and CBI – and often one or more state bodies are involved. Many disputes in recent years have concerned nationalised industries and public sector employees such as teachers, nurses, doctors, postmen. There are often other public agencies involved as well – for example, the Advisory Conciliation and Arbitration Service (ACAS – previously it was part of the Department of Employment). These public bodies pose special problems for journalists and the media – because these bodies are in some senses neutral, devoted explicitly to the public good, and in practice accorded considerable respect by journalists; on the other hand not only are national specialist journalists prone to be suspicious of all central government agencies, but such journalists often suspect that some of these government agencies are unilaterally pursuing their own contentious and partisan departmental policies.[2]

Not only is the field of industrial relations devoid of a single clear neutral news path between two and only two sides, but the extremely political flavour of the field is of a lop-sided character. The Trade Unions in Britain have a special relationship to the Labour Party so that in a sense within this field the Labour Party is permanently in government. And, somewhat like a governing Party, the Unions usually make the major news. The 'events' criterion favours the somewhat unusual; thus Unions tend to supply a flow of newsworthy events, whilst managements preside over unnewsworthy normalcy.

---

1   Jeremy Tunstall, *The Media are American* London: Constable, 1977.

2   For a more detailed discussion of specialist correspondents' experiences of dealings with government and civil servants, see Jeremy Tunstall, *Journalists at Work*, London: Constable, 1971, pp 173–201.

Not only is the press faced with great difficulties in deciding how to be neutral or objective, but industrial relations is a field about which knowledge is very unevenly distributed. Many readers will know something about their own Union or at least their own shop steward, but how much can they be assumed to know about any other aspects?

Not all news fields have the same predominant goals. The present author has previously argued (on the basis of interviews with Editors, advertising and circulation managers, as well as correspondents) that the labour field operates under a *mixed goal*. This mixture is made up of:

(*a*) A circulation element, which is stronger in fields like Crime or Football, but is present in labour news – because many readers are Union members and because industrial relations events affect people both as general public and as consumers of particular goods and services.

(*b*) An advertising goal element. There is no very close connection (of the gardening, fashion or motoring kind) but there is an important body of job advertising – especially in the provincial dailies and prestige nationals, and also in popular dailies like the *Daily Mirror*. In the case of regional dailies one reason for the existence of full-time labour correspondents is the job advertising section.

(*c*) A prestige element. Industrial relations coverage is widely seen in Britain as an essential part of serious coverage – in somewhat the same way as political coverage (although the extreme example of prestige coverage lies in staff foreign correspondents).

But since the advertising and prestige elements are in practice rather vague, the circulation goal becomes very often the main one. Labour stories, it seems probable, will usually be assessed on 'hard news' value and anticipated readership interest.

The goals of labour news coverage can be contrasted with the goals which operate in financial coverage. Financial coverage also has a vague prestige flavour and some political overtones, but it differs organisationally in crucial respects. Financial news has a *direct* connection with advertising – in the sense that financial news in many papers occupies a special section alongside special financial advertising; because it attracts this special advertising, financial news does not have to attract so large or so general an audience as does most other news. It can be assumed that its readers have a special interest in, and some sympathy for and knowledge of, financial news.

Since financial stories have a separate section of the paper which is usually known and fixed well ahead of each day's stories, financial stories do not have to compete against the whole run of stories on the day for space. Thus, compared with financial stories – which of course include management and the management end of industrial relations – labour stories have to 'fight their way into the paper'. Those who write labour stories are encouraged to appeal to the widest possible span of the readership (wider even than football which in practice appeals mainly to men and can realistically assume previous knowledge); they have to make the minimum assumption of relevant knowledge which the particular publication makes for any field of news.

Labour news, then, covers an extremely complex reality – which happens not to fit too easily either with general news values or with *national* media – and deliberately makes the minimum assumption of previous knowledge. And although daily papers in Britain may have labour specialists, *generalist* journalists also play a big part. Specialist labour correspondents' copy is typically sub-edited by generalist sub-editors – in contrast to foreign, sports, and financial news which on most national newspapers have specialist sub-editors; on many papers the main political stories are also subbed by specialist, or at least senior, sub-editors. In addition much labour news comes from regional correspondents, local stringers and local agencies – all of whom are generalists. Labour stories are also written by generalist feature writers.

One other peculiarity of labour news as seen by newspapers is its reputation as a 'hard news' and *late* news field. Certain news fields are regarded as having a rather features flavour – education is an example; education is not full of sudden events and gets a rather background 'soft news' kind of coverage. Labour is regarded, however, along with politics, as strong in hard and late news. Just as politics supplies sudden surprises, 10 pm Parliamentary votes and instant conflict, so labour news is believed to be full of sudden events – late night and early morning votes, instant conflict, and crisis 'marathon' meetings. This kind of reputation is, for both labour and political news, part of a generally high status in newspapers. To a large extent this reputation for producing sudden and late events may reflect the reality of audience interest and the reality of how decisions do emerge. To some extent the supply of instant events may reflect decisions made within newspapers – many news 'events' are in practice shaped and timed, if not entirely staged, with media coverage in view.

Regardless of how exactly it comes about, this late news reputation of labour news extends into broadcasting and indeed is even magnified there. TV and radio news try to carry later news than the newspapers with which they compete. Early morning mass meetings, mid-day statements, or late night marathon negotiations may fit these criteria quite well.

Evening papers in turn with copy times in late morning try to update the big audience early morning radio programmes; while national and regional morning papers with edition times from mid-evening to after midnight seek out events which postdate the evening television bulletins.

The media seem to have some preference for 'running stories' which run for a few days, reach a crescendo and then fall off – only to start up again at a later date. Industrial relation stories can easily be presented in this way – although once again it could be that some industrial 'events' are partly shaped thus to attract media coverage.

1.4 The weakness of the unions in relation to the press

One of the commonest Union complaints (noted by Lippmann in 1922 and by many others since) is that the Unions only get covered when strikes are happening or threatened, whereas their constructive activities get little coverage. A related complaint is that the basic 'facts' which appear in the press about industrial relations come from management, while the Unions provide conflict-laden 'events' which become news.

The aspects of industrial relations which become news typically involve large companies (size of work force or scale of disruption being itself a criterion of news significance), nationalised industries, and agencies of the central government. These large companies and public sector organisations happen to be the very ones in which information generally (planning, scientific expertise, and social research) as well as public relations are present on the very largest scale found anywhere in an industrial society. By contrast even the largest trade unions are fairly small organisations in terms of their total headquarters staff, in terms of specialised research and information, and in the scale of their public relations.

Some of the largest trade unions do not have one single employee dealing entirely in public relations. The Transport and General Workers Union in 1975 had no PR department and no single official dealing exclusively with press and broadcasting. The General and Municipal Workers Union had two full-time staff concerned with these functions; the Amalgamated Union of Engineering Workers had one PR officer. These three Unions with some four million members thus together had only three PROs.

In contrast to this pattern in the large general unions, some of the white collar unions had much stronger PR staffs, especially in relation to their overall size. ASTMS had six full-time PR personnel. White collar unions also tended to have a much more activist approach to public relations, often seeing PR as a way of recruiting new members. NUPE during the 'pay beds' disputes in the health service had six full-time press staff devoted to the single issue. The National Union of Teachers had one of the largest PR sections with a staff of nine in 1975.[1]

PR weakness as such, however, is only one of a number of inter-related ways in which Unions are weak in relation to the press and in competition with management and government:

(a) Resources: Not only do Unions not have elaborate PR or research staffs, but their poverty makes them vulnerable in other ways. Unions have, on the whole, less good legal advice at least in the press relations area. Journalists know that they are more likely to be taken to court for a legal infringement by management than by a union.

(b) Expertise: In the supply of 'factual' and neutral information management inevitably has many advantages. Most of what most people would think of as relevant 'facts' are in their nature management facts – output, future sales plans, profits, costs; even in the area of employment itself management has a personnel staff to tell it about productivity, earnings, overtime and the like. Unions do not.

(c) Access to the general media: Although Unions get more coverage in the labour stories, this is at least partly because management is often deliberately keeping a low profile, while more than one group of Union leaders are using the general media in an attempt to mobilise their support. But management gets sheltered access to the financial pages on a regular basis.[2] Moreover management can use other sorts of 'sheltered' access such as conventional paid advertising or a supplement in the *Financial Times* padded out with informative but rather uncritical articles. Nor must one forget the trade press – which is also heavily (or in the case of controlled circulation magazines entirely) dependent on advertising from the industry in question.

1   The Glasgow University Media Group, *Bad News*, London: Routledge and Kegan Paul, 1976, pp 205–43.
2   'Sheltered' in two senses. Firstly in the sense that fixed financial space is available, especially in the 'quality' papers for financial news. Secondly, in the sense that management views are defined as central on financial news pages, but Union views as only marginal.

(d) Internal House Publications: Larger companies typically have quite an elaborate battery of these. Trade Unions have these as well but they usually do not reach the bulk of rank and file members. In Blumler's sample of Yorkshire Trade Union members only 31% claimed to have read their own union's journal and to know its name.[1] Management also outstrips the Unions especially in house papers directed at 'publics-in-contact', local influentials, dealers and so on.

On the part of the General Secretaries and some other senior officials within major Unions, the lack of emphasis on conventional public relations is presumably deliberate. Since there is often contention for power between elected members of Union executives, any PR apparatus which existed would in turn become a focus for such contention. There are other advantages in the senior full-time officials being their own public relations officers.

Access to national publicity is in many conflict situations one of the few immediately available weapons possessed by a trade union national official, and it is an asset which may improve with use. The more publicity, the more public recognition, the stronger the publicity weapon. Such access enables Union leaders to capitalise on their one major publicity advantage – the generally friendly attitude of the national Labour correspondents. National media publicity enables a Union leader simultaneously to reach all the publics he wishes to reach – nationally spread members, local members and officials, his Union national executive, the politicians, the civil servants and the employers. During disputes and strikes the national media (plus the local daily media) are the only effective way to reach the members involved.

Trade Unions, at the national level, are primarily *negotiating* bodies; and even in routine annual negotiations the resort to publicity is a routine tactic. Here national trade union leaders are to some extent working in partnership with journalists – in somewhat the same way that many MPs to some extent work in partnership with their local lobby correspondents.[2]

Labour correspondents are typically friendly with the leaders of one or more major factions within each big Union; these 'friendships' vary and change according to personal preference, beliefs, compatibility and the way in which the publicity-for-information exchange evolves. But journalists are obviously most interested in the leading Union figures, because news values point in this direction. All news stories involve an element of contrivance, and there may be an element of journalists deliberately 'building up' certain Union leaders in return for information given and statements made.

Union leaders may win the publicity battles but lose the publicity wars. Their national publicity may lead to unrealistic expectations among some members and resentment and rival publicity from others. By making public statements during the course of negotiations they may easily mislead their own supporters as to what is actually happening in negotiating terms – for instance members of a Union may not realise that the Union leader who is publicly telling them to return to work is at the same time vigorously pressing their cause on management, or threatening to make the strike official. There must also be a danger

---

1 Jay Blumler and Alison Ewbank, 'Trade Unionists, the Mass Media and Unofficial Strikes', *British Journal of Industrial Relations* 8, 1970, p 54.
2 Jeremy Tunstall, *The Westminster Lobby Correspondents*, London: Routledge, 1970.

that media publicity comes to play such an important part in the general style of certain trade union leaders as to inhibit efficient management, and the realistic pursuit of viable goals.

Or to put it in Donovan language: If the national system of bargaining has become 'increasingly empty', national media publicity may exaggerate this trend still further.

1.5 Bias, conflict, neutrality and class

Sometimes bias is so blatant that at least in retrospect it can be agreed to have existed. In the early 1850's for example nearly all of the British press was opposed to the very existence of Trade Unions. The Amalgamated Society of Engineers was referred to in 1852 as 'a heartless and vulgar tyranny' and a 'Self-created despotism' by *The Economist* and the *Manchester Guardian*.[1] If bias exists today it takes somewhat subtler forms. Most of the people who have conducted detailed investigations on this topic in Britain are to the left of centre in their own political views, but virtually all agree that if bias exists at all it takes somewhat ambiguous forms. Of course ambiguity is not an accidental but an essential element in the news – it enables a publication to appeal to readers of different persuasions and partly underlies the much documented finding of 'selective perception' among the audience. It is essential to the neutral news approach that no final moral is attached to the end of the story; the reader is left free either to mutter that Smith is indeed a scoundrel or to cry out that Smith is indeed a hero.

Some brief observations can be made on four central terms:

'Bias' implies two-sides reporting and some would say that it also implies a true or perfect version. As Walter Lippmann observed in *Public Opinion* over fifty years ago, this is only possible where there is a good machinery of record such as turns out election results and stock exchange prices. In most cases there is no perfect version and thus what constitutes bias is uncertain.

'Neutrality' raises similar problems; it is not possible at least in most cases. Anglo-Saxon journalists may operate as if neutrality were possible, which is not the same thing as saying that it is possible. Neutrality is part of the occupational ideology of journalists and like other ideologies it masks interests; in this case an obviously relevant interest is the interest of journalists in being the 'professional' definers of where neutrality is, or how one can act 'as if' neutrality existed.

'Conflict': Few would deny that conflict is important in news values. But the media seem to define some kinds of conflict as more benign than others. The difference between inter-union rivalry and inter-company rivalry is relevant here. Why is it that Unions 'conflict', 'clash' and 'poach' whereas Companies merely 'compete' with each other? Companies compete or conflict via markets (for their products and their shares) or in Lippmann's term 'a machinery of record'. We are back to ambiguity once more; it can be argued that companies on the financial pages compete in a nice gentlemanly positive way. But do they? If mortal wounds are evidence of the ferocity of conflict, then do not more companies than Unions die?

---

1 Hamilton Fraser, *Trade Unions and Society: The struggle for acceptance, 1850–1880*, London: Allen and Unwin, 1974, p 200.

'Class': One of the oddities of British industrial relations coverage is that for a supposedly class-obsessed nation we manage to discuss our industrial relations in non-class language, or in language less class-obsessed than one might expect in say France or Italy where both Unions and press follow the party-sectarian pattern. Who are portrayed as the losers in British industrial relations? More often the customers,[1] the public or the nation than, say, the working class or the bosses. One has only to consider what a straightforward class conflict model of British industrial relations would look like to recognise that some quite different model actually prevails.

---

1 Three of the six most common themes in industrial relations stories in 1975 were 'loss of output due to dispute', 'inconvenience or danger to public' and 'loss of work by non-disputants'. Denis McQuail, *Analysis of Newspaper Content*, Cmnd 6810–4, p 127.

2 Industrial Relations News : Content and Correspondents

2.1 The content of press and broadcast industrial relations news

How much industrial relations news there is and what aspects of industrial relations are covered is obviously the core of the subject.

The coverage of industrial relations in the national newspapers is the subject of a separate report by Denis McQuail. Much of this section then merely summarises points from that report plus sections of the McQuail content analysis dealing with other publications than national daily newspapers. This section will also make some brief mentions of broadcast news. Nine general questions about industrial relations will be considered:

2.1.1 *Does the press carry excessive amounts of industrial relations news?*

In 1975 all national dailies, apart from the *Morning Star*, devoted between 1·9% (*Daily Mirror*) and 3·4% (*Financial Times*) of their total *editorial* space to industrial relations. This hardly appears an excessive quantity, especially when compared with sport – even papers like *The Times* and *The Guardian* devoted four times as much space to sport as to industrial relations, and the popular national dailies devote over nine times as much to sport. Both the *Daily Mirror* and *The Sun* devote more space to pictures of nude females than to all industrial relations.[1]

The amounts of total *editorial space* devoted to industrial relations in various sorts of newspapers in 1975 was approximately as follows:

Morning Star	11·9%	of total
Quality national dailies	3·1%	editorial space.
Daily Mail and *Daily Express*	3·0%	
Provincial mornings (England, Scotland and Wales)...	2·4%	
Daily Mirror and *The Sun*	2·0%	
Provincial evenings	2·0%	
National Sundays	0·8%	

Thus the quality national dailies and the two more serious popular national dailies all devote about 3% of editorial space to industrial relations, while about 2% is the figure for the provincial dailies and the two most popular national dailies.

Unfortunately it is not possible to make exact comparisons with broadcasting – either with news bulletins as such or with broadcasting more broadly. The

---

1   Denis McQuail, *Analysis of Newspaper Content*, Cmnd 6810–4, p 28.

Glasgow University Media Group's recent study of television news, *Bad News*, shows 'industrial' news constituting between 13·1% and 18·6% of all *items*[1] (not time) in the major weekday bulletins (p 98). In sharp contrast to the national Sunday newspapers, which collectively devote a lower proportion to industrial material, on television the proportion rises at weekends – accounting for between 19·4% and 25% (BBC 1) of news bulletin items on weekends in the first half of 1975. There are indications, however, that these Glasgow authors use a definition of 'industrial' wider than the 'industrial relations' definition of McQuail and wider also than one used by Hartmann, who found for April–May 1973 that the main BBC evening TV news devoted 6% of viewing time, and the main ITN news 4%, to industrial relations. Hartmann's study included newspapers and radio as well, and his overall pattern was as follows:[2]

Daily Mirror, Daily Express and *Daily Telegraph*	about 2% of editorial space
Coventry Evening Telegraph	about 4%
ITN TV News (10 pm)	about 4%
BBC TV News (9 pm)	about 6%
BBC Radio 4 (1 pm)	about 9%
Morning Star	about 12%

If the comparison between *news bulletins* and the whole editorial content of a newspaper is accepted then the accusation of 'too much industrial relations' coverage seems more relevant to broadcasting than to press, more relevant to BBC than to ITN and probably more relevant to radio than to TV.

One possible explanation for the overall picture is that journalists collectively see industrial relations as typically providing 'hard news' stories and as providing on many days one of the strongest single available stories. McQuail (op. cit. see p 111) finds that industrial relations typically provide 1·4 'large items' (21 column cms or more) on the front page of any national daily – in other words industrial relations typically provides either one or two of the larger front page stories; he also finds that on about one day in four industrial relations provides the 'splash' main front page headline story. Television news bulletins give rather similar prominence. The Glasgow authors find that 'industrial' is the third biggest category of news item – just behind foreign and political and far ahead of both economics and sport (p 95):

'... industrial stories ... on both channels ... cluster in the first half of the programme and occupy the largest proportion (41%) of second items on BBC 1 and the largest proportion of third items on ITN' (pp 113, 118).

This judgment of the top industrial relations item as typically the second or third 'strongest' story of the moment might thus explain why it occupies a larger proportion of television bulletins which are so much shorter than newspapers; the point is often made that a TV news bulletin is equivalent to a newspaper front page – where indeed industrial relations news appears to be

---

1 Industrial items had average durations between 1 min 10 secs (BBC 1) and 1 min 40 secs (ITN); this was close to the overall average so the *item* criterion does not greatly alter the general picture.

2 The figures in the original are given only in approximate form – and are for total space including advertising; the press figures here have been converted on the assumption of 50% editorial in the nationals, 50% in the *Coventry Evening Telegraph* and 100% in the *Morning Star*. See Paul Hartmann, 'Industrial Relations in the News Media', *Industrial Relations Journal*, Winter 1975, pp 5–6.

more prominent than in the newspaper overall. If this typical second or third ranking operates also in radio, the one-and two-minute radio bulletin will give industrial relations the greatest *proportional* pre-eminence.

Industrial relations is regarded as a 'hard news' area – such an area being implicitly defined by journalists as one which provides many sudden and relatively factual and relatively unpredictable events. The *recency* and *unpredictability* criteria within this reputation would also explain why the *fastest* medium – radio – may use its speed to give this field high emphasis; the next fastest medium is, of course, television. This speed factor would explain the low coverage by weekly and national Sunday newspapers both of which have a big gap between their final printing deadlines and the average time of being read.[1]

Paradoxically, then, newspapers seem to be less guilty than broadcasting of producing 'too much' industrial relations news. Indeed the accusation that they carry too little might have more substance.

Nevertheless even if the 'too much' coverage accusation is not very credible, the belief that there is something 'wrong' about media coverage of industrial relations overall appears to have more substance. The newspapers most read by urban working class people – the *Daily Mirror*, *The Sun* and the provincial evenings – carry the least industrial relations news; the local weekly papers, where one might expect to find positive coverage of local industrial relations, or the Sunday papers where one might expect more leisured consideration of background aspects – neither of these sorts of publication carry much industrial news. But each day there tend to be one or two big industrial relations stories on the radio headlines, on the newspaper front pages and near the top of the evening television news.

2.1.2 *Are strike stories too prominent within industrial relations coverage?*

The McQuail content analysis distinguishes helpfully between 'disputes' and 'strikes'. In national daily newspapers in 1975 36% of all industrial relations coverage was of 'disputes, stoppages and industrial action generally' (McQuail op. cit. p 116). However within this 'disputes' category, 'strikes' account for only 61% of coverage; some stories are about picketing, or working to rule and 13% are of 'unspecified action' – a remarkable finding in itself. One dispute story in eight does not even specify the type of dispute!

Thus 'strikes' accounted for only 22% of all industrial relations coverage – and well below 1% of the total editorial content of national newspapers in 1975.

In television the proportion is significantly higher. According to the Glasgow authors (p 169) all three channels devoted 39–40% of industrial relations coverage to strikes. But TV journalists can still reply that – even within the restrictions of TV news – three-fifths of industrial stories are not about strikes.

The criticism is widely made that settlements of disputes receive much less coverage than the disputes they settle. An example of this criticism is provided by NALGO in its evidence to the Royal Commission. The figures quoted are for a limited official strike against British Waterways Board in 1974; the strike, say NALGO, received 800 column inches of coverage, of which only 25 inches dealt with the settlement. The McQuail content analysis found the higher, but still not very high, proportion of 12% of all strike stories involving news of settlements (McQuail op. cit. p 118).

---

1 Sundays print earlier than morning dailies and, research indicates, are read later.

But it is not entirely obvious that 12% is such a low figure. Strikes, like negotiations, are often a 'running story' spread over several days. The McQuail content analysis (based on a random sample of separate days) has no data on the *duration* of particular strike stories. But the Glasgow authors have such data for national TV news coverage; for selected stories which received TV news coverage on all three channels (a reasonable definition of what TV news regards as a major strike story) ITN ran the story on average for 6·3 days and BBC 1 for 6·2 days.

An obvious difference between a strike and a settlement is that while the strike usually lasts a number of days, the settlement occurs on only one day. Two other obvious points can be made in defence of settlements getting only 12% of strike coverage. One is that in a sense much of the 'strike' coverage is also 'settlement' coverage – discussions of what terms will settle the strike. A second point is that audiences can be expected to be interested in a big strike for some days in succession, whereas if the settlement produces the end of the strike the audience will not want this news repeated for more than 24 hours. Indeed, since newspaper Editors assume that readers also get news from radio and TV, it can be argued that readers will be interested in press stories on the settlement for less than 24 hours.

In the light of this point the 'not enough news of settlements' criticism perhaps needs re-formulating into a positive demand for retrospective explanatory discussion of the settlement – or in journalistic terms, *feature* (or current affairs) coverage after the strike ends rather than *news* coverage of the settlement.

2.1.3 *Is industrial relations coverage unduly concentrated on a few industries?*
The criticism is made that industrial relations news focuses excessively on a few industries – such as car manufacture – and ignores many others. The Glasgow authors make this particular criticism in extremely severe terms. In the first half of 1975, they report, the motor vehicle industry – with 2·1% of the labour force – received a quarter of all industrial coverage on the TV news. Just three industries – motor vehicles, transport and public administration – received three-quarters of the industrial disputes coverage over a 22-week period.

The McQuail content analysis, which deals with the whole of the same year, 1975, rather than the first 22 weeks, finds a similar but less extreme pattern in the press.

Table 2.1

Percentage of all national newspaper strike coverage devoted to two industries, 1975

Industry	National Newspapers Percentage of all strike items	Percentage of working days lost	Percentage of working population
Vehicles	29	19	3
Transport and Communications	29	7	7
Two Industries Combined	58	26	10

Source: McQuail, op cit, p 131.

370

Table 2.1 shows that two industries accounted in 1975 for 58% of national newspaper strike items but only 26% of national working days lost and 10% of the working population.

Such figures can be regarded as evidence of excessive concentration on a few industries. But they can be defended on the grounds that these industries did account for one-quarter of 'days lost', because news must inevitably focus on something, and because these industries are well-known, affect consumers and workers in other industries, and can reasonably be regarded as key industries.

2.1.4 *Do the unions get a fair say in industrial relations coverage?*
Once again the Glasgow authors argue very forcibly that the actual nature of coverage favours management against workers. One example they quote is that managers are usually interviewed talking quietly and articulately in offices or studios, whereas strikers or workers are accosted at the factory gates and are often inaudible.

The press has no exact equivalent of television's craving for pictures of 'all the news that moves'. Nor can the argument that trade unions don't get a fair 'say' be justified on the press evidence. A more valid criticism might be that trade union spokesmen incriminate themselves by their own attributed statements. Of all 'participants' in national daily press industrial relations stories 32% were union officials, 5% TUC spokesmen and 4% shop stewards or convenors – 41% in all; in contrast government and official spokesmen contributed 24% of participants, while managers and employers made up only 13%. Trade Union officials bulk even larger among those whose words are quoted in the press. And in 1975 all of the four most frequently named participants were trade union leaders; among the ten people most frequently named, seven were union leaders, three were Cabinet ministers, and none employers (McQuail op. cit., p 141). Industrial relations is thus presented in the press as an activity engaged in firstly by union leaders, and secondly by government spokesmen, while managers and employers remain relatively anonymous in the background.

2.1.5 *Is industrial relations presented as being primarily a national or a local phenomenon?*
The evidence here is perhaps not very clear cut. In the national press (as TV) national union leaders are very prominent, but they are often presented in relation to local disputes. A content analysis of London editions of national newspapers cannot reveal what industrial relations coverage the same national newspapers carry in the editions which reach the north of England.

The McQuail content study does contain useful data on the provincial dailies. Provincial morning newspapers do, it seems, give a little more of their industrial relations coverage to national than to non-national coverage. This is perhaps to be expected in view of the general character of provincial mornings and their dependence on the Press Association. But provincial evenings give a roughly opposite weighting – some 60% of their industrial relations news being regional or local. Since the evenings have bigger circulations, provincial newspaper readers do receive a quite heavily non-national view of industrial relations.

2.1.6 *Comparisons with financial coverage*
One criticism is that industrial relations coverage gives a less full and much less sympathetic view of trade unions than the financial coverage provides about management. In terms of sheer space in the press it is difficult to argue about

this in the case of national quality dailies, national Sundays and provincial morning newspapers. In these more serious publications industrial relations gets slightly more space than in the popular press, but this is enormously outweighed by financial and economic coverage which gets from four to nine times as much space.

The data in Table 2.2 emphasise that it does make a tremendous difference which combination of papers you read, as to what balance of industrial relations and financial news is offered to you. In particular anyone strongly sympathetic to trade unions who reads one national quality daily and one provincial morning will find, on average, his industrial relations news outweighed seven times by the space given to financial and economic news. Local and regional trade union leaders tend do to read just this combination of newspapers.

Table 2.2

Percentage of all editorial space devoted to industrial relations and financial/economic coverage

	4 National Quality Dailies	4 National Popular Dailies	7 National Sundays	17 Provincial Mornings (Eng, Sc, Wales)	12 Provincial Evenings (Eng, Sc, Wales)
	%	%	%	%	%
Industrial Relations	3·1	2·5	0·8	2·4	2·0
Financial/ Economic	28·5	2·3	4·2	9·4	2·5

Source: McQuail, op cit.

2.1.7 *Is industrial relations news excessively uniform?*
One of the most commonly repeated themes in the McQuail content analysis is that industrial relations coverage appears to operate on a set of news values very uniformly held between otherwise very different newspapers. The Glasgow authors repeatedly make the same point as between television channels and they also confirm that TV news values for industrial relations stories are similar to those exhibited by the national press and the Press Association. How this uniformity comes about is discussed in the next subsection but one.

2.2 Major strikes and the role of the press

Whether or not Britain is really unusually strike-prone, there have been some big strikes since 1970 and one miners' strike has been used by a Prime Minister as the occasion for calling a General Election (an election which he lost). Some of these unusually big strikes – like dramatic news stories in other fields – may play a special part in the view which people have both of industrial relations and of industrial relations coverage. Another reason for looking at them is that some of the sparse literature on industrial relations press coverage happens to take this form.

2.2.1 *The Engine Tuners' strike at BLMC in early 1975*
This lasted for one month. As described by the Glasgow authors (who recorded the relevant materials on videotape) the television news coverage of both BBC and ITN was unfairly critical of the tuners; their argument as to the unfairness of this coverage rests heavily upon the 'Ryder Report' published later in 1975

which put the blame for many of BLMC's ills, including strikes and other stoppages, on mismanagement.

2.2.2 The Ford Halewood Strike of March–April 1971

This strike lasted nine weeks and accounted for 2 million 'striker days'. Richard Hyman, a lecturer in Industrial Relations from Warwick University, lists several aspects of the strike which are of broader relevance. The strike was unofficial throughout, although it had the obvious sympathy of national and local full-time Union (TGWU and AEUW) officials. The strike, according to Hyman, could only be understood as part of a struggle for control over shop-floor conditions. And 'the "quality" press was unanimous that the Halewood stoppage was provoked by management action'. According to Hyman, however, 'the "populars" virtually ignored the dispute – perhaps because it could not readily be presented in terms of the stereotype of "wildcat" action by "greedy" workers'.[1]

Another author in a full length book on the same strike says that a weekly strike bulletin was produced at Dagenham and less frequent bulletins at the other Ford sites – Swansea, Halewood and Leamington. But:

'The fact is that throughout the strike communications were poor. Union leaders and shop stewards talked to the rank and file almost exclusively through the Press and television – media over which they had no control.'[2]

But the great complexity of these events is illustrated by the fact that a third independent authority has a somewhat different view.[3]

2.2.3 The Pilkington Strike of April–May 1970

This strike lasted seven weeks. The book on the strike[4] is unusual in several ways. It is perhaps the most detailed account of a recent British strike; and its

---

1 Richard Hyman, Strikes, Collins/Fontana, 1972, pp 16, 152.

2 John Matthews, Ford Strike: the Workers' Story, Panther, 1972, pp 115–16.

3 This view comes from Dr Robert Houlton, a well-known writer and broadcaster on industrial relations (and a former journalist), who was a lecturer at Liverpool University at the time. Dr Houlton writes:
'I am unhappy about the quote from Hyman. There were two strikes at Halewood during 1971 separated by a couple of days. The first was the strike over "parity" with the "other car workers" which was the culmination of a long campaign by the shop stewards and by the T&GWU (which published the wage claim as a leaflet and distributed it on the shop floor). When the workers heard of the management response to the claim (which they felt was just) they began walking out of the factory – often with the shop stewards pleading with them to come back and at least hold a meeting. This strike was settled by Jones and Scanlon outside the normal bargaining machinery meeting the management and agreeing a deal which was then put to the whole of the membership via a postal ballot. When the workers returned to Halewood they faced a concerted attempt by the lower ranks of management to "take on" the shop stewards and demonstrate their control (remember the Jones/Scanlon deal had been a blow to the shop stewards who felt that they had been stabbed in the back). The result was one steward, John Dillon, was sacked and after an initial hesitation the whole of the Halewood plant went out on strike again. This was the strike about control over shop floor conditions.
The coverage of the populars was not as Hyman maintains tantamount to ignoring the disputes – and the Sunday Times, Financial Times, The Times and The Guardian were, in my memory, quite favourable to the workers' claims especially in light of Ford's need for a stoppage to sort the Cortina Mk III production line out in Dagenham. The World in Action team did an extremely favourable programme about the stoppage . . . and it was brought to the public notice that Ford was a multinational and might be pursuing policies which were not in the interest of the host community!
I would dispute Matthews' claim that communications through the strike were poor. In Liverpool mass meetings were held at the stadium and given considerable coverage by local radio. But many of the workers realised that they were in for a long strike – as a result the rank and file would propose that the next meeting should be held "in two months' time" rather than the week or fortnight that the shop stewards proposed.'

4 Tony Lane and Kenneth Roberts, Strike at Pilkingtons, Collins/Fontana, 1971.

authors pay special attention to the press coverage. The authors make no secret of their sympathy for the Rank and File Strike Committee and their hostility towards both Pilkington and the main relevant Union (the GMWU) at the national level. The authors are especially critical of the then General Secretary of the GMWU (Lord Cooper) and its then national industrial officer responsible for the glass industry – David Basnett; however they have taken some trouble also to look at the strike from Mr Basnett's point of view and even manage – among the many barbs – a few words of praise. The study is exceptional in one key respect – these authors actually used crude surveys to monitor the evolution of opinion among the strikers as the strike progressed. These surveys reveal that the shifts in opinion were continuous yet subtle and illustrate the appalling difficulties of anyone's knowing what is really happening during a strike in terms of opinion among the strikers. The authors preface their highly partisan, but perceptive, observations on the press as follows: 'The press generally was not popular with any of the "generals" during the strike'. The GMWU did not praise any papers, while Pilkingtons and the Rank and File Strike Committee both liked the *Financial Times* and disliked the popular press:

'None of the papers were *openly* hostile towards the strikers, and needless to say none of them were favourably disposed either . . . One paper, *The Guardian*, came very near to supporting the strikers – without actually expressing support in so many words. Several, the *Daily Express*, the *Daily Sketch* and *The Sun*, came very near to open hostility without actually expressing it either.

Yet despite the leanings of some reporters, despite the editorial policies of the different papers, all of the press without exception managed to convey the impression that the whole thing was really rather lamentable . . . The industrial status quo, in other words, always came out on top. This of course should not surprise anyone for the press itself is part of the status quo . . . Strikes are never written about from the point of view of the striker. It may be that from time to time a pay claim is seen as justified and that the press is unanimous in this view, but a strike in its pursuit is nevertheless regarded as a matter for regret . . . As the press is presently constituted there is not much joy in it for the striker – the most he can hope for is the strained neutrality of papers such as *The Financial Times* . . ..

In a strike where the war is waged with words between people who are not speaking to each other, the press assumes a crucial role . . . But the press was more than a 'despatch rider' lathering from Ghent to Aix (or from Pilks head office to the RFSCHQ in the Cotham Arms) for the despatch rider had a mind of his own . . . Since the press was the main bearer of first hand news, the way in which it presented its news had very real consequences for the way people thought and hence for the course of the strike.

One particular aspect of press coverage particularly incensed both Pilkingtons and the RFSC – the massive coverage given to 'violence on the picket lines' in the fifth and seventh weeks of the strike. Both were incensed because they thought it to have been blown up out of all proportion – though for different reasons. The firm because they thought it deterred a lot of people from returning to work; the RFSC because they thought it brought discredit upon them and branded them as 'thugs' and 'hooligans'.

There might well have been something in Pilkingtons' views. In the sixth week when we conducted our survey we asked all those who favoured a return to work (54%) why they had not done so. Well over half of these (63%) gave reasons such as 'fear', 'afraid of violence', 'afraid for my family' etc. Some eight days previous to these answers the *Daily Mirror* (more widely read in St Helens than any other national daily) was producing headlines: STRIKERS IN BIG CLASH AS SHIFT ENDS (6 May) and STRIKEBREAKERS BEATEN BY FEAR (7 May) . . ..

Right wing papers have left wing reporters and vice-versa . . . some reporters are more prone to sub-editing than others; some papers sub-edit more than others; some reporters are more sympathetic to one side or another than other reporters. Indeed during the strike different reporters writing for the same paper leaned one way or another to such an extent that the apparent 'line' of the paper could vary from day to day . . ..

The 'generals' – the RFSC, the GMWU, and Pilkingtons – were probably much more selective in the way they looked at the press than was the rank and file striker – they read the 'pops' to get some indication of how the 'general public' were being informed, and read the 'heavies' for their own information.

The 'heavies' were relied upon not only because they tended to give fairly full accounts of what the parties had said and done, but also because they presented the story in an unemotional manner . . ..

A reading of the 'heavy' features by the RFSC allowed them, with some justification to conclude that on the whole they came out of it rather well . . . Pilkingtons did rather less well . . . The GMWU came off worst of all for hardly any commentator at any time could find a good word for it . . .

The feature writers in the 'heavies' were usually experienced industrial reporters . . . If we did not always accept their judgments we had at least to accept that they were reasoned. The RFSC took a similar view and consequently took them seriously.'[1]

Lane and Roberts in discussing the press coverage of the Pilkington strike confine their remarks almost entirely to the coverage of the national press – presumably because they, like it, are aiming at a national audience. The national newspapers to which they are referring are in most cases Manchester editions.

St Helens happens to be on the edge of the circulation areas of four evenings – based in Manchester, Liverpool, Preston and Bolton;[2] the authors themselves clearly preferred the coverage of the Labour reporter of the Preston-based *Lancashire Evening Post*. In most strike situations a single local evening will have easily the highest circulation among the strikers.

What general conclusions can one draw from these case studies of strikes?

(a) Not all strike coverage is hostile to strikers. The quality papers in general and *The Financial Times* and *The Guardian* in particular and Granada television programmes have, at least in some major strikes, been favourable to the strikers. These papers may be favourable to the strikers but hostile to the national Union; and in the Pilkington case the GMWU might accuse the journalists of having unreasonably encouraged the strikers to the point of setting up a breakaway union – but without warning them that breakaway unions in Britain almost invariably wither.

---

1 Tony Lane and Kenneth Roberts, op cit, pp 71–82.
2 According to ENAB, the *Liverpool Echo* sells the most copies in St Helens.

(*b*) The press is much more important than television during the life of a long strike because the press covers it day by day, whereas television only swoops down occasionally in pursuit of dramatic film coverage.

(*c*) In a strike situation the employers, the strikers and the national union communicate with each other to a considerable extent via the editorial columns, over which they have no direct control. Because it can give a lot of space to a local event the local daily must be important – and presumably the less the strike interests the nationals the more crucial is the coverage of the local daily.

(*d*) All the 'generals' in a strike face the same dilemma as do British politicians – they do not have their own media.

(*e*) While it is obviously naïve to attribute strikes simply to poor 'communications', the Pilkington case does suggest that at least one popular newspaper exaggerated 'violent' incidents in a manner which may have protracted the strike.

(*f*) In a strike the key piece of information is what the strikers think and this is something which none of the 'generals', nor the press, knows.

2.3 Labour correspondents

The uniformity of news values which operate in any specialist field of journalism is largely channelled through, and partly shaped by, the specialist group of journalists in question.

There are some reasons why the specialist group of correspondents may in this particular case be especially influential in collectively shaping the kind of news which appears about the field in question. These reasons include the following:

(i) In contrast to other important and high status fields of news, in this case Editors of national newspapers have little alternative to relying on their correspondents. In foreign news there are high status news agencies, whereas in Fleet Street eyes the PA service carries low status. In national politics Editors have political experts in addition to lobby correspondents (such as leader writers), there are other relevant specialists, and some Editors have their own political sources. This is not so in industrial news.

(ii) Public relations personnel are relatively unimportant in this field, making it difficult for other journalists to cover the field casually.

(iii) Personal relations between journalists and sources are unusually important, partly because trade union leaders are their own professional trouble shooters and PROs.

(iv) Industrial news is more unpredictable on more days of the year than is the case in most fields of news – and the more unpredictable an event, the more it fits with definitions of news broadly held by all journalists.

(v) In these circumstances industrial relations correspondents are more dependent upon each other than is the case in most other fields; this dependence involves small and large acts of colleaguely help, as well as dependence upon the collective group decision as to what the main stories and 'angles' are on any particular day.

(vi) Since the main actors in this field, the Trade Union leaders, are themselves professional crisis managers for whom the current ranking of most urgent crises is largely carried out by the media, it is improbable that any rival definition of news values can prevail. News editors and Editors are also dependent on the same collective operation of news values.

(vii) This is not to suggest that correspondents cynically create the news or conspire as to what is most important. They tend to agree anyway because on any single day news values held in common usually point to one or two obvious stories. But if any single correspondent wants to escape this collective decision he cannot easily do so.

Since colleague behaviour between journalists probably impinges here in an extreme form it is worth looking at how these correspondents work. The data relate to 1968 and have not appeared before in this detail.[1]

Although called Labour (or industrial) correspondents these journalists only devoted 75% of their time to labour news, the rest going to national and economic planning and to the Labour Party – they traditionally cover the Labour Party's annual conference and its NEC meetings, because of the prominence of leading trade unionists in both cases. As seen by other specialists, the labour field has the third highest status – after foreign and lobby correspondence. This was the most overwhelmingly pro-Labour among the specialist fields apart from the Education correspondents.

The majority of these journalists would advise a son to enter journalism. Like other specialists their main experience of tension at work was in dealing with their own employing office and not with their news sources. They all belonged to the NUJ but thought it had only a little beneficial impact on their work. The majority thought the Press Council had 'no impact' at all on their work.

The average labour specialist was aged in his late thirties – it was the youngest of the higher status fields. About half had continued full-time education beyond age 19 – somewhat more education than specialists overall. Few had ever worked in the major provincial centres of Manchester or Glasgow, while about half had started on weekly newspapers in the South of England. Thirty was the average age for becoming a national labour specialist; most had been general reporters. Almost all had done some labour reporting before becoming full-blown specialists, and on average they had had 'fairly strong' previous interest in the field.

Labour correspondents thought themselves to the left of their newspapers, but nearly as many thought 'about the same' or 'depends on the issue'. Any picture of the labour specialists being far to the left of other journalists is not accurate; but national Editors expected labour specialists to be to the left. Like most other specialists they were fairly definite that they would be free *not* to write a particular story (although of course someone else might be willing, or agency copy could be used). With somewhat less unanimity they denied being restricted from writing stories they favoured.

The typical labour specialist spent 'half to three-quarters' of his time in his office in London; he found the coverage (space) given to his field by his paper 'satisfactory' but not 'very satisfactory'. Some 80% of stories were initiated by the correspondents themselves (typically working in a team of two or three in the case of a national daily) and about 80% of copy produced appeared in print although a few said that only half or less was used. Most thought the level of seriousness of their output about right, while some thought it not quite serious enough. (The latter response might get more support today.) Labour

---

1 These data are taken from questionnaires completed by 23 national Labour correspondents for the study which resulted in: Jeremy Tunstall, *Journalists at Work*, London, Constable, 1971.

377

specialists worked for and talked to their news desks daily but only spoke to the Editor 'weekly or monthly'. They claimed to work about 50 hours a week. Their busiest time of day for morning paper men was 5 to 7 pm – making them (along with Crime specialists) the second latest of the home news fields. This is in line with the 'hard news' reputation of the field.

Labour was not one of the better paid specialist fields – and combining salary, expenses and extra earnings it was the second lowest renumerated of all the specialist fields (Education, a young field, being the lowest). It was especially poorly endowed with opportunities for extra earnings – labour men complained that there were plenty of extra writing offers but mainly from Union publications short of funds!

In terms of contact with their audience, each labour specialist received only four letters from readers a week – the lowest figure for any domestic news field. But half the Labour specialists said they had at some time seen some readership research.

Their most time consuming activities went in this order:
1 Telephoning sources.
2 Writing stories.
3 Dealing with documents, reading material.
4 Interviewing sources.
5 Talking to other journalists.
6 Communal meetings with sources, press conferences.

Their reported level of 18 telephone calls made and 8 received per day was fairly typical of specialists in general. The picture of the labour men tethered to their desks is also supported by their pattern of travel or non-travel. They were, apart from the Lobby, one of the most London-bound of all the domestic fields – with only 34 days a year spent in the provinces. Much even of this time was spent at seaside conferences of big Unions and the Labour Party. The labour men had spent only ten working days abroad – also a low figure for specialists at large.

Like other specialists, most labour men thought there were certain 'key individuals' in their fields but there was not any single especially powerful source. Most said that there was only 'a little' payment to news sources – and only then in special cases such as an unofficial strike group which claimed to need the money for basic operating expenses. Labour men thought that the major decisions in their field were 'sometimes' made by civil servants – an indication of the significance of economic planning, and perhaps nationalised industries, in their work.

They received about 20 separate pieces of unsolicited material through the mail each day – some of this would be Union journals and the like but formal PR was also involved. In 1968 in fact the Ministry of Labour's PRO had an extremely vigorous style (and a legendary reputation) which included as well as literature sent by mail and messenger, much telephoning through the day to inform correspondents of late developments in negotiations.

The labour men found themselves attending about three press conferences or briefings per week; most of these were semi-public on-the-record affairs but there were also regular 'not for attribution' meetings for instance with the TUC chairman.

The labour men concentrated very heavily on national negotiations – so that when they did venture out onto the street it would be the street outside a Union headquarters in the Euston Road, London, rather than the backstreets of Derby. They spent a fair amount of time waiting for such meetings to break up or in going to interview national or regional union leaders involved in negotiations. Quite often they subsequently had a drink across the street with Union men – much less often with the management side. This appeared to be the group of specialists who consumed the most drink in the line of duty.

Labour specialists are heavy readers of the serious parts of other newspapers – after their own field they read news from the Lobby, then foreign news, then financial and diplomatic. Even fields like Education and Aviation received attention because they have labour 'angles'. All specialists were asked to rate the seriousness of competition provided by the other publication. The labour specialists in 1968 collectively ranked the national labour coverage in terms of quality in this order:

1	The Guardian
2	The Times
2	Financial Times
2	Daily Express
5	Daily Mail
5	The Daily Telegraph
7	The Sun
8	Morning Star
8	Sunday Telegraph
10	Daily Mirror
10	Daily Sketch
10	Evening Standard
10	The Observer
10	The Sunday Times

As with other aspects of these data, the precise order would, some years later, undoubtedly be different. But it is much less likely that there would have been any change in two aspects shown here: Firstly the national journalists covering this field have the most respect for the coverage of the more *serious* newspapers. Secondly the field is seen very much in terms of *daily* coverage.

Labour journalism had a reputation among other journalists as one in which a great deal of co-operation occurred between competitors. Almost all the labour specialists were prepared to state that they were competing against such a partnership of journalists on two or more papers. Since all of the relevant personnel have now changed there is no harm in revealing that *The Times* number one man worked with an opposite number on the *Financial Times*; *The Times* number two worked with the *Daily Mail*. It is also no secret that *Financial Times* and *Guardian* journalists have over the years often worked together in various fields including this one. This kind of arrangement is inevitably known by some news sources because they see things said to one paper popping up elsewhere as well. In the labour field there could be some anxiety about *Financial Times* and *Guardian* co-operation when it is remembered that these two apparently divergent papers, which carry a heavy responsibility in some highly charged industrial relations situations, may in practice be just one journalist.

The general atmosphere among labour journalists was claimed by them to be harmonious. Relations with news sources can never be totally harmonious especially since news sources often are vying with each other for publicity; moreover this is a field in which, as one labour specialist put it, 'you taste blood'. But the labour journalists in general describe their relations with Union leaders as friendly, even if tinged with some caution. Of course while the national labour man is chatting to the General Secretary in London, 'our Midlands correspondent' may be reporting an unofficial strike meeting in Coventry.

All the labour journalists were men and most lived in the outer London suburbs. The majority did not invite their news informants to their homes; like other specialists they normally had two days off each week – on one of which they were 'on call', usually for telephone consultation only. They were somewhat less likely than most specialists to say their friends were other journalists – nevertheless about *one-third* of their friends were journalists and if other communications occupations were included this raised the level to about *one-half* of all friends. Whether this is a high level is once more a matter of opinion; but clearly their London commuter life style was much closer to that of a full-time national level Union official than to the shop steward in Leeds.

Labour journalism is slightly unusual in one final respect. This is a field which quite a lot of journalists leave before the age of 40. There was a big turnover before 1968, and a big one has occurred since. This seems to happen because – more than in most specialist fields – the journalists want to leave and there are other jobs available to them. They want to leave partly because there is a widespread attitude that this is not a field to stay in all one's life. Other jobs on offer have included a number of very senior PRO jobs in the public sector especially; some labour journalists move over into political journalism or foreign correspondence and become star columnists or feature writers. Others become news executives or MPs. But one job that few take on is being PRO to a trade union.

3 Uses of, and attitudes towards, Industrial relations news

3.1 The general public

The SCPR survey on the General Public and its attitudes to the Provincial Press[1] contains information on attitudes to press coverage of industrial relations. The conventional wisdom of journalists – that most people are not very interested in industrial relations until they are inconvenienced in some way – receives substantial support in this survey. Only 16% of respondents said they were 'very' interested in news about trade union affairs – this placed trade unions ninth on a list of eleven selected topics in terms of reader interest (p 37). A higher proportion were interested in news about 'business and industry' (p 37). Amongst those 'very' or 'fairly' interested in trade union news – nearly half the sample – television was regarded as the most important source, with national morning newspapers a close second, and local evening papers well behind. The press was thought relatively more important in the case of 'business and industry' news (p 33).

The readers of provincial evenings were the group of readers most likely to say they looked at news about 'local trade union affairs', but much higher proportions looked at news about the local Council, and other news categories in the local evening (p 46).

Overall the general public sample perceived the provincial press as being a little biased to the Conservative side (p 69). But this diversion from neutrality is seen as quite small. Asked specifically what they would expect papers to do 'when employers and unions disagree', the usual expectation is of 'both sides' being fully given. Twenty per cent of provincial evening readers and 42% of local weekly paper readers said their paper 'does not print much at all' on such matters (p 76). The public in general does not think that either side in industrial disputes gets more space. There is one exception: 'Very strong Labour' supporters (less than a third of all Labour supporters) are somewhat inclined to think provincial evenings favour the employers – but even among this highly partisan group only 23% hold such a view.

There is, then, in this survey strong evidence against the view that the general public, or even a sizeable minority of it, think that Unions are unfairly treated in the press.

3.2 Community influentials

The SCPR survey on local 'Influentials' presents an interestingly different picture. 'News about local trade union activities' is the one topic that is quite frequently mentioned by members of all groups as being treated badly by the provincial press (p 219).

---

1 See *Attitudes to the Press* Cmnd 6810–3.

This is a very important finding, because these local influentials are in a good position to observe the local press – as readers and as prominent people locally whose own activities are reported. On the subject of trade union coverage they (leaving aside the trade union influentials) are an unusually independent set of observers, who collectively combine this independence with an unusually high level of sophisticated knowledge of the local press. The sample contains 51 Councillors, 52 Council officials, 97 managing directors, 100 local trade union secretaries and 50 head teachers of local schools.

All groups of influentials are heavy readers of both the national and provincial press. They tend to find the local press reasonably good but they also have some scepticism about it. Most topics are considered to be at least fairly well covered in the local press, with local trade union affairs being the main exception. The influentials collectively think the provincial evenings (in contrast to mornings) and local weeklies are least good at covering 'news of local trade union activities' (p 196).

From a list of seven topics, 'news of local trade union activities' was chosen by easily the highest percentage of the whole sample as being 'very badly' or 'fairly badly' covered by the provincial press. *Higher proportions of both Council officials and Managing-directors chose trade unions affairs as being badly covered than chose any other topic.* Trade union secretaries shared this view. This was also the topic chosen by the second highest proportion among Councillors and Head teachers.

Table 3.1.

Provincial Press treatment of particular topics

Proportion of papers treating topic very badly or fairly badly	Managing Directors %	Council Officials %	All Influentials %
News of local Trade Union activities ...	25	26	36
News of local industrial disputes ...	19	14	17
Activities of Conservative Party on Council	9	14	12
Activities of Labour Party on Council...	8	17	19
News of local industry	12	10	13
Local educational matters	10	10	16
Local town redevelopment	7	10	11

Source: SCPR Influentials, p 197.

The level of dissatisfaction is not dramatic, but when managing-directors, council officials and local trade union secretaries agree to this extent in their criticism, it is worth considering what precisely the complaint is. The complaint is not primarily about coverage of *disputes* – criticism of disputes coverage is much less than for coverage of 'local trade union activities'. Nor is the criticism about 'news of local industry'.

The complaint primarily concerns lack of general coverage of local trade unions. It is not that disputes as such should be covered any differently, but that there should be more general coverage. Asked about which single topic out of seven topics was worst treated, much the highest figure (29%) for any single topic went to 'news of local trade union activities' (p 197). And of reasons given for this, the overwhelming leader among a list of eight was 'insufficient coverage' – given by 52% of those making any criticism (p 198).

Answers to other questions give some clues as to how this perceived lack of coverage comes about. The local trade union secretaries, from their own replies, emerge as the least active of all the five groups of influentials in themselves approaching the local papers:

'The trade union secretaries were the least likely of all groups to have any contact with the regional evening papers and were also more likely to talk to them only when approached' (p 199).

Trade union secretaries when they do have contact with the local press are likely to contact a journalist, whereas managing directors are more likely to contact the Editor (p 201). Local trade union secretaries are much less likely to issue press statements than are council officials or managing directors (p 201). Although trade union secretaries were critical of press accuracy and especially of biased editing (p 207), they were relatively reluctant to complain (p 208).

By all of the influential groups – including managing directors – the local press is seen either as neutral or as Conservative; 35% of the managing directors see the local dailies as Conservative, while only 5% see them as Labour (p 218). Council officials, head teachers and Councillors, to very similar extents, also see the local dailies as either neutral or Conservative. Local press comments on disagreements between employers and unions were seen by all influential groups, except managing directors, to be either neutral or to favour the employers (p 221).

Altogether, then, the accusation against the local press in the trade union field is not one of major bias – although the general influentials' view is that there is some bias. The main sin is believed to be a sin of omission. And although the other influentials do not offer any explanation for this sin of omission, what appears to happen is that local trade union leaders lack public relations support and do not themselves actively supply news to the local press; moreover what the local union leaders do not supply, the local press insufficiently (as seen in the criticism) seeks out.

3.3 Local Trade Union officials and members

The trade union 'influentials' were mainly district or divisional secretaries from the thirty largest British trade unions. Their experience of the local press can be compared with a survey carried out in the Yorkshire area in 1968[1]. They obtained information from 714 trade unionists in just four unions – the Engineers, GMWU, NALGO and SOGAT. The sample included members, shop stewards, local branch officials and full-time officers (including nearly all the full-time officers of these unions in Yorkshire). This study reveals a very different pattern of media use between full-time officials and the other three categories; in terms of attitudes towards media coverage the shop stewards and branch officials are relatively close to the membership at large, while full-time officials hold very much more critical views, especially of the press.

The full-time officials are shown to adopt a much more typically middle-class pattern of media use than are the others. In contrast to the shop stewards, the full-time officials are more likely to choose *The Sun* (then still operated by IPC under terms agreed with the TUC) and to read a quality paper, especially *The Guardian*. The officials watch TV less and, when they do watch, favour BBC more; they are more attached to the radio news. There is a paradox in the attitudes which go with this behaviour. The media which the officials follow,

---

1 Blumler and Ewbank, op cit.

(with the possible exception of the BBC) seem to many other observers to be on the whole more favourable to the Unions than are the media followed by the stewards. But whereas criticism from the other Union levels is confined mainly to press coverage of strikes, the full-time officials differed radically in also thinking that the entire press (but not TV) is anti-Union.

The full-time officials were almost certainly more aware of the whole range of the press – including the quality papers and their financial pages. In searching the financial pages for information to be used in negotiations with managements, the full-time officials may well have come to see the press at large as pro-management. They may have found television relatively uncritical partly because they didn't watch it so much and did not *study* it for Union purposes.

It would be interesting to have comparable information for Union officials at the national level. But clearly they will be much less likely to read a local (non-London) evening of the kind which exists in all provincial cities. It is also fairly safe to predict that national Union officials will be heavy readers of the press, especially the quality press such as *The Guardian* and *Financial Times*. National union leaders based in London will read *London* editions of the nationals. In view of their long irregular hours, their fireman functions, and their

Table 3.2

Yorkshire shop stewards, full-time union officials and the media 1968

PRESS	Shop Stewards %	Full-time Officials %	Branch Officials %	Members %
Read Local Evening	71	68	76	74
Read *Daily Express*	31	18	25	28
Read *The Sun*	17	42	24	11
Read *The Guardian, The Daily Telegraph* and *The Times*	7	45	10	7
Read quality Sunday	18	68	16	14
BROADCAST	%	%	%	%
Light TV viewer or no TV ...	19	47	30	22
Watch mainly BBC TV	24	44	16	19
Watch TV news most evenings ...	56	32	47	56
Hear radio news most days ...	58	71	57	48
ATTITUDES	%	%	%	%
Press is anti-Union...	29	68	35	21
Television is anti-Union	17	16	12	10
Press is either unbiased or pro-Union	57	26	55	52
Television is either unbiased or pro-Union	75	71	75	72
Press gives strikes too much attention	51	68	67	49
Television gives strikes too much attention	30	26	35	35
Number of respondents	235	38	51	360

Source: Jay Blumler and Alison Ewbank, op cit.

propensity to travel to crisis situations, they may follow more radio (which carries the latest news) and less television to an even greater extent than do regional Union officials. Thus national Union officials will inhabit a different sort of media world from their members and shop stewards. Moreover national union officials deal directly with the media and thus become – somewhat like politicians – themselves semi-professional media men. But this deep involvement will be largely confined to contact with selected press journalists and the personnel of a limited range of broadcast programmes. With this intimate and involved knowledge of certain sectors of journalism may go the attitude – often expressed by politicians also – that 'the media are fair to me personally but unfair more broadly about the the causes I represent'.

4 Differing diagnoses and solutions

4.1 National/local and other paradoxes

One of the reasons why people find it so difficult to change each other's minds about any aspect of the press is that the press has always been fundamentally to do with politics. If journalism at large is rooted in politics this is even more so of Labour journalism. It is inevitable, consequently, that Labour journalism must be controversial, ambiguous, seen through political spectacles.

All political dramas in democratic countries have a media sub-plot. Think of any major political drama concerning an American President or a British Prime Minister and you think also of its accompanying media sub-plot. The reason is quite simple. A major political drama is only such because it puts in question the loyalty of political supporters. Since voters receive their national political information almost entirely via the media it is impossible for this source – or these sources – of information not to be sucked into the controversy. Members of the public observing the political drama through spectacles of a particular political tint also receive a tinted view of the media which carry the messages.

Nor is there anything unusual within journalism in the national Labour correspondent's concern with the national political end of industrial relations. Most fields of serious journalism are really the 'Politics of . . . ' aviation, education, etc. Moreover whether or not the 'formal system' of industrial relations has become increasingly 'unreal', national Trade Union leaders have in the last 40 or 50 years become increasingly involved in formulating national economic policy. And if you regard Labour correspondents in the national press as Trade Union Leader correspondents – which is what they have perhaps always been – then it could be argued that they should be covering the ('real') political and economic planning activities of trade union leaders rather than their (somewhat less 'real') industrial relations activities.

But if national Labour correspondents have become slightly less involved in industrial relations coverage, the regionally based correspondents now almost certainly do substantially more industrial relations coverage than was the case 30 years ago. This has several aspects:

1 Even on the national newspapers regionally based correspondents probably do more of the industrial relations coverage than they used to, because of the increase in *unofficial* strikes in the postwar period and the relative absence of the old set-piece planned official strike (which was more common in times when wages were being cut).

2 There has been a massive increase in regional television and radio news, which includes coverage of labour relations in the main local industries. The local press has to compete.

387

3   There has been a substantial increase in the number of labour specialists on provincial dailies. The tide of specialisation is running quite fast on these papers and in the urban settings upon which most provincial dailies (evenings especially) concentrate the industrial field is – after local politics – an obvious field for specialisation. On provincial mornings there is a labour element in the increased financial and business coverage. Another possible reason is pressure from the advertising department for news relevant to lucrative job advertising.[1]

But perhaps most importantly the provincial dailies have undergone a revolution in make-up, so that some look as good as popular nationals. Now they are starting to try to read as well as popular nationals; and industrial relations news is – after local politics which has been transformed and which Fleet Street does not understand – one most obvious field in which they can try to beat the Fleet Street populars.

4   While Fleet Street has been cutting back on journalists in general the provincial dailies have been building up (fuelled with their larger and larger share of advertising revenue) in several fields of which industrial relations is one. Consequently there is now a supply in each main region of correspondents and stringers who know about local industry and labour.

Thus in some respects we may be already getting industrial relations coverage which conforms reasonably well with reality as described by Donovan. The bulk of the population gets its *industrial relations* news from local newspapers and from regional TV and radio, while it gets news of the *national political* doings of trade union leaders in the national newspapers, radio and TV.

What will happen in the future? If Britain moves over to the pattern found in every other significant industrial nation except Japan – and has the bulk of its daily papers produced outside the capital – then, one could argue, the scene will be set for realistic industrial relations coverage in *the* press, which will then be primarily a provincial press.

Nor is this national-local axis the only focus of ambiguity and paradox. Almost every conceivable aspect of the connection between industrial relations and the press is encrusted with paradox:

– Some of the sketchiest trade union coverage occurs in the *Daily Mirror*, a paper notionally friendly to the trade unions, while some of the coverage most respected by trade union leaders occurs in the *Financial Times*.

– The general charge of superficial, sensational and excessively strike-orientated coverage is perhaps most true of broadcasting, but television coverage is regarded by most trade unionist members as fair and objective.

– The most sensational and superficial coverage of all may appear on radio, but this aspect of radio has attracted little research and little criticism.

– One of the most common accusations made by national union leaders is of excessive industrial relations coverage and within it of excessive strike coverage, whereas among local union Secretaries strike coverage is regarded as fair, while the major grievance is the general lack of coverage.

---

1   £75m of recruitment advertising was placed in newspapers in 1975. This was 41% of all classified advertising and the bulk of it went into provincial newspapers. *Advertising Quarterly*, Summer 1976, p 44.

- National union leaders who might appear to get the fullest and most friendly treatment and who read the publications which contain the least superficial coverage are nevertheless those who make the strongest complaints.
- The management side contains equal paradoxes. The CBI at the national level makes the complaint of excessive strike coverage, while local managing directors think that strikes are fairly covered although unions at large are not.
- Nor is the national Civil Service exceptionally consistent in this area. The main public relations effort of the Ministry of Labour was for years devoted to providing journalists with a rapid supply of information about strikes and negotiations. The Treasury, which complains about the unfortunate consequences abroad of excessive strike coverage, makes no systematic attempt to monitor the actual press coverage which occurs abroad. The Treasury press office devotes less than a fifth of its time to the foreign press.[1]

The one conclusion which would clearly be inconsistent with the data collected by the Royal Commission is that there is 'no problem' here. The problem may be poorly stated in the evidence put to the Commission by the trade unions at the national level. The trade union evidence – with the exception of that from one or two of the white collar unions – is badly thought out and argued. But in this respect it does not greatly differ from the CBI's 7 page document with its pleasant, if not too relevant, concluding quotation from the *Areopagitica*.

While one can hardly accept the 'Union Case' one also clearly cannot accept the CBI case.

The problem is that there are so many problems. Apart from the national-local complications just mentioned these problems can be seen from several view points such as:

(a) The National-interest-overseas-implications case

(b) The Trade Unions

(c) Management and business

(d) The press, and other media.

Each viewpoint, since it reveals a somewhat different set of problems, suggests a somewhat different set of solutions. But since there is some overlap in the problems there is some overlap also in the suggested solutions. These solutions broadly are of two kinds: firstly possible structural, legal or other strategic changes. Second, possible changes of a persuasive, tactical or educational kind.

4.2 Overseas repercussions of industrial relations coverage

Does the industrial relations coverage in the British press get taken up and further exaggerated by the press in other lands, with Britain receiving a 'strike prone' reputation abroad? The difficulties in answering such a question are familiar ones: Is the coverage 'excessive' or is it not too brief? Are not foreign correspondents most likely to rely on the serious British newspapers whose industrial relations coverage is regarded by many people as fairly sober and realistic?

Does Britain even have a 'strikeprone' reputation abroad? In the absence of relevant data, it is difficult to know, and thus the discussion tends to fall back on anecdotal evidence. It may be that this used to be the case but is now less so. My own guess would be that the proportion of 'strike prone' coverage

---

1 Interview with Head of Information, HM Treasury, 14 July 1976.

has diminished in the last ten years both in the British press (especially the popular nationals) and in the press coverage of Britain abroad. My own guess would be that Ulster has – ever since the killings began – been the leading focus of foreign news coverage of the UK; in the mid 1970s also the pound may have edged the Trade Unions out as the leading British economic story as reported abroad.

Foreign correspondents based in London must initially find themselves scanning the British media to discover something which will 'grab them in New York' or interest them in Munich or Milan or Marseilles. Like news editors of British nationals based in London scanning what's on offer from the British provinces, foreign correspondents want a story which has drama or violence or some special appeal for the folks back home. In the case of foreign news it has to fit into, or relate to, some kind of existing stereotype. 'Strike-prone' coverage may fit into one stereotype of Britain held in many foreign countries – namely that Britain is a class conscious society. Industrial relations may be the field which offers the best supply of 'events' which can be given this construction.

But in recent years the Ulster troubles have probably on more days in the year supplied events which fit news values in general – violence, death, conflict – but which also fit another stereotype. This is the stereotype of Britian's restless celtic fringe – Britain having lost its Empire is now about to lose its Celts. Moreover there are ethnic and religious factors which give Ulster cultural meaning abroad – the Catholic as underdog appeals to Europeans and Americans in general and may appeal to the Catholic press in Europe, and to the big city press in the Eastern United States in particular. It also seems a fair prediction that Scotland will receive a large and probably increasing share of foreign media coverage of Britain. Even on the general economic front the 'British disease' can be even more easily illustrated through exchange rate stories. The floating of sterling has breathed life into that particular 'machinery of record'.

Many other countries complain that foreign press coverage of them is 'unfair'. There has for many years been a recurring complaint in the United States that foreign coverage portrays the USA as dominated by racial violence, murder and *industrial conflict*.[1] In France there is the complaint that excessive attention is paid to regional separatism, police brutality and industrial strife. In Germany there have been complaints that excessive media attention from abroad has been paid to both right wing and left wing political extremists.

There is a substantial body of evidence to suggest that American political assassinations – not only of the Kennedys but also of Martin Luther King and Malcolm X – have received world wide media coverage beyond almost any other events in recent years and that these events have become known within hours in many parts of the world well beyond the normal reach of mass media; for example these events became known in mountainous areas of Tanzania and Colombia into which word of mouth communication carried them beyond the reach of media in a matter of hours. Such coverage, and such audience interest, could be said to lead to a negative stereotype of the United States which stresses the assassination of political figures.

The position of foreign correspondents in London is, however, different from that of correspondents based in most other world capitals in that London is

---

1 The American complaint about excessive coverage of industrial conflict is made especially against communist media in Eastern Europe and elsewhere.

the home of a dominant *national* press. Although correspondents in Paris have a big capital city press into which to dip they know that the bulk of the circulation goes to non-Parisian papers. Correspondents in Bonn must read newspapers from other cities – such as Frankfurt, Munich and Hamburg; correspondents in Rome read papers originating in Milan and Turin because this is where the two leading Italian dailies are based. But correspondents based in London probably give rather little attention to the British provincial press, especially since they can obtain in London the same non-regionalised Press Association service on which provincial dailies rely for much of their national news.

In policy terms what could be done about this if anything? It might be possible for the Foreign Office, if it so desired, to supply foreign correspondents in London with free copies of, say, the *Yorkshire Post*. Courses could be held about the structure of the British press – emphasizing perhaps such subleties as that, with *Manchester* editions taken into account, even today the majority of British adults' reading of dailies is of dailies published outside London. Such courses might perhaps most effectively be aimed at press relations and newspaper clipping personnel in the London Embassies – since they presumably account for much of the selection process from the British media which ultimately reaches foreign policy makers, and they observe the British press in a more second hand manner than do foreign correspondents based in London.

However, the lack of any *prestige* provincial daily is clearly the obvious reason why foreign correspondents in London will tend to ignore the British provincial media – and the more 'realistic' view of industrial relations[1] and much else which such a paper might provide. But there is no such single obvious choice as the *Manchester Guardian* used to provide. If there is a major switch of emphasis away from Fleet Street towards the provincial dailies, it is safe to predict that one or two provincial dailies will achieve a prestige reputation and the accolade of being read each day by foreign correspondents based in London.

4.3 Union diagnoses and dilemmas

If the problem is seen as one of 'lack of communication' between Union and members or Union and Shop Stewards then presumably the loss of the *Daily Herald* was a loss indeed. Since the TUC is understandably reluctant to launch a new national daily, this kind of concern might best focus upon the fate of Fleet Street papers which may be closing. The *Evening Standard, The Guardian* and *The Observer* are probably all too heavily weighted to the South East and/or ABC readers, to be much use for the purpose. Of the weaker nationals those with the most promising current readership profiles might be the *Sunday People* and the *Daily Express*. The *Daily Express* would probably be the best bet – at perhaps half its present sinking circulation. It would not be essential for the TUC as such to purchase (or launch) a paper. It could be done by a group of Unions and other business interests. Another argument would be that it would be cheaper and preferable to launch a new paper in the wake of Fleet Street deaths – this would presumably bring benefits in terms of manning levels, but the promotional launch costs of a major new publication are usually large in amount and extend long in time.

---

1 For example if one reads the *Yorkshire Post* it is difficult to make the common mistake (made perhaps even by Mr Edward Heath) of regarding the National Union of Mineworkers as a monolithic body. The YP coverage emphasises the Yorkshire miners who are often at odds with NUM national leadership.

If both of the above are regarded as needlessly grandiose or traditional, another option would be to pursue 'sheltered' access to the general media. In view of the legal restrictions on broadcast advertising, without new broadcast legislation this in practice means using the press. The most obvious way of securing this is through advertising – Unions could buy display advertising space or they could use advertising to secure 'special supplements', or the equivalent (gardening column alongside garden product advertising) found in the populars. An obvious benefit of this practice would be that Unions nationally (and regionally) could advertise in local dailies as a routine practice during strikes. This would strengthen the official hand in unofficial strikes – if that is thought desirable. This policy could be pursued by a direct state subsidy to Trade Unions (presumably on a membership basis) either wholly or partly earmarked for advertising purposes. It should be popular with advertising managers in the press.

Of course one basic fact makes co-operation between Unions in this field difficult to achieve. This is the *competitive* element in the relations between Unions – their interests conflict and this is even more obvious in the publicity field than elsewhere. So long as individual Unions give almost all their emphasis to publicising their own Unions, the advantage will tend to lie with the white collar Unions. They are already better at PR, their memberships represent blocks of readership in which the press (and advertisers) are more interested and they are strategically located in the economy, often (as in the case of civil service unions) closely identified with the public good, and able to provide press stories which are highly persuasive. Within the Union movement, then, one way of putting the point is: Are the white collar unions willing to help the manual unions to achieve better publicity?

Within particular unions in most cases the only people who can in practice alter the publicity situation are the General Secretaries or their immediate colleagues. In a typical largish union the General Secretary is a national figure or is at least prominent enough to receive a lot of press and perhaps television coverage. Usually he is supported by a fairly minimal PR apparatus; this concentrates the publicity on him personally; at the regional and branch level press relations efforts are also minimal. At the regional and local level the Union is no match for the large employing organisation which typically has a PR apparatus and also a Chief executive with better access to higher levels of the press than do all but a very few local union spokesmen. (Each region of course has its own famous regional union personalities – the regional officers of one or two unions especially important in the region, but these are 'national' type exceptions to the usual provincial rule). Consequently in status, in negotiations and from day-to-day, many local union officials feel unfairly covered by the local press and powerless – in terms of information, advertising, status, prestige, or press relations skill – to do anything about it. The dilemma for the national leadership, obviously, is that if more effective press relations did exist at the regional or local level, this would to some extent divert publicity and influence in the union away from the centre.

Whatever solution or combination of solutions may be chosen it seems obvious that the national leaders of the largest unions must take the initiative and choose some from the available alternatives:

(a) To set up a major nationally spread press segment owned or controlled in the trade union interest.

(b) To organise various forms of 'sheltered' access into the dominant media.

(c) To engage in a large public relations expansion including the establishment of significant press relations staffs at national and regional, and perhaps even at local, levels.

4.4 Management and business

If the dissatisfaction expressed by the 97 managing directors in the 'influentials' survey is more representative of management than is the CBI's evidence, then management and business overall must consider doing something to ensure better coverage of industrial relations, especially in the provincial press.

The dilemma for management is clearly that if the unions become too effective at press relations this will unduly strengthen their hand in bargaining. But it is presumably in the long term interests of management that unions should be able to express themselves effectively and that they should not be too disillusioned with the dominant forms of mass media. Such disillusion already leads to 'underground' papers of an industrially militant kind and 'new technology' is making these increasingly easy to produce.

'Better communication' will not necessarily solve anything, but in this area several sorts of co-operation might have something to offer. Some areas are:

– Business management overall controls a lot of press space through direct advertising and supplements and also influences heavily through this – and through its predominance in supplying information – most of the financial, business and industrial news. There are many possible ways in which unions could be given a share of this sheltered and semi-sheltered space.

– Press relations activities are an area where management – in both the commercial and public sectors – enormously predominates. Management could lend bits of these facilities to unions and could train union personnel in relevant skills.

– Management could supply funds to unions in some indirect way – for instance via a foundation or educational grants – to improve union expertise in press relations.

– If management deemed it advisable, support could be given to establishing trade union publications – either daily or non-daily, either national or regional. One way of doing this would be for certain organisations to sign long-term advance advertising contracts (on a circulation and inflation linked formula).

But perhaps the strategic decision for management collectively is the extent to which it does or does not wish to cede to the Unions some special kind of legitimacy as a unique interest in the land. It is possible to argue that Unions are just another interest and deserve no special favours. It is possible to disagree and say that the Unions in Britain must be given more effective power (as both Conservative and Labour Governments have at times in the recent past argued) and more legitimacy. In provincial press terms the local Unions might become a 'duty' area of interest – often dull, perhaps, but things which must be given day-to-day coverage because of their unique position and unique legitimacy.

If the 'unique legitimacy' point is granted, then the significance of the media – as special conferrers of legitimacy both nationally and locally – is self-evident. It is the 'legitimacy' step which is not self-evident, a value judgement which management must consider.

393

Another way of putting the same point is to consider which areas of national political and economic life do get special press treatment. One such, fairly obviously, is government – both nationally and locally. Another is the courts.

These are the two classic areas of specialised newspaper reporting. A third area is business and finance – heavily covered in all the serious papers, and with its own specialised daily newspaper, the *Financial Times*. If the Trade Unions are to be regarded as a unique interest in the land they must then have the 'extra fair' coverage which a union equivalent of the *Financial Times* would provide *and/or* they need to be covered as thoroughly and rationally as politics and the courts, nationally and locally.

4.5 Journalism, the press and industrial relations

It could be argued that in a field like industrial relations national specialists should be either more or less educated than the level found in 1968 (of about half being graduates). Also amenable to change is the basic stock of information or training to which all or most journalists could be exposed. For example the basic NCTJ training scheme could include an element devoted entirely to industry and/or to industrial relations – this would probably accord quite well with the local realities of reporting which confront most trainee journalists.

It seems improbable that the NUJ would object to such an emphasis, while critics of the NUJ might (or might not) think that such instruction would have a benign influence. Such training might within a few years have a substantial influence on sub-editors, feature writers and general reporters.

It could also be argued that the training scheme has in the past given too much emphasis to literacy as opposed to numeracy. Simple numeracy is necessary in a field like industrial relations (as in sport, politics and of course financial coverage); most people will be able to remember reading an industrial relations story in which the elementary arithmetic of a wage claim seemed to contain errors. The suggestion here is not that all journalists should have to pass even O level maths or that numeracy should be substituted for literacy – merely that consideration might be given to the view that *both* simple numeracy and simple literacy are qualifications relevant to journalism in general and to fields like industrial relations in particular.

In Britain journalism training courses have mainly been confined to exercises aimed at the lower levels of the occupation. There have been few 'courses' aimed at the middle and upper middle levels of journalism – from which industrial relations coverage largely emerges. Courses dealing with the border areas of industrial relations and financial journalism or with press coverage of strikes would be examples which might have appeal.

Two suggestions have already been made on strike coverage. Firstly the possibilities for 'sheltered access' to local media by the major parties to the strike might be considered – this, of course, to be in addition to, not instead of, ordinary news coverage. Secondly it would be possible for journalists to use very crude survey techniques to obtain evidence on the emergence of opinion – two reporters could in a single day easily conduct quite an effective survey and the consequence would be a major news story. This would be an alternative to reporters hanging about the strike headquarters or to the common 'I talked to Mrs Jones, wife of a typical striker' colour feature story.

Even though the Royal Commission's Interim Report wants to enable 'as many national newspapers as possible to continue publication', it still may be worth considering the probable consequences of certain papers disappearing. The *Daily Express* has been mentioned already. *The Guardian* is another vulnerable daily and it clearly has a special position in the national coverage of industrial relations. Impressionistic evidence suggests that this newspaper is often the one which provides the most common ground for the various – often contending – groupings within the Trade Unions. It is safe to predict, therefore, that the loss of this paper would be bitterly resented by the TUC, while the current readership of this paper (containing many southern, non-Labour voting and ABC1 readers) would make a TUC purchase, or even support, probably unviable. In addition to its special position in national press coverage of industrial relations, *The Guardian* also holds a special position in broadcast news. It is only a slight exaggeration to state that BBC notions of neutrality involve steering between *The Daily Telegraph* and *The Guardian*.[1] In industrial relations news especially it would become much more difficult to operate 'neutrally' without *The Guardian* as one of the steering aids.

The social distance between London and the provinces appears to be quite large within the great Trade Unions; but it may be equally large within journalism, including industrial relations journalism. One of the oddities of the British press is that while much of the provincial press is owned from London by groups also owning national publications there is very little interchange between national and provincial publications – at least for journalists. One view, of course, would be that provincial groups of the size of Associated, Thomson, United, or Westminster are only acceptable so long as they are editorially separated from the national publications. If this view is favoured then any interchange of journalists must be unacceptable.

However the opposite view would be that just as *The Times* uses some journalists from its Supplements and does some sharing with *The Sunday Times*, a similar amount of sharing with Thomson Regional Newspapers would be desirable.

Another media model which might be considered would be the BBC 'attachment' system by which personnel are posted temporarily to a programme without long-term obligation. Or might there not be some advantage in, say, *The Times* number two labour specialist changing jobs for a few weeks with the labour man on the Newcastle *Evening Chronicle*?

It can also be argued that British journalism at the higher levels is even further biased towards a South East view than might at first appear. Tunstall found that three-quarters of all national specialist correspondents had originally entered journalism in London, the London suburbs, elsewhere in the South of England, or overseas. Many of these journalists had never worked outside the South, few had any experience of industry and their closest friends came either from the media or from jobs very remote from manufacturing industry[2].

4.6 Lack of a public debate on the media

Very little exists in Britain in the way of a continuing public debate on the media. There is nothing comparable to the many Journalism Reviews in the United States, or to *Presse Actualité* in France. Such pronouncements as do appear

1 See Philip Schlesinger, *Putting Reality Together: The BBC News*, London: Constable, forthcoming.
2 Jeremy Tunstall, *Journalists at Work*, London: Constable, 1971, pp 99, 258–9.

have to fight for space in the general national media – the consequence is a scattering of snippets. In considering a topic like the press coverage of industrial relations there is virtually nothing available in published form which falls anywhere in the large territory between a half column in a national newspaper or an article in a strictly academic social science journal. The gap must partly explain the frankly inadequate evidence submitted to the Commission on this topic even by the TUC and the CBI.

Columbia Journalism Review and the numerous other American publications have a national constituency in the university journalism schools – approximately 70,000 students are 'majoring' in journalism or communications at present in the USA. *Presse Actualité* was originally a house magazine, directed by the Roman Catholic press group which still owns the publication, to its amateur sales network around France; its readership is now heavily weighted towards schoolteachers.[1] Neither of these sets of circumstances exists in Britain. Thus if such a publication is thought desirable for Britain some means would be needed to support it.

The lack of such publications in Britain means that in practice journalists and others involved in the press have no means of discussing complex subjects – of which the press coverage of industrial relations is a good case – and of moving towards some kind of possible solutions. If such a publication existed one inevitable line of discussion would be as to what could be done about more 'positive' and less 'hard news' coverage now. Ideas to emerge in such discussions might include:

- More feature writing, including retrospective 'now that the strike is over' pieces.
- More 'columns' in which one person returns to the subject again and again perhaps on a particular day each week.
- Perhaps more coverage of industrial relations stories by a range of specialists and reporters each covering different aspects.

Such a publication would also be able to examine the way in which particular stories had been covered by the specialist labour correspondents and might be able both to document and to challenge the consensus news values which operate there. Finally such a publication could look at the press relations activities of the Trade Unions and point out to the Trade Union movement some of the structural consequences of the highly personal PR style of certain prominent Union leaders.

4.7 Conclusion

No single aspect of industrial relations news is dramatically unfair or biased, but the entire mosaic of news is unfair to the trade unions. 'Unfairness' must be comparative. The obvious other field for comparison is the 'other side' of industry, which is so much more fairly treated. This comparative difference is documented in several parts of the content analysis; it is also supported by the opinions of a sub-sample of 97 managing directors.

The media mosaic which overall is unfair to the trade unions derives from polarisation in Britain between national and local, 'quality' and 'popular', press and broadcast media:

---

1 Information supplied by Jean C Texier of *Presse Actualité* and author of *La Presse Quotidienne Francaise*, Paris: Armand Colin, 1974.

1 The national popular newspapers with the highest trade union readership largely ignore or sensationalise industrial relations.

2 Local weekly newspapers which give most positive and intimate coverage to local events and interests do not extend this coverage to include much about local industrial relations.

3 Television is in many ways like the national popular press in its coverage; its film-dependent character is at the core of its superficiality, but these very qualities make for credibility. Some dissatisfaction with TV industrial news may be attributed to the press because of a strong popular belief that TV news either is not, or cannot be, untrue.

4 The serious daily newspapers give the only tolerably fair and adequate coverage of industrial relations, but this appears alongside still fairer and very much more adequate coverage of business.

5 Britain has one of the strongest trade union movements in Western Europe, but is unusual in Europe in lacking any significant press owned or controlled either by the trade unions or by a related political party or co-operative movement.

6 Dissatisfaction within the TUC and the Labour movement was one major factor leading to the setting up of this Royal Commission on the Press. The inquiries of the Commission in the view of this writer, show that the dissatisfaction – even if poorly expressed – does spring from treatment which overall is indeed unfair. Were the Royal Commission not to recommend some fairly major measures to alter this situation, the TUC would feel even more dissatisfied and would be able to point to Commission documentation to support its case.

7 The Royal Commission has two alternatives:

(a) To take the view that the sort of case made out in this paper is not sufficiently convincing.

(b) The second alternative is to recommend ways in which the unions could receive fairer coverage.

8 If the latter course is chosen the main options seem to be one or more of:

(a) Some kind of significant Trade Union controlled element in the general sale British press.

(b) Some legal provision for 'sheltered access' via advertising and/or editorial in the existing press.

(c) A recommendation that the press at all levels should give much more background, positive, feature, column and investigative coverage to the subjects of industrial relations, trade unions, occupations, professions and employment generally.

(d) A programme of educational measures to teach journalists about industry, industrial relations and trade unions.

Printed in England for Her Majesty's Stationery Office by Oyez Press Limited
Dd 586784 K18 8/77